SOCIOECONOMIC STATUS, PARENTING, AND CHILD DEVELOPMENT

MONOGRAPHS IN PARENTING

Marc H. Bornstein, Series Editor

Borkowski, Ramey, and Bristol-Powers   Parenting and the Child's World: Influences on Academic, Intellectual, and Social-Emotional Development

Bornstein and Bradley   Socioeconomic Status, Parenting, and Child Development

Cowan, Cowan, Ablow, Johnson, and Measelle   The Family Context of Parenting in Children's Adaptation to School

Bornstein   Parenting: Essential Readings

For more information on LEA titles, please contact
Lawrence Erlbaum Associates, Publishers, at www.erlbaum.com.

SOCIOECONOMIC STATUS, PARENTING, AND CHILD DEVELOPMENT

Edited by

Marc H. Bornstein
National Institute of Child Health and Human Development

and

Robert H. Bradley
University of Arkansas at Little Rock

LAWRENCE ERLBAUM ASSOCIATES, PUBLISHERS
2003   Mahwah, New Jersey   London

Senior Acquisitions Editor: Bill Webber
Editorial Assistant: Erica Kica
Cover Designer: Kathryn Houghtaling Lacey
Production Manager: Marianna Vertullo
Full Service Compositor: TechBooks
Text and Cover Printer: Sheridan Press

This book was typeset in 10/12 pt. Times Roman, Bold, and Italic.
The heads were typeset in Americana, Italic and Bold.

Lawrence Erlbaum Associates, Inc., Publishers
10 Industrial Avenue
Mahwah, New Jersey 07430

Library of Congress Cataloging-in-Publication Data

Socioeconomic status, parenting, and child development / edited by Marc H. Bornstein
    and Robert H. Bradley.
        p.   cm.—(Monographs in parenting series)
    Includes bibliographical references and indexes.
    ISBN 0-8058-4242-X (alk. paper)
      1. Parenting.   2. Parent and child.   3. Child development.   4. Socioeconomic status.
    I. Bornstein, Marc H.   II. Bradley, Robert H., 1946–   III. Series.

    HQ775.8 .S63   2003
    649′.1—dc21   2002026382

Books published by Lawrence Erlbaum Associates are printed on
acid-free paper, and their bindings are chosen for strength and
durability.

Printed in the United States of America
10   9   8   7   6   5   4   3   2   1

For

Bernice, Gilbert, Helen, Lea, and Jon

M.H.B.

Harold, Margaret, Rozalyn, and Suzanne

R.H.B.

. . . who have taught us the lessons and joys of parenting . . .

Contents

Series Foreword
Monographs in Parenting

Parenting is fundamental to the survival and success of the human race. Everyone who has ever lived has had parents, and most adults in the world become parents. Opinions about parenting abound, but surprisingly little solid scientific information or considered reflection exists about parenting. *Monographs in Parenting* intends to redress this imbalance: The chief aim of this series of volumes is to provide a forum for extended and integrated treatments of fundamental and challenging contemporary topics in parenting. Each volume treats a different perspective on parenting and is self-contained, yet the series as a whole endeavors to enhance and interrelate studies in parenting by bringing shared perspectives to bear on a variety of concerns prominent in parenting theory, research, and application. As a consequence of its structure and scope, *Monographs in Parenting* will appeal, individually or as a group, to scientists, professionals, and parents alike. Reflecting the nature and intent of this series, contributing authors are drawn from a broad spectrum of the humanities and sciences—anthropology to zoology—with representational emphasis placed on active contributing authorities to the contemporary literature in parenting.

Parenting is a job whose primary object of attention and action is the child—children do not and cannot grow up as solitary individuals—but parenting is also a status in the life course with consequences for parents themselves. In this forum, parenting is defined by all of children's principal caregivers and their many modes of caregiving. *Monographs in Parenting* encompass central themes in parenting ...

Who Parents?

Biological and adoptive mothers, fathers, single-parents, and divorced and remarried parents can be children's principal caregivers, but when siblings, grandparents, and nonfamilial caregivers mind children their parenting is pertinent as well.

Whom Do Parents Parent?

Parents parent infants, toddlers, children in middle-childhood, and adolescents, but special populations of children include multiple births, preterm, ill, developmentally delayed or talented, and aggressive or withdrawn children.

The Scope of Parenting

Parenting includes genetic endowment and direct effects of experience that manifest in parents' beliefs and behaviors; parenting's indirect influences take place through parents' relationships with each other and their connections to community networks; and the positive and negative effects of parenting are both topics of concern.

Factors that Affect Parenting

Evolution and history; biology and ethology; family configuration; formal and informal support systems, community ties, and work; social, educational, legal, medical, and governmental institutions; economic class, designed and natural ecology, and culture—as well as children themselves—each helps to define parenting.

The Nature, Structure, and Meaning of Parenting

Parenting is pleasures, privileges, and profits as well as frustrations, fears, and failures.

Marc H. Bornstein
Series Editor

SOCIOECONOMIC STATUS, PARENTING, AND CHILD DEVELOPMENT

Socioeconomic Status, Parenting, and Child Development: An Introduction

In the long history of research on child well-being, few constructs have received greater attention than socioeconomic status (SES). Although social scientists do not fully agree on precisely what SES represents, and they have proposed multiple different mechanisms linking SES to child well-being, there is near universal agreement that higher SES children have access to more of the resources needed to support their positive development than do lower SES children. For young children, it is assumed that much of the influence of SES on development is mediated directly through what parents afford by way of financial and human capital. As children age, SES increasingly operates through the social capital afforded by parents and through neighborhood–community connections and resources. Despite considerable support for such broad generalizations, many questions remain regarding relations among SES, parenting, and child development. "What is the best way to measure SES in a complex, rapidly changing world?" "What aspects of parenting carry most of the SES effect for children of different ages and for different domains of development?" "How does neighborhood SES, in combination with family SES, affect parenting?" "children's behavior and development?" "How does SES vary in its effect on child well-being as a function of ethnicity, geography, and immigration status?" "Which components of SES exert the most potent influences on children's health, competence, and adjustment, and how does each component function to influence the child's developmental course?" The chapters in this volume attempt to address such questions with particular emphasis on how parenting mediates SES-child development relations.

The authors represent an array of different disciplines, and they approach the issue of SES, parenting, and child development from a variety of perspectives. Accordingly, their take on how SES matters in the lives of children varies. Even so, these chapters, considered as a whole, attest to the value of systematically examining the components of SES, and how each flows through an array of specific parenting practices and resources both within and outside the home environment to help shape the course of child development. The result is a more fully delineated picture of how SES impacts the lives of children in the 21st century, a picture that contains a road map for the next generation of studies of SES and its role in the rapidly evolving ecology of family life.

It is accepted as axiomatic by contemporary social scientists that parenting is intimately implicated in the relation between socioeconomic status and child development. The question is, How? Addressing that question is the focus of this volume. In some respects this volume represents a return to the roots of scholarship on SES. The term *socioeconomic status* has historically denoted the relative position of individuals, families, or groups in stratified social systems where some societal values (e.g., occupational prestige, education, economic resources, power, information) are not uniformly distributed. The complex processes of social stratification, in turn, hierarchically classify people according to their access of those values.

A one-dimensional view of social stratification proposes economics as the key dimension to understanding stratification. However, contributors to this collection tend not to view SES as one dimensional. As a group they subscribe to a multidimensional view of social stratification that takes into account other dimensions like education, occupational prestige, financial resources, power, and knowledge. Many also accord value to subjective feelings about one's position vis-à-vis others in society (subjective SES) as being significant in family life. In effect, the view of SES generally espoused by contributors in this volume represents an extension of the branches of inquiry on SES, parenting, and child development so that the inquiry more fully envelopes current bioecological conceptions of children and how they become the individuals they are. SES entails a synergy of social and economic forces that pull from assets internal to the individual and assets contained in the surrounding ecology. Through time the individual is transformed as is the relation between the individual and constituent components of the ecology. For the most part, high SES creates circumstances that lead to adaptive functioning. It enables the individual to more fully realize adaptive capacities and behavioral tendencies. It also protects the individual from the ravages of incompetence and maladaptive behavioral tendencies. By contrast, low SES constrains individuals from achieving maximum adaptive functioning and may exacerbate problems connected with maladaptive tendencies. For children, what parents do and what parents afford by way of physical, social, and material resources both internal and external to the family are presumed to be among the major paths connecting SES to adaptive functioning. Contributions to this volume attempt to illuminate those paths.

This volume is divided into two parts. Part I concerns the constructs and measurement of SES, and Part II the functions and effects of SES. Each part presents four substantive chapters on the topic followed by an interpretive and constructively critical commentary.

Ensminger and Fothergill set the recent historical stage of SES study in an examination of the last decade of research in *Child Development*, the *American Journal of Public Health*, and the *Journal of Health and Social Behavior* to illustrate how SES is measured and used in studies of parenting and child development. Different journals, with different histories, interests, and intended audiences, have all emphasized SES, if to different degrees and for different purposes. The authors report no consensus on how best to measure SES; indeed, they observed a wide variety of different approaches to the measurement of SES across the three journals. They also find that components of SES (notably education, occupation, and income) were used in studies of child well-being more often than composite SES indices such as Hollingshead Four-Factor Index of Social Status. Their review shows that SES has been used as a descriptor of a study population, an independent variable, a dependent variable, a control variable, and in attempts to unconfound the relation between SES and other factors in developmental study. By far, the most popular use of SES has been as a descriptor of a study population. Along the way, the authors find that in much of the literature SES is often (unfortunately) confounded with race and ethnicity. Of course, different fields and their respective scientific journals emphasize different aspects and uses of SES. The authors conclude with a series of recommendations for the use and effectiveness of SES in developmental science.

Bornstein, Hahn, Suwalsky, and Haynes offer a detailed exploration of linkages among SES, parenting, and child functioning during infancy. They focus on six parenting processes as potential mediators of relations between SES and five aspects of infant behavior. Specifically, in a series of structural equation models, Bornstein and his colleagues look at relations between two major SES composite indices—the Hollingshead Four-Factor Index of Social Status and the Duncan Socioeconomic Index of Occupations—in relation to six parenting processes and five infant behavior outcomes. They then analyze the role of these two SES composites and also decompose each composite into its constituents (education, occupation, and income). They find that maternal education largely accounts for SES effects on child behavioral outcomes during infancy and that it does do so through several parenting channels. They further delineate relations between SES and child behavior by including in their models several maternal factors with known relations to child outcomes: maternal age, intelligence, personality, and employment.

Duncan and Magnuson also argue for a differentiated conceptualization of SES, one where the focus falls on the constituent components, including education, occupation, and income. Accordingly, they contend that it makes sense to study the separate effects of these components of SES. The authors define the main components of SES and then indicate their effects on parenting and child development. In doing so, they discuss the significance of natural experiments (beyond correlational designs) in pinning down how SES influences parenting and child development. Further to this point, Duncan and Magnuson emphasize the difficulties of finding experimental studies of SES in relation to parenting and child development and the need and importance to implement such basic research in the area.

Immigration currently looms large in developmental considerations as, according to Fuligni and Yoshikawa, approximately 20% of American children have at least one foreign-born parent. Fuligni and Yoshikawa point out that SES is not the same in all populations, and they focus on immigrant families as an example. They present guidelines for understanding the ins and outs of SES in immigrant families, pointing out that traditional socioeconomic indicators may not have the same meaning for immigrant families as for U.S.-born families. The history of American immigration policy has exerted significant effects on the nature and distribution of the socioeconomic characteristics of the contemporary foreign-born population in the United States, and a preference system within American foreign policy has favored family unification and occupational qualifications. As a consequence, different immigrant groups have varied in their admission to the United States, and socioeconomic variability in the foreign-born population in America is ascribable at least in part to American immigration policy. Fuligni and Yoshikawa frame the socioeconomic resources of immigrant families in terms of Coleman's taxonomy of human capital, financial capital, and social capital. In terms of human capital, of which educational attainment is a principal representation, all immigrant groups come from societies with lower overall levels of educational attainment than U.S.-born, but relatively speaking immigrants in some societies may come from higher or lower normative educational strata. As a consequence, absolute and relative levels of education have different meanings for U.S.- and foreign-born parents, and it could be the case that perceived aspirations of immigrant parents with a high school degree are equivalent to those of American parents with a college degree. Different immigrant groups also exhibit different levels of obligations, expectations, and trustworthiness so that immigrant parents may lack traditional measures of human and financial capital but compensate with a strong supply of social capital from their families and communities. In the end, measurement indicators of SES appear to vary between immigrant and native-born families. As a consequence, it may be necessary to obtain separate estimates of education, occupation, and income because they do not serve well as proxies for one another among immigrant families.

In her commentary on Part I, Hoffman observes that the influences of SES on child development are so pervasive as to be unavoidable. SES, she writes, often needs to be controlled or considered as a moderator. First, Hoffman takes up two issues, namely assessment of components of SES and whether a general measure of SES exists and is useful. In evaluating income, occupation, and education, Hoffman points out that each measure has advantages and disadvantages that must be considered when enlisting one or the other component of SES as the measure of social class to be used in research in the social sciences. Hoffman also points out that for certain studies individual indicators of SES may not capture the full spectrum of resources implied by SES; thus, it may be valuable to have a general measure of SES. To meet this need, she evaluates the Hollingshead Four-Factor Index of Social Status critically examining its advantages and disadvantages for developmental science. Hoffman also addresses the issue of confounds between ethnicity and SES (with special reference to African Americans). In the final paragraphs of her commentary, Hoffman reiterates the importance of considering multiple and variant construals of SES for immigrant populations to the United States. How SES is measured, and what it means to these populations, need to be considered carefully in the studies that marshal SES factors as explanations or as controls.

Authors in Part II turn their attention to functions and effects of SES on parenting and child development. Hoff raises four key questions with respect to the role of SES in parenting and child development. Her first question is whether there are SES-related differences in parent-to-child speech, for which she supplies ample data that support a response in the affirmative. Specifically, she shows that higher-SES mothers sustain conversation longer with their children, elicit more conversation from their children, and are more responsive to their children's conversational contributions. When Hoff raises the next question about what causes these differences, she finds that SES-related differences in speech are general and not specific to child-directed or adult-directed speech. The third question Hoff poses is whether there are SES-consequent related differences in children's language development, and she finds that children's vocabulary growth at 2 and amount and lexical richness of speech produced in conversation and standardized productive vocabulary at 4 differ by SES. These findings beg the fourth question: Are SES-related differences in child language a reflection of parent-to-child speech? To this, Hoff answers yes. Children in different SES groups experience different language environments that affect their own language. Hoff's results focus on mid- and upper-SES and so do not include low SES or poverty samples; nonetheless, SES-related differences are in evidence. High-SES and mid-SES children differ in their vocabulary and language, and SES shapes children's language-learning environments and thus influences the development of their language.

Bradley and Corwyn use seven waves of data from the National Longitudinal Survey of Youth to examine relations among components of SES, two aspects of the parenting environment (stimulation, maternal responsiveness), and child competence and adjustment in three major ethnic groups from early childhood through adolescence. They find low to moderate correlations between SES and measures of child development in all groups. Correlations between SES and measures of competence were greater than correlations with measures of behavioral adjustment. Bradley and Corwyn also report low to moderate correlations between SES and learning stimulation in all groups, but stronger relations for European American than African American children. Relations between SES and maternal responsiveness were somewhat lower, and learning stimulation partially mediated the relation between SES and competence at all age levels; all these relations varied somewhat by ethnic group, but the basic pattern of findings was similar. The authors' analyses further show that learning stimulation during middle childhood and adolescence mediates the SES-competence relation net the amount of learning stimulation received in the prior developmental period; however, there is little evidence that learning stimulation is related to changes in competence from one developmental period to the next. By contrast, maternal responsiveness is an inconsistent mediator of the SES-competence relation, with relations varying in terms of the component of SES examined and the developmental period. Their evidence suggests that the relation between SES and behavioral adjustment of children is quite complex. There was evidence that learning stimulation mediated the relation between SES measures and behavior problems net earlier levels of learning stimulation, especially for European Americans; by contrast, there was little evidence that maternal responsiveness mediated the relation. Further analyses indicated that the availability of learning stimulation may afford children protection against behavior problems by developing higher levels of competence, thus allowing them to remain connected to schools and other social institutions. Finally, Bradley and Corwyn's results indicated that family process mediates relations between maternal education and child outcomes to a greater extent than relations between occupational status and child outcomes.

The chapter by Gottfried, Gottfried, Bathurst, Guerin, and Parramore uses the extensive data set from the Fullerton Longitudinal Study (FLS) to address several key questions about SES, parenting, and child development. They include the nature of relations among SES factors, the consistency of relations of SES to various domains of psychological development, and relations of SES to family environment. In the main, Gottfried and his colleagues found that SES is a pervasive and important general construct in child development. In the FLS, a family's SES in infancy predicted key aspects of children's development through high school. The Hollingshead Index proved to be a consistently reliable measure of SES over almost two decades of investigation. However, the components of SES used to compose the Hollingshead Index behaved differently and, notably, on account of its instability, mother's occupational status was not a predictor of child outcome the way other components of the Hollingshead were. Despite its pervasive role in the child's development, SES accounted for no more than 20% of the variance in child outcomes. And, most noteworthy and in accord with other findings from other investigators in the field, Gottfried and associates report that maternal education has the most consistent relation to child outcome.

Leventhal and Brooks-Gunn follow by presenting three theoretical models for understanding how neighborhood influences may be transmitted to children and youth; they are through institutional resources, parental relationships, and the norms and collective efficacy model. Institutional resources in the neighborhood are important to children's health and development. Institutional resources include learning activities, social and recreational activities, childcare, schools, health care services, and employment opportunities. As an example, neighborhood SES, like family SES, is associated with access to institutional resources, as well as the quality of the resources obtained. Parental relationships include parental characteristics, support networks, behavior, and the home environment, and these may transmit neighborhood effects to children and youth. The authors found that families that moved to more affluent neighborhoods used less harsh behavior than families that remained in poor neighborhoods. Finally, norms and collective efficacy operate at the community level through informal institutions, peers, and physical threats. To flesh out these models, the authors appeal to data from the Moving to Opportunity for Fair Housing Demonstration, the program whose overarching goal was to examine the impact of residential relocation on child and family outcomes. Leventhal and Brooks-Gunn document the results of this nationwide study for residential mobility, as well as parent and child mental and physical health. Their data afford the opportunity to examine how a major shift in neighborhood SES alters child and adolescent development.

In his commentary on Part II, Lerner raises the critical question of causal mechanisms by which SES influences parenting and child development. In reply Lerner offers a developmental systems perspective that warns theoreticians and researchers alike about the artificial and dangerous split between sociogenic, psychogenic, or biogenic theories on the one hand and SES, parenting, and child development on the other. Rather, Lerner proposes that the linkages among SES, parenting, and child development need to be understood in the context of a dynamic, developmental systems theory of human development. First, Lerner discusses and critiques each of the individual perspectives. Against this backdrop, he then explains the principles and mechanisms of action of developmental systems models. These models take a relational, synthetic approach to understanding the multiple levels of organization involved in human development. This view features the active participation of human beings in their own development. The central tenet is that relations among variables (from genes to environment) not splits (between nature and nurture) lay at the core of developmental process. As Lerner points out, an important implication of this new perspective taking on SES is its policy implications. Lerner culminates his commentary with an analysis of implications of split and relational perspectives on linkages among SES, parenting, and child development both for parenting efficacy and for social programs and social policy.

For over 60 years, SES has been regarded as one of the most important antecedents of children's well-being. A substantial body of literature on SES and child well-being has emerged from diverse disciplines in the health and social sciences since World War II. From the outset, there was the belief that SES had both direct (access to certain types of resources) as well as indirect (mostly through the quality of parenting received) impacts on children's patterns of growth and development. Some putative mechanisms linking SES to aspects of child well-being were articulated in the 1960s and 1970s (such as the link between parental education, the quality of language to which children were exposed, and children's cognitive development). The list of mechanisms has been expanded every decade since, with recent emphasis not only on identifying new parenting mediators of SES but mediators of the link between SES and specific parenting practices (e.g., parental distress as a mediator of the link between low SES and harsh parenting) and mediators of the link between parenting practices and global child outcomes (e.g., time spent in academic activities as a mediator of parental efforts to encourage achievement and achievement test scores). Even so, many mechanisms remain undelineated and even more have been tested on only a few age or ethnic groups.

A number of more recent advances in research traditions and theoretical formulations regarding relations between children's environments and their well-being now call for a reexamination of how SES is implicated in children's development. First, there has been a shift in the focus of studies that examine relations between children's contexts and aspects of well-being. Most no longer examine SES holistically, choosing instead to concentrate on individual aspects (e.g., economic status, education, occupation, and neighborhood of residence). Second, ecological theories of human development postulate that relations between features of context (such as SES) and children's development are themselves affected by other aspects of context (e.g., culture, linkages between home and school or health services). Third, living systems theories postulate dynamic relations among components of context themselves (e.g., level of education may partially determine level of occupation, level of occupation may partially determine level of income, and area of residence may partially determine access to employment). Likewise, living systems theories postulate dynamic relations among aspects of development, such that SES influences on one developmental system may be moderated by another developmental system or mediated through impacts on another developmental system. Ecological and living systems perspectives have generated many studies pertaining to moderation (group differences) and mediation (pathways) vis-à-vis linkages between SES and child development through parenting. But, scholars have only begun to touch the surface of complex moderated mediation and mediated moderation effects. Fourth, decision theory, certain self theories, and theories pertaining to the cognitive construal of circumstances suggest potentially new mechanisms linking SES to aspects of child well-being (e.g., both parents and children make conscious decisions about events and circumstances and their relations to life goals). Fifth, recent research and theory about specific components of SES identify potentially meaningful new mechanisms (e.g., household income–poverty) linking SES to aspects of child well-being. Sixth, life-course theory suggests the value of examining how various aspects of SES, singly and in combination across time, affect patterns of development. That is, most previous research has not examined issues surrounding the timing of particular components of SES on specific aspects of well-being, the chronicity of particular components of SES on specific aspects of well-being, or the combination of particular components of SES on specific aspects of well-being at different developmental periods. "Does area of residence make a greater difference during adolescence than infancy?" Seventh, during the 1980s and 1990s issues were raised about how best to measure SES— and there remain questions about whether the measures that best serve the needs of psychologists are the same as those that best serve the needs of sociologists, economists, or epidemiologists.

In sum, there is contemporary need to carefully reexamine rich relations between SES and child well-being, with emphasis on integrating what has become a somewhat splintered approach to research in the field. There is a need to reconsider the direct impact of SES conditions on child well-being and the indirect impact of SES on child well-being through parenting practices and activities. There is a need to reconsider these issues in light of current theories pertaining to how context affects the course of development and how development emerges over the life course. In the process of reconsidering how parenting is implicated in relations between SES and various aspects of child development, scholars need to bear in mind the principles of parallel, convergent, and reciprocal causation. The principle of parallel causation stipulates that several different processes or factors may be sufficient, but not necessary, to produce a particular developmental outcome. The principle of convergent causation stipulates that a particular process may be necessary but not sufficient to produce a particular outcome; its effect depends on the presence of a second factor. The principle of reciprocal causation stipulates that bidirectional influences among several factors interacting across time are required to produce a particular developmental outcome. Consideration of these principles in terms of their applicability to the central question of this volume should provide fodder for social scientists through the early decades of the 21st century. And, finally, there is need to reconsider issues pertaining to the measurement of SES for various purposes and different disciplines, including measurement equivalence across sociocultural groups. This last issue is of particular relevance given that SES indicators are currently contained in all the major national health, education, and human development studies.

Throughout the history of science, there has been the necessary (if sometimes reluctant) dance between theory and measurement in regard to scientific constructs. Right now there is no theory of SES (precisely what it is and how it works in relation to other constructs) that social scientists fully agree upon. Therefore, how the various components of SES (e.g., education, occupation, and income) should be joined, or if they should be joined at all for purposes of scientific study, remains somewhat elusive.

This volume addresses many of these reconsiderations by presenting cutting-edge thinking and research on linkages among SES, parenting, and child development. As this collection shows, SES retains considerable appeal among social scientists of various stripes today (from psychologists to economists, from linguists to sociologists, from anthropologists to epidemiologists)—just as it did in the mid-20th century. If anything, that appeal may grow in the coming years as the mobility of class and immigration become more profound in society. Where two decades ago we perhaps appeared to have reached consensus (if not certainty) on how SES affects some aspects of child development, now new mysteries emerge as conditions and people change. The face of SES changes with time. But the challenge (and the imperative) to understand its role in the lives of children and families remains unchanged.

Socioeconomic Status, Parenting, and Child Development derives from original presentations delivered at a workshop of the same name held in Minneapolis, Minnesota. The workshop was sponsored by the National Institute of Child Health and Human Development. We are especially grateful to Dr. Owen M. Rennert and Dr. Duane F. Alexander of the National Institute of Child Health and Human Development for sponsoring the workshop and for their continuing support of research into all facets of human growth and childrens' health. Thanks too to the production staff at LEA for continuing professionalism and excellence.

I

SES: Measurement and Ecology

1

A Decade of Measuring SES: What It Tells Us and Where to go From Here

Margaret E. Ensminger and Kate E. Fothergill

Department of Health Policy and Management,
The Bloomberg School of Public Health,
The Johns Hopkins University

INTRODUCTION

Numerous studies have demonstrated the relation of socioeconomic status (SES) to health, psychological well-being, and attainment of socially and culturally derived goals. Theoretical and empirical work have emphasized that families' socioeconomic situations have an impact on how parents rear their children (Bronfenbrenner & Morris, 1997; Elder, 1996; Elder & Conger, 2000; Kohn 1977). Individual development is shaped by the processes that are influenced by SES and that occur in key social contexts, including families, schools, and neighborhoods (Alwin & Thornton, 1984; Bidwell & Friedkin, 1989; Blau & Duncan, 1967; Demo & Acock, 1996; Duncan, Brooks-Gunn, & Klebanov, 1994). Social class has been one of the most robust predictors of health status for both adults and children (Bunker, Gomby, & Kehrer, 1989; Pappas, Queen, Hadden, & Fisher, 1993; Williams, 1990).

In addition to the direct effects of SES on outcomes that influence families and children, SES may also interact with other variables, moderating or mediating the influence of other key variables (Conger, Ge, Lorenz, & Simons, 1994; McLoyd, Jayartine, Ceballo, & Borquez, 1994; Sampson & Laub, 1994). For example, in a longitudinal study examining pathways to high school dropout, Ensminger and Slusarcick (1992) found that the influence of maternal education on high school

13

graduation was through its interaction with individual characteristics. Having a mother with at least a high school education increased the likelihood that males who performed poorly in first grade or who had low educational expectations as adolescents would graduate from high school.

Furthermore, excluding the consideration of SES in studies on children and families ignores the diversity and economic variation that exists in the United States (MacPhee, Kreutzer, & Fritz, 1994). We cannot understand the full range of normal development if ethnic or socioeconomic diverse samples are not included in the studies that provide the basis for developmental science. Yet, despite the evidence of the importance of SES on developmental and health outcomes, it is not clear that there is much research on the effects of SES on growth and development or that SES is taken into account in other than the most elementary way.

For example, in the 1970s, Kohn (1977) described how the experiences in the course of doing one's work could influence the values related to child rearing. His study was of a nationally representative sample of men. Yet, surprisingly little has been written since that time on whether and how SES influences parenting (for an important exception see the work of Menaghan and colleagues: Menaghan, Kowaleski-Jones, & Mott, 1997; Menaghan & Parcel, 1997).

In this chapter, we investigate the ways that SES is utilized and measured in research on children and adolescents. First, we review past work that has analyzed the child development literature with regard to the inclusion of SES measures. Second, we highlight some important issues pertaining to the measurement of SES, such as the source of information and the type of measure used. Next, we review articles published in three select journals over the past decade to assess the use and measurement of SES in studies of parents, children, and adolescents. Finally, we summarize the literature review findings and make some recommendations for the field.

PAST REVIEWS OF THE CHILD DEVELOPMENT LITERATURE

Over the last 20 years, various content analyses have documented trends in research on SES and child health and development. These reviews have discussed the theoretical origins of SES measures, the common measures used today, the use of the measures (e.g., sample descriptors, control variables), SES's confounding relationship with measures of race, and the precision of SES measures (Berrios & Hagen, 2000; Graham, 1992; Hagen & Conley, 1994; MacPhee, et al., 1994; McLoyd & Randolph, 1985; Smith & Graham, 1995). In addition to providing background on SES measurement in family research, these analyses highlight key areas in need of improvement.

First, in a review of articles published from 1991 through 1993 in *Journal of Marriage and the Family* and select psychology and sociology journals, Smith and Graham (1995) concluded that most researchers are not concerned about the theoretical and methodological issues related to using measures of SES. For example, theories of stratification, such as functionalism or Marxism, could inform research design, and Weber's dimensions of stratification could help identify which measure will be most precise in particular circumstances. Yet, different theories of stratification and their implications are seldom referred to in the family or childrearing literature. In addition, this review concluded that there is a lack of systematic effort to identify which SES measures are most powerful in predicting family behaviors. The authors suggested that the three most common measures of SES—education, income, and occupation—may have differential effects, depending on the outcome of study (Smith & Graham, 1995; for a more detailed discussion of measurement issues, see the following section in this chapter).

Second, past content analyses also reveal a dearth of research on diverse samples. In a special 1994 issue of *Child Development* focused on poverty, MacPhee and colleagues (1994) reviewed nine journals, three each from child development, adolescent development, and parenting or socialization, between the years 1982 to 1991. They found that measures of family background were lacking for a significant minority of studies, and less than a third of the studies included low-income or ethnically diverse subjects. The authors noted that this absence of information on the samples significantly reduced the external validity of many of the studies.

In a review of the ethnicity of children studied in *Child Development* from 1980 to 1993, Hagen and Conley (1994) found that a number of studies offered no information on the backgrounds of their participants. The number of studies with unspecified samples decreased between 1990 and 1993, during which time most studies reported European American or predominantly European-American participants. According to a separate study comparing trends in *Child Development* to those in *Developmental Psychology* between 1991 and 1999, *Developmental Psychology* was even less likely to include studies on minority children and youth (Berrios & Hagen, 2000). Although these analyses found diversity to be lacking, Hagen et al. (2000), in a review of over 60 years of *Child Development*, found that since 1980, "white, middle class children continue to be very well represented, but increases in studies predominantly involving racially and ethnically diverse children are dramatic, as are increases in studies on atypical or at-risk children."

McLoyd and Randolph (1985), in their analysis of trends in *Child Development* studies on African American children between 1936 to 1980, found that the specification of social class was highest between 1971–1975, but after 1975 it decreased substantially. The authors hypothesize that the increase between 1971 and 1975 was partly due to social and political changes, such as the federal antipoverty programs and federal support for research in this area, but they did not speculate as to what caused the subsequent decline. Wilson (1987) hypothesized that the controversy surrounding the Moynihan report (1965) "had the effect of curtailing serious research on minority problems in the inner city for over a decade, as liberal scholars shied away from researching behavior construed as unflattering or stigmatizing to particular racial minorities" (p. 4).

Third, in relation to failing to specifiy the class composition of African-American study samples, researchers of race also often fail to control for SES in the analyses. This is problematic because in the United States race and SES are highly correlated, and the lack of such controls can lead to misleading findings. Nonetheless, in the aforementioned analysis of more than 40 years of research on African-American children, McLoyd and Randolph (1985) found that there was a confounding of race and social class in 23% of the studies.

In a review of six psychological journals between 1970 and 1989, Graham (1992) noted that the research on African American populations was weakened by the lack of reporting on SES. In addition to finding fewer than one-half of the studies specifying the participants' SES, she found that, "Even among those studies that did measure SES, it was not necessarily the case that this variable was appropriately examined as a factor in the analyses" (p. 634). She pointed out that researchers tended to compare low-income African Americans to middle-income European Americans without controlling for the effect of SES. She recommended that comparative racial studies should be required to report SES information and to test for interactions between race and SES.

These analyses summarize general trends identified thus far in the study of SES within family research. Most important, they highlight necessary improvements in SES research: the consideration of theory, methods, and type of measurement. The following section provides additional details on critical measurement issues. Special attention was given to these issues because the subsequent literature review focuses on SES measurement.

SES MEASUREMENT ISSUES

Several articles have reviewed both the concepts and the measures of SES as they exist in the social science literature. Smith and Graham (1995) gave theoretical and historical background to SES measurement, including a discussion of shifts in gender roles that impacts whose status should be measured. They also gave examples of how different theoretical positions of social stratification might influence the hypotheses and interpretations of results of family researchers.

In articles in *Child Development* focused specifically on the measurement of SES and ethnicity, Entwisle and Astone (1994) and Hauser (1994) posed guidelines for researchers. Entwisle and Astone recommended measures of income, mothers' education, and household and family structure to be asked of parents. Hauser (1994) suggested gathering information about the major adult earner in the household, in order to ascertain the education, labor force status, and occupational position of that person. Hernandez (1997) discussed the utility of using standard census questions on household composition, family income, educational attainment, race and ethnicity, and employment so that information can be compared with national population data.

In an excellent review of measurement of social class, Liberatos, Link, and Kelsey (1988) concluded that there is no one best SES measure. They suggest nine criteria for selecting measures: conceptual relevance, the possible role of social class in the study, the applicability of the measures to the specific populations being studied, the relevance of a measure to the time period of study, the reliability and validity of the measures, the number of indicators included, the level of measurement, the simplicity of the measure, and comparability with other studies.

An issue in the measurement of SES is whether scales or separate indices are preferable. The consensus seems to be that multiple components should be measured, but that these should be used in analyses separately rather than combined into one scale (Bornstein, Hahn, Suwalsky, & Haynes, chap. 2, this volume; Duncan & Magnuson, chap. 3, this volume; Entwisle & Astone, 1994; Krieger, Williams, & Moss, 1997; Liberatos, et al., 1988; Mechanic, 1989). For example, Liberatos et al. (1988) concluded that the three indicators of social class most commonly used—occupation, education, and income—appear to be related to health, yet are not themselves highly intercorrelated. Each indicator is often associated with health outcomes independent of the other two. Similarly, Smith and Graham (1995) cited findings from several studies that suggest that in family research one SES variable may have considerably more power than another to account for a specific outcome.

An implicit assumption in the literature is that SES measures are based on individual characteristics. Increasingly, this assumption is being challenged. Krieger et al. (1997) argued that both households and neighborhoods influence the social resources available to individuals and often characterize aspects of living conditions that are not captured by individual measures. The impact of neighborhood on developmental outcomes of children and adolescents has been of growing interest in the child and adolescent literature (Duncan et al., 1994; Levanthal & Brooks-Gunn, 2000).

We now turn to review how SES is used in research on parents and children. Specifically, we examine whether SES is used by investigators as an independent or control variable that potentially influences the questions under study, a dependent variable in the research, or as a descriptor of the study population. When SES is measured, we also note how it is measured, the level of the measurement, and the source of the SES information. For illustrative purposes, we compare and contrast three journals from different disciplines and targeting different audiences.

REVIEW OF SES USE
IN SELECT JOURNALS

Three journals were selected for review based on their representation of different perspectives in the field of child health and development: *Child Development, American Journal of Public Health*, and *Journal of Health and Social Behavior. Child Development* was chosen as the premier U.S. publication focusing on children and development. While it is not discipline specific, many of the journal's articles are written from a developmental psychology perspective, and most of the articles concern children or adolescents. *The American Journal of Public Health* was chosen for its focus on health and its multidisciplinary approach. Many of the articles are based on populations of children, adolescents, or both. The *Journal of Health and Social Behavior* is one of the journals sponsored by the American Sociological Association. It examines health and behavior issues from a sociological perspective, and it reports findings from all age groups, including children.

This study analyzed 10 years of literature from 1991 to 2000. For analysis of *Child Development*, which is published six times per year and focuses entirely on children, researchers randomly selected two issues per year for review. The only exception to the random selection was the purposeful inclusion of *Child Development*'s special April 1994 issue on poverty. As the *American Journal of Public Health* designates many of its monthly issues to a specific topic, we selected two issues per year from those issues specifically focused on children and adolescents or SES-related constructs. We reviewed all issues of *Journal of Health and Social Behavior* in this time period because it is published only four times a year and includes fewer articles about children. The final analysis included 40 *Journal of Health and Social Behavior*, 20 *Child Development*, and 20 *American Journal of Public Health* issues, for a total of 80 journal issues over the 10-year period.

The goal of the study was to evaluate the status of the use and the discussion of SES in the literature pertaining to children and adolescents. Each journal was screened for articles meeting the following criteria: (1) they concerned children or adolescents; (2) they were based on empirical data; and (3) they were conducted on U.S. human populations. Excluded from the study were literature reviews, editorials, and other articles not based on primary research, articles on studies conducted outside the United States, studies of animals, and studies of adults only. (Although not included in the data analysis, we looked for overview, conceptual, or review articles on SES as background for the work.) We reviewed a total of 926 articles, and, of these, 471 met the criteria for inclusion. Most articles that failed to meet the criteria were not about children, adolescents, or both.

The analysis next reviewed each article to determine if and how it included SES. Of the 471 articles on children and youth in the United States, there were a total of 359 (76%) articles that included some type of discussion of SES. For each article that did include SES, we coded its use as: (1) basic sample descriptor without a description of measures used to determine SES; (2) detailed sample descriptor including measurement description; and (3) independent, outcome, or control variable. Each article was also reviewed for the types of SES measures used. We categorized the SES indicators as to the kinds of measures that were used: (1) education; (2) occupation; (3) income; and (4) participation in means-tested programs. Whether the level of each measure was individual or aggregate was noted. We also noted whether SES scales such as the Hollingshead Four-Factor

Index of Social Status (Hollingshead, 1975) were used. Also included in our coding was the source of the SES information and whether there was a discussion on the rationale for the SES measurement.

In addition to this detailed analysis of these three journals, we also examined the *Child Development Abstracts and Bibliography* between 1990 and 2000. *Child Development Abstracts and Bibliography* is published three times a year and includes abstracts from over 100 professional journals relating the growth and development of children. We noted how often any indication of SES or common measures of SES were included in the the subject index of each *Child Development Abstracts and Bibliography* issue in order to determine the extent of SES inclusion over this 10-year period. All articles on SES or SES-related constructs per year were counted and then any trends in coverage of SES over time could be observed.

Analysis of Three Journals

Of the 80 journal issues reviewed, *Child Development* had the highest proportion of articles (73%) focused on children and youth, 47% (133/283) of the *American Journal of Public Health* articles, and 20% (51/251) of the *Journal of Health and Social Behavior* articles met this criterion. Of the total 471 research articles on U.S. children and youth, 359 (76%) included any mention of SES. Articles in *Journal of Health and Social Behavior* were most likely to discuss SES, with 88% of the 51 articles including SES. Similarly, 84% of the 287 articles reviewed in *Child Development* discussed SES, but only 55% (73/133) of the articles in *American Journal of Public Health* had some mention of SES (Figure 1.1).

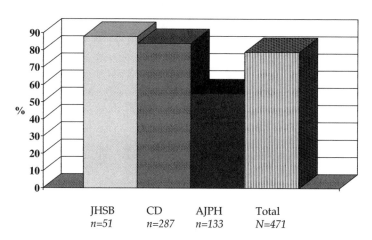

JHSB=Journal of Health and Social Behavior; CD=Child Development; AJPH=American Journal of Public Health

FIGURE 1.1. Proportion of articles on U.S. children and youth that include SES 1991–2000.

Use of SES

We next reviewed the 359 articles including SES to assess how it is used. Almost all (87%) of the articles used SES as either a basic or detailed descriptor of the sample population. More specifically, 51% of the articles provided detailed descriptions of the SES measures used to describe the samples, but 36% gave only a basic description, such as European American, middle-class sample. Forty-five percent of the 359 studies included SES in the analysis, either as an independent, outcome, or control variable.

The use of SES varied by journal. The *Journal of Health and Social Behavior* articles were most likely to include SES as an independent–outcome–control variable in the analysis (87% of its studies). In comparison, only 58% of *American Journal of Public Health* articles and 37% of *Child Development* articles included SES as a variable in the analysis. The use of SES as a sample descriptor was more similar across journals: 91% of the articles in both *Journal of Health and Social Behavior* and *Child Development* used SES to describe the sample, and 73% of *American Journal of Public Health* articles included SES in the sample description (Figure 1.2). In all three journals, the sample descriptions were more likely to be detailed than basic, although 44% of *Journal of Health and Social Behavior*, 38% of *Child Development*, and 25% of *American Journal of Public Health* included only a basic description of the sample, with no mention of the SES measures used. *Child Development* was most likely to report European American, middle-class samples, and *American Journal of Public Health* was the most likely to include samples of lower-SES populations and minorities. The *Journal of Health and Social Behavior* was most likely to mention that its samples were representative of

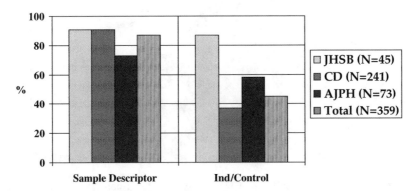

JHSB=Journal of Health and Social Behavior; CD=Child Development; AJPH=American Journal of Public Health

FIGURE 1.2. Proportion of articles using SES as sample descriptor and independent–control variable: 1991–2000.

either the U.S. population or the state or local population of interest in the study; it did not include many studies of one race or income stratum.

We also reviewed the literature for changes in the use of SES over time. Across all three journals, between 1991 and 2000, the use of SES as an independent, outcome, or control variable in the analysis increased slightly from 42% in 1991–92 (combined) to 53% in 1999–2000 (combined). The use of SES as a sample descriptor decreased from 96% in 1991–92 to 84% in 1999–2000.

Comparing the changes over time for each journal, we found no consistent trends. Between 1991–92 and 1999–2000, the use of SES as an independent, outcome, or control variable increased in *Child Development* (26% to 40%) and *American Journal of Public Health* (64% to 73%), but it decreased in *Journal of Health and Social Behavior* from 100% to 80%. The use of SES as a sample descriptor decreased in all three from 96% to 93% in *Child Development*, 100% to 80% in *Journal of Health and Social Behavior*, and 91% to 60% in *American Journal of Public Health*.

SES Measures

Overall, education was the most common indicator of SES across all journals. It was used in 45% of the 359 articles with SES included. Income was used in 28% of the articles, occupation was used in 14% of the articles, and participation in various means tested programs was used in 12% of the articles (Figure 1.3). Aggregate indicators of SES were generally rare, with articles in *American Journal of Public Health* (15%) most likely to use this type of measure. Articles in *Child Development* were much more likely to include SES scales, the most common of

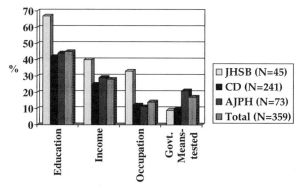

JHSB=Journal of Health and Social Behavior; CD=Child Development; AJPH=American Journal of Public Health

FIGURE 1.3. Proportion of articles that use education, income, occupation, means-tested indicators, or all of SES.

which was the Hollingshead Four-Factor Index of Social Status (Hollingshead, 1975), compared to articles in *Journal of Health and Social Behavior* (9%) or *American Journal of Public Health* (4%). Four articles in *Journal of Health and Social Behavior* included measures designed specifically for use with adolescents. Neither of the other two journals reported special measures for any populations.

Sources of SES Information

Throughout the 10-year period and consistent across all three journals, the majority of SES measures were obtained through interviews or surveys with parents, most often the mother. Other less frequent sources of SES information included reports by the closest adult to the youth, self-reports by the youth, and multiple secondary sources, such as school and hospital records, birth and death certificates, U.S. Census information, and area resource files.

Discussion of SES Measurement

In general, very few articles in any of the three journals included a discussion of measurement issues, such as measurement validity, advantages of certain measures over others, or the importance of including SES in the study. We found this type of discussion in only seven *Journal of Health and Social Behavior* articles, six *Child Development* articles, and three *American Journal of Public Health* articles.

Child Development Abstracts and Bibliography, 1990–2000

We next reviewed the *Child Development Abstracts and Bibliography* from 1990–2000 to assess how often SES or its related constructs were included as primary variables of interest in a variety of child development and public health journals (about 100 journals are abstracted). The portion of articles related to SES remained consistent at 1 or 2% each year throughout the decade. We counted any articles that were included in the categories of SES or any of the common measures (such as education or income) for SES. Overall, of the total 11,015 articles abstracted over these 10 years, only 137 (1%) were categorized by SES or common SES measures, and this was consistent over the 10-year period.

In addition, we examined how many of the SES-related articles were included in the journal articles dedicated to theory and methods. Between 1991 and 2000, only 11 of the SES articles were categorized as theoretical or methodological. Of these 11 articles, six were from *Child Development*; three were from the special issue on poverty that *Child Development* published in 1994; and two were the special articles on SES measures solicited by the editors of *Child Development* and published in 1994.

CONCLUSIONS

In the literature that we reviewed, investigators seem to be aware of the importance of describing their study population in terms of various indicators of SES, most typically education or income, less often occupation. There was less interest and discussion of the potential influence of SES on the outcome variables that were being assessed. The articles in *Journal of Health and Social Behavior* were most likely to use SES as an independent or control variable. It is understandable that SES would be key because a major focus in the sociological literature concerns the impact that social class or SES has on the life circumstances and life chances of people.

In the literature in *Child Development* that often requires intensive measurement with small samples, the major use of SES was to control its influence by using relatively homogeneous samples. This is a reasonable and defensible research-design strategy. However, given the pervasiveness of this research-design strategy, then more attention needs to be paid to the external validity of the studies. When the participants in the research were from middle-class populations, very few of the articles discussed who was not represented or the problem of generalizability. However, when the research participants were from lower-SES communities, there were more likely to be cautions that the study findings may not apply to all populations. We reviewed one article that evaluated whether a scale that had been developed on a middle-class population was valid and reliable for a lower-class population, but in general there were not many examples of this in the literature that we reviewed.

The measurement of SES did not receive much attention in this literature. We found no instances in which the article discussed why certain sources of information were used rather than others, the validity or reliability of the SES measures, or the limitations of certain SES measures. For example, the few articles that depended on adolescent reporters of family SES did not question whether adolescents were likely to know the SES information that was being requested (most often parental education). Across all journals, very few articles discussed the value of including SES and the merits of one measure over another. Often the article would describe the population in one or two sentences and not include the source of the information, or how the categorization was made. Perhaps this is less important in articles where SES is being used to describe the study population. However, when SES is used as an independent variable, the source and kind of measure may potentially be quite important. As is known from health research with adults, different measures of SES may relate differentially to the outcomes being measured (Liberatos et al., 1988; Mechanic, 1989).

We found little standardization of the SES measures in the literature. The Hollingshead scale was the most frequently cited standard measure that was reported, but most articles did not use the Hollingshead scale. As discussed earlier, the authors of several review articles suggest using SES measures separately in analyses rather than as a composite measure. However, this recommendation was made for those studies in which SES is being used as a causal variable. There has been little study of the use of composite measures in studies of children and families. In a study of the reliability and validity of SES measures of adolescents, Ensminger et al. (2000) found that a composite measure of adolescent-reported items correlated highly with mothers' reports of family income and may be useful as a way to overcome the difficulties in the limited information that adolescents can report.

The most frequently used SES measure in the literature is mother's education. It is easily collected and questions concerning level of education are not refused to the extent that questions concerning family income are (but see Duncan & Magnuson, chap. 3, this volume). For example, Demo and Acock (1996) reported that 17.5% of the mothers in the National Survey of Families and Households did not answer the question on family income.

There are important limitations to this review. First, we reviewed selected articles in only three journals. Many journals other than the three we examined focus on the development and well-being of children and adolescents. An adolescent journal may have had more articles that included SES as a causal or control variable. In addition, there have been several key books published in the past decade that have focused on the impact of SES or poverty on children's lives. These were not represented in the review. One reason we examined the *Child Development Abstracts and Bibliography* was to partially overcome this limitation.

Second, our time frame was only one decade. Thus, we were not able to chart time trends for more than one decade. There have been important reviews from earlier time periods and we tried to take advantage of these in designing our review.

Finally, we offer several recommendations based on our review. First, we need to focus more on how social resources and SES can influence childrearing, children's health, and transitions over the life course. Whereas the review indicates that investigators recognize the need to describe their study populations in terms of SES, there is much less attention paid to SES as a causal influence. There were some excellent examples of this in the literature we reviewed, but, given the importance that social resources seem to have for the development and well-being of children, more understanding and attention are needed. There was especially little attention paid to how normal development may (or may not) vary by SES. Increasingly, there has been more attention in the literature to the importance of context as suggested by Bronfenbrenner (1979). Yet, there has been little focus on the interaction of the broader social context (including neighborhoods and schools) with the family resources on the health and developmental outcomes of children.

Second, the field of child development would benefit from knowing more about the generalizability of studies of relatively homogeneous populations (often European American and middle class). How much is this research generalizable to other populations? There is very little systematic study of this issue in the literature.

Third, there should be more focus on the measures of SES and the source of these measures. Suprisingly, little attention has been paid to these issues. The measurement and source of information may or may not matter, but we do not have the evidence to know the answer. Specifically, when adolescents are used as the source of family background information, we need validated methods of obtaining youth reports of SES. Only recently have researchers begun to modify SES measures for use with adolescents, such as the new version of the MacArthur Scale of Subjective Social Status (Goodman et al, 2001). We also need more study of whether measures are culturally appropriate for populations other than those that the measures were developed.

Fourth, there is very little speculation or discussion in the child and parenting literature as to how or why SES may matter. There seemed little attempt to examine how social class influences child rearing. Interest in the implications of social stratification for family life seems missing in the literature that we reviewed. Smith and Graham (1995) reported a similar conclusion from their content analysis of the family literature.

Finally, recommendations for interdisciplinary research are becoming trite, but in this area active collaboration between sociologists and economists who have thought about SES with developmental scientists who know about children and parenting would seem to have the opportunity to reap large rewards.

ACKNOWLEDGMENTS

This work was supported by National Institute of Mental Health (Grant RO1 MH52336) and National Institute on Drug Abuse (Grant RO1 DA06630). The authors thank Marc Bornstein and Robert Bradley for their helpful comments on several drafts of the manuscript.

REFERENCES

Alwin, D. F., & Thornton, A. (1984). Family origins and the schooling process: Early versus late influence of parental characteristics. *American Sociological Review, 49*, 784–802.

Berrios, M. N., & Hagen, J. W. (2000). *Trends in research in two leading journals: Developmental Psychology and Child Development.* Presentation at Student Research Opportunity Program, Columbus, OH, August 2000.

Bidwell, C. E., & Friedkin, N. E. (1989). The sociology of education. In N. J. Smelser (Ed.), *Handbook of sociology* (pp. 449–472). Newbury Park, CA: Sage Publications.

Blau, P. M., & Duncan, O. D. (1967). *The American occupational structure.* New York: Wiley.

Bronfenbrenner, U. (1979). *The ecology of human development: Experiments by nature and design.* Cambridge, MA: Harvard University Press.

Bronfenbrenner, U., & Morris, P. A. (1997). The ecology of developmental processes. In W. Damon (Ed.), *Handbook of child psychology* (5th ed., pp. 993–1028). New York: Wiley.

Bunker, J. P., Gomby, D. S., & Kehrer, B. H. (1989). *Pathways to health: The role of social factors.* Menlo Park, CA: Henry J. Kaiser Family Foundation.

Coleman, J. S. (1988). Social capital in the creation of human capital. *American Journal of Sociology, 94* (Supplement 1988), S95–S120.

Conger, R. D., Ge, X., Elder, G. H., Lorenz, F. O., & Simons, R. L. (1994). Economic stress, coercive family process, and developmental problems of adolescents. *Child Development, 65,* 541–561.

Demo, D. H., & Acock, A. C. (1996). Family structure, family process, and adolescent well-being. *Journal of Research on Adolescence, 6,* 457–488.

Duncan, G. J., Brooks-Gunn, J., & Klebanov, P. K. (1994). Economic deprivation and early childhood development. *Child Development, 65,* 296–318.

Elder, G. (1996). Human lives in changing societies: Life course and developmental insights. In R. B. Cairns, G. H. Elder, Costello, E. J., & McGuire, A. (Eds.), *Developmental science* (pp. 31–62). New York: Cambridge University Press.

Elder, G. H., & Conger, R. D. (2000). *Children of the land: Adversity and success in rural America.* Chicago: University of Chicago Press.

Ensminger, M. E., & Slusarcick, A. L. (1992). Paths to high school graduation or dropout: A longitudinal study of a first-grade cohort. *Sociology of Education, 65,* 95–113.

Ensminger, M. E., Forrest, C. B., Riley, A. W., Myungsa, K., Green, B. F., Starfield, B., & Ryan., S. A. (2000). The validity of measures of socioeconomic status of adolescents. *Journal of Adolescent Research,* Vol. 15, No. 3, May 2000, pp. 392–419.

Entwisle, D. R., & Astone, N. M. (1994). Some practical guidelines for measuring youth's race–ethnicity and socioeconomic status. *Child Development, 65,* 1521–1540.

Goodman, E., Adler, N. E., Kawachi, I., Frazier, A. L., Huang, B., & Colditz, G. A. (2001). Adolescents' perceptions of social status: Development and evaluation of a new indicator. *Pediatrics,* Vol. 108, No. 2, August 2001.

Graham, S. (1992). Most of the subjects were white and middle class. *American Psychologist, 47*(5), 629–639.

Hagen, J. W., & Conley, A. C. (1994). Ethnicity and race of children studied in child development, 1980–1993. *Newsletter of the Society for Research in Child Development,* Spring 1994.

Hagen, J. W., Germak, M. C., McCartney, J. R., & Lignell, B. W. (2000, June). *Research on children: Trends in substantive areas and subject characteristics.* Presented at the 5th National Head Start Research Conference, Washington, DC.

Hauser, R. M. (1994). Measuring socioeconomic status in studies of child development. *Child Development, 65,* 1541–1545.

Hernandez, D. J. (1997). Child development and the social demography of childhood. *Child Development, 68,* 149–169.

Hollingshead, A. B. (1975). *Four-factor index of social status.* New Haven, CT: Yale University.

Kohn, M. L. (1977). *Class and conformity: A study in values.* Second Edition. Chicago, IL: The University of Chicago Press.

Krieger, N., Williams, D. R., & Moss, N. E. (1997). Measuring social class in U.S. public health research: Concepts, methodologies, and guidelines. *Annual Review of Public Health, 18,* 341–378.

Leventhal, T., & Brooks-Gunn, J. (2000). The neighborhoods they live in: The effects of neighborhood residence on child and adolescent outcomes. *Psychological Bulletin, 126,* 309–337:

Liberatos, P., Link, B. G., & Kelsey, J. L. (1988). The measurement of social class in epidemiology. *Epidemiologic Reviews, 10,* 87–121.

MacPhee, D., Kreutzer, J. C., & Fritz, J. J. (1994). Infusing a diversity perspective into human development courses. *Child Development, 65,* 699–715.

McLoyd, V. C., Jayartine, T. E., Ceballo, R., & Borquez, J. (1994). Unemployment and work interruption among African American single mothers: Effects on parenting and adolescent socioemotional functioning. *Child Development, 65,* 562–589.

McLoyd, V. C., & Randolph, S. M. (1985). Secular trends in the study of Afro-American children: A review of *Child Development,* 1936–1980. In A. B. Smuts & J. W. Hagen (Eds.), *Monographs of the Society for Research in Child Development,* 50(4–5, Serial No. 211).

Mechanic, D. (1989). Socioeconomic status and health: An examination of underlying processes. In J. P. Bunker, D. S. Gomby, & B. S. Kehrer (Eds.), *Pathways to health: The role of social factors* (pp. 9–26). Menlo Park, CA: The Henry J. Kaiser Family Foundation.

Menaghan, E. G., Kowaleski-Jones, L., & Mott, F. L. (1997). The intergenerational costs of parental social stressors: Academic and social difficulties in early adolescence for children of young mothers. *Journal of Health and Social Behavior,* 38(1), 72–86.

Menaghan, E. G., & Parcel, T. L. (1997). Social sources of change in children's home environments: The effects of parental occupational experiences and family conditions. *Journal of Marriage and the Family,* 57(1), 69–84.

Moynihan, D. P. (1965). *The Negro family: The Case for National Action.* Washington, DC: Office of Policy, Planning and Research, U.S. Department of Labor.

Pappas, G., Queen, S., Hadden, W., & Fisher, G. (1993). The increasing disparity in mortality between socioeconomic groups in the United States, 1960 and 1986. *New England Journal of Medicine,* 329(2):103–109.

Sampson, R. J., & Laub, J. H. (1994). Urban poverty and the family context of delinquency: A new look at structure and process in a classic study. *Child Development,* 65, 523–540.

Smith, T. E., & Graham, P. B. (1995) Socioeconomic stratification in family research. *Journal of Marriage and the Family,* 57, 930–941.

Williams, D. R. (1990). Socioeconomic differentials in health: A review and redirection. *Social Psychology Quarterly,* 53(2):81–99.

Wilson, W. J. (1987). *The truly disadvantaged: The inner city, the underclass, and public policy.* Chicago: University of Chicago Press.

2

Socioeconomic Status, Parenting, and Child Development: The *Hollingshead Four-Factor Index of Social Status* and the *Socioeconomic Index of Occupations*

Marc H. Bornstein, Chun-Shin Hahn,
Joan T. D. Suwalsky, and O. Maurice Haynes

National Institute of Child Health and Human Development

INTRODUCTION

Human parenting expresses itself and child development unfolds in multiple enveloping contexts, an important one being socioeconomic status (SES) (Bronfenbrenner & Morris, 1998; Lerner, Rothbaum, Boulos, & Castellino, 2002). Indeed, SES is thought to relate to variation in a host of biobehavioral through social ecological variables in family research (Argyle, 1994; Bradley & Corwyn, 2002; Hoff, Laursen, & Tardif, 2002). Distal variables like SES could affect child development directly or they could influence proximal variables like parenting beliefs and behaviors and thereby affect child development indirectly (Bornstein, 2002; Eccles, 1993; McLoyd, 1998). Little is known, however, about which specific features of SES influence which specific aspects of parenting and child development. In this chapter, we compare the two most prominent multivariate measures of SES and their components, and using structural equation modeling we assess simultaneous direct and indirect paths of influence from these two indexes of SES, and from their components, to multiple maternal behaviors and, in turn, to multiple infant behaviors.

Socioeconomic Status, Parenting, and Infancy

Many sociodemographic factors are relevant to parenting and child development, including ethnicity, race, and residence (Garcia Coll & Pachter, 2002; Hernandez, 1997; McLoyd, 1998). SES is a key sociodemographic marker variable (Entwisle & Astone, 1994; Hernandez, 1997; Hoff et al., 2002), and social status is associated with variation in parenting and child development (e.g., Palacios, 1990; Sameroff & Feil, 1985). SES is usually stable across a child's life (the first 17 years in Gottfried, Gottfried, Bathurst, Guerin, & Parramore, chap. 8, this volume). Lynd and Lynd (1929, 1937) described associations between social status and childrearing in *Middletown*, and Kohn (e.g., 1963; Kohn & Schooler, 1983) focused on how SES influenced parents, proposing that differences in parents' occupations engender differences in their childrearing values which, in turn, are associated with differences in parent-child relationships (Floyd & Saitzyk, 1992). Recent studies of parental beliefs have shown that high-SES mothers give higher estimates of their children's capacities and earlier age estimates for their children's attainment of developmental milestones than do low-SES mothers (e.g., Mansbach & Greenbaum, 1999; Ninio, 1988; Von der Lippe, 1999). In the behavioral realm, lower-SES mothers tend to be more controlling, restrictive, and disapproving, whereas higher-SES mothers tend to be less punitive and more tolerant of interruptions from their children (Hart & Risley, 1995; Kelley, Sanchez-Hucies, & Walker, 1993). Lower-SES parents provide generally more chaotic, disorganized, and unstructured environments than do higher-SES parents (Garrett, Ng'andu, & Ferron, 1994; Gottfried, 1984; Hart & Risley, 1992; Ninio, 1980). Higher-SES parents engage in more authoritative and lower-SES parents in more authoritarian relationships with their children (Gecas, 1979; Hess, 1970). Higher-SES parents act and talk with their young children more than lower-SES parents (Hart & Risley, 1995; Hoff-Ginsberg, 1991); they provide their infants with higher levels of emotional and verbal responsivity and afford their children more opportunities for variety in daily stimulation, more appropriate play materials, and more stimulation overall (Bradley & Corwyn, 2002). In turn, encouragement of verbal communication by higher-SES mothers is associated with child self-expression—babies from higher-SES families produce more sounds and words than do babies from lower-SES families (Hart & Risley, 1995; Papoušek, Papoušek, & Bornstein, 1985), and higher-SES mothers have children who possess higher level language skills (Hoff, chap. 6, this volume). More generally, Bradley, Corwyn, and Whiteside-Mansell (1996) reported that SES relates to intellectual and academic performance from infancy through middle childhood in a variety of cultures.

The specification of SES plays other key roles in developmental science. For example, it is essential to document the sociodemographic characteristics of study participants (see Bell & Hertz, 1976; Gottfried, 1985), to describe the characteristics of the study sample adequately, and to ensure proper comparability and generalizability. In spite of these several motives and its increasing popularity, the use of SES in developmental science and family research is still ad hoc and loose in operationalization and measurement (Smith & Graham, 1995).

SES Measurement

Components of SES

As currently conceived, SES is a multidimensional construct that is indexed by three quantitative factors having to do with parents, namely educational achievement, occupational status, and financial income, used alone or in combination (DeGarmo, Forgatch, & Martinez, 1999; Edwards & Bagozzi, 2000; Gottfried, 1985; Krieger, Williams, & Moss, 1997; Liberatos, Link, & Kelsey, 1988; Meudell, 1982; Smith & Graham, 1995; White, 1982). *Education* is perhaps the most common indicator of SES (Ensminger & Fothergill, chap. 1, this volume; Entwisle & Astone, 1994), as it is associated with many lifestyle traits, connotes level of acquired knowledge and cultural tastes (Liberatos et al., 1988), and is stable in adulthood (Gottfried et al., chap. 8, this volume; Hollingshead, 1975). Parental (particularly maternal) education has been associated with parenting beliefs and behaviors across ethnic groups and cultures (Alwin, 1984; Duncan & Brooks-Gunn, 1997; Kelly et al., 1993; Kohn, 1963; Laosa, 1980; Menaghan & Parcel, 1991; Tardif, 1993; Wright & Wright, 1976). For example, maternal education is associated with quantity and quality of speech to children and the nature of parental discipline practices. Maternal education correlates with SES as a whole ($r = .69$ in Bradley, Caldwell, Rock, & Ramey, 1989), and maternal and paternal education are also highly correlated (see Kalmijn, 1991). *Occupational status*, a second component of SES, is illustrative of the "skills and power" that people bring to their labor force participation as they function productively in society; occupation is also normally stable throughout adulthood (Hauser, 1994; Hollingshead, 1975; Otto, 1975). Occupation is associated with parenting behaviors (e.g., DeGarmo et al., 1999; Greenberger & O'Neill, 1991; Kohn & Schooler, 1983; Menaghan & Parcel, 1991). However, occupation is a somewhat problematic indicator of SES (Entwisle & Astone, 1994). For example, many women (particularly new mothers) self-exempt from labor force participation (e.g., Gottfried et al., chap. 8, this volume), and men's and women's occupations have different prestige and remunerate differently (Crompton, 1993; Kilbourne, England, & Beron, 1994). *Income*, the third main constituent of SES, provides families the wherewithal they must have to meet the physical needs and provide material resources for their children. There is conflicting evidence as to whether income per se is reliably or meaningfully associated with parenting or child development (Blau, 1999; Bradley, Mundfrom, Whiteside, & Caldwell, 1994; Conger & Elder, 1994; DeGarmo et al., 1999; Duncan & Brooks-Gunn; 1997; Garrett et al., 1994; Hitchcock & Oliver,

1976). Moreover, measuring monetary compensation is often precarious because income exhibits short-term variation (Duncan, 1988), questions about income, which is sensitive information, often suffer from item nonresponse (Entwisle & Astone, 1994; Hauser, 1994), and mothers' income may be especially unreliable (Gottfried et al., chap. 8, this volume).

Notably, Liberatos et al. (1988) and Gazeboom and Treiman (1996) observed that education, occupation, and income are not highly correlated and that each of these indicators is differentially associated with different child outcomes.

Instruments

Many instruments are available to measure family SES. The best known and most widely adopted measures (Ensminger & Fothergill, chap. 1, this volume; Ribas, 2001; Smith & Graham, 1995) are the Hollingshead Four-Factor Index of Social Status (HI; Hollingshead, 1975) and the Socioeconomic Index of Occupations (SEI; Duncan, 1961; Nakao & Treas, 1990, 1992). For example, Ribas (2001) reviewed the PsycArticles database and found that the HI was used in 259 articles published between 1988 and 2001 (the Hollingshead Two-Factor Index of Social Position, its predecessor, was used in an additional 108) and variants of the SEI were used in 51 articles. In recent reviews, Entwisle and Astone (1994) and Hauser (1994) recommended the SEI as a preferred measure of family SES. Other instruments are the Prestige Scale (Siegel, 1971), the Standard International Occupational Prestige Scale (Treiman, 1977; see also Ganzeboom & Treiman, 1996), the Socioeconomic Index for Occupations in Canada (Blishen, Carroll, & Moore, 1987), and the International Socio-Economic Index of Occupational Status (Ganzeboom, De Graaf, & Treiman, 1992).

The Hollingshead Four-Factor Index of Social Status is based on the education and occupation of each employed householder in a home. A householder is defined as a person who has or shares financial responsibility for maintaining the home and supporting the family members living there (Hauser, 1994). Homemakers, students, and unemployed individuals are not included in the calculations, with one exception: If there is no employed adult in the household, the HI is based on the one (unemployed) person most likely to be considered the householder. Occupation is keyed to approximately 450 titles and codes from the 1970 United States Census and is graded on a 9-point scale (Appendix 2.1). Education is based on the number of years of school achievement and is scored on a 7-point scale (Appendix 2.2). To determine the HI for an individual, scores on the two scales are weighted and summed; the education score is weighted by 3 and the occupation score is weighted by 5; the sum of the weighted scale scores results in a HI score ranging from 8 to 66. For families with more than one householder, individual HI scores are averaged to obtain a single family HI.

The Socioeconomic Index of Occupations updates Duncan's (1961) Socioeconomic Index, a frequently used ordinal measure of occupational prestige. The original SEI used age-standardized education and income levels of male occupational incumbents from the 1950 United States Census to predict occupational prestige. The SEI and its revisions constitute preferred descriptions of the socioeconomic ranking of occupations (e.g., Featherman & Hauser, 1977; Featherman & Stevens, 1982; Stevens & Cho, 1985). In particular, a 1989 study (Nakao & Treas, 1990) updated prestige scores assigned to occupations to reflect both occupational evaluations and the 1980 occupational classification system for 503 detailed occupational categories. In 1992, Nakao and Treas updated SEI scores for all detailed categories in the 1980 census occupational classification by regressing 1989 prestige scores on age-adjusted education and income levels of full-time incumbents to yield weights that would predict prestige. The prestige scores used were the proportion of respondents rating an occupation a 5 or above in the 1989 NORC General Social Survey (Nakao & Treas, 1990). SEI scores are computed to reflect the education required by occupations as well as the income and prestige that accompanies those occupations. Education weights more heavily in total-based than in male-based SEI scores, indicating sex-differences in prestige. SEI scores range from 0 to 100.

The Present Study

SES contributes to the short- and long-term goals parents have for their children, the practices parents employ in attempting to meet their goals, and, consequently, the everyday contexts of development experienced by children. Here we report direct and indirect relations among multiple measures of parental SES, multiple indexes of maternal parenting, and multiple indicators of infant development. In terms of SES, we examined the HI and SEI, the two most popular composite measures of SES, and we analyzed the role of their constituent components in predicting parenting and infant behaviors. Composite measures of SES and their constituent components may bear somewhat different relations to outcomes. With respect to the role of parenting, we examined the effects of SES on the most prominent maternal behaviors towards infants as they have been posited to mediate or be moderated by distal ecological variables, such as SES in their relations with child development. Infancy is an especially appealing and revealing time to investigate these relations. During the very first years of life, almost everything a child experiences and learns depends on his or her immediate environment and on what parents provide physically, emotionally, intellectually, and materially (Bornstein, 2002; Bradley, 2002). The infant, however, is also thought to be buffered in early development from variation in experience (McCall, 1981; Waddington, 1962).

    In this study of SES, mothering, and infancy, we exercised several precautions. First, we treated SES as a continuous variable and recruited a sample whose scores covered a wide range. Treating SES as a categorical variable diminishes its explanatory power, and a restricted range may attenuate otherwise meaningful effects of SES. Second, we studied SES in a European American one-child, mostly two-parent sample. Many variables including ethnicity, single-parent status, and family size that do not define SES per se covary with SES (see Harwood, Lyendecker, Carlson, Asencio, & Miller, 2002; McAdoo, 2002; Moore & Brooks-Gunn, 2002; Weinraub, Horvath, & Gringlas, 2002), making it difficult to disentangle these other influences from SES. Third, we used observational measures of parent and infant behaviors; SES is thought to relate to the accuracy of self-reports of parenting (many parenting instruments depend on verbal skills, for example; Holden & Edwards, 1989). Last, we used structural equation modeling to discern direct and indirect effects of the HI and SEI and their components on multiple mother and infant behaviors, considered simultaneously.

THE HI AND SEI *QUA* MEASURES OF SES

Participants

Altogether, 324 European American mother–infant dyads—149 mothers and their daughters and 175 mothers and their sons—participated in this study. Mothers were recruited through mass mailings and newspaper advertisements. The main inclusion criteria were: (1) mothers were at least 18 years of age and were of European American origin; (2) infants were firstborn only children; (3) infants were 5 months of age when observed; and (4) infants weighed at least 2500 g at birth and were healthy at the time of the study. Mothers were asked to provide demographic information on infant gender, birth weight, and health, and parental age, education, occupation, marital status, and number of hours of maternal employment per week outside the home.

Mothers' ages ranged from 18.1 to 43.1 years, $M = 29.7$ years, $SD = 5.8$. Ninety-three percent, $n = 301$, of the mothers were married at the time of the study; 19 adolescent and 4 adult women were not married. For 11 of these 23 families (7 of the teens and all of the adults), the baby's father was living in the home. For the entire sample, fathers' ages ranged from 18.1 to 58.2 years, $M = 32.2$ years, $SD = 6.6$. On average, infants were 163.3 days of age at the time of the observation, $SD = 6.8$. At birth, all were of normal weight, $M = 3542.5$ g, $SD = 469.2$, and the first children in their families, 306 by birth and 18 by domestic adoption.

Of the 324 participating mothers, 17 had not completed high school, 41 had completed high school, 71 had partial college, 195 had completed college, and, of those, 97 had completed university graduate programs, $M = 5.7$ on the HI 7-point education scale, $SD = 1.2$. At the time of observation, 61.7% of the mothers were employed outside of the home; those who were — $n = 200$ — worked an average of 30.8 hours per week, $SD = 14.2$. Fifteen mothers were employed in positions classified as skilled trades or lower; 14 were either sales workers or small business owners; and 45, 44, 45, and 37 mothers were employed in semiprofessional, minor, lesser, and major professional occupations, respectively, $M = 6.9$ on the HI 9-point occupation scale, $SD = 1.7$; $M = 62.6$ on the SEI, $SD = 22.5$.

Mean nonmaternal householder (typically the father, but in 14 cases grandparents or other relatives in addition to both parents, one parent, or neither parent of the infant) education ranged from 2 to 7 on the HI education scale, $M = 5.7$, $SD = 1.2$. Thirteen had not completed high school, 49 had completed high school, 60 had partial college, 197 had completed college, and, of those, 106 had completed university graduate programs. Occupational status of nonmaternal householders ranged from 1 to 9 on the HI occupation scale, $M = 6.7$, $SD = 2.2$, and from 14 to 92 on the SEI, $M = 64.0$, $SD = 20.7$. Sixty-six were employed in positions classified as skilled trades or lower; 20 were either sales workers or small business owners; and 42, 51, 57, and 83 were employed in semiprofessional, minor, lesser, and major professional occupations, respectively.

For 310 families, the HI was calculated based on the education and occupational status of either mother, $n = 5$; father, $n = 116$; or both, $n = 189$. For the families with single adult mothers, the HI was based on one or both parents (and, in one case, also the maternal grandparents). For the families with unmarried adolescent mothers, the HI was based on one or both of the parents in nine cases, on parent(s) and one or more maternal grandparents in four cases, and solely on the maternal grandparents in six cases. The SEI was calculated using the same householders who were used in the computation of the HI. A male householder was assigned the male-based SEI score for his occupation. The SEI for a female householder was estimated as twice the SEI score assigned her based on the total sample less the SEI score assigned her based on the sample of males only. For families with more than one householder, individual SEI scores were averaged to yield a family score.

Methods

Prior to data collection, the mother was instructed that the observer was interested in observing her infant's usual activities at a time when the mother was at home and solely responsible for her baby. Dyads were videotaped by a single observer for 1 hour in the home setting when the infant was awake. The mother was asked to go about her normal routine and to disregard the observer insofar as possible. Typically, no other people were present in the home during the visit. Mothers' verbal intelligence and personality traits were also assessed, but on a separate visit.

From the videotape of the home visit, the first 50 minutes were coded using mutually exclusive and exhaustive coding systems that assessed 12 maternal and 15 infant behaviors using real-time observation coding procedures. (For details of the video/audiorecording, data coding, and scoring, see Bornstein, Tamis-LeMonda, Suwalsky, Rahn, & Ludemann, 1991.) Coders were first trained to reliability on consensus coding, and between 14% and 21% of the sample (depending on domain) was afterward coded independently to obtain reliability. For all behaviors that were continuously coded, *kappa* (κ; Cohen, 1960, 1968) was used; for time-sampled behaviors, the Intra-Class Correlation (ICC: McGraw & Wong, 1996) was used.

Six maternal domains were identified, encompassing 12 primary parenting tasks and abilities required of the mother of a young infant: nurture (feed/burp/wipe, bathe/diaper/dress/groom, and hold), physical and verbal encouragement of gross motor skills (to sit/stand and to roll/crawl/step), social exchange (encourage attention to mother, social play, express affection), didactic interaction (encourage attention to the object world), provision of the material environment (including quality and quantity of play materials), and speech to child. Appendix 2.3A gives details of behavioral and context indicators and scoring reliabilities for these domains.

Five infant domains, representing 15 key developmental and performance competencies that are critical to successful adaptation of the infant in the middle of the first year of life were identified: physical development (prelocomotion-upper body, prelocomotion-lower body, locomotion, and sitting), social interaction (look at mother, smile, alert expression), exploration (look, touch, mouth, and extent and efficiency of exploration), nondistress vocalization, and distress communication (negative facial expression and negative vocalization). Appendix 2.3B gives details of behavioral indicators and scoring reliabilities for these domains.

The means and standard deviations for each domain score and its indicators are listed in Table 2.1.

Evaluation of the Visit

Although mothers may interact more or differently with their children when they know they are being observed, this effect does not vary as a function of SES (Hoff et al., 2002). Nonetheless, as a check against such threats to validity, at the conclusion of the home visit the mother and the observer independently evaluated the observation session by marking a series of 8-point, *range* $= 0$ to 7, graphic rating scales, randomly ordered with respect to valence but recoded in ascending order. According to the observers' evaluation, mothers were relaxed, $M = 5.3, SD = 1.5$, and did not engage in activities that seemed preplanned, $M = 1.2, SD = 1.4$; infants appeared alert, $M = 5.1, SD = 1.9$; and not fussy, $M = 2.1, SD = 1.8$. Mothers also reported that they felt relatively comfortable being videotaped, $M = 5.2, SD = 1.5$, and that they talked to their child no more or less than usual, $M = 3.1, SD = 1.3$. According to both the mother and the observer, infants showed only moderate interest in the observer, $M = 3.0, SD = 1.6$; $M = 3.5, SD = 1.9$, and camera, $M = 3.4, SD = 1.8$; $M = 3.6, SD = 1.8$. Mothers reported that their child's, $M = 5.6, SD = 1.8$, and their own, $M = 5.1, SD = 1.7$, behavior during the session was characteristic of their normal routine. These data suggest that the observation procedures yielded data that are representative and generalizable.

TABLE 2.1
Domain Scores for Mothers and Infants and Their Indicators ($N = 324$)

	Domain Scores		Frequency		Duration	
	M	SD	M	SD	M	SD
Maternal behaviors						
Nurture	.00	.64	—	—	—	—
Feed/burp/wipe	—	—	—	—	442.43	377.26
Bath/diaper/dress/ groom/other	—	—	—	—	230.55	247.35
Hold	—	—	—	—	925.51	534.19
Physical	.12	.09	—	—	—	—
Encourage to sit/stand[a]	.21	.16	—	—	—	—
Encourage to roll/ crawl/step[a]	.03	.05	—	—	—	—
Social	.00	.68	—	—	—	—
Encourage attention to mother	—	—	21.41	14.77	199.70	162.89
Social play	—	—	15.01	13.18	99.10	102.09
Express affection	—	—	19.67	14.28	72.37	81.33
Didactic	.00	.91	—	—	—	—
Encourage attention to objects	—	—	30.05	18.99	295.48	241.78
Material	.00	.61	—	—	—	—
Quality of objects provided[b]	.00	.82	—	—	—	—
Quantity of objects provided[b]	.00	.85	—	—	—	—
Language[c]	.00	.86	—	—	—	—
Speech to child	—	—	239.55	102.87	668.14	394.68
Infant behaviors						
Physical development	−.05	.75	—	—	—	—
Prelocomotion–upper body[d]	2.67	.74	—	—	—	—
Prelocomotion–lower body[d]	1.73	.85	—	—	—	—
Locomotion[d]	2.16	1.52	—	—	—	—
Sitting[d]	2.46	.91	—	—	—	—
Social	.00	.65	—	—	—	—
Look at mother	—	—	49.38	25.39	210.54	145.77
Smile	—	—	10.67	11.82	23.46	30.59
Alert expression	—	—	—	—	2156.66	328.47
Exploration	.00	.61	—	—	—	—
Look at object	—	—	120.78	37.05	1027.64	389.30
Touch object	—	—	69.86	40.21	662.48	391.60
Mouth object	—	—	37.91	27.01	312.44	226.86
Extent of exploration[b]	.00	.90	—	—	—	—
Efficiency of exploration[b]	.00	.85	—	—	—	—

(Continued)

TABLE 2.1
(Continued)

	Domain Scores		Frequency		Duration	
	M	SD	M	SD	M	SD
Vocalization	.00	.92	—	—	—	—
Nondistress vocalization	—	—	123.58	61.52	283.34	194.98
Distress communication	.00	.90	—	—	—	—
Negative facial expression	—	—	10.61	10.79	48.10	72.89
Distress vocalization	—	—	11.50	15.62	64.75	100.09

[a] Mean proportion of intervals.
[b] Mean standard score.
[c] Residual controlling for mothers' self-evaluation of the amount of talking during the observation.
[d] Mean highest level.
Note. Duration is in sec.

We evaluated these scales for use as covariates prior to the main analyses. In order to qualify as a covariate, the scale scores had to correlate meaningfully (explain at least 5% of the variance with relations in an expected direction) and significantly, $p < .05$, with the domain scores. Only one significant correlation between mothers' self-evaluations and their behaviors emerged. Mothers who reported that they talked to their child more often than usual directed more speech to their child during the observation, $r(297) = .24$, $p < .001$; therefore, the residual of the mother language domain score, controlling for her self-evaluation of amount of talking, was computed and used in all analyses.

RELATIONS BETWEEN THE HOLLINGSHEAD FOUR-FACTOR INDEX OF SOCIAL STATUS AND THE SOCIOECONOMIC INDEX OF OCCUPATIONS

The sample represented a range from low to upper-middle SES. The mean HI across all families was 50.6, $SD = 12.6$; *range* = 14 to 66, and the mean SEI was 63.2, $SD = 19.8$; *range* = 14 to 95. The zero-order correlation of the HI and SEI was $r(322) = .89$, $p < .001$ (see Figure 2.1). This correlation compares well with intercorrelations among the SES indexes as previously reported by Gottfried (1985): Duncan with Siegel, $r = .87$; Duncan with Hollingshead, $r = .79$; and Siegel with Hollingshead, $r = .73$, all $ps < .001$. Clearly, all these indexes of SES overlap and share large proportions of variance; however, they cannot be considered interchangeable (Gottfried, 1985).

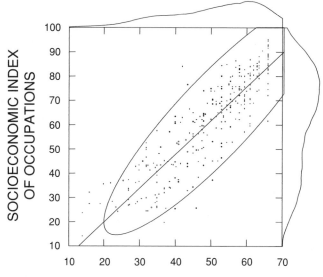

FIGURE 2.1.   The line represents the linear regression of SEI on HI
($N = 324$). Marginal kernel curves show skewness is only slightly
greater in HI than in SEI. The 95% sample confidence ellipse en-
closes all but a few stray points, especially at the lower end of
the scales. The size of the points, which correspond to the influence of each point on the correlation, also indicates no unduly
influential points.

THE HOLLINGSHEAD FOUR-FACTOR INDEX OF SOCIAL STATUS AND MOTHER AND INFANT BEHAVIORS

Preliminary analyses and the data analytic plan are detailed in Appendix 2.4, including a discussion of the structural equation modeling, identification of potential
covariates, and treatment of variables. In the first section, we report models with
HI as the predictor of mother and infant behaviors, followed by separate models
with each of the four components of HI as the primary predictor. In addition, we
tested each of the final models with HI or mothers' education as the predictor for
cross-group invariance in mothers of girls and mothers of boys. Furthermore, we
evaluated separate models controlling for covariations among mothers' education
and education and occupational status of nonmaternal householders, and among
mothers' education, IQ, and personality, respectively. In each model, we evaluated
the effects of the primary predictor controlling for its covariation with maternal
age and hours of employment. Maternal age correlated with the HI, $r(322) = .62$,
$p < .001$, and each of its components. Employment correlated with the HI and

mothers' education and occupation, $r(322, 322, 198)$s $= .14, .22,$ and $.25, ps <$ .05, .001, and .001, respectively. Evaluation of the measurement model of maternal domain scores is presented in Appendix 2.5; it resulted in two first-order factors (dyadic and extradyadic focus). Because correlation coefficients between all pairs of infant domain scores were small (with the exception of the correlation between infant physical and exploration, $r = .34,$ the absolute magnitudes of all other correlations ranged from .00 to .16), and the ratio of aggregated shared variances to aggregated shared plus aggregated unique variances for all pairs of infant domain scores was low (Kaiser-Meyer-Olkin measure $= .47$), no factor structure was evident for the infant variables.

Zero-order Correlations

Table 2.2 presents zero-order correlations of the HI and its components with maternal and infant domains of behavior. The HI and occupational status of nonmaternal householders were related to all maternal domains, except mother nurture and material. Mothers' education was related to all maternal domains, except mother nurture. Mothers' occupational status and education of nonmaternal householders were related to mother physical and language domains. Neither the HI nor any components was related to infant behaviors based on their zero-order correlation.

Structural Equation Modeling

Full Sample

To study the direct and indirect effects of the HI on infant behavior, with indirect effects mediated by maternal behaviors, and to control for the covariations between HI and maternal age and employment in predicting maternal behaviors, the data were evaluated in structural equation models. An initial model (see Figure 2.2) was tested that contained—other than the paths in the measurement model for maternal domain scores, the covariations between HI and maternal age and maternal employment, and between maternal age and employment—direct paths from HI and maternal age and employment to dyadic and extradyadic focus latent variables, from the dyadic focus latent variable to infant physical (negative) and social, from the extradyadic focus to infant physical and exploration, from the error term of mother physical to infant physical and exploration, and from infant vocalization (negative) and distress communication to mother nurture. (In this and other models, covariances between the error terms for infant social and vocalization and exploration and distress communication were included.) The a priori model did not fit the data, S-B $\chi^2(64) = 130.22, p < .001,$ Robust CFI $= .91,$ RMSEA $= .06, 90\%$ CI $= (.04, .07).$ The Wald tests suggested dropping several paths, and the Lagrange multiplier tests suggested possible additional paths.

TABLE 2.2
Zero-Order Correlations of the Hollingshead Index and Its Components with Maternal and Infant Behaviors

	Hollingshead Index N = 324	Mothers' Education N = 324	Mothers' Occupational Status n = 200	Nonmaternal Householder Education N = 319	Nonmaternal Householder Occupational Status N = 319
Maternal domains					
Nurture	.06	.03	.04	.10	.08
Physical	.22***	.19***	.15*	.22***	.22***
Social	.13*	.12*	.04	.11	.15**
Didactic	.13*	.12*	.10	.10	.14**
Material	.10	.11*	.01	.07	.10
Language	.30***	.36***	.15*	.30***	.26***
Infant domains					
Physical	.06	.05	.03	.07	.05
Social	.01	.03	.04	.02	.03
Exploration	−.00	.01	−.04	.01	.00
Vocalization	.02	.06	.04	.07	.02
Distress communication	.03	.02	−.03	.03	.07

$* p \leq .05; ** p \leq .01; *** p \leq .001.$

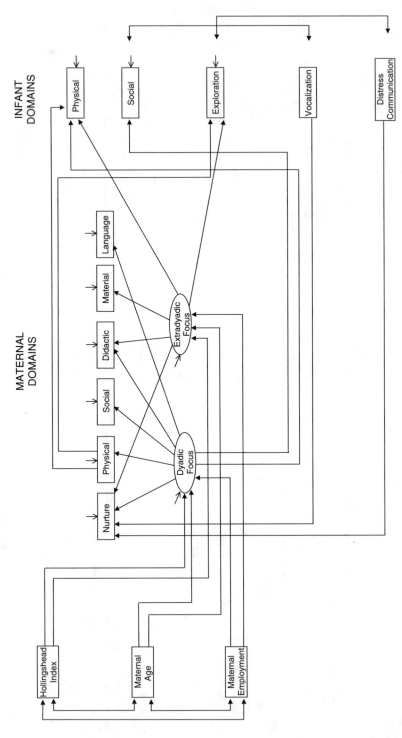

FIGURE 2.2. Hypothetical model of causal relations among HI, maternal age, maternal employment, and mother and infant behaviors.

Figure 2.3 presents the standardized solution to the structural portion of the final, sequentially constructed model, S-B $\chi^2(63) = 79.24$, $p \leq .08$, Robust CFI = .98, RMSEA = .03, 90% CI = (.00, .05). The model reproduced observed correlations with an average absolute standardized error of .03. All parameters estimated in the model were significant at the .05 level or better. Of primary interest in this model are the paths from HI to maternal behaviors and the indirect effects of HI on infant behaviors. HI related significantly to dyadic focus controlling for the relations of HI with maternal age and employment. Controlling for relations with maternal age and employment, HI also had direct effects on mother physical and material domains. Mothers with a higher HI more often encouraged their infants' physical development and provided their infants with more objects, objects with more stimulating features for exploration, or both. Significant effects of HI on five maternal domains were mediated by dyadic focus. Mothers with a higher HI spent a longer time nurturing their infants (standardized indirect effect = .04, $p < .05$), more often encouraged their infants' physical development (standardized indirect effect = .08, $p < .01$), engaged in more social exchanges (standardized indirect effect = .13, $p < .01$) and didactic interactions (standardized indirect effect = .13, $p < .01$) with their infants, and spoke more to their infants (standardized indirect effect = .11, $p < .01$). Two infant behaviors contributed to the time mothers spent in nurturing them. Mothers whose infants vocalized nondistress less often or communicated distress more often spent longer nurturing their infants.

Controlling for relations of HI and employment to maternal age, older mothers spoke more to their infants. Mothers' employment related significantly to extradyadic focus controlling for relations with HI and maternal age. Controlling for relations of maternal employment on HI and maternal age, significant effects of mothers' employment on mother nurture, didactic, and material were mediated by extradyadic focus. Mothers who worked more hours spent more time nurturing their infants (standardized indirect effect = .09, $p < .05$), engaged in fewer didactic interactions (standardized indirect effect = $-.08$, $p < .05$), and provided their infants with fewer objects, objects with fewer stimulating features for exploration (standardized indirect effect = $-.09$, $p < .05$), or both. Controlling for relations with HI and maternal age, mothers' employment had a direct effect on mothers' didactic domain. Mothers who worked more hours engaged in fewer didactic interactions with their infants. In addition, mothers who worked longer hours had infants who communicated distress more often during the observation.

With regard to the indirect effects of HI on infant behaviors, infants from higher HI families exhibited a lower level of gross motor development (standardized indirect effect = $-.03$, $p \leq .05$) but engaged in more social exchanges (standardized indirect effect = .07, $p < .01$), with both effects mediated by dyadic focus. Mothers' employment had negative indirect effects on infant physical development (standardized indirect effect = $-.06$, $p < .05$) and exploration (standardized indirect effect = $-.11$, $p < .05$). Infants of mothers who worked more hours exhibited a lower level of gross motor development and engaged in less exploring, with both effects mediated by extradyadic focus.

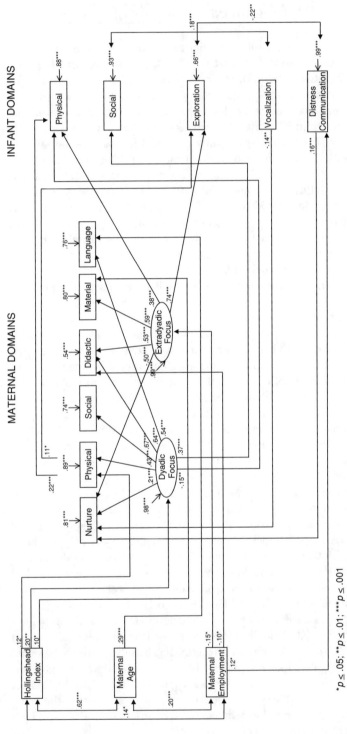

FIGURE 2.3. Standardized solution for the final model for relations among HI, maternal age, maternal employment, and mother and infant behaviors (*N* = 324). (In this and subsequent figures, numbers associated with single-headed arrows are standardized path coefficients; numbers associated with double-headed arrows are standardized covariance estimates. Arrows associated with dependent variables are error or disturbance terms.)

*p ≤ .05; **p ≤ .01; ***p ≤ .001

44

Child Gender

To test whether the final model fit equally well for mothers of girls and mothers of boys, we constructed a series of nested multisample models that sequentially introduced constraints on path coefficients, factor loadings, and covariances (Bentler, 1995; Bollen, 1989). For the test of cross-group invariance, a preliminary test in which no parameter estimates were constrained to be equal fit the data, suggesting that more restrictive models were appropriate. Results from multisample models in which factor loadings, path coefficients, and covariances were constrained to be equal suggested that there were two factor loadings and two path coefficients that differed for mothers of girls and mothers of boys. When these four constraints were released, a good fit was achieved, $\chi^2(148) = 168.32$, $p \leq .12$, CFI = .98, RMSEA = .02, 90% CI = (.00, .03). The four constraints that showed gender differences were the factor loadings from dyadic focus to mother physical (standardized factor loading = .36, $p < .001$, for mothers of girls and .47, $p < .001$, for mothers of boys) and from dyadic focus to mother didactic (standardized factor loading = .59, $p < .001$, for mothers of girls and .68, $p < .001$, for mothers of boys), and the path coefficients from the error term of mother physical to infant exploration (standardized coefficient = .20, $p < .01$, for girls and .06, $p \leq .32$, for boys) and from infant distress communication to mother nurture (standardized coefficient = .29, $p < .001$, for mothers of girls and .05, $p \leq .43$, for mothers of boys). Girls whose mothers more often encouraged their physical development (that part of the variance in mother physical that was unrelated to the latent variable of dyadic focus) engaged in more exploring, and the distress communications of girls led to their mothers' nurturing behaviors. No such relations existed in mother–son dyads. Although the magnitudes of the factor loadings differed statistically, all were significant and in the same direction for mothers of girls and mothers of boys. These gender differences were limited to the relations of dyadic focus with mother physical and didactic, between mother physical and infant exploration, and between infant distress communication and maternal nurturant behaviors, and so the main HI relations to maternal behavior and infant development held equally for girls and boys.

Components of the Hollingshead Four-Factor Index of Social Status and Mother and Infant Behaviors

The HI is constructed of four components: maternal education and occupation, and nonmaternal householder education and occupation. In the analyses that follow, we aimed to find the component(s) of the HI that underlay the direct or indirect effects of the HI on mother and infant behavioral domains by examining each component of the HI in predicting mother and infant domains of behavior. With this aim in mind, we limit this discussion to the direct and indirect effects of each component of the HI on mother and infant domains.

Maternal Education

Figure 2.4 presents the standardized solution to the final model with mothers' education as the predictor, S-B $\chi^2(64) = 82.45$, $p \leq .06$, Robust CFI $= .98$, RMSEA $= .03$, 90% CI $= (.00, .05)$. The model reproduced observed correlations with an average absolute standardized error of .03. Controlling for its relation to age and employment, mothers' education related significantly to dyadic focus. Controlling for relations with age and employment, mothers' education also had a direct effect on mother material. Mothers with more education provided their infants with more objects, objects with more stimulating features for exploration, or both. Effects of mothers' education on five maternal domains, mediated by dyadic focus, were significant. Mothers with more education spent a longer time in nurturing (standardized indirect effect $= .05$, $p < .01$), more often encouraged physical development (standardized indirect effect $= .10$, $p < .001$), engaged in more social exchanges (standardized indirect effect $= .15$, $p < .001$) and didactic interactions (standardized indirect effect $= .15$, $p < .001$), and spoke more to their infants (standardized indirect effect $= .12$, $p < .001$). With regard to the effect of mothers' education on infant behaviors, infants of more educated mothers exhibited a lower level of gross motor development (standardized indirect effect $= -.03$, $p < .05$) but engaged in more social exchanges (standardized indirect effect $= .08$, $p < .01$), with both effects mediated by dyadic focus.

Maternal Occupational Status

This model was based on the 200 mothers who were working outside the home at the time of study. Figure 2.5 presents the standardized solution to the final model with mothers' occupational status as the predictor, S-B $\chi^2(69) = 78.56$, $p \leq .20$, Robust CFI $= .98$, RMSEA $= .03$, 90% CI $= (.00, .05)$. The model reproduced observed correlations with an average absolute standardized error of .04. Controlling for its relations to mothers' age and employment, mothers' occupational status did not relate to any maternal behaviors; nor were there direct or indirect effects of mothers' occupational status on infant behaviors.

Nonmaternal Householder Education

Figure 2.6 presents the standardized solution to the final model with education of nonmaternal householders as the predictor, S-B $\chi^2(65) = 92.00$, $p \leq .02$, Robust CFI $= .96$, RMSEA $= .04$, 90% CI $= (.02, .05)$. The model reproduced observed correlations with an average absolute standardized error of .03. Controlling for relations with maternal age, education of nonmaternal householders related to dyadic focus. Controlling for relations with maternal age, education of nonmaternal householders also had a direct effect on mother physical domain. Mothers from families with more educated nonmaternal householders encouraged their infants' physical development more. Effects of education of nonmaternal

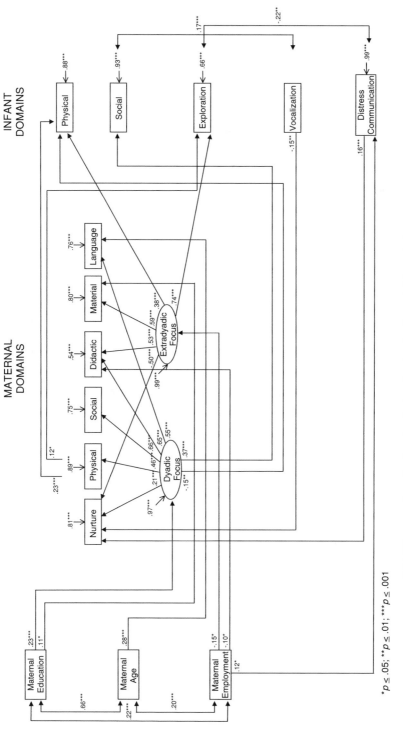

FIGURE 2.4. Standardized solution for the final model for relations among maternal education, age, employment, and mother and infant behaviors ($N = 324$).

$*p \leq .05; **p \leq .01; ***p \leq .001$

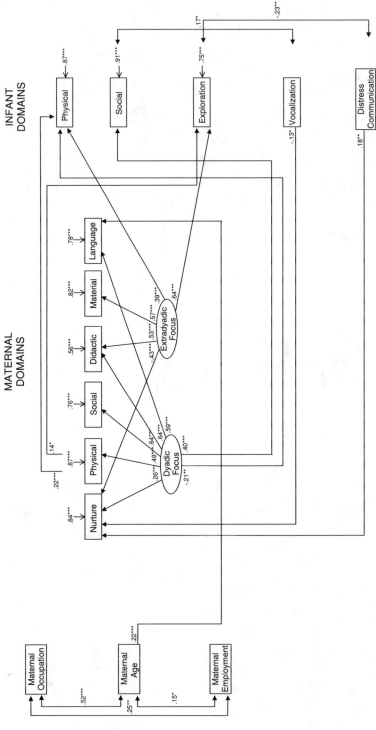

FIGURE 2.5. Standardized solution for the final model for relations among maternal occupational status, age, employment, and mother and infant behaviors (*N* = 200).

*p ≤ .05; **p ≤ .01; ***p ≤ .001

48

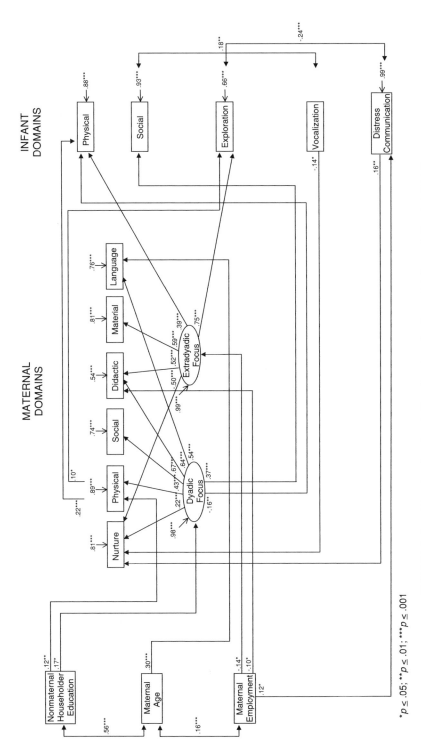

FIGURE 2.6. Standardized solution for the final model for relations among nonmaternal householder education, maternal age, maternal employment, and mother and infant behaviors (N = 319).

*p ≤ .05; **p ≤ .01; ***p ≤ .001

householders on the five maternal domains, mediated by dyadic focus, were significant. Mothers from families with more educated nonmaternal householders spent a longer time nurturing (standardized indirect effect = .04, $p < .05$), more often encouraged their infants' physical development (standardized indirect effect = .07, $p < .05$), engaged in more social exchanges (standardized indirect effect = .12, $p < .01$) and didactic interactions (standardized indirect effect = .11, $p < .01$), and spoke more to their infants (standardized indirect effect = .09, $p < .05$).

Infants from families with more educated nonmaternal householders engaged in more social exchanges (standardized indirect effect = .06, $p < .05$), with the effect mediated by dyadic focus.

Nonmaternal Householder Occupational Status

Figure 2.7 presents the standardized solution to the final model with occupational status of nonmaternal head(s) of the household as the predictor, S-B $\chi^2(65) = 115.44$, $p \leq .001$, Robust CFI = .93, RMSEA = .05, 90% CI = (.03, .06). The model reproduced observed correlations with an average absolute standardized error of .04. Controlling for relations with maternal age, occupational status of nonmaternal householders related to dyadic focus. Controlling for relations with maternal age, occupational status of nonmaternal householders also had a direct effect on mother physical. Mothers from families with nonmaternal householders with higher occupational status encouraged their infants' physical development more. The direct effect of occupational status of nonmaternal householders on mother material was only marginally significant ($p = .059$). Effects of occupational status of nonmaternal householders on five maternal domains, mediated by dyadic focus, were significant. Mothers from families with nonmaternal householders with higher occupational status spent a longer time in nurturing their infants (standardized indirect effect = .04, $p < .05$), encouraged their infants' physical development more (standardized indirect effect = .06, $p < .01$), engaged in more social exchanges (standardized indirect effect = .14, $p < .01$) and didactic interactions (standardized indirect effect = .13, $p < .01$), and spoke more to their infants (standardized indirect effect = .11, $p < .01$).

Infants from families with nonmaternal householders with higher occupational status exhibited a lower level of gross motor development (standardized indirect effect = $-.03$, $p < .05$) but engaged in more social exchanges (standardized indirect effect = .08, $p < .01$), with both effects mediated by dyadic focus.

Maternal Occupational Status Re-visited

In contrast to the results of mothers' education (Figure 2.4) and the education and occupational status of nonmaternal householders (Figures 2.6 and 2.7), the model based on the 200 mothers who were working outside the home indicated

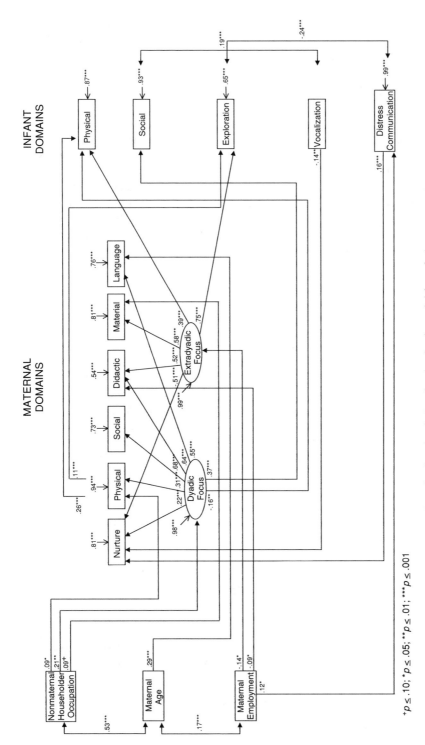

FIGURE 2.7. Standardized solution for the final model for relations among non-maternal householder occupational status, maternal age, maternal employment, and mother and infant behaviors (*N* = 319).

+*p* ≤ .10; *p* ≤ .05; **p* ≤ .01; ***p* ≤ .001

that mothers' occupational status (Figure 2.5) did not relate to any of the maternal behaviors. We suspected that this attenuation was caused by the reduction of the sample size, and thus we built a model with mothers' education as the co-predictor with the same 200 mothers. The final model fit the data, S-B $\chi^2(79) = 78.21$, $p \leq .50$, Robust CFI = 1.00, RMSEA = .00, 90% CI = (.00, .04). The model reproduced observed correlations with an average absolute standardized error of .04. Controlling for relations with age, employment, and occupational status, mothers' education related to dyadic focus (standardized path coefficient = .27, $p < .001$). Effects of mothers' education on all maternal domains with the exception of mother material, mediated by dyadic focus, were significant at the .05 level or better. This model suggests that, after relations with maternal education, age, and employment were accounted for, the nonsignificant role of mothers' occupational status in predicting maternal behaviors is probably not ascribable to a reduction in power to detect an effect.

Nonmaternal Householder Education and Occupation Re-visited

The foregoing analyses indicated significant effects of mothers' education and the education and occupational status of nonmaternal householders on mother and infant behaviors. Specific relations between particular components of the HI and maternal behaviors may be difficult to discern because components of the HI are usually highly intercorrelated. For this sample, zero-order correlations between mothers' education and the education of the nonmaternal householder was $r(317) = .77$, $p < .001$ (see too Kalmijn, 1991), and that between mothers' education and the occupational status of the nonmaternal householder was $r(317) = .70$, $p < .001$. The following analyses evaluated the unique impact of mothers' education on their own behaviors. To this end, we included the education and occupational status of nonmaternal householders simultaneously with mothers' education in one model as co-predictors of mother and infant behaviors, controlling for maternal age and employment.

The final model fit the data: S-B $\chi^2(87) = 104.83$, $p \leq .09$, Robust CFI = .99, RMSEA = .03, 90% CI = (.00, .04). The model reproduced observed correlations with an average absolute standardized error of .03. Figure 2.8 shows the model. Controlling for relations with the education and occupational status of nonmaternal householders, as well as maternal age and employment, mothers' education related significantly to dyadic focus. Effects of mothers' education on all maternal domains, with the exception of mother material mediated by dyadic focus, were significant at the .05 level or better. Mothers with more education spent more time in nurturing their infants, more often promoted their physical development, engaged in more social exchanges and more didactic interactions, and spoke to their infants more. Controlling for relations with education and occupational status of nonmaternal householders, as well as maternal age and employment,

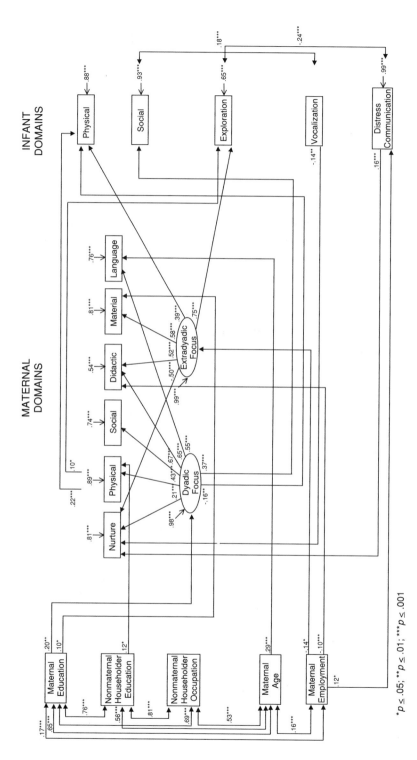

FIGURE 2.8. Standardized solution for the final model for relations among maternal education, age, employment, nonmaternal householder education and occupation, and mother and infant behaviors (N = 324).

*p ≤ .05; **p ≤ .01; ***p ≤ .001

mothers' education had a direct effect on mother material. Mothers with more education provided their infants with more objects, objects with more stimulating features to explore, or both. Controlling for relations with mothers' education, the occupational status of nonmaternal householders, and maternal age, the education of nonmaternal householders related significantly to mother physical. Mothers from families with more educated nonmaternal householders encouraged their infants' physical development more. Controlling for relations with maternal education and age as well as the education of nonmaternal householders, the occupational status of nonmaternal householders did not relate to any mother behaviors.

Infants of more educated mothers exhibited lower levels of gross motor development (standardized indirect effect $= -.03$, $p < .05$) but engaged in more social exchanges (standardized indirect effect $= .08$, $p < .01$), with both effects mediated by dyadic focus.

Mothers' Education and Mother and Infant Behaviors Controlling for Intelligence and Personality

Maternal Education, Intelligence, and Personality Re-visited

Finally, with respect to the HI, we asked whether mothers' education predicts mothers' own behaviors independent of their intelligence and personality traits. This model was based on 244 mothers from whom we were able to obtain maternal verbal intelligence scores as measured by the Peabody Picture Vocabulary Test-Revised (PPVT-R Form L; Dunn & Dunn, 1981; $M = 108.43$, $SD = 16.67$) and personality traits as measured by the Jackson Personality Inventory (JPI; Jackson, 1976). For purposes of this analysis, we computed the Big Five personality factors from the JPI following Paunonen and Jackson's (1976) model. The Openness factor consisted of the JPI Breadth of Interest, $M = 48.32$, $SD = 10.20$, and Innovation scales, $M = 50.30$, $SD = 9.65$. The Neuroticism factor consisted of the Anxiety, $M = 48.34$, $SD = 9.86$, Interpersonal Affect, $M = 48.35$, $SD = 8.57$, and Conformity, $M = 47.02$, $SD = 8.99$, scales. The Extraversion factor consisted of the Self-esteem, $M = 53.56$, $SD = 8.82$, and Social Participation $M = 46.79$, $SD = 8.91$, scales. These three factors were computed as the principal components of their constituent scales. The scale score Responsibility, $M = 56.73$, $SD = 7.11$, was taken as a single index of Trustworthiness, and the scale score Organization, $M = 54.74$, $SD = 9.44$, was taken as a single index of Conscientiousness. At the zero-order level, only maternal verbal intelligence, $r(242) = .62$, $p < .001$, and Openness, $r(242) = .23$, $p < .001$, were significantly related to mothers' education. Both were significantly related to the mother physical ($r(242) = .15$, $p < .05$, for verbal intelligence and $r(242) = .14$, $p < .05$, for Openness) and mother language

($r(242) = .30$, $p < .001$, for verbal intelligence and $r(242) = .16$, $p < .05$, for Openness) domains.

In the structural equation model, we added maternal verbal intelligence and Openness as co-predictors with mothers' education, age, and employment in predicting mother and infant behaviors. Figure 2.9 shows that the final model fit the data: S-B $\chi^2(88) = 108.18$, $p \leq .07$, Robust CFI = .97, RMSEA = .03, 90% CI = (.00, .05). The model reproduced observed correlations with an average absolute standardized error of .04. Mothers' education significantly covaried with age, employment, verbal intelligence, and Openness. Controlling for relations with maternal age, employment, verbal intelligence, and Openness, mothers' education related to dyadic focus. Effects of mothers' education on all maternal domains with the exception of mother material, mediated by dyadic focus, were significant at the .05 level or better. Infants of more educated mothers exhibited a lower level of gross motor development (standardized indirect effect $= -.04$, $p < .05$) but engaged in more social exchanges (standardized indirect effect $= .08$, $p < .01$), with both effects mediated by dyadic focus. Controlling for relations with maternal education, age, and Openness, maternal verbal intelligence related to mother language. There were no direct or indirect effects of maternal verbal intelligence on infant behaviors. Controlling for its relations to mothers' education, age, and verbal intelligence, Openness did not relate to any maternal behaviors, nor were there direct or indirect effects of mothers' Openness on infant behaviors.

Child Gender

The consistent and unique predictive validity of mothers' education on mother and infant behaviors prompted inquiry into whether the final model with mother's education as the predictor (Figure 2.4) fit equally well for the mothers of girls and mothers of boys. A preliminary multisample test, in which no parameter estimates were constrained to be equal, fit the data, suggesting that more restrictive tests were appropriate. Results from multisample models in which factor loadings, path coefficients, and covariances were constrained to be equal suggested that there were two path coefficients that differed for mothers of girls and mothers of boys. When these two constraints were released, a good fit was achieved, $\chi^2(151) = 183.72$, $p \leq .04$, CFI = .96, RMSEA = .03, 90% CI = (.01, .04). The two constraints that showed gender differences were the path coefficients from error term of mother physical to infant exploration (standardized coefficient $= .21$, $p < .01$, for girls and .04, $p \leq .48$, for boys) and the path coefficient from infant distress communication to mother nurture (standardized coefficient $= .29$, $p < .001$, for mothers of girls and .06, $p \leq .40$, for mothers of boys). Girls whose mothers more often encouraged their physical development (that part of variance in mother physical that was unrelated to the latent variable of dyadic focus) engaged in more exploring, and the distress communications of girls led to their mothers' nurturing behaviors. No such relations existed in mother-son dyads.

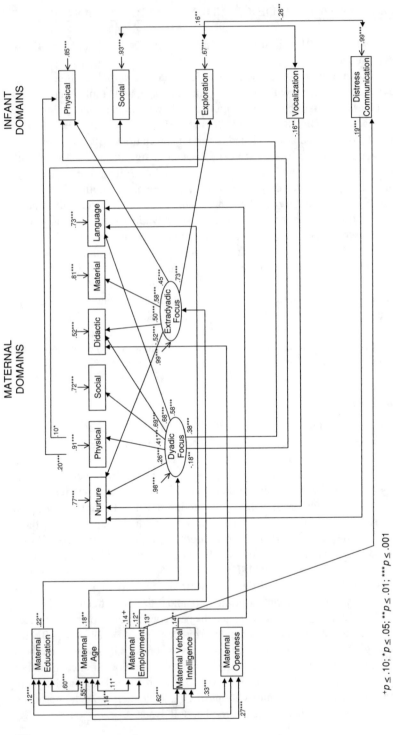

FIGURE 2.9. Standardized solution for the final model for relations among maternal education, age, employment, intelligence, openness, and mother and infant behaviors (N = 244).

+p ≤ .10; *p ≤ .05; **p ≤ .01; ***p ≤ .001

56

THE SOCIOECONOMIC INDEX
OF OCCUPATIONS AND MOTHER
AND INFANT BEHAVIORS

Preliminary analyses and the data analytic plan for our approach to the SEI are detailed in Appendix 2.4. In the first section, we report models with SEI as the predictor of mother and infant behaviors, followed by separate models with each of the two components of the SEI as the primary predictor. In addition, we tested the final model with the SEI as the predictor for cross-group invariance in mothers of girls and mothers of boys. To make models for SEI comparable with those for HI, we evaluated the effects in each model of the primary predictor controlling for covariation with maternal age and hours of employment. Maternal age correlated with the SEI, $r(322) = .59$, $p < .001$, and each of its components. Employment correlated marginally with maternal SEI, $r(198) = .13$, $p = .059$.

Zero-order Correlations

Table 2.3 presents zero-order correlations of SEI and its components with maternal and infant behaviors. The SEI and maternal SEI were related to mother physical and language. Nonmaternal householder SEI was related to all maternal domains, except mother nurture and didactic domains. Nonmaternal householder SEI was also related to infant physical development. No other correlations emerged between the SEI or any of its two components and infant domains.

TABLE 2.3
Zero-Order Correlations of Family SEI and Its Components with Maternal
and Infant Behaviors

	SEI *N = 324*	*Maternal SEI* *n = 200*	*Nonmaternal Householder SEI* *N = 319*
Maternal domains			
Nurture	.04	.08	.04
Physical	.19***	.16*	.19***
Social	.11†	.03	.14*
Didactic	.08	.07	.09
Material	.11	−.01	.12*
Language	.23***	.14*	.23***
Infant domains			
Physical	.08	−.00	.13*
Social	−.05	−.05	−.01
Exploration	−.00	−.04	.01
Vocalization	.06	.06	.07
Distress communication	.06	−.00	.08

† $p = .056$; * $p \le .05$; ** $p \le .01$; *** $p \le .001$.

Structural Equation Modeling

Full Sample

To study the direct and indirect effects of the SEI on mother and infant behaviors, with indirect effects on infant behaviors mediated by maternal behaviors, and to control for covariations between the SEI and maternal age and maternal employment in predicting maternal behaviors, the data were evaluated in structural equation models. An initial model (see Figure 2.10) of the direct and indirect effects of SEI on mother and infant behaviors was tested that was analogous to the initial model for HI (see Figure 2.2) with HI replaced by SEI. The a priori model did not fit the data, S-B $\chi^2(64) = 139.72$, $p < .001$, Robust CFI = .90, RMSEA = .06, 90% CI = (.05, .07). The Wald tests suggested dropping several paths, and the Lagrange multiplier tests suggested consideration of a number of additional paths.

Figure 2.11 presents the standardized solution to the structural portion of the final, sequentially constructed model, S-B $\chi^2(64) = 87.30$, $p \le .03$, Robust CFI = .97, RMSEA = .03, 90% CI = (.01, .05). The model reproduced observed correlations with an average absolute standardized error of .03. All parameters estimated in the model were significant at the .05 level or better.

Of primary interest in this model are paths from the SEI to maternal behaviors and indirect effects of the SEI on infant behaviors. Controlling for relations with maternal age, SEI had direct effects on mother physical and material domains. Mothers with a higher SEI more often encouraged their infants' physical development and provided their infants with more objects, objects with more stimulating features for exploration, or both. Two infant behaviors contributed to the time mothers spent in nurturing them. Mothers whose infants vocalized nondistress less often or communicated distress more often spent longer nurturing their infants.

Controlling for relations with SEI and maternal employment, maternal age related significantly to mothers' dyadic focus. Significant effects of maternal age on five maternal domains were mediated by dyadic focus. Older mothers spent a longer time nurturing their infants (standardized indirect effect = .04, $p < .05$), more often encouraged their infants' physical development (standardized indirect effect = .08, $p < .05$), engaged in more social exchanges (standardized indirect effect = .12, $p < .01$) and didactic interactions (standardized indirect effect = .11, $p < .01$) with their infants, and spoke more to their infants (standardized indirect effect = .09, $p < .01$). Controlling for relations of the SEI and employment to maternal age, older mothers also spoke more to their infants. Mothers' employment related significantly to their extradyadic focus controlling for relations with maternal age. Controlling for relations with maternal age, mothers' employment had a direct effect on mother didactic domains. Mothers who worked more hours engaged in fewer didactic interactions with their infants. Significant effects of mothers' employment on mother nurture, didactic, and material were mediated by

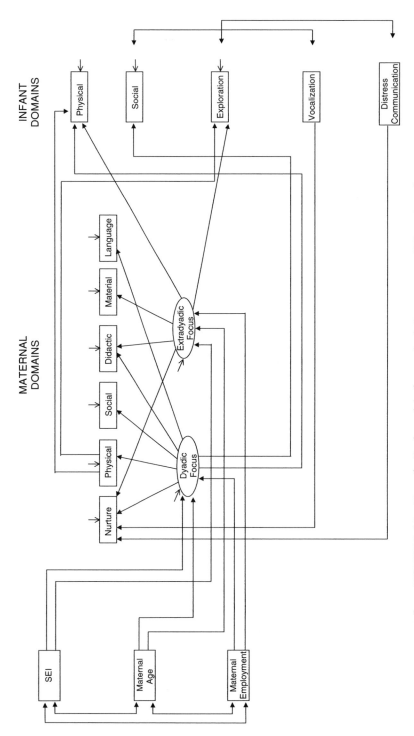

FIGURE 2.10. Hypothetical model of causal relations among SEI, maternal age, maternal employment, and mother and infant behaviors.

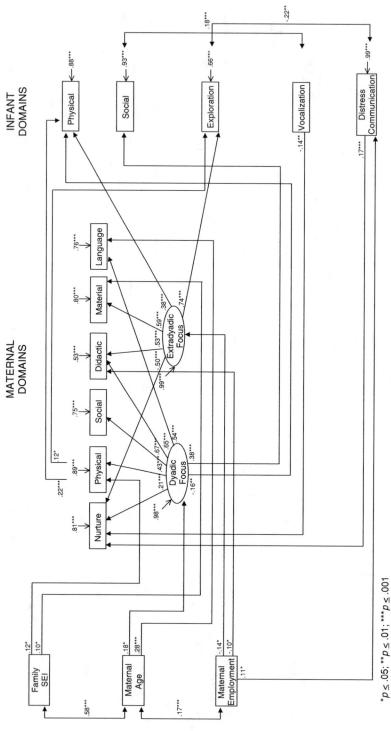

MATERNAL DOMAINS

INFANT DOMAINS

FIGURE 2.11. Standardized solution for the final model for relations among SEI, maternal age, maternal employment, and mother and infant behaviors (*N* = 324).

*p ≤ .05; **p ≤ .01; ***p ≤ .001

60

extradyadic focus. Mothers who worked more hours spent more time nurturing their infants (standardized indirect effect $= .09$, $p < .05$), engaged in fewer didactic interactions (standardized indirect effect $= -.08$, $p < .05$), and provided their infants with fewer objects, objects with fewer stimulating features for exploration, or both (standardized indirect effect $= -.08$, $p < .05$). In addition, mothers who worked longer hours had infants who communicated distress more often during the observation.

With regard to the indirect effects of maternal age on infant behaviors, infants of older mothers engaged in more social exchanges (standardized indirect effect $= .07$, $p < .05$), with the effect mediated by dyadic focus. There were no direct or indirect effects of SEI on infant behaviors. Mothers' employment had negative indirect effects on infant physical development (standardized indirect effect $= -.05$, $p < .05$) and exploration (standardized indirect effect $= -.11$, $p < .05$). Infants of mothers who worked more hours exhibited a lower level of gross motor development and engaged in less exploring, with both effects mediated by extradyadic focus. There was no indirect effect of SEI on any infant behavior.

Child Gender

To test whether the final model fit equally well for mothers of girls and mothers of boys, we constructed a series of nested multisample models that sequentially introduced constraints on factor loadings, path coefficients, and covariances (Bentler, 1995; Bollen, 1989). For the test of cross-group invariance, a preliminary test, in which no parameter estimates were constrained to be equal, fit the data, suggesting that more restrictive models were appropriate. Results from multisample models in which factor loadings, path coefficients, and covariances were constrained to be equal suggested that there were two factor loadings and two path coefficients that differed for mothers of girls and mothers of boys. When these four constraints were released, a good fit was achieved, $\chi^2(149) = 177.32$, $p \leq .06$, CFI $= .96$, RMSEA $= .02$, 90% CI $= (.00, .04)$. The four constraints that showed gender differences were the factor loadings from dyadic focus to mother physical (standardized factor loading $= .36$, $p < .001$, for mothers of girls and .48, $p < .001$, for mothers of boys) and from dyadic focus to mother didactic (standardized factor loading $= .59$, $p < .001$, for mothers of girls and .69, $p < .001$, for mothers of boys), and the path coefficients from the error term of mother physical to infant exploration (standardized coefficient $= .20$, $p < .01$, for girls and .07, $p \leq .27$, for boys) and from infant distress communication to mother nurture (standardized coefficient $= .29$, $p < .001$, for mothers of girls and .06, $p \leq .41$, for mothers of boys). Girls whose mothers more often encouraged their physical development (that part of the variance in mother physical that was unrelated to the latent variable of dyadic focus) engaged in more exploring, and the distress communications of girls led to their mothers' nurturing behaviors. No such relations existed in mother–son dyads. Although the magnitudes of the factor loadings differed statistically, all were significant and in the same direction for mothers of girls and mothers of boys. These gender differences were limited to relations of dyadic focus with mother physical and didactic, between mother physical and infant exploration, and between infant distress communication and maternal nurturant behaviors, and so the main SEI relations to maternal behaviors held equally for girls and boys.

In the analyses that follow, we examined each component of the SEI in predicting mother and infant behavior.

Maternal SEI and Mother and Infant Behaviors

This model was based on the 200 mothers who were working outside of the home at time of study. Figure 2.12 presents the standardized solution to the final model with mother SEI as the predictor, S-B $\chi^2(70) = 80.87$, $p \leq .18$, Robust CFI = .97, RMSEA = .03, 90% CI = (.00, .05). The model reproduced observed correlations with an average absolute standardized error of .04. Controlling for its relation with maternal age, maternal SEI did not relate to any maternal behaviors; nor were there direct or indirect effects of maternal SEI on infant behaviors.

Nonmaternal Householder SEI

This model was based on the 319 families for which data from nonmaternal householders were used to calculate SEI scores. Figure 2.13 presents the standardized solution to the final model with SEI of nonmaternal head(s) of households as the predictor, S-B $\chi^2(63) = 82.70$, $p \leq .05$, Robust CFI = .97, RMSEA = .03, 90% CI = (.01, .05). The model reproduced observed correlations with an average absolute standardized error of .03. Controlling for relations with maternal age, nonmaternal householder SEI had direct effects on mother physical and material domains. Mothers from families with a higher nonmaternal householder SEI more often encouraged their infants' physical development and provided their infants with more objects, objects with more stimulating features for exploration, or both. Controlling for relations with maternal age, nonmaternal householder SEI had a direct effect on the infant physical domain. Infants from families with a higher nonmaternal householder SEI exhibited a higher level of gross motor development.

SEI and Maternal Education Re-visited

In each of the three models, SEI did not relate to dyadic focus, whereas maternal age did. Note that in models with the HI and each of its components as the predictor, maternal age did not relate to dyadic focus. We suspected that the effect of maternal age, in models with SEI as the predictor, on dyadic focus was actually carried by its significant correlation with mothers' education. The zero-order correlation between maternal age and education was $r(322) = .66$, $p < .001$. In the following

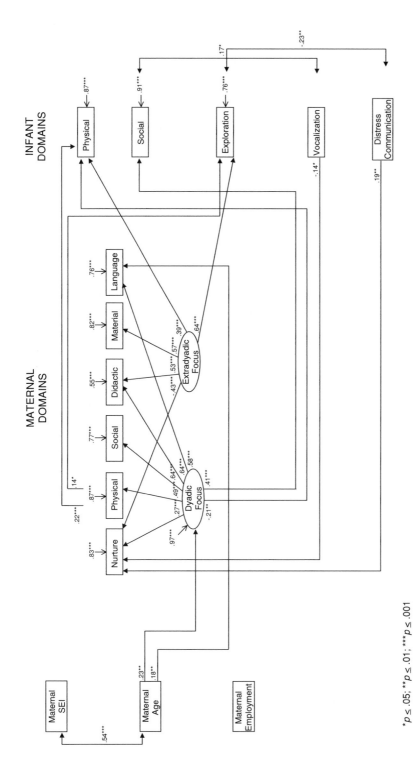

FIGURE 2.12. Standardized solution for the final model for relations among maternal SEI, age, employment, and mother and infant behaviors (N = 200).

*p ≤ .05; **p ≤ .01; ***p ≤ .001

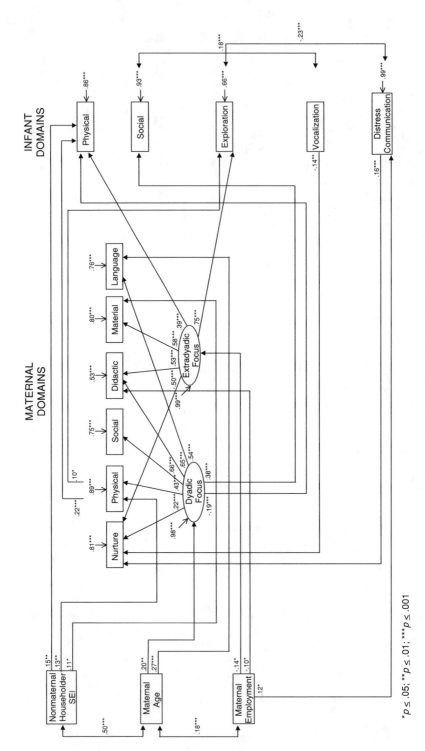

FIGURE 2.13. Standardized solution for the final model for relations among nonmaternal householder SEI, maternal age, maternal employment, and mother and infant behaviors (N = 319).

*p ≤ .05; **p ≤ .01; ***p ≤ .001

64

analyses, we included mothers' education in each of the three models with family SEI, maternal SEI, or nonmaternal householder SEI as co-predictors in predicting mother and infant behaviors, while controlling for their covariation with maternal employment, to assess the relative impact of mothers' education, age, and SEI score on maternal behaviors. The final models fit the data: S-B $\chi^2(75) = 96.58$, $p \leq .05$, Robust CFI = .98, RMSEA = .03, 90% CI = (.01, .05) for the model with maternal education, SEI, and maternal employment, as predictors; S-B $\chi^2(82) =$ 92.37, $p \leq .20$, Robust CFI = .98, RMSEA = .03, 90% CI = (.00, .05) for the model with maternal education, maternal SEI, and maternal employment as the predictors; and S-B $\chi^2(74) = 90.82$, $p \leq .09$, Robust CFI = .98, RMSEA = .03, 90% CI = (.00, .04) for the model with maternal education, nonmaternal householder SEI, and maternal employment as predictors. Controlling for its relation with maternal age, employment, and SEI, maternal education related significantly to dyadic focus (standardized path coefficients = .20, .27, and .22, in the models with SEI, maternal SEI, and nonmaternal householder SEI as co-predictors, respectively, $ps < .01, .001$, and .01). Effects of mothers' education on all maternal domains, with the exception of mother material mediated by dyadic focus, were significant at .05 level or better in all three models. In the model with maternal education and SEI as predictors, controlling for its relations with maternal education and age, SEI related to mother physical (standardized path coefficient = .11, $p <$ .05) and material domains (standardized path coefficient = .11, $p < .05$). In the model with maternal education and maternal SEI as predictors, controlling for its relations with maternal education and age, maternal SEI did not relate to any maternal or infant behaviors. In the model with maternal education and nonmaternal householder SEI as predictors, controlling for its relations with maternal education and age, nonmaternal householder SEI related to mother physical (standardized path coefficient = .12, $p < .05$) and material (standardized path coefficient = .12, $p < .05$), and to infant physical (standardized path coefficient = .15, $p < .01$).

SES, MEASUREMENT, AND MOTHER AND INFANT BEHAVIORS

It is no longer the case that parenting is seen to relate to children's development narrowly; rather, a more ecumenical view is that factors outside the family (e.g., schools, residence, and ethnicity) predict variation in parenting and child development (e.g., Belsky, 1984; Bornstein, 2002; Lerner et al., 2002; Leventhal & Brooks-Gunn, 2000; McLoyd, 1998). In particular, SES is associated with family attributes that are themselves differentially esteemed in society. Moreover, since World War II, transformations in several of these demographic characteristics have profoundly affected family life in the United States (Hernandez, 1997), rendering a need for constant attention to sociodemographics in social science research. In this study, we assessed relations of the two most prominent contemporary measures of

SES, the Hollingshead Four-Factor Index of Social Status and the Socioeconomic Index of Occupations, as well as their components, to multiple domains of mother and infant behavior. We found that the HI and SEI correlate with each other but that they differentially predict maternal domains of behavior. The HI predicted dyadic focus, physical, and material directly and all maternal domains (except material) indirectly, whereas the SEI predicted only physical and material directly. The HI predicted infant physical and social domains of behavior indirectly, and the SEI only infant social indirectly. Both instruments predicted equally well in families with girls and families with boys, and in families where mothers were working and not.

We further analyzed how components of the HI and SEI individually predicted maternal and infant behaviors. It could be that composite indexes of SES are more than the sum of their constituent parts and affect parenting and child development as monolithic variables that cannot be meaningfully decomposed (Featherman, Spenner, & Tsunematsu, 1988; White, 1982). Or, it could be that a monolithic multivariate index of SES is an imperfect proxy for a small variety of specific factors that bear independent and differential relations to parenting and child development (Bronfenbrenner, 1958). If so, composite indexes, like the HI and SEI, may cloud the separate sources of effect that individual indicators bear on parent and child outcomes (DeGarmo et al., 1999; Magnuson & Duncan, 2002; Smith & Graham, 1995). For example, Bradley et al. (1989) found that parental occupation related to some subscales (e.g., responsivity) of the HOME inventory (a measure of the quality of the physical and social environment), but occupation's relations to others (e.g., organization) were more tenuous. Thus, an index of SES might provide little explanatory power if it is not parsed into its component parts—education, occupation, and income—and the predictive validity of each part investigated separately (Burns, Homel, & Goodnow, 1984; DeGarmo et al., 1999).

In the present study, when examined separately, the multiple factors that compose SES were found to bear different relations to mother and infant behaviors. Of the four HI components, maternal education was a unique and consistent predictor of both maternal and infant behaviors. Maternal education behaved most like the composite HI, whereas nonmaternal householder education, maternal occupational status, and nonmaternal householder occupational status did not. Although nonmaternal householder occupation and education predicted maternal behaviors directly, when maternal education was introduced as a simultaneous co-predictor, maternal education turned out to be the most robust predictor. Maternal SEI did not predict either mother or infant behaviors, and family SEI and nonmaternal householder SEI predicted some maternal behaviors directly (physical and material). Insofar as the HI contains education scores, the HI composite then proved to be a more robust predictor of maternal behavior and infant development.

Our data support the conclusion that SES is not more than the sum of its constituent parts and that SES does not function as a coherent, indivisible factor in these aspects of early family life. In particular, we found (like others; Aubret, 1977;

Haveman & Wolfe, 1995; Smith, Brooks-Gunn, & Klebanov, 1997) that maternal education was the most robust individual sociodemographic predictor of mother and infant behavior. Although Liberatos et al. (1988) concluded that there is no one best measure of SES, maternal education seems to be the best stand-in for SES at large. Thus, various components of composite SES indexes should not be considered interchangeable. They should be analyzed separately rather than combined into a single scale (Entwisle & Astone, 1994; Krieger et al., 1997; Liberatos et al., 1988), and a preliminary conclusion for our SE models would be that many of the correlations that emerged between nonmaternal householder education and occupation and parenting/infant behaviors are probably carried by the correlation between maternal education and nonmaternal householder education/occupation. This means that which SES measure an investigator selects has important implications for research findings.

Evidence has accumulated that specific experiences in young children's lives relate to specific features of their development (Bornstein, 2002; Collins, Maccoby, Steinberg, Hetherington, & Bornstein, 2000). With respect to parenting and early child development, maternal education was first among equals among various components of SES. These findings move child development and parenting research (at least with regard to mothering) away from strict reliance on the HI or the SEI (instruments which both remain unpublished) to a minimal (and perhaps adequate) reliance on maternal education as a relevant marker for SES. In early life at least, the HI and SEI predict less of parenting or infancy apart from maternal education per se. Similarly, Bradley and Corwyn (chap. 7, this volume) found that maternal education showed as strong or stronger relations with children's PPVT and PIAT scores as the SEI. Of course, how well the HI and SEI predict has no implication for how well they represent SES or whether either or both would predict parenting or child development beyond infancy; we are presently investigating these questions.

Although maternal education was an effective distal influence on parenting and to a degree on infant development, it is also possible that maternal education is associated with other individual-differences factors that affect parenting and infancy (Belsky, 1984; Hoff et al., 2002). For example, an individual-differences factor related to SES in the amount of talk addressed to children may be mothers' general level of talkativeness. High-SES mothers talk more than low-SES mothers in conversation with adults (Hoff-Ginsberg, 1991, 1992). To distinguish this and other individual-differences factors in parenting from education effects per se, we included in our analyses assessments of maternal verbal IQ and personality traits. Maternal education predicted parenting dyadic focus, verbal IQ predicted language, but personality factors from the Big Five were not predictive. Thus, the maternal education effects we observed obtained apart from presumably shared genetic endowment with the child. Of course, genetic endowment can be expected to influence infant parenting and infant development (Rowe, 1994), but our data show independent influences of maternal education.

The predictive power of maternal education accords with other reports in the literature. First, most previous investigations in infancy have used maternal education as the main stand-in measure of SES. Parental education is the most "popular single indicator of social class" (Liberatos et al., 1988, p. 97), and "epidemiologists have . . . selected education as the measure of choice" for SES (p. 117; see also Meudell, 1982; Smith & Graham, 1995). Baxter (1994) found that a woman's level of formal education shaped her subjective class identity in the United States, as well as in Australia, Norway, and Sweden (see also Abbott, 1987; Jackman & Jackman, 1983). Second, achieved maternal education is an appropriate representative variable for conceptual reasons. In the first months of life, mothers are primary caregivers to their babies (Barnard & Solchany, 2002; Bornstein, 2002; Parke, 2002), and alternative SES measures of maternal occupation and income during this particular period can be expected to be more variable and less valid (Gottfried et al., chap. 8, this volume). Psychometrically, education is adequately representative of SES as a whole, it is accurately reported, it has established short-term reliability, and it is more stable than are occupation or income (see Hauser & Featherman, 1977; Liberatos et al., 1988; Susser, Watson, & Hopper, 1985). Clearly, too, it is quick and easy to obtain information about maternal education. Third, maternal education has been shown to bear a close and systematic relation to individual variation in parenting behaviors (Alwin, 1984; Kelly et al., 1993; Kohn, 1963; Wright & Wright, 1976) and, through this relation, to exert an impact on child health (DeSai & Alva, 1998; Green, 1970) and development (Dollaghan et al., 1999; Hitchcock & Oliver, 1976; Hoff-Ginsberg & Tardif, 1995; Mercy & Steelman, 1982) across a range of child ages and across ethnic groups (Ramey & Ramey, 1999; Sandqvist, 1995; Sonnander & Claesson, 1999; Terrisse, Roberts, Palacio-Quintin, & MacDonald, 1998). The findings we report here should give additional impetus to policy makers that a consistent focus on educational achievement will stand parenting and the next generation in good stead. In these respects it is heartening that the last quarter of the 20th century witnessed consistent increases in mothers' educational attainments. Between 1975 and 1997, for example, the proportion of U.S. children living with mothers who had graduated from college improved from 14% to 24% (National Research Council, 2000).

Level of education has real meaning, first, for mothers, and, next for the human capital (Coleman, 1988) mothers provide their children. Increases in education presumably improve parents' perspectives on their lives, enhance their own cognitive and literacy skills, and may spill over to increased feelings of mastery and competence in the sense that education helps parents organize their lives and mobilize their resources efficaciously with respect to their goals (Duncan & Magnuson, chap. 3, this volume; Michael, 1972). Education is regularly associated with greater knowledge about childrearing and child development (Bornstein, Hahn, Suizzo, & Haynes, 2001; Pagani, Boulerice, Vitaro, & Tremblay, 1999; Pettit, Laird, Dodge, Bates, & Criss, in press; Sampson & Laub, 1994). Education is associated with a more verbal childrearing style (Hoff, chap. 6, this volume), and education places parents in a position to provide their children with a cognitively enriched environment (Menaghan & Parcel, 1991). More educated parents are thought to be more effective co-teachers, in the sense that they cooperate with teachers and the school system (Epstein & Sanders, 2002) and know more about schooling and school work (Alexander, Entwisle, & Bedinger, 1994). Thus, parents' education not only benefits their own lives but has manifest advantages for their children's lives as well.

Whether and how environmental conditions influence infant development is a central issue for studies of infant status, individual differences, and the predictive validity of such measures. SES may affect child development directly, but parenting variables could mediate or be moderated by SES in their relations with child development (e.g., DeGarmo et al., 1999; Laosa, 1983; McLoyd, 1998). As Hart and Risley (1995) observed, young children's developmental achievements reflect educational and material advantages that are associated with SES as much as they do the cumulative individual experiences their parents provide. Perhaps children of wealthy parents are advantaged in cognitive development because of their wealth per se or because parenting mediates between influences of SES on the one hand and individual variation in child cognitive development on the other.

Parental education tends to correlate with children's educational achievement (.40 to .60 depending on age and prediction interval; McCall, 1977). However, correlations of SES indicators (within the normal range) with neurodevelopmental assessments of infants and younger children, such as the Bayley Scales, are typically low (Gottfried, 1985). Child assessments in the first 18 months tend to evaluate primarily motor competence and cognitive information processing (Bornstein, 1989; Fagan, 1992), neither of which has revealed relations to SES (Fagan & Singer, 1983; Mayes & Bornstein, 1995; McCall, 1979; O'Connor, Cohen, & Parmelee, 1984). Gottfried's (1985) review showed that SES begins to correlate with children's developmental status between 18 and 42 months of age. In a later study, however, Roberts, Bornstein, Slater, and Barrett (1999) tested infants on a variety of cognitive tasks at three-monthly intervals between 9 and 18 months, and the same children returned at 27 months to complete the Bayley Mental Development Index. They found that children's eventual cognitive performance was associated with parental education from 12 months on, but not earlier.

It is not surprising, therefore, that in the present study SES variables did not relate directly to the behaviors of 5-month-old infants. We found that, although SES (actually, maternal education) related to maternal behavior, SES (maternal education) only inconsistently related to only some infant behaviors, and SES (maternal education) related to those infant behaviors only indirectly through maternal behaviors. That is, proximal maternal behaviors were better predictors of infant behaviors than were distal sociodemographic indicators, including maternal education. On arguments such as canalization (Waddington, 1962, 1966), distal or proximal contextual experiences such as these are not supposed to directly influence infant behavior. On the other hand, the fact that maternal behaviors relate to infant behaviors suggests that the canalization perspective requires some revision.

This investigation focused on SES relations to mother and infant behaviors. Much less is known about SES in relation to fathers' or other caregivers' interactions with infants (Clarke-Stewart & Allhusen, 2002; Parke, 2002). Moreover, we studied mothers in only one culture. The effects of SES are believed to be moderated by culture (Fuligni & Yoshikawa, chap. 4, this volume; Gutierrez, Sameroff, & Karrer, 1988; Harwood, Leyendecker, Carlson, Asencio, & Miller, 2002; Williams & Collins, 1995). For example, among European Americans, lower-SES mothers are more concerned with their young children's proper demeanor and higher-SES mothers with their young children's self-actualization, whereas Puerto Rican mothers of all SES levels are primarily concerned with proper demeanor (Harwood, Schoelmerich, Ventura-Cook, Schulze, & Wilson, 1996). Likewise, education can have different meanings and implications in different ethnic groups (Fuligni & Yoshikawa, chap. 4, this volume). Thus, relations of SES and education to mother and infant behaviors in different cultures require close examination.

Studying the role of SES and its constituents, as we have done, is crucial to studies of family functioning and children's development. Identifying antecedents of parenting in SES and its components, as we have done, in turn permits social policy to target the most effective means to influence and alter parenting and child development to the good.

ACKNOWLEDGMENTS

We thank E. Beatty, D. Clay, and C. Varron for assistance. Requests for reprints should be sent to Marc H. Bornstein, Child and Family Research, National Institute of Child Health and Human Development, National Institutes of Health, Suite 8030, 6705 Rockledge Drive, Bethesda MD 20892-7971, U.S.A. Email: *Marc_H_Bornstein@nih.gov.*

APPENDIX 2.1

Hollingshead Index Occupational Status Scale

(1) Farm Laborers/Menial Service Workers
(2) Unskilled Workers
(3) Machine Operators and Semiskilled Workers
(4) Smaller Business Owners, Skilled Manual Workers, Craftsmen, and Tenant Farmers
(5) Clerical and Sales Workers, Small Farm and Business Owners
(6) Technicians, Semiprofessionals, and Small Business Owners

(7) Smaller Business Owners, Farm Owners, Managers, and Minor Professionals

(8) Administrators, Lesser Professionals, and Proprietors of Medium-Sized Businesses

(9) Higher Executives, Proprietors of Large Businesses, and Major Professionals

APPENDIX 2.2

Hollingshead Index Education Scale

(1) Less than 7th grade

Highest grade completed:_____

(2) 7th, 8th, or 9th grade

(3) 10th or 11th grade

Which one(s) completed?_____

(4) High school graduate or GED

Which?_____

(5) Partial college (at least 1 year completed); or has completed specialized training

Number of years of college completed:_____

Type of college degree received:_____

Type of specialized training:_____

Years of specialized training completed:_____

(6) Standard college or university graduate

Type of degree received:_____

(7) Graduate professional training (graduate degree completed)

Type of degree received:_____

APPENDIX 2.3

A. Behavioral and Context Indicators and Scoring Reliabilities
for Maternal Domains

Mother nurture is the mean standard aggregate of the following three indicators. Feed/burp/wipe is the sum of the durations of two behaviors: the total length of the time the mother fed her infant and the total length of time the mother burped or wiped her infant. Bath/diaper/dress/groom/other is the sum of the durations of five behaviors: bathing the infant; checking or changing the infant's diaper; dressing the infant; grooming the infant; and attending to the infant's health needs. Hold is the total length of time the mother supported some or all of her infant's weight with her body. The overall κ for the domain score was .92.

Mother physical is the mean of the following two indicators. Encourage to sit/stand is the mean proportion of consecutive 10-minute intervals in which the mother verbally and physically encouraged her infant to sit or stand. Encourage to roll/crawl/step is the mean proportion of consecutive 10-minute intervals in which the mother verbally and physically encouraged her infant to roll, crawl, or step. The mean ICC for the domain score was .74.

Mother social is the mean standard aggregate of the following three indicators. Encourage attention to mother is the mean standard aggregate of the number of times and total duration the mother attempted to draw her infant into face-to-face interaction with herself. Social play is the mean standard aggregate of the number of times and total duration the mother directed verbal or physical behavior to her infant for the purpose of amusing the infant (i.e., to elicit smile, positive vocalization, laughter, or motoric excitement). Express affection is the mean standard aggregate of the number of times and total duration the mother expressed affection or positive evaluation to her infant either physically or verbally. Transformation: $\log_{10}$. The overall κ for the domain score was .70.

Mother didactic is made up of a single indicator. Encourage attention to objects is the mean standard aggregate of the number of times and total duration the mother physically moved her infant or an object so that her infant could see or touch it, or verbally referred to an object-related event or activity. Transformation: $\log_{10}$. κ for didactic was .72.

Mother material is the mean aggregate of the following two indicators. Quality (responsiveness) of objects is the mean standard aggregate of the number and proportion of highly responsive objects within reach of the infant. Quantity of objects is the mean standard aggregate of the variety, density, and consistency of toys, books, and household objects that were within the infant's reach. The mean ICC for the domain score was .91.

Mother language is made up of a single indicator. Speech to child is the mean standard aggregate of the number of times and total duration the mother used adult-directed speech (i.e., normal intonation patterns) and child-directed speech (i.e., speech marked by short sentences, repetition, and high and more variable intonation—motherese) to address the infant. κ for language was .71.

B. Behavioral Indicators and Scoring Reliabilities for Infant Domains

The infant physical score is the mean standard aggregate of four possible indicators that assess gross motor development. Each of four scales consisted of behavioral abilities, ordered from least mature to most mature, and the highest level of competence observed on each scale was recorded for each consecutive 10-minute period. The mean highest level observed in the first five segments was computed as the indicator score. Prelocomotion-upper body is the mean highest level of ability to control and coordinate the upper body while in a prone position, ranging from level 1 (infant lifts head and shoulders for more than 5 consecutive seconds) to level 5 (infant is able to reach with one arm, shift weight, and remain balanced). Prelocomotion-lower body is the mean highest level of ability to control and coordinate the lower body while in a prone position, ranging from level 1 (infant lies with legs extended and hips resting on the supporting surface) to level 4 (infant assumes the full crawl position with weight supported on knees and lower legs). Locomotion is the mean highest level of deliberate, unassisted movement, ranging from level 1 (infant lifts legs when placed in a supine position) to level 11 (infant actively creeps across the room). Sitting is the mean highest level of ability to control the body while in a sitting position, ranging from level 1 (infant sits with back rounded and head unsteady when fully supported in an inclined sitting position) to level 8 (infant rotates from prone position to a balanced sitting position with weight on buttocks and without assistance). For each 10-minute interval, if the infant was never in the physical position necessary to exhibit a given skill, no rating was made for that skill; in the case of some skills for some infants, no ratings were made in any 10-minute period because the infant was never placed in the required position. The mean standard aggregate score is composed of indicators of all skills that were assessed in at least one 10-minute period. As such, it represents the general performance of gross motor functioning in the infant. Transformation: reciprocal of square root; the product of the reciprocally transformed variable was multiplied by −1 in all analyses. The mean ICC for the domain score was .92.

Infant social is the mean standard aggregate of the following three indicators. Look at mother is the mean standard aggregate of the number of times and total duration the infant looked at the mother's face. Smile is the mean standard aggregate of the number of times and total duration the infant emitted a clear, unambiguous smile. Alert expression is the total length of time the infant's facial expression indicated interest, concentration, staring, or wide-eyed alertness. Transformation: square root. The overall κ for the domain score was .63.

Infant exploration is the mean aggregate of the following five indicators. Look at object is the mean standard aggregate of the number of times and total duration the infant looked at any discrete object or body part other than a face. Touch object is the mean standard aggregate of the number of times and total duration the infant actively and purposefully handled an object by grasping it and moving it or by directly exploring the object using the palm or fingers of the hand (e.g., patting, rubbing, etc.). Mouth object is the mean standard aggregate of the number of times and total duration a discrete object other than a bottle or pacifier came into contact with the infant's mouth. Extent of exploration is the mean standard aggregate of the variety, density, and consistency of objects mouthed or touched. Efficiency of exploration is the mean standard aggregate of the variety, density, and consistency of objects mouthed or touched. The overall domain κ was .71. Mean ICC for extent and efficiency of exploration was .93.

Infant vocalization is made up of a single indicator. Nondistress vocalization is the mean standard aggregate of the number of times and total duration the infant expressed a positively or neutrally toned vocalization. Transformation: cubic. κ for nondistress vocalization was .69.

Infant distress communication is the mean standard aggregate of two indicators. Negative facial expression is the mean standard aggregate of the number of times and total duration the infant displayed a distressed, angry, or frowning countenance. Distress vocalization is the mean standard aggregate of the number of times and total duration the infant produced vocalizations that indicated protest, anger, complaint, or upset. Transformation: reciprocal of square root; the product of the reciprocally transformed variable was multiplied by -1 in all analyses. The overall κ for the domain score was .67.

APPENDIX 2.4

Preliminary Analysis and Data Analytic Plan

Prior to any analysis, univariate distributions for all variables were examined for nonnormalcy and the presence of outliers; and all variables in the model with HI or SEI as the predictor were assessed for multivariate outliers (Bollen, 1989; Cook & Weisberg, 1999; Fox, 1997). Several mother and infant domain scores required transformation to approximate normality and reduce the number and influence of outliers (see Appendix 2.3). Transformed variables were used in all analyses and models; for clarity, untransformed means are presented in Table 2.1. In the structural equation models, univariate measures of kurtosis and normalized estimates of Mardia's (1970) multivariate coefficient indicated no significant problems of nonnormality in the a priori or final models, and no additional cases were identified as multivariate outliers that contributed disproportionately to parameter variances.

Bivariate plots and curve estimation regression statistics were first carried out and confirmed that both the HI and SEI had linear effects on the mother and infant behavioral measures used in the analyses and that no curvilinear effects existed between either of the SES measures and the mother and infant behaviors. To assess whether and how SES predicted infant behaviors mediated by maternal behaviors, structural equation models were fit to the data in two steps. In the first step, a measurement model representing the hierarchical factor structure of maternal parenting underlying the six maternal domains was fit (see Appendix 2.5). In the second step, direct or indirect effects of SES (HI, SEI, and each of their components) on infant behaviors were investigated with indirect effects mediated by maternal behaviors; in these models, maternal age and hours working per week outside the home (employment) were considered as potential covariates in predicting maternal behaviors. Each model was tested for its fit to the data using a maximum likelihood function and following the mathematical model of Bentler and Weeks (1980) as implemented in EQS (Bentler, 1995). Model fit was assessed using multiple, convergent indices, including the robust Satorra-Bentler (1988, 1994) scaled chi-square statistic, robust comparative fit index (Robust CFI; Bentler, 1990), and root mean square error of approximation (RMSEA; Browne & Cudeck, 1993) and its 90% confidence intervals.

For the model with HI or SEI as the predictor, an initial structural equation model that represented hypothesized relations was tested for its fit to the data. If the a priori model did not fit the data, re-specifications of the models were planned using the following strategy. First, to simplify the model, all nonsignificant paths in the a priori model were dropped based on the multivariate Wald statistics. When all remaining estimated parameters in the model were significant, single paths were then added sequentially to the model. At each step, the standardized residual covariance matrix was studied, together with Wald and Lagrange multiplier tests, and potential paths were evaluated for their theoretical plausibility and empirical probability (Bentler, 1995; Bollen, 1989). Finally, models for each of the four components of the HI and each of the two components of the SEI as the predictor were generated by post-hoc modifications of the final model. Models that are constructed by sequentially testing the addition and removal of paths, even when selection of paths is guided by theoretical relevance and plausibility, tend to exploit ungeneralizable relations in the data. For this reason, the final modified model is treated as having tentative explanatory value, suggesting relations for testing in future research.

APPENDIX 2.5

Latent Constructs of Maternal Parenting

An a priori model in which all maternal domains load, without covarying errors, on a single mothering factor was first fit to the data: S-B $\chi^2(9) = 84.30$, $p < .001$, Robust CFI = .72, RMSEA = .16, 90% CI = (.12, .19). The overall χ^2 test and the RMSEA indicated that the model left considerable covariation unexplained, and one domain, mother nurture, had a nonsignificant, negative loading on the single factor. Examining the standardized residual covariance matrix and the significant parameters suggested by the Lagrange multiplier test, we then postulated that a model with two factors was necessary to account for the data. Mother physical, social, didactic, and language were expected to load positively on a factor representing Dyadic Focus in parenting; didactic and material were expected to load positively on a factor representing Extradyadic Focus in parenting, whereas nurture was expected to load negatively. However, this postulated hierarchical factor structure also failed to account for significant covariation, S-B $\chi^2(8) = 27.15$, $p < .001$, Robust CFI = .93, RMSEA = .08, 90% CI = (.05, .12). The Lagrange multiplier test suggested that mother nurture also cross-loaded on both first-order factors, and a modified model, with this path added, fit the data well, S-B $\chi^2(7) = 9.57$, $p \leq .21$, Robust CFI $= .99$, RMSEA $= .03$, 90% CI $= (.00, .08)$. The model reproduced observed correlations with an average absolute standardized error of .04. All loadings of the maternal behaviors on their respective first-order factors were significant at the .001 level or better.

REFERENCES

Abbott, P. (1987). Women's social class identification: Does husband's occupation make a difference? *Sociology, 21,* 91–103.

Alexander, K. L., Entwisle, D. R., & Bedinger, S. D. (1994). When expectations work: Race and socioeconomic differences in school performance. *Social Psychology Quarterly, 57,* 283–299.

Alwin, D. F. (1984). Trends in parental socialization values: Detroit, 1958–1983. *American Journal of Sociology, 90,* 359–381.

Argyle, M. (1994). *The psychology of social class.* London: Routledge.

Aubret, F. (1977). Prediction of elementary school success. *Enfance, 2,* 141–166.

Barnard, K. E., & Solchany, J. E. (2002). Mothering. In M. H. Bornstein (Ed.), *Handbook of parenting Vol. 3. Status and social conditions of parenting* (2nd ed., pp. 3–25). Mahwah, NJ: Lawrence Erlbaum Associates.

Baxter, J. (1994). Is husband's class enough? Class location and class identity in the United States, Sweden, Norway, and Australia. *American Sociological Review, 59,* 220–235.

Bell, R. Q., & Hertz, T. W. (1976). Toward more comparability and generalizability of developmental research. *Child Development, 47,* 6–13.

Belsky, J. (1984). The determinants of parenting: A process model. *Child Development, 5,* 83–96.

Bentler, P. M. (1990). Comparative fit indexes in structural models. *Psychological Bulletin, 107,* 238–246.

Bentler, P. M. (1995). *EQS structural equations program manual.* Los Angeles, CA: BMDP Statistical Software, Inc.

Bentler, P. M., & Weeks, D. G. (1980). Linear structural equations with latent variables. *Psychometrika, 45,* 289–308.

Blau, D. M. (1999). The effect of income on child development. *The review of economics and statistics, 8,* 261–276.

Blishen, B. R., Carroll, W. K., & Moore, C. (1987). The 1981 socioeconomic index for occupations in Canada. *Canadian Review of Sociology and Anthropology, 24,* 465–488.

Bollen, K. A. (1989). *Structural equations with latent variables.* New York: Wiley.

Bornstein, M. H. (1989). Stability in early mental development: From attention and information processing in infancy and language and cognition in childhood. In M. H. Bornstein & N. A. Krasnegor (Eds.), *Stability and continuity in mental development: Behavioral and biological perspectives* (pp. 147–170). Hillsdale, NJ: Lawrence Erlbaum Associates.

Bornstein, M. H. (2002). Parenting infants. In M. H. Bornstein (Ed.), *Handbook of parenting Vol. 1. Children and parenting* (2nd ed., pp. 3–43). Mahwah, NJ: Lawrence Erlbaum Associates.

Bornstein, M. H., Hahn, C.-S., Suizzo, M.-A., & Haynes, O. M. (2001). *Mothers' knowledge about child development and childrearing.* Unpublished manuscript, National Institute of Child Health and Human Development.

Bornstein, M. H., Tamis-LeMonda, C. S., Suwalsky, J. T. D., Rahn, C., & Ludemann, P. M. (1991). *Mother-Infant interaction: A manual for observation and analysis.* Unpublished manuscript, National Institute of Child Health and Human Development. Betherda, MD.

Bradley, R. H. (2002). Environment and parenting. In M. H. Bornstein (Ed.), *Handbook of parenting Vol. 2 Biology and Ecology of Parenting* (2nd ed, pp. 281–314). Mahwah, NJ: Lawrence Erlbaum Associates.

Bradley, R. H., Caldwell, B. M., Rock, S. L., & Ramey, C. T. (1989). Home environment and cognitive development in the first 3 years of life: A collaborative study involving six sites and three ethnic groups in North America. *Developmental Psychology, 25*, 217–235.

Bradley, R. H., & Corwyn, R. F. (2002). Socioeconomic status and child development. *Annual Review of Psychology, 53*, 371–399.

Bradley, R. H., Corwyn, R. F., Whiteside-Mansell, L. (1996). Life at home: Same time, different places. *Early Development and Parenting, 5*, 251–269.

Bradley, R. H., Mundfrom, D. J., Whiteside, L., & Caldwell, B. M. (1994). A reexamination of the association between HOME scores and income. *Nursing Research, 43*, 260–266.

Bronfenbrenner, U. (1958). Socialization and social class through time and space. In E. E. Maccoby, R. M. Newcomb, & E. L. Harley (Eds.), *Readings in social psychology* (pp. 400–425). New York: Holt, Rinehart, & Winston.

Bronfenbrenner, U., & Morris, P. A. (1998). The ecology of developmental processes. In R. M. Lerner (Ed.), W. Damon (Series Ed.), *Handbook of child psychology: Vol. 1. Theoretical models of human development* (5th ed., pp. 993–1028). New York: Wiley.

Browne, M. W., & Cudeck, R. (1993). Alternative ways of assessing model fit. In K. A. Bollen & J. S. Long (Eds.), *Testing structural equation models* (pp. 136–162). Newbury Park, CA: Sage.

Burns, A., Homel, R., & Goodnow, J. (1984). Conditions of life and parental values. *Australian Journal of Psychology, 36*, 219–237.

Clarke-Stewart, K. A., & Allhusen, V. D. (2002). Nonparental caregiving. In M. H. Bornstein (Ed.), *Handbook of parenting Vol. 3 Status and Social Conditions of Parenting* (2nd ed., pp. 215–252). Mahwah, NJ: Lawrence Erlbaum Associates.

Cohen, J. (1960). A coefficient of agreement for nominal scales. *Education and Psychological Measurement, 20*, 37–46.

Cohen, J. (1968). Weighted kappa: Nominal scale agreement with provision for scaled disagreement or partial credit. *Psychological Bulletin, 70*, 213–220.

Coleman, J. S. (1988). Social capital in the creation of human capital. *American Journal of Sociology, 94*, S95–S120.

Collins, W. A., Maccoby, E. E., Steinberg, L., Hetherington, E. M., & Bornstein, M. H. (2000). Contemporary research on parenting. *American Psychologist, 55*, 218–232.

Conger, R. D., & Elder, G. H. (1994). *Families in troubled times*. Hawthorne, NY: deGruyter.

Cook, R. D., & Weisberg, S. (1999). *Applied regression including computing and graphics*. New York: Wiley.

Crompton, R. (1993). *Class and stratification: An introduction to current debates*. Cambridge, England: Polity Press.

DeGarmo, D. S., Forgatch, M. S., & Martinez, C. R. (1999). Parenting of divorced mothers as a link between social status and boys' academic outcomes: Unpacking the effects of socioeconomic status. *Child Development, 70*, 1231–1245.

Desai, S., & Alva, S. (1998). Maternal education and child Health: Is there a strong causal relationship? *Demography, 35*, 71–81.

Dollaghan, C. A., Campbell, T. F., Paradise, J. L., Feldman, H. M., Janosky, J. E., Pitcairn, D. N., & Kurs-Lasky, M. (1999). Maternal education and measures of early speech and language. *Journal of Speech Language and Hearing Research, 42*, 1432–1443.

Duncan, G. J. (1988). The volatility of family income over the life course. In P. Baltes et al. (Eds.), *Life span development and behavior* (Vol. 9). Hillsdale, NJ: Lawrence Erlbaum Associates.

Duncan, G. J., & Brooks-Gunn, J. (Eds.). (1997). *Consequences of growing up poor*. New York: Russell Sage.

Duncan, O. D. (1961). A socioeconomic index for all occupations. In A. L. Reiss, Jr. (Ed.). *Occupations and social status*. New York: The Free Press.

Dunn, L. M., & Dunn, L. M. (1981). *Peabody Picture Vocabulary Test -Revised Manual.* Circle Pines, MN: American Guidance Service.

Eccles, J. S. (1993). School and family effects on the ontogeny of children's interests, self-perceptions, and activity choice. In J. Jacobs (Ed.), *Nebraska symposium on motivation, 1992: Developmental perspectives on motivation* (pp. 145–208): Lincoln, NE: University of Nebraska Press.

Edwards, J. R., & Bagozzi, I. P. (2000). On the nature and direction of relationships between constructs and measures [Electronic version]. *Psychological Methods, 5,* 155–174.

Entwisle, D. R., & Astone, N. M. (1994). Some practical guidelines for measuring youth's race–ethnicity and socioeconomic status. *Child Development, 65,* 1521–1540.

Epstein, J. L., & Sanders, M. G. (2002). Family, school, and community partnerships. In M. H. Bornstein (Ed.), *Handbook of parenting Vol. 5. Practical parenting* (2nd ed., pp. 407–437). Mahwah, NJ: Lawrence Erlbaum Associates.

Fagan, J. (1992). Intelligence: A theoretical viewpoint. *Current Directions in Psychological Science, 1,* 82–86.

Fagan, J., & Singer, L. (1983). Infant recognition memory as a measure of intelligence. *Advances in Infancy Research, 2,* 31–78.

Featherman, D. L., & Hauser, R. (1977). *The process of stratification: Trends and analysis.* New York: Academic Press.

Featherman, D. L., Spenner, K. I., & Tsunematsu, N. (1988). Class and the socialization of children: Constancy, change, or irrelevance? In E. M. Heatherington, R. M. Lerner, & M. Perlmutter (Eds.), *Child development in life-span perspective* (pp. 67–90). Hillsdale, NJ: Lawrence Erlbaum Associates.

Featherman, D. L., & Stevens, G. (1982). A revised socioeconomic index of occupational status: Application in analysis of sex differences in attainment. In R. Hauser, A. Haller, D. Mechanic, & T. Hauser (Eds.), *Social structure and behavior* (pp. 141–181). New York: Academic Press.

Floyd, F. J., & Saitzyk, A. R. (1992). Social class and parenting children with mild and moderate mental retardation. *Journal of Pediatric Psychology, 17,* 607–631.

Fox, J. (1997). *Applied regression analysis, linear models and related methods.* Thousand Oaks, CA: Sage.

Ganzeboom, H. B. G., De Graaf, P. M., & Treiman, D. J. (1992). A standard international socioeconomic index of occupational status. *Social Science Research, 21,* 1–56.

Ganzeboom, H. B. G., & Treiman, D. J. (1996). Internationally comparable measures of occupational status for the 1988 international standard classification of occupations. *Social Science Research, 55,* 201–239.

Garcia Coll, C. T., & Pachter, L. M. (2002). Ethnic and minority parenting. In M. H. Bornstein (Ed.), *Handbook of parenting Vol. 4. Applied parenting* (2nd ed., pp. 1–20). Mahwah, NJ: Lawrence Erlbaum Associates.

Garrett, P., Ng'andu, N., & Ferron, J. (1994). Poverty experiences of young children and the quality of their home environments. *Child Development, 65,* 331–345.

Gecas, V. (1979). The influence of social class on socialization. In W. R. Burr, R. Hill, F. I. Nye, & I. L. Reiss (Eds.), *Contemporary theories about the family, Vol. 1* (pp. 365–404). New York: The Free Press.

Gottfried, A. W. (1984). Home environment and early cognitive development: Implications for intervention. In A. W. Gottfried (Ed.), *Home environment and early cognitive development* (pp. 329–342). New York: Academic Press.

Gottfried, A. W. (1985). Measures of socioeconomic status in child development research: Data and recommendations. *Merrill-Palmer Quarterly, 31,* 85–92.

Green, I. W. (1970). Manual for scoring socioeconomic status for research on health behaviors. *U.S. Public Health Reports, 85,* 815–827.

Greenberger, E., & O'Neil, R. (1991, April). *Characteristics of fathers' and mothers' jobs: Implications for parenting and children's social development.* Paper presented at the biennial meeting of the Society for Research in Child Development, Seattle, WA.

Gutierrez, J., Sameroff, A. J., & Karrer, B. M. (1988). Acculturation and SES effects on Mexican-American parents' concepts of development. *Child Development, 59*, 250–255.

Hart, B., & Risley, T. R. (1992). American parenting of language-learning children: Persisting differences in family-child interactions observed in natural home environments. *Developmental Psychology, 28*, 1096–1106.

Hart, B., & Risley, T. R. (1995). *Meaningful differences in the everyday experience of young American children*. Baltimore, MD: Paul H. Brookes.

Harwood, R., Leyendecker, B., Carlson, V., Asencio, M., & Miller, A. (2002). Parenting among Latino families in the U.S. In M. H. Bornstein (Ed.), *Handbook of parenting Vol. 4. Applied parenting* (2nd ed., pp. 21–46). Mahwah, NJ: Lawrence Erlbaum Associates.

Harwood, R. L., Schoelmerich, A., Ventura-Cook, E., Schulze, P. A., & Wilson, S. P. (1996). Cultural and class influences on Anglo and Puerto Rican mothers' beliefs regarding long-term socialization goals and child behavior. *Child Development, 67*, 2446–2461.

Hauser, R. M. (1994). Measuring socioeconomic status in studies of child development. *Child Development, 65*, 1541–1545.

Hauser, R. M., & Featherman, D. L. (1977). *The process of gratification: Trends and analyses*. New York: Academic Press.

Haveman, R., & Wolfe, B. (1995). The determinants of children's attainments: A review of methods and findings. *Journal of Economic Literature, 23*, 1829–1878.

Hernandez, D. J. (1997). Child development and the social demography of childhood. *Child development, 68*, 149–169.

Hess, R. D. (1970). Social class and ethnic influences upon socialization. In P. H. Mussen (Ed.), *Carmichael's manual of child psychology, 3rd ed., Vol. 2* (pp. 457–557). New York: Wiley.

Hitchcock, D. C., & Oliver, L. I. (1976). Intellectual development and school achievement of youths 12–17 years: Demographic and socioeconomic factors. *Vital and Health Statistics, 158*, 65.

Hoff, E., Laursen, B., & Tardif, T. (2002). Socioeconomic status and parenting. In M. H. Bornstein (Ed.), *Handbook of parenting Vol. 2. Biology and Ecology of Parenting* (2nd ed., pp. 231–252). Mahwah, NJ: Lawrence Erlbaum Associates.

Hoff-Ginsberg, E. (1991). Mother-child conversation in different social classes and communicative settings. *Child Development, 62*, 782–796.

Hoff-Ginsberg, E. (1992). How should frequency in input be measured? *First Language, 12*, 233–245.

Holden, G. W., & Edwards, L. A. (1989). Parental attitudes toward child rearing: Instruments, issues, and implications. *Psychological Bulletin, 106*, 29–58.

Hollingshead, A. B. (1975). *The four-factor index of social status*. Unpublished manuscript, Yale University, New Haven, CT.

Jackman, M., & Jackman, R. (1983). *Class consciousness in the United States*. Berkeley: University of California Press.

Jackson, D. N. (1976). *Jackson personality inventory manual*. Port Huron, MI: Research Psychologists Press.

Kalmijn, M. (1991). Shifting boundaries: Trends in religious and educational homogamy. *American Sociological Review, 65*, 786–800.

Kelly, M. L., Sanchez-Hucles, J., & Walker, R. (1993). Correlates of disciplinary practices in working-to middle-class African-American mothers. *Merrill-Palmer Quarterly, 39*, 252–264.

Kilbourne, B., England, P., & Beron, K. (1994). Effects of individual occupational and industrial characteristics on earnings: Intersections of race and gender. *Social Forces, 72*, 1149–1176.

Kohn, M. L. (1963). Social class and parent-child relationships: An interpretation. *American Journal of Sociology, 68*, 471–480.

Kohn, M. L., & Schooler, C. (1983). *Work and personality: An inquiry into the impact of social stratification*. Norwood, NJ: Ablex.

Krieger, N., Williams, D. R., & Moss, H. W. (1997). Measuring social class in U.S. public health research: Concepts, methodologies, and guidelines. *Annual Review of Public Health, 18*, 341–378.

Laosa, L. M. (1980). Maternal teaching strategies in Chicano and Anglo-American families: the influ-
    ence of culture and education on maternal behavior. *Child Development, 51*, 759–765.
Laosa, L. M. (1983). School, occupation, culture and family. In E. Sigel & L. Laosa (Eds.), *Changing
    Families* (pp.79–135). Plenum.
Lerner, R. M., Rothbaum, F., Boulos, S., & Castellino, D. R. (2002). Developmental systems perspective
    on parenting. In M. H. Bornstein (Ed.), *Handbook of parenting* (2nd ed., Vol. 2, pp. 285–309).
    Mahwah, NJ: Lawrence Erlbaum Associates.
Leventhal, T., & Brooks-Gunn, J. (2000). The neighborhoods they live in: The effects of neighborhood
    residence upon child and adolescent outcomes. *Psychological Bulletin, 126*, 309–337.
Liberatos, P., Link, B. G., & Kelsey, J. L. (1988). The measurement of social class in epidemiology.
    Epidemiologic Reviews, 10, 87–121.
Lynd, R. S., & Lynd, H. M. (1929). *Middletown: A study in American culture.* New York: Harcourt
    Brace.
Lynd, R. S., & Lynd, H. M. (1937). *Middletown in transition: A study in cultural conflicts.* New York:
    Harcourt Brace.
Magnuson, K. A., & Duncan, G. J. (2002). Parents in poverty. In M. H. Bornstein (Ed.), *Handbook
    of parenting Vol. 4. Applied parenting* (2nd ed., pp. 95–121). Mahwah, NJ: Lawrence Erlbaum
    Associates.
Mansbach, I. K., & Greenbaum, C. W. (1999). Developmental maturity expectations of Israeli fathers
    and mothers: Effects of education, ethnic origin, and religiosity. *International Journal of Behavioral
    Development, 23*, 771–797.
Mardia, K. V. (1970). Measures of multivariate skewness and kurtosis with applications. *Biometrika,
    57*, 519–530.
Mayes, L. C., & Bornstein, M. H. (1995). Infant information-processing performance and maternal
    education. *Early Development and Parenting, 4*, 91–96.
McAdoo, H. P. (2002). African American parenting. In M. H. Bornstein (Ed.), *Handbook of parenting
    Vol. 4. Applied parenting* (2nd ed., pp. 47–58). Mahwah, NJ: Lawrence Erlbaum Associates.
McCall, R. (1977). Childhood IQ's as predictors of adult educational and occupational status. *Science,
    197*, 482–483.
McCall, R. (1979). Individual differences in the pattern of habituation at 5 and 10 months of age.
    Developmental Psychology, 15, 559–569.
McCall, R. (1981). Nature-nurture and the two realms of development: A proposed integration with
    respect to mental development. *Child Development, 52*, 1–12.
McGraw, K. O. , & Wong, S. P. (1996). Forming inferences about some intraclass correlation coeffi-
    cients. *Psychological Methods, 1*, 30–46.
McLoyd, V. C. (1998). Socioeconomic disadvantage and child development. *American Psychologist,
    53*, 185–204.
Menaghan, E. G., & Parcel, T. L. (1991). Social sources of change in children's home environments:
    The effects of parental occupational experiences and family conditions. *Journal of Marriage and
    the Family, 57*, 69–94.
Mercy, J. A., & Steelman, L. C. (1982). Family influence on intellectual attainment of children.
    American Sociological Review, 42, 532–542.
Meudell, M. B. (1982). Household social standing: Dynamic and static dimensions. In P. H. Rossi
    & S. L. Nock (Eds.), *Measuring social judgements: The factorial survey approach* (pp. 69–83).
    Beverly Hills, CA: Sage.
Michael, R. T. (1972). The effect of education on efficiency in consumption. New York: Columbia
    University Press.
Moore, M. R., & Brooks-Gunn, J. (2002). Adolescent parenthood. In M. H. Bornstein (Ed.), *Handbook
    of parenting Vol. 3. Status and social conditions of parenting* (2nd ed., pp. 173–214). Mahwah, NJ:
    Lawrence Erlbaum Associates.
Nakao, K., & Treas, J. (1990). *Computing 1989 occupational prestige scores (General Social Survey
    Methodological Report No. 70).* Chicago: University of Chicago.

Nakao, K., & Treas, J. (1992). *The 1989 socioeconomic index of occupations: construction from the 1989 occupational prestige scores (General Social Survey Methodological Report No. 74).* Chicago: University of Chicago.

National Research Council. (2000). *From neurons to neighborhoods: The science of early child development.* Washington, DC: National Academy of Sciences Press.

Ninio, A. (1980). Picture-book reading in mother-infant dyads belonging to two subgroups in Israel. *Child Development, 51,* 587–590.

Ninio, A. (1988). The effects of cultural background, sex, and parenthood on beliefs about the timetable of cognitive development in infancy. *Merrill-Palmer Quarterly, 34,* 369–388.

O'Connor, M. J., Cohen, S., & Parmelee, A. H. (1984). Infant auditory discrimination in preterm and full-term infants as a predictor of 5-year intelligence. *Developmental Psychology, 20,* 159–165.

Otto, L. B. (1975). Class and status in family research. *Journal of Marriage and the Family, 37,* 315–332.

Pagani, L., Boulerice, B., Vitaro, F., & Tremblay, R. E. (1999). Effects of poverty on academic failure and delinquency in boys: A change and process model approach. *Journal of Child Psychology and Psychiatry, 40,* 1209–1219.

Palacios, J. (1990). Parents ideas about the development and education of their children: Answers to some questions. *International Journal of Behavioral Development, 13,* 137–155.

Papoušek, M., Papoušek, H., & Bornstein, M. H. (1985). The naturalistic vocal environment of young infants: On the significance of homogeneity and variability in parental speech. In T. M. Field & N. Fox (Eds.), *Social Perception in Infants* (pp. 269–297). Norwood, NJ: Ablex.

Parke, R. D. (2002). Fathers and families. In M. H. Bornstein (Ed.), *Handbook of parenting Vol. 3. Status and social conditions of parenting* (2nd ed., pp. 27–73). Mahwah, NJ: Lawrence Erlbaum Associates.

Paunonen, S. V., & Jackson, D. N. (1996). The Jackson Personality Inventory and the five-factor model of personality. *Journal of Research in Personality, 30,* 42–59.

Pettit, G. S., Laird, R. D., Dodge, K. A., Bates, J. E., & Criss, M. M. (in press). Antecedents and behavior-problem outcomes of parental monitoring and psychological control in early adolescence. *Child Development.*

Ramey, C. T., & Ramey, S. L. (1999). Prevention of intellectual disabilities: Early interventions to improve cognitive development. In S. J. Ceci, W. M., Williams, et al., (Eds.), *The nature–nurture debate: Essential readings* (pp. 147–163). Walden, MA: Blackwell.

Ribas, R. C. (2001). *Indexes of socioeconomic status in psychological research: A brief review.* Unpublished manuscript, Universidade Federal do Rio de Janeiro.

Roberts, E., Bornstein, M. H., Slater, A. M., & Barrett, J. (1999). Early cognitive development and parental education. *Infant and Child Development, 8,* 49–62.

Rowe, D. C. (1994) *The Limits of Family Influence: Genes Experience and Behavior.* New York: Guilford.

Sameroff, A. J., & Feil, L. A. (1985). Parental concepts of development. In I. E. Sigel (Ed.), *Parental belief systems: The psychological consequences for children* (pp. 83–105). Hillsdale, NJ: Lawrence Erlbaum Associates.

Sampson, R. J., & Laub, J. H. (1994). Urban poverty and the family context of delinquency: A new look at structure and process in a classic study. *Child Development, 65,* 523–540.

Sandqvist, K. (1995). Verbal boys and mathematical girls: Family background and educational careers. *Sandinavia Journal of Educational Research, 39,* 5–36.

Satorra, A., & Bentler, P. M. (1988). *Scaling corrections for statistics in covariance structure analysis.* Los Angeles: UCLA Statistics Series #2.

Satorra, A., & Bentler, P. M. (1994). Corrections to test statistics and standard errors in covariance structure analysis. In A. Von Eye & C. C. Clogg (Eds.), *Latent variable analysis: Applications for developmental research* (pp. 399–419). Thousand Oaks, CA: Sage.

Siegel, P. M. (1971). *Prestige in the American occupational structure.* Unpublished manuscript, University of Chicago.

Smith, J. R., Brooks-Gunn, J., & Klebanov, P. K. (1997). Consequences of living in poverty for young children's cognitive and verbal ability and early school achievement. In G. J. Duncan & J. Brooks-Gunn (Eds.), *Consequences of growing up poor* (pp. 132–189). New York: Russell Sage.

Smith, T. E., & Graham, P. B. (1995). Socioeconomic stratification in family research. *Journal of Marriage and the Family, 57,* 930–941.

Sonnander, K., & Claesson, M. (1999). Predictors of developmental delay at 18 months and later school achievement problems. *Developmental Medicine and Child Neurology, 41,* 195–202.

Stevens, G., & Cho, J. H. (1985). Sociometric indexes and the new 1980 census occupational classification scheme. *Social Science Research, 14,* 142–168.

Susser, M., Watson, W., & Hopper, K. (1985). *Sociology in medicine.* New York: Oxford University Press.

Tardif, T. (1993). *Adult-to-child speech and language acquisition in Mandarin Chinese.* Unpublished doctoral dissertation, Yale University, New Haven, CT.

Terrisse, B., Roberts, D. S. L., Palacio-Quintin, E., & MacDonald, B. E. (1998). Effects of parenting practices and socioeconomic status on child development. *Swiss Journal of Psychology, 57,* 114–123.

Treiman, D. J. (1977). *Occupational prestige in comparative perspective.* New York: Academic Press.

Von der Lippe, A. L. (1999). The impact of maternal schooling and occupation on child-rearing attitudes and behaviours in low income neighbourhoods in Cairo, Egypt. *International Journal of Behavioral Development, 23,* 703–729.

Waddington, C. H. (1962). *New patterns in genetics and development.* New York: Columbia University Press.

Waddington, C. H. (1966). *Principles of development and differentiation.* New York: Macmillan.

Weinraub, M., Horvath, D. L., & Gringlas, M. B. (2002). Single parenthood. In M. H. Bornstein (Ed.), *Handbook of parenting Vol. 3. Status and social conditions of parenting* (2nd ed., pp. 109–140). Mahwah, NJ: Lawrence Erlbaum Associates.

White, K. R. (1982). The relation between socioeconomic status and academic achievement. *Psychological Bulletin, 91,* 461–481.

Williams, D. R., & Collins, C. (1995). U.S. socioeconomic and racial differentials in health: Patterns and explanations. *Annual Review of Sociology, 21,* 349–386.

Wright, J. D., & Wright, S. R., (1976). Social class and parental values for children: A partial replication and extension of the Kohn thesis. *American Sociological Review, 41,* 527–537.

3

Off With Hollingshead: Socioeconomic Resources, Parenting, and Child Development

Greg J. Duncan and Katherine A. Magnuson
Northwestern University

INTRODUCTION

Socioeconomic status (SES) is an amorphous concept used in different ways by different social science disciplines. Parental education, occupation, and family income are the most common markers for SES. Some developmentalists combine education and occupation in the widely used four factor Hollingshead Social Status Index whereas others use single indicators as measures of SES (Ensminger & Fothergill, chap. 1, this volume). Although there are often substantial correlations between SES measures, parenting practices, and children's health, ability, and behavior, the causal impacts of these components are less clear, as are the processes by which SES affects development (Belsky, Hertzog, & Rovine, 1986; Brooks-Gunn & Duncan, 1997; Hoff-Ginsberg & Tardif, 1995).

We argue that developmental research is ill served by an aggregated, simplified, or superficial, treatment of SES. In 2000, some 1.4 million American adults with a college degree were poor (U.S. Bureau of the Census, 2001a). Is their SES high or low? With both schooling levels and poverty increasing over the past quarter century, should we consider trends in the socioeconomic status of Americans to be positive or negative? What is the occupation-based SES of the families of the many teen mothers who have virtually no work experience? If a highly educated, stay-at-home mother divorces and finds her family income falls by one-half, has her SES fallen as well (Mueller & Parcel, 1981)? Does the SES of the family of a mid-career professional who is downsized from his or her job remain high during the subsequent spell of unemployment?

Volatility in income, occupation, and family circumstances is surprisingly common among American families (Duncan, 1988; Featherman & Spenner, 1988), which belies the presumption that SES is a permanent characteristic of families. It is ironic that developmental research often takes great care in measuring the temporal vagaries of developmental trajectories and their microsystem correlates, but usually ignores fluctuations in the components of family SES.

Disregarding changes in income, occupation, and even occasionally education has been motivated by the argument that these changes are idiosyncratic and can be relegated to our models' error terms (Hauser, 1994). That is, these fluctuations may constitute anomalies of little lasting consequence for children. Accordingly, some researchers have used measures of SES that mask or reduce the relative contribution of the individual components of education, employment, occupation, and education in favor of a more reliable measure (Mueller & Parcel, 1981). For example, the Hollingshead Four Factor Index (Hollingshead, 1975)[1] measure provides an overall SES score that is a weighted average of an individual's education and occupation. In the case of a family with two parents only one of whom is employed, the index is based on the employed parent's individual score. In the case of a family with two employed parents, the index is based on the average of the parents' individual scores. Creating a weighted combination of education and occupation, rather than including both as independent constructs reduces the ability of researchers to understand the distinct contribution of both dimensions to parenting and children's development.

Developmental studies sometimes include only one SES indicator (Elo & Preston, 1996; Ensminger & Fothergill, chap. 1, this volume). This is appropriate if a researcher is particularly interested in studying how that one component of SES, for example education or income, affects children's outcomes. However, inclusion of a single SES indicator should not be viewed as an adequate approach to controlling for SES or understanding the effects of SES on child outcomes. The research we review suggests that changes in the components of SES systematically and differentially affect parenting and children's outcomes. Components of

---

[1]Hollingshead's four factor index is an update of his two factor index that was criticized by social stratification scholars for its lack of validity and practicality (Haug, 1977: Hauser & Warren, 1997). It is important to note that the Four Factor Index of Social Status (Hollingshead, 1975) is more accurately described as a two-factor index of education and occupation with guidelines for computing the scale for families of different circumstances (e.g., dual earners and single-parent households). The rational behind many of the scale's conventions are not presented in the short unpublished manuscript. For example, education is scored on a seven-point scale whereas occupation is scored on a nine-point scale, and the final scores are then unevenly split into five strata.

SES may act in concert to affect children's lives, but each has distinct impacts and is not interchangeable with the others. Consequently, combining components of SES or measuring only one dimension is misguided until we better understand their individual effects.

Similarly ill served are the policy lessons that might come out of SES-based developmental research. There are no treatments for enhancing overall SES; policies abound for enhancing specific components of SES (e.g., income transfers, job training). Imposing immigrant restrictions on eligibility for the food stamp program or expanding the earned income tax credit for working families has a direct, short-run impact on the financial but no other SES component of affected families. Policies designed to promote high school completion or community-college enrollment affect completed schooling, although they may eventually improve occupational standing and income as well. Forecasting the differential impacts on children of imposing job- or schooling-related welfare reforms requires knowledge of their separate causal impacts on development.

We begin with an explanation of how economic, education, and occupational components of SES each constitute distinct constructs with distinct theoretical linkages to developmental outcomes. All are related in some way to a conception of family's resources, but each is distinct in ways that may be consequential for parenting practices and child outcomes. Its relative neglect in the psychological literature leads us to feature the economic component of SES in this discussion.

We next review evidence on trends in SES indicators for children and find both encouraging and discouraging developments. Most encouraging is that the average schooling level of parents of young children has increased substantially over the past several decades. Income inequality has increased as well, simultaneously producing more affluent and more poor children.

Evidence on the causal connections between these SES components, parenting, and child outcomes is summarized in the following section. We first address the issue of whether SES differences merely reflect differential genetic endowments and argue that they do much more than that. In the case of income, the literature suggests that the causal impact of economic deprivation on children's development is overstated by simple comparisons of poor and non-poor children. But economic resources do matter, and poverty early in childhood appears to be more detrimental to long-run development than poverty later in childhood. The strong correlations between parental education levels, parenting, and child development reflect an uncertain combination of genetic factors, concrete skills acquired by parents in school, and personality traits that lead parents to acquire more schooling and to rear children who are healthier and more successful. Similarly, the modest correlations between parental occupation and parenting probably reflect the direct influences of the job characteristics on parents as well as characteristics of the parents' personal endowments that affect their occupational attainment, parenting practices, and their children's outcomes.

We end with a discussion of some of the potential data-collection and analytic implications of taking SES more seriously in parenting and developmental research.

DEFINITIONS AND THEORIES OF SES-BASED RESOURCES

At the heart of the possible linkages between SES and children's development are the differing resources available to families at different socioeconomic levels (Brooks-Gunn, Brown, Duncan, & Moore, 1995; Haveman & Wolfe, 1994). We first review conceptions of economic resources and then turn to education and occupation.

Economic Resources

Economic models of child development (e.g., Becker, 1981) view families with higher economic resources as being better able to purchase or produce important inputs into their young children's development (e.g., nutritious meals; enriched home learning environments and childcare settings outside the home; safe and stimulating neighborhood environments), and, with older children, higher-quality schools and college education. The degree to which these inputs are purchased is presumed to vary with their cost, household income, and parents' preferences for purchases that meet their own needs. The efficiency with which parents and children are able to translate inputs into positive developmental outcomes is presumed to vary with both their innate and their acquired (e.g., formal schooling) abilities (Michael, 1982).

Household Income

Household income is the sum of income from all sources received by all members of the household over some time period, typically a calendar year or month. When combined with a measure of household wealth (see the following), a household's income measures its ability to provide its children with food, shelter, a quality home, or childcare environment, and a safe and stimulating community setting. Adjustments for the inclusion of near-cash sources of income such as food stamps and payments from the earned income tax credit, and subtraction of taxes paid, produce a better approximation of a household's disposable income. Division of household income by household size or, better yet, a poverty threshold based on household size produces a more refined measure of its per capita command over resources referred to as an income-to-needs ratio (Citro & Michael, 1995).

Contrary to popular belief, and in comparison to other SES-based measures, family income is quite volatile across a family's life cycle in general, and a child's childhood, in particular (Duncan, Brooks-Gunn, Yeung, & Smith, 1998). On average, family incomes increase as children age, but average patterns conceal a great deal of year-to-year volatility, making it important to measure economic resources during the particular childhood stage in which income-based SES influences are sought. This income instability makes a single year's measure of household income a somewhat erroneous measure of a household's permanent income, and suggests that data collections consider some combination of multi-year income measurement, or measurement of wealth, occupation, or other correlates of permanent income.

Wealth

Wealth is the point-in-time stock of a household's financial assets, including both liquid forms such as money in a savings account, as well as illiquid forms such the net equity tied up in an owned home. Wealth is the net amount held in accounts and assets—the difference between the market value of that asset and whatever remaining debt the household owes on that asset. In contrast to income, which consists of a flow of resources over some time period, wealth is a stock concept and makes sense only at a distinct point in time. Income and wealth are positively correlated but distinct, as can be seen in the case of a divorced, home-owning mother with a low cash income but substantial wealth in the form of net equity tied up in the home.

Hourly Earnings

This is earnings per hour worked, usually obtained by dividing labor-market earnings received over some time period by the total number of hours worked during that time. Workers paid by the hour have an hourly wage rate that may differ between regular and overtime hours.

Perhaps surprisingly, some economists would nominate the hourly wage rate as the best summary measure of SES. This is because they conceive of the hourly wage as a good measure of an individual's stock of skills—the productivity of his or her time either at work or at home.[2] How an individual chooses to allocates

---

[2]It is unlikely that productivity at home and at work is identical for all individuals. However, factors that determine such productivity (e.g., formal skills and age-related experience) are similar in both settings (Michael, 1972). Although individuals not currently working have zero labor-market earnings, they still have a positive wage rate—the amount per hour they could earn if they did work.

time between market work and childcare and other home-production activities depends on a host of idiosyncratic factors such as family structure and local-area employment conditions. But the product of the hourly wage and 16 waking hours measures the total value of those waking hours, regardless of how they happen to be divided between paid and unpaid work.

Poverty

Social scientists have proposed many household-income-based definitions of economic deprivation (Citro & Michael, 1995). The official U.S. definition of poverty is based on a comparison of a household's income with a threshold level of income that varies with family size and inflation. In 2000, the respective thresholds for two-, three-, and four-person families were $11,590, $13,738, and $17,603 (U.S. Bureau of the Census, 2001b). Households with incomes below these thresholds are considered poor, whereas households with incomes above the thresholds are considered not poor. A household's poverty status is assumed to apply to each household member. Thresholds are adjusted each year for inflation, but not for changes in living standards of the general population.

According to opinion polls, official poverty thresholds are lower than the amounts of money—typically around $20,000—judged by Americans as necessary to get along in their community, to live decently, or to avoid hardship (Vaughn, 1993). A detailed ethnographic study of family budgets by Edin and Lein (1997) identified $16,500 as the approximate income level that enables a thrifty three-person family to live without severe hardship.

How persistent is poverty? We speak easily of the poor as if they were an ever-present and unchanging group. Indeed, the way we conceptualize the poverty problem or the underclass problem seems to presume the permanent existence of well-defined economic groups within American society. In fact, as already noted, longitudinal data have always revealed a great deal of turnover among the poor, as events like unemployment and divorce push families into poverty, and reemployment, marriage, and career gains pull them out (Duncan et al., 1984). More than one-quarter of the individuals living in poverty in one year report incomes above the poverty line in the next, and considerably less than one-half of those who experience poverty remain persistently poor over many years. A clear majority of poverty spells are short (60% last less than three years). A substantial but small subset of poor families experiences longer-run poverty (14% of poverty spells last eight or more years; Bane & Ellwood, 1986). As with all poverty, persistent poverty is not evenly distributed across ethnic groups. Long-term poverty rates for minority children are especially high, with nearly one-quarter of African American children living in persistent poverty (U.S. Department of Health and Human Services, 1997). An important implication of economic mobility among the poor is the need to distinguish between impacts of transitory and persistent poverty.

Formal Education

Human capital constitutes a second form of SES-based family resources, and includes the collection of parental skills acquired in both formal and informal ways that have value either in the labor market or at home (Becker, 1975). Formal schooling is the most familiar and most studied form of human capital, although it is not the only form. A large body of literature has attempted to gauge the labor-market value of the skills acquired through additional years of schooling (Mincer, 1974) but less is known about the non-pecuniary returns to schooling (Michael, 1982). An individual's hourly earnings are presumed by economists to correspond to the value of the human capital that an individual brings to the labor market.

Parents' formal education may well influence children's well being by shaping parent-child interactions. When compared to less educated parents, parents who have acquired more formal schooling tend to provide a more cognitively stimulating home learning environment and have a more verbal and supportive teaching style (Laosa, 1983; Richman, Miller, & Levine, 1992). These differences are considered very consequential in explaining why children of less-educated parents perform less well on measures of cognitive development than children of more highly educated parents (Harris, Terrel & Allen, 1999). Although most developmental researchers have pointed to parent–child interactions as the primary mediator of parental education's effects on children, the skills acquired through formal education may enhance parents' abilities to organize their daily routines and resources in a way that enables them to effectively accomplish their parenting goals (Michael, 1972).

Occupation

Human capital also refers to a much broader set of skills than those learned though formal education. Skills such as intellectual flexibility, verbal communication, and decision-making accumulate throughout a lifetime. In the 1960s and 1970s, social psychologists and sociologists sought to describe how occupations and job characteristics contribute to and detract from human capital through the life course (Kohn, 1959, 1969; Kohn & Schooler, 1973).

Occupations are a much-studied component of SES, with higher-status occupations typically conferring higher earnings, more control, and more prestige on workers holding them (Jencks, Perman, & Rainwater, 1988). Research has focused on occupation as an important aspect of SES because they are closely related to education and earnings and, compared with single-year income, may better measure a family's permanent economic position. However, research on occupational transitions throughout the life course suggests that career mobility patterns are dynamic (Featherman & Selbee, 1988; Featherman & Spenner, 1988).

Of greatest interest is the fact that research has found that job conditions appear to shape workers' values and personalities (Kohn, 1959, 1969; Kohn & Schooler, 1973, 1982). Characteristics of high prestige jobs such as highly complex tasks and autonomy are associated with an orientation toward self-direction and intellectual flexibility, whereas low complexity jobs are associated with an orientation toward conformity. Based on correlational evidence, researchers have argued that job conditions determine worker's personality and values. Workers acquire values and skills on the job and generalize them to other areas of life (Kohn & Schooler, 1982). More recent work has also suggested that job characteristics shape employees cognitive skills, rather than or in addition to their personalities (Menaghan & Parcel, 1991; Parcel & Menaghan, 1994). In particular, low-prestige jobs with low autonomy, routinized tasks, and little opportunity for substantively complex work may erode parents' cognitive skills, whereas high-prestige jobs promote initiative, thought, and decision-making skills.

Much of the motivation for studying occupational influences on human capital was to better understand the intergenerational transmission of social inequality. Therefore, from the very beginning researchers argued that acquired values, orientations, or cognitive skills were passed on to children through parenting practices. For example in the case of values, class differences in the value of autonomy have been linked to class differences in parental goals, and subsequently parenting practices (Kohn, 1969; Luster, Rhoades, & Haas, 1989). Higher-SES parents are more likely than lower-SES parents to use shame, guilt, and reasoning as disciplinary strategies, strategies that emphasize a child's autonomy, and less likely to use commands and imperatives, strategies that emphasize children's conformity (Kohn, 1969). In the case of cognitive skills, theory suggests that characteristics of parental employment influence children primarily through the home learning environment, because parents with lower cognitive skills provide a less cognitively stimulating home learning environment (Menaghan & Parcel, 1991).

TRENDS IN SES INDICATORS

Different components of SES have exhibited divergent trends in the United States. As compared with 25 years ago, young children today are more likely to have better-educated parents, live in families with incomes either below or well above the poverty line, and live with one parent (Shonkoff & Phillips, 2000).

Family Poverty and Affluence

As of 2000, some 16.2% of U.S. children were poor, a figure that is several percentage points lower than in the early 1990s, but still higher than 25 years before (U.S. Bureau of the Census, 2001c). Poverty is considerably more prevalent among children now than 25 years ago; in 1974, 15% of children were poor. This rate changed little during the remainder of the 1970s, jumped to 22% by 1984, and fell back below 20% only in 1997. Poverty rates were much higher in 2000 for African American (31%) and Latin American (28%) than European American (13%) children, in part because poverty increased much more for minority children. To the extent that low incomes prevent parents from buying things that promote healthy development, these trends do not bode well for the development of children, especially minority children. However, the number of affluent children also increased between 1974 (5%) and 1997 (14%). Thus, in 1997 when compared with 1974, the United States was home to both more poor and more affluent children.

Parental Schooling

Educational attainment of the parents of young children increased substantially between 1975 and 1998 (Figure 3.1, adapted from Shonkoff & Phillips, 2000, Figure 10-3). The proportion of children whose mothers had not graduated from high school dropped nearly by nearly half, from 30% to 17%, although the proportion whose mothers had graduated from college nearly doubled, from 13% to 24%. Trends in fathers' schooling also show increases in attainment, although not quite as dramatic. To the extent that parental education influences the quality

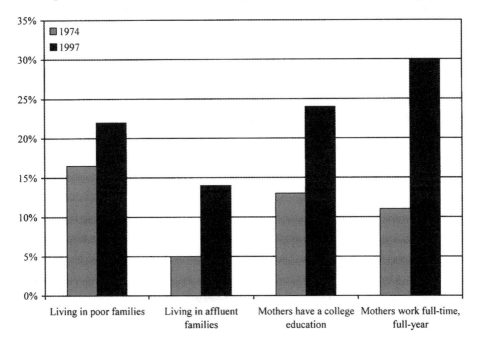

FIGURE 3.1. Demographic data on parental schooling, income, and maternal employment for young children (adapted from Shonkoff and Phillips, 2000, Figure 10–3).

of parenting and children's home environments, as well as enhances parental careers and earnings, these trends bode well for the healthy development of young children.

Changes in parental schooling levels among young African American children were even more favorable than among Caucasian children, although in 1998 racial and ethnic inequalities in educational attainment were still evident. A much larger fraction of African American (21%) than European American (8%) children had mothers who had not completed high school, and nearly half (45%) of young Hispanic children had mothers who lacked a high school degree. The low schooling levels of Hispanic immigrant parents largely explain the low maternal schooling levels of Hispanic parents as a whole.

Parental Employment

Increases in paid maternal employment over the past quarter century are one of the most dramatic—and best-known—social trends. Between 1974 and 1997, the proportion of young children with mothers working full-time, year-round nearly tripled, from 11% to 30% (Figure 3.1). At between 36% and 41%, the proportion of young children with a mother working part-time changed relatively little over that period. A much larger share of young Hispanic (48%) than European American (29%) or African American (29%) children lived with mothers who did not work for pay in 1997.

In contrast, paternal employment among children living with their fathers changed relatively little between 1974 and 1997, with modest increases (73% to 81%) in full-time work and corresponding decreases in part-time work. Over the 25-year period, very small (4% to 7%) and relatively constant fractions of fathers living with their young children were not working.

DOES SES MATTER
FOR CHILDREN'S DEVELOPMENT?

Many studies, books, and reports have reported correlations between children's SES and various measures of child achievement, health, and behavior. In the case of poverty, for example, the risk for poor in comparison to nonpoor children is: 2.0 times as high for grade repetition and high-school dropout; 1.4 times for learning disability; 1.3 times for a parent-reported emotional or behavior problems; 3.1 times for a teenage out-of-wedlock birth; 6.8 times for reported cases of child abuse and neglect; and 2.2 times for experiencing violent crime (Brooks-Gunn & Duncan, 1997).

These kinds of correlations say little about the true causal connections between SES and child outcomes. As compared with nonpoor children, for example, poor children have a much higher risk of low school achievement, but that fact does not mean that increasing the incomes of poor parents would automatically improve children's school achievement. Many important variables in developmental models are, at least in part, determined or influenced by the actions of individuals, or the parents of the individuals whose development is being studied. Consequently, the correlation between these determined or influenced contextual variables and developmental outcomes may be the result of difficult-to-measure characteristics of the individuals themselves or, in the case of young children, of parents. Omitting these unmeasured child or family characteristics is likely to bias nonexperimental estimates of SES on children's outcomes (Duncan, Magnuson, & Ludwig, 1999).

For example, researchers worry that nonexperimental data will impart an upward bias to estimates of the effect of maternal education on children's outcomes (Resnick, Corley, & Robinson, 1997). This is because more highly educated mothers are likely to be advantaged in other ways that may positively affect their children's development, but that are not typically measured and included in the estimation models (Rosenzweig & Wolpin, 1994). For example, most studies of the effect of education lack a good measure of the mother's genetically endowed cognitive ability. By omitting this variable, researchers may mistakenly attribute positive children's outcomes to maternal schooling rather than to mothers' personal endowments, thereby possibly overestimating the effect of maternal schooling on children's school outcomes.

The Challenge of Behavioral Genetics

Behavioral geneticists raise two distinct challenges to the view that SES resources affect children's development. First, they argue that because SES is, in part, caused by parents' genetic endowments, an analysis relating children's family SES to their achievement that does not somehow adjust for parent and child genetic endowments risks misattributing to SES causation that ought to be attributed to genetic influences (e.g., Rowe, 1994). This argument has merit and adds genetic influences to a long list of potentially important factors that deserve attention in studies that seek estimates of the causal effects of SES components on children's development.

Some compelling data on the independent role of SES come from a recent adoption study that compared the pre- versus post-adoption IQs of children adopted into low-, middle- and high-SES families (Duyme, Dumaret, & Tomkiewicz, 1999). All of the adopted children had low IQs (in the 60–86 range) prior to adoption and were adopted between ages 4 and 6. IQ growth was strikingly different by SES (defined by father's occupation), with the gains associated with adoption into high- and middle-SES families much larger than the IQ gains for children adopted into low-SES families. Furthermore, the authors were able to discount differential selection as a possible cause of the differences. Thus, the evidence suggests that something about SES—unrelated to genetic endowment—was responsible for the differential gains.

A second challenge from behavioral genetics is based on the fact that the correlations in abilities and personalities of twins and other siblings reared apart are almost as large as correlations of siblings who grow up together. Indeed, in this accounting, children's shared environments account for very little (almost always less than 10%, usually less than 5%) of the variability of ability and personality found in the population (Bouchard, Lykken, McGue, Segal, & Tellegren, 1990). Some have concluded from this evidence that the developmental consequences of persistent family environmental influences such as SES or parenting are remarkably small (Scarr, 1992).

An alternative view is that the nature and effects of family socioeconomic influences vary sufficiently across time and among siblings that SES resources are more properly conceived as nonshared environmental influences. Only if a family's economic status were constant across the childhoods of siblings would the economic component of SES be shared by all siblings. Previously mentioned longitudinal studies based on nationally representative data have shown that family income is quite volatile (Duncan, 1988); Duncan et al. (1998) showed that siblings several years apart in age often experience quite different childhood incomes.

Moreover, it is quite possible that the effects on child development of SES components such as economic conditions and single-parent family structure depend on the stage of childhood in which they are experienced. For example, both divorce and economic deprivation may be more detrimental if they occur in childhood rather than adolescence, although the stigma that may accompany parental welfare receipt may be felt more by older than younger children. If so, then the extent to which siblings share SES conditions shrinks and the extent to which SES influences are better conceived as part of the nonshared family environment grows (Teachman, Duncan, Yeung, & Levy, in press).

Experimental Studies of Family Economic Resources and Children's Development

Much of the literature on the causal effects of household income on parenting children has methodological shortcomings. Family income is not reported in many data sources that contain crucial information about child outcomes. Even in data sets containing measures of income, parenting, and developmental outcomes, it is usually the case that the income measurement covers only a portion of childhood, often adolescence. Moreover, even when the required data are available the analyses of such data rarely go beyond using correlational techniques to estimate causal impacts.

Experimental designs involving manipulation of family incomes are better able to establish the causal nature of associations between household income and child well-being because the differences in income are not associated with child or parent characteristics (Duncan et al., 1999). Unfortunately, these types of experiments are extremely rare. In four income-maintenance experiments in the 1960s and

1970s, treatment families received an income supplement that varied with the family's income from work and other sources. Impacts on preschool children and parenting practices were not assessed. School performance and attendance were affected positively in some sites for elementary-school-age children, but not for high school-age adolescents. In two sites reporting high school completion and advanced education, these were higher for the experimental group (Institute for Research on Poverty, 1976; Kershaw & Fair, 1976; Salkind & Haskins, 1982; U.S. Department of Health and Human Services, 1983).

A number of experiments begun in the early to mid-1990s implemented various packages of welfare-to-work programs, some of which augmented family economic resources and others did not, and whose evaluations tracked family process and child well-being (Morris, Huston, Duncan, Crosby, & Bos, 2001). In all cases, participants were randomly assigned to a treatment group that received the welfare-reform package or to a control group that continued to live under the old Aid to Families with Dependent Children (AFDC) rules.

Evidence compiled by Morris et al. (2001) comes from five experiments: (1) the National Evaluation of Welfare to Work Strategies (NEWWS), which evaluated child impacts of both labor-force attachment and human-capital development treatments in Atlanta, Grand Rapids, and Riverside (Hamilton, 2000; McGroder, Zaslow, Moore, & LeMenestrel, 2000); (2) the Minnesota Family Investment Program, which combined participation mandates, make-work-pay incentives, and services in a way that constitutes a somewhat more generous version of Minnesota's current Temporary Aid for Needy Families (TANF) program (Gennetian & Miller, 2000; Miller, Knox, Aupos, & Hunter-Mann, 1997); (3) the Canadian Self-Sufficiency Project, which, by offering a very generous but temporary (three-year) earnings supplement for full-time work, is a pure make-work-pay approach (Morris & Michaelopolous, 2000); (4) Milwaukee's New Hope Project, which combined various make-work-pay strategies with some employment services (Bos et al., 1999); and (5) Florida's Family Transition Program (FTP), which offered a small earnings supplement, a participation mandate and fairly intensive case management (Bloom et al., 2000).

Comparable analyses of these data by Morris and colleagues (2001) revealed that welfare reforms that both increased work and provided financial supports for working families generally promoted children's achievement and positive behavior. In contrast, welfare reforms that mandated work but did not support it financially had few impacts—positive or negative—on children. Also of interest is the lack of consistent experimental impacts across all types of programs with respect to parental reports of parenting practices across a range of measures such as warmth and monitoring.

Welfare reform impacts on children depended crucially on the ages of the children studied. Elementary-school children were helped by the reforms that increased family resources and, for the most part, not harmed by unsupportive ones. For adolescents, more limited evidence suggested that even generous reforms that promoted maternal employment may have caused detrimental increases in school problems and risky behavior (Morris et al., 2001).

Nonexperimental Studies of Family Economic Resources and Children's Development

Despite these experiments, whether family resources affect child development remains a controversial issue that has generated a large nonexperimental literature (Blau, 1999; Brooks-Gunn & Duncan, 1997; Haveman & Wolfe, 1995; Mayer, 1997). Duncan and Brooks-Gunn (1997) provided a recent look at links between poverty and development by coordinating analyses of 12 groups of researchers working with 10 different developmental data sets. Most of these data sets offer longitudinal measurement of parental family income, as well as measurements of the achievement, behavior, and health of individuals at various points in life. Bias is reduced, but almost certainly not eliminated, with controls for parental education, family structure, age of the mother at the birth of the child, and several other demographic measures.

On the whole, the results suggest that family income may have substantial but decidedly selective associations with children's attainments. The selective nature of effects included the following: (1) family income had much larger associations with measures of children's ability and achievement than with measures of behavior, mental health, and physical health; (2) family economic conditions in early childhood appeared to be more important for shaping ability and achievement than did economic conditions during adolescence; (3) the association between income and achievement appeared to be nonlinear, with the biggest impacts at the lowest levels of income; and (4) persistent poverty has stronger negative associations with child outcomes than does transitory poverty.

Concerned that including measured covariates is an insufficient correction for potential biases associated with the omission of unmeasured factors such as parental ability or mental health, a few recent empirical studies linking income and child development have employed more sophisticated techniques. Using the Panel Study of Income Dynamics and the National Longitudinal Survey of Youth, Mayer (1997) provided a set of tests for omitted-variable bias, including the addition of measures of parental income after the measurement of the child outcome, as well as using only those components of parental income that are fairly independent of the actions of the family. In both cases, Mayer found large reductions in the estimated impact of parental income, leading her to conclude that much of the estimated effect of income in the literature is spurious.

As Mayer herself pointed out, these arguments have some potential flaws. If families anticipate future income changes and adjust their consumption accordingly, and the consumption changes benefit or hurt children, then future income does indeed play a causal role. The likely measurement error in income sources such as dividends and interest will impart a downward bias in their coefficients. Moreover, because interest and dividends are almost universally absent from the income packages of families at or below the poverty line, these exogenous income sources are not useful for estimating the impact of income increments to low-income families.

Blau (1999) used data from the National Longitudinal Survey of Youth to estimate a number of models relating income and other aspects of parental family background to children's ability and achievement test scores as well as behavior problems. These outcomes are assessed for most children in middle childhood. Among his approaches are family fixed-effect models that relate within-family differences in test scores to within-family differences in the income histories of the individual children. He employs two alternative measures of income: income (and, for some models, wage rates) during the calendar year prior to the developmental assessment and average household income of the mother over all years from 1979 to 1991 in which the data were available. In general, he finds small and insignificant effects of current income and larger (though still modest) effects of long-run income.

Although Blau attempted to address the omitted variable bias issue, his measures of income failed to recognize the possibility that the timing of parental income during childhood may be important. He implicitly assumed that families can smooth their consumption perfectly and that parental income during early childhood is equivalent (in terms of affecting child development) to income received in other stages of childhood.

Duncan et al. (1998) used data from the Panel Study of Income Dynamics to relate completed schooling and nonmarital childbearing to average household incomes in early and middle childhood and adolescence. Their models allow for differential effects of income according to the childhood stage in which it is received and are motivated by the hypothesis that the malleability of young children's development and the overwhelming importance of the family (as opposed to school or peer) context prior to school entry make economic conditions in early childhood more consequential for shaping children's ability and achievement than conditions later in childhood. Their models estimate the effects of income in early childhood, controlling for income in middle childhood and adolescence. These kinds of controls should go a long way in producing the kinds of omitted-variable adjustments Mayer and Blau strove for.

As hypothesized, early childhood emerges as the stage in which income appears to matter most. For example, controlling for income later in childhood, as well as for demographic characteristics of households, Duncan et al. (1998) estimated that a $10,000 increment to income averaged over the first five years of life for children in low-income families is associated with a 2.8-fold increase in the odds of finishing high school. This estimated effect was much larger than the corresponding estimated effects of increases in income measured later in childhood.

In summary, although previous correlational research has found consistent and substantial links between parental income and child well-being, the causal nature of the association has not been well established. Studies that manipulate families' economic resources experimentally support the hypothesis of a causal role. In nonexperimental research, researchers have employed a wide variety of ways to correct for some of the potential for omitted variable biases in their study designs. However, the potential differences of income's effect with respect to timing during childhood, and the greater importance of increases to income at the lower end of the income distribution suggest that prior research has not adequately answered the question of whether increasing parents' incomes would affect children's development.

Parental Education

Substantively large and statistically significant positive correlations among parental schooling levels, parent teaching styles, home learning environment, and children's achievement and behavior are among the most replicated results from developmental studies. Haveman and Wolfe's (1995) review of published studies suggested that maternal educational attainment is more closely related to children's academic performance than fathers' educational attainment, and parents' completion of high school, or a year or two of post-secondary education appears to have a larger effect than additional years of post secondary education beyond that level.

Nevertheless, surprisingly little is known about the causal nature of these associations (Mercy & Steelman, 1982). Most work in this area does not establish that these findings are attributable to mothers' relative schooling per se, as opposed to genetic differences or other characteristics that differentiate individuals who acquire different levels of schooling. In fact, there is a long list of spurious factors that could be driving the maternal education–child development correlation. Most obvious among these factors is cognitive ability. For example, Borduin and Henggeler (1981) argued that differences in parent–child interactions typically attributed to education or social class are due to mothers' and children's verbal IQ rather than SES. Few studies attempt to control statistically for maternal cognitive ability and the many other factors that might bias nonexperimental estimation strategies, but those that do find that these control reduce the association between maternal education and children's outcomes (e.g., Rosenzweig & Wolpin, 1994; Yeates, MacPhee, Campbell, & Ramey, 1983).

Two noteworthy studies have tried to account for the confounding correlations among parental genes, parental educational attainment, children's genes, and children's outcomes by using research designs that account for the genetic similarities among parents and children. Using a sample of adopted adolescents and matched biological children in two parent families, Neiss and Rowe (2000) estimated the proportion of the association between parental education and children's' verbal IQ that is attributable to genetics and to education per se. They found that parental education was significantly but modestly associated with adolescents verbal IQ.

The correlation between maternal education and child's verbal IQ was .16, and the correlation between paternal education and child's IQ was .18.

Behrman and Rosenzweig (in press) differentiated between parents' genetic endowments and their educational attainment by comparing the children of monozygotic twin parents. They take advantage of the fact that twins sometimes complete different levels of education despite having the same genes. By relating differences in twin parents' education to differences in their children's educational attainment they attempt to isolate the effect of parental schooling on children's schooling. Using samples of 424 twin mothers and 244 fathers born between 1936 and 1955 with children and at least one child 18 years of age or older, the authors find that maternal schooling does not have a beneficial effect on children's educational attainment. However, the authors caution that their findings may be context dependent. The mothers in their sample who attained more education were more likely to work out of the home, and this may have had an offsetting negative effect on children. In contrast, they do find that paternal schooling has a positive effect on their children's schooling. An additional year of paternal schooling would raise their child's educational attainment by slightly more than a third of a year.

We know of only one study of the impacts of mothers' schooling on children's development that involves experimental manipulation of mothers' schooling. Magnuson and McGroder (2001) exploited that fact that the National Evaluation of Welfare to Work Strategies Child Outcome Study randomly assigned welfare recipients with young children to either an education-, work-focused program group, or to a control group that received no additional assistance. Magnuson and McGroder took advantage of the experimental design by using an instrumental variable approach to estimate the affect of maternal schooling on 5- to 7-year old children's academic school readiness. They estimate that an additional nine months of schooling causes a quarter of a standard deviation increase on a test of young children's academic school readiness and a similar-sized reduction in academic problems such as grade retention.

Two additional studies have taken advantage of the fact that young mothers often acquire more formal schooling between the births of first and subsequent children to estimate whether achievement and behavior differences between earlier- and later-born siblings are related to increases in mother's formal schooling. These studies also provide contradictory evidence. Kaestner and Corman (1995) used this approach in an analysis of scores on the Peabody Individual Achievement Tests (PIATs) and found no consistent effect of increased maternal education on children's achievement scores.

In contrast, Rosenzweig and Wolpin (1994) found that an additional year of maternal schooling did have a modestly positive and marginally significant effect on children's PIAT scores. Interestingly, they found that mothers' enrollment during a child's first three years had a significant and large positive effect on children's scores on the Peabody Picture Vocabulary Test (PPVT), a measure of receptive vocabulary.

Parental Occupation

Despite modest associations between occupation, values, and parenting practices, we have found no convincing evidence that these associations are causal. Furthermore, much of this work has stopped short of relating parenting values and parenting practices to children's developmental outcomes (e.g., Harwood, 1992; Holden, 1995; Sigel, 1992).

Like research on the connections between child outcomes and both education and income, much of this work is correlational and likely suffers from biases owing to omitted variables and reverse causality. Researchers often overlook important confounding conditions that might be driving both a parent's selection of a job and parenting behavior. For example, because of their educational experiences, highly educated parents may be both more likely to obtain prestigious jobs and to value self-direction. An example of reverse causality is that the value of self-direction may be driving both job selection and parenting values. For example, a parent who is self-directed may seek out a high autonomy job and employ parenting practices that emphasize autonomy.

In an effort to reduce these biases, some researchers have included important baseline covariates in their estimation models (e.g., Parcel & Menaghan, 1994) and modeled reciprocal effects of job characteristics on parental values, cognitive skills, or personality traits (Kohn & Schooler, 1982). These efforts suggest that job characteristics have a substantively small yet statistically significant effect on workers' values, orientations, and cognitive skills, and that personalities and skills of workers have substantial effect on their job conditions. In addition, some research has suggested that class-based differences in values have declined over time, and that differences may be more the result of education than occupation (Alwin, 1984; Wright & Wright, 1976). These findings suggest that the rather small effects of job characteristics on parents may not be as consequential for parenting practices as previously thought and brings into question the causal nature of the associations among job characteristics, parenting practices, and child outcomes. Without more convincing evidence, we have little way of evaluating whether the modest differences in parental values or cognitive skills that may be causally associated with job characteristics have any meaningful influence on children's development.

A Broader View of SES

There is a long list of additional dimensions of SES that may influence parenting practices and children's development. For example, the quality of parents' schooling may be as important for parenting and family management as its quantity. To the extent that social class, racism, or cultural differences persist across generations, grandparental characteristics may matter as well, even after accounting for whatever advantages or disadvantages parents may have acquired from those grandparents (Phillips et al., 1998). Neighborhood conditions may affect children independently of family conditions (Brooks-Gunn, Duncan, & Aber, 1997; Jencks & Mayer, 1990).

Phillips et al. (1998) used nationally representative data on children born to younger mothers to assess the comparative importance of some of these additional dimensions. Their developmental outcome, measured at ages 5 or 6, is the child's score on the PPVT, a test of receptive vocabulary. They found that, when combined with the child's age, gender, and race, parental schooling levels accounted for 29% of the variation in test scores. The addition of measures of the quality of the mother's schooling increased this explained variance to 32%; and a set of grandparental measures boosted the explained variance to 36%. Thus, parental schooling levels capture most, but not all, of the explanatory power of a broader set of SES measures.

CONCLUSIONS

We have argued that developmental studies that seek to study directly, control for, or stratify by SES are ill served by the traditional Hollingshead-based approach. SES is too multifaceted to be captured by a single index or even a multi-factor index. Furthermore, latent-factor logic is not useful here. Household income, parental education, and occupational standing are distinct theoretical constructs, with distinct impacts on children's development and subject to manipulation through very different policy interventions.

How to do justice to the multi-faceted nature of SES in empirical studies? Entwisle and Astone (1994) and Hauser (1994) provided excellent summaries of how sociologists conceive of SES, with explicit recommendations for survey questions and coding. In the case of schooling, their recommendation is for two questions, the first on highest educational degree attained and the second, asked only of high school dropouts, on highest grade in school completed.

In the case of occupation, the recommendation is for a handful of questions regarding labor-force status and a description of the occupation and industry of the usual job. An elaborate classification of occupations and industries has been developed over the years by sociologists in academia and the U.S. Census Bureau (Entwisle & Astone, 1994).

We take issue with their modest recommendations regarding income questions and their characterization of such questions as always subject to high levels of nonresponse. Duncan and Peterson (2001) contended that this conventional wisdom regarding survey questions on economic characteristics is wrong. They pointed to many examples of successful surveys that gather high-quality income data without suffering unduly from high rates of either item or case nonresponse. Their analysis highlighted the need to motivate both respondents and interviewers, probe reluctant respondents with easier-to-answer follow-on questions, and ask questions that do not overburden respondents' memories. They presented a series of recommendations regarding both very short and longer sequences of survey questions on household income, hourly earnings, and wealth.

All told, these recommendations perhaps add between about two and five minutes of questions for survey-based studies that seek to gather adequate information about SES. Ten minutes of questions would gather much richer information about the components of income, household wealth, or both.

Is it worth gathering the needed information? We hope that our arguments convince readers that it is, particularly for studies that aspire to estimating the causal role played by SES in affecting the parenting and developmental outcomes of interest.

But what about developmental research that merely seeks to control for SES in its pursuit of other analytic goals, or that needs a simple division of a sample on SES in order to estimate its moderational role? Here too there is a compelling need for adequate measurement of the components of SES. Turning the problem on its head, suppose that an economic or sociological study of children sought to control for or stratify by maternal self-esteem. Would developmentalists be convinced if that study attempted to do so with a three or four item self-esteem scale or, worse yet, a more general summary index of maternal mental health that captured some but not all of the variance of a more complete scale? Attention to important constructs requires careful measurement, and the components of socioeconomic status are no exception.

ACKNOWLEDGEMENTS

We are grateful to the Family and Child Well-being Research Network of the National Institute of Child Health and Human Development (2 U01 HD30947-07) for supporting this research. Some of the material presented here parallels that found in the "Family Resources" chapter of the National Research Council/Institute on Medicine's (Shonkoff & Phillips, 2000) book *From Neurons to Neighborhoods*, to which both Duncan, as co-author, and Magnuson, as research assistant, contributed. We are grateful to Deborah Phillips, Jack Shonkoff, Steve Raudenbush and other committee members for their many helpful suggestions on this work. In addition, we are grateful for helpful comments from Lois Hoffman, Richard Lerner, Kris Moore, Marc Bornstein, and Robert Bradley.

REFERENCES

Alwin, D. F. (1984). Trends in parental socialization values: Detroit, 1958–1983. *American Journal of Sociology, 90*, 359–382.

Bane, M. J., & Elwood, D. (1986). Slipping in and out of poverty: The dynamics of spells. *Journal of Human Resources, 21*, 1–23.

Becker, G. S. (1975). *Human capital*. New York: National Bureau of Economic Research.

Becker, G. S. (1981). *A treatise on the family*. Cambridge, MA: Harvard University Press.

Behrman, J. R., & Rosenzweig, M. (in press). Does increasing women's schooling raise the schooling of the next generation. *American Economic Review*.

Belsky, J., Hertzog, C., & Raine, M. (1986). Causal analyses of multiple determinants of parenting: Empirical and methodological advances. In M. Lamb, A. L. Brown, & B. Rogoff (Eds.), *Advances in Developmental Psychology, Volume 4* (153–202). Hillsdale, NJ: Lawrence Erlbaum Associates.

Blau, D. M. (1999). The effect of income on child development. *The Review of Economics and Statistics, 8*, 261–276.

Bloom, D., Kemple, J. J., Morris, P., Scrivener, S., Verma, N., & Herndra, R. (2000). The Family Transition program: Final report on Florida's initial time-limited welfare program. New York: Manpower Demonstration Research Corporation.

Borduin, C. M., & Henggeler, S. W. (1981). Social class, experimental setting and task characteristics as determinants of mother-child interactions. *Developmental Psychology, 17*, 209–214.

Bos, H., Huston, A., Granger, R., Duncan, G., Brock, T., & McLoyd, V. (1999). *New hope for people with low incomes: Two-year results of a program to reduce poverty and reform welfare*. New York: Manpower Demonstration Research Corporation.

Bouchard, T., Lykken, D., McGue, M., Segal, N., & Tellegen, A. (1990). Sources of human psychological differences: The Minnesota study of twins reared apart. *Science, 250*, 223–228.

Brooks-Gunn, J., & Duncan, G. (1997). The effects of poverty on children and youth. *The Future of Children, 7*, 55–71.

Brooks-Gunn, J., Duncan, G. J., & Aber, J. L. (Eds.) (1997). *Neighborhood Poverty: Context and Consequences for Children*. Vol. II. New York: Russell Sage.

Citro, C., & Michael, R. (Eds.). (1995). *Measuring poverty: A new approach*. Washington, DC: National Academy Press.

Duncan, G. J., Coe, R., Corcoran, M., Hill, M., Hoffman, S., & Morgan, J. (1984). *Years of poverty, years of plenty*. Ann Arbor, MI: Institute for Social Research.

Duncan, G. J. (1988). The volatility of family income over the life course. In P. Baltes, D. Featherman, & R. M. Lerner, (Eds.), *Life-span development and behavior* (pp. 317–358). Hillsdale, NJ: Lawrence Erlbaum Associates.

Duncan, G., & Brooks-Gunn, J. (Eds.). (1997). *Consequences of growing up poor*. New York: Russell Sage.

Duncan, G., Brooks-Gunn, J., Yeung, J., & Smith, J. (1998). How much does childhood poverty affect the life chances of children? *American Sociological Review, 63*, 406–423.

Duncan, G., Magnuson, K., & Ludwig, J. (1999). *The endogeneity problem in developmental studies*. Evanston, IL: Northwestern University.

Duncan, G. J., & Petersen, E. (2001). The long and short of asking questions about income, wealth and labor supply. *Social Science Research, 30*, 248–263.

Duyme, M., Dumaret, A. C., & Tomkiewicz, S. (1999). How can we boost IQs of "dull children"?: A late adoption study. *Proceedings of the National Academy of Sciences, 96*, 8790–8794.

Edin, K., & Lein, L. (1997). *Making ends meet*. New York: Russell Sage.

Elo, I. T., & Preston, S. H. (1996). Educational differentials in mortality: United States, 1979–85. *Social Science and Medicine, 42*, 47–57.

Entwisle, D. R., & Astone, N. (1994). Some practical guidelines for measuring youth's race/ethnicity and socioeconomic status. *Child Development, 65*, 1521–1540.

Featherman, D. L., & Selbee, L. K. (1988). Class formation and class mobility. In M. W. Riley (Ed.), *Social structure and human lives* (pp. 247–264). Newbury Park, CA: Sage.

Featherman, D. L., & Spenner, K. I. (1988). Class and the socialization of children: Constancy, change or irrelevance. In E. Mavis Hetherington, R. M. Lerner, & M. Perlmutter (Eds.), *Child Development in Life-span Perspective* (pp. 67–90). Hillsdale, NJ: Lawrence Erlbaum Associates.

Gennetian, L., & Miller, C. (2000). *Reforming welfare and rewarding work: Final report on the Minnesota Family Investment Program.* New York: Manpower Demonstration and Research Corporation.

Hamilton, G. (2000). *Do mandatory welfare-to-work programs affect the wellbeing of children? A synthesis of child research conducted as part of the national evaluation of welfare-to-work strategies.* Washington, DC: U.S. Department of Health and Human Services,.

Harris, Y. R., Terrel, D., & Allen, G. (1999). The influence of education context and beliefs on the teaching behavior of African American mothers. *Journal of Black Psychology, 25,* 490–503.

Harwood, R. L. (1992). The influence of culturally derived values on Anglo and Puerto Rican mothers' perceptions of attachment behavior. *Child Development, 63,* 822–839.

Haug, M. R. (1977). Measurement in social stratification. *Annual Review of Sociology, 3,* 51–77.

Hauser, R. M. (1994). Measuring socioeconomic status in studies of child development. *Child Development, 65,* 1541–1545.

Hauser, R., & Warren, J. (1997). Socioeconomic indexes for occupations: A review, update, and critique. *Sociological Methodology, 27,* 177–298.

Haveman, R., & Wolfe, B. (1994). *Succeeding generations: On the effect of investments in children.* New York: Russell Sage.

Haveman, R., & Wolfe, B. (1995). The determinants of children's attainments: A review of methods and findings. *Journal of Economic Literature, 23,* 1829–1878.

Hoff-Ginsberg, E., & Tardif, T. (1995). Socioeconomic status and parenting. In M. Bornstein (Ed.) *Handbook of parenting, Vol. 4.* (pp. 161–187). Mahwah, NJ: Lawrence Erlbaum Associates.

Holden, G. W. (1995). Parental attitudes towards childrearing. In M. H. Bornstein (Ed.), *Handbook of parenting, Vol. 3: Status and social conditions of parenting* (pp. 359–392). Mahwah, NJ: Lawrence Erlbaum Associates.

Hollingshead, A. A. (1975). *Four-factor index of social status.* Unpublished manuscript, Yale University, New Haven, CT.

Institute for Research on Poverty (1976). *The rural income maintenance experiment.* Madison, WI: University of Wisconsin.

Jencks, C., & Mayer, S. (1990). The social consequences of growing up in a poor neighborhood. In L. Lynn & M. McGeary (Eds.), *Inner-city poverty in the United States* (pp. 111–186). Washington, DC: National Academy Press.

Jencks, C. S., Perman, L., & Rainwater, R. (1988). What is a good job? A new measure of labor market success. *American Journal of Sociology, 93,* 1322–57.

Kaestner, R., & Corman, H. (1995). *The impact of child health and family inputs on child cognitive development.* National Bureau of Economic Research Working Paper #5257.

Kershaw, D., & Fair, J. (1976). *The New Jersey income maintenance experiment. Vol. 1.* New York: Academic Press.

Kohn, M. L. (1959). Social class and the exercise of parental authority. *American Sociological Review, 24,* 352–366.

Kohn, M. L. (1969). *Class and conformity: A study in values.* Homewood, IL: Dorsey Press.

Kohn, M. L., & Schooler, C. (1982). Job conditions and personality: A longitudinal assessment of their reciprocal effects. *American Journal of Sociology, 87,* 1257–1285.

Kohn, M. L., & Schooler, C. (1973). Occupational experience and psychological functioning: An assessment of reciprocal effects. *American Psychological Review, 38,* 97–118.

Laosa, L. (1983). School, occupation, culture and family. In E. Sigel & L. Laosa (Eds.), *Changing Families* (pp. 79–135). New York: Plenum.

Luster, T., Rhoades, K., & Haas, B. (1989). The relation between parental values and parenting behavior: A test of the Kohn Hypothesis. *Journal of Marriage and the Family, 51,* 139–147.

Magnuson, K. A., & McGroder, S. (2001, March) From ABE to 123s: The effect of maternal education on children's school readiness. Poster presented at the Population Association of America, Washington, DC.

Mayer, S. (1997). *What money can't buy: The effect of parental income on children's outcomes.* Cambridge, MA: Harvard University Press.

McGroder, S. M., Zaslow, M. J., Moore, K. A., & LeMenestrel, S. M. (2000). *National evaluation of welfare-to-work strategies impacts on young children and their families two years after enrollment: Findings from the child outcomes study.* Washington, DC: U.S. Department of Health and Human Services.

Menaghan, E. G., & Parcel, T. L. (1991). Social sources of change in children's home environments: The effects of parental occupational experiences and family conditions. *Journal of Marriage and the Family, 57,* 69–94.

Mercy, J. A., & Steelman, L. C. (1982). Family influence on intellectual attainment of children. *American Sociological Review, 42,* 532–542.

Michael, R. T. (1972). *The effect of education on efficiency in consumption.* New York: Columbia University Press.

Michael, R. T. (1982). Measuring non-monetary benefits of education: A survey. In W. W. McMahon & T. G. Geske (Eds.), *Financing education: Overcoming inefficiency and inequality* (pp. 119–149). Chicago: University of Illinois Press.

Miller, C., Knox, V., Auspos, P., & Hunter-Manns, J. (1997). *Making welfare work and work pay: Implementation and 18 month impacts of the Minnesota family investment program.* New York: Manpower Demonstration Research Corporation.

Mincer, J. (1974) *Schooling, experience and earnings.* New York: National Bureau of Economic Research.

Morris, P. A., Huston, A. C., Duncan, G. J., Crosby, D. A., & Bos, J. M. (2001). *How welfare and work policies affect children: A synthesis of research.* New York: Manpower Demonstration Research Corporation.

Morris, P., & Michaelopolis, C. (2000). *The self sufficiency project at 36 months: Effects on children of a program that increased parental employment and income (executive summary).* New York: Social Research and Demonstration Corporation.

Mueller, C. W., & Parcel, T. L. (1981). Measures of socioeconomic status: Alternatives and recommendations. *Child Development, 52,* 13–30.

Neiss, M., & Rowe, D. C. (2000). Parental education and child's verbal IQ in adoptive and biological families in the national longitudinal study of adolescent health. *Behavior Genetics, 30,* 487–495.

Parcel, T. L., & Menaghan, E. G. (1994). *Parents' jobs and children's lives.* New York: deGruyter.

Phillips, M., Brooks-Gunn, J., Duncan, G., Klebanov, P., & Crane, J. (1998). Family background, parenting practices, and the black-white test score gap. In C. Jencks & M. Phillips (Eds.), *The black-white test score gap* (pp. 103–144). Washington, DC: Brookings.

Resnick, S., Corley, R., & Robinson, J. (1997). A longitudinal twin study of intelligence in the second year. *Monographs of the Society for Research in Child Development, 62.* Chicago: University of Chicago Press.

Richman, A. L., Miller, P. M., & LeVine, R. A. (1992). Cultural and educational responsiveness in maternal responsiveness. *Developmental Psychology, 4,* 614–621.

Rosenzweig, M. R., & Wolpin, K. I. (1994). Are there increasing returns to intergenerational production of human capital? Maternal schooling and child intellectual development. *Journal of Human Resources, 29,* 670–693.

Rowe, D. C. (1994). *The limits of family influence: Genes, experience and behavior.* New York: Guilford.

Salkind, N. J., & Haskins, R. (1982). Negative income tax: The impact on children from low-income families. *Journal of Family Issues, 3,* 165–180.

Scarr, S. (1992). Developmental theories for the 1990s: Development and individual differences. *Child Development, 63,* 1–19.

Shonkoff, J. P., & Phillips, D. A. (Eds.). (2000). *From neurons to neighborhoods: The science of early childhood development.* Washington, DC: National Academy Press.

Sigel (1992). The belief-behavior connection: A resolvable dilemma? In I. E. Sigel, A. V. McGillicuddy-DeLisi, & J. J. Goodnow (Eds.), *Parental belief systems: The psychological consequences for children* (pp. 433–456). Hillsdale, NJ: Lawrence Erlbaum Associates.

Teachman, J., Duncan, G., Yeung, W. J., & Levy, D. (2001). Covariance structure models for fixed and random effects. *Sociological Methods and Research*, 2, 271–288.

U.S. Bureau of the Census (2001a). Table 7: Years of school completed by people 25 years and over, by age, race, household relationship, and poverty status: 2000 [on-line]. Available: [http://www.ferret.bls.census.gov/macro/032001/pov/new07_005.htm]

U.S. Bureau of the Census (2001b). Poverty thresholds in 2000, by size of family and number of children under 18 years [on-line]. Available: [http://www.census.gov/hhes/poverty/threshld/thres00.html]

U.S. Bureau of the Census (2001c). Poverty status of people, by age, race, and hispanic origin: 1959–2000 [on-line]. Available: [http://www.census.gov/hhes/poverty/histpov/hstpov3.html]

U.S. Department of Health and Human Services. (1983). *Overview of the Seattle-Denver income maintenance experiment and final report*. Washington, DC: Author.

U.S. Department of Health and Human Services. (1997). *Indicators of welfare dependence annual report to Congress*. Washington, DC: Author.

Vaughn, D. (1993). Exploring the use of the public's views to set income poverty thresholds and adjust them over time. *Social Security Bulletin*, 56, 22–46.

Wright, J. D., & Wright, S. R. (1976). Social class and parental values for children: A partial replication and extension of the Kohn thesis. *American Sociological Review*, 41, 527–537.

Yeates, K. O., MacPhee, D., Campbell, F. A., & Ramey, C. T. (1983). Maternal IQ and home environment as determinants of early childhood intellectual competence: A developmental analysis. *Developmental Psychology*, 19, 731–739.

4

Socioeconomic Resources, Parenting, and Child Development Among Immigrant Families

Andrew J. Fuligni
University of California, Los Angeles

Hirokazu Yoshikawa
New York University

INTRODUCTION

Children from immigrant families represent one of the fastest growing groups of children in the United States today. After almost four decades of rising immigration since the 1965 changes in immigration laws, approximately one-fifth of American children have at least one foreign-born parent (Hernandez & Charney, 1998). This proportion is expected to grow in the years ahead, as the 1990s saw a record number of immigrants enter the United States. Children from immigrant families also constitute the vast majority of children with Latin American and Asian backgrounds, two of the fastest growing ethnic minority groups in the United States (Rumbaut, in press). Given the notable presence of children from immigrant families in the general population, as well as the significant challenges they face as newcomers to the United States, it is imperative for social scientists to understand how this unique group adjusts and becomes integrated into American society.

Critical to any analysis of children's adjustment is a clear understanding of the roles played by families' socioeconomic resources. Yet such an understanding, difficult to achieve even under the most ideal circumstances, is especially challenging for studies of immigrant families because their socioeconomic characteristics need

107

to be considered in light of the fact that these families have made a transition to
a new society. Many of the socioeconomic features of immigrant families, such
as the educational level and occupational skills of the parents, were developed in
countries other than the United States. Immigrant families often demonstrate socialization and behavior patterns that are more closely tied to their native cultural
backgrounds than to the norms of contemporary American society (Bornstein &
Cote, 2001; Fuligni, 1998). As a result, traditional socioeconomic indicators may
not have the same meaning for immigrant families as they do for American-born
families, at least in terms of the environmental features and socialization processes
these indicators are thought to capture. Our intent in this chapter is to discuss how
to conceptualize and measure the socioeconomic resources of immigrant families, in terms of how they may shape parenting and children's development, by
presenting some of the issues one should consider when studying this population.

The chapter is divided into three major sections. In the first section, we describe how both the history and the current features of American-immigration
policy have shaped the socioeconomic distribution of the current foreign-born
population. Second, we present some of the issues involved when assessing socioeconomic resources and their role in parenting and development by discussing
the measurement of human, financial, and social capital among immigrant families.
In the final section, we close the chapter with some general conclusions and recommendations for future study of this increasingly prominent group of American
families.

IMMIGRATION POLICY
AND SOCIOECONOMIC VARIABILITY

In order to study the socioeconomic resources of immigrant families, one must
begin with an understanding of how the history of American immigration policy
has had a significant effect on the nature and distribution of socioeconomic characteristics of the current foreign-born population. First, the preference system by
which immigrants are permitted entry into the United States, in conjunction with
a particular group's immigration history, has contributed to the dramatic socioeconomic variation according to national origin in the current foreign-born population.
In 1965, the United States dramatically altered its immigration policy so that specific groups were no longer excluded according to their national origin (Portes &
Rumbaut, 1996). Similar quotas were established for each country, and a preference system was established in order to determine which petitioners from each
nation would be allowed to enter the United States. The preference system has
several specific levels of priority, but it employs two basic criteria: family reunification and occupational qualifications. First priority is given to those potential
immigrants who already have family members in the United States, after which
preference is given to individuals who possess occupational skills deemed valuable

or lacking within the American workforce. In general, individuals admitted under family reunification provisions tend to be from lower socioeconomic strata in their countries of origin than those who enter by means of occupational preference.

The preference system interacts with a group's immigration history to produce large socioeconomic variations among the foreign born according to national origin (Portes & Rumbaut, 1996). Immigrants from Mexico, because they had been permitted to enter the United States prior to 1965, were more likely than those from Asia and Africa to enter under family reunification provisions in the late 20th century. In contrast, immigration from Asia and Africa was highly restricted prior to 1965. As a result of there being relatively few Asian and African immigrants already living in the United States, immigrants from these two regions have tended to enter the country under occupational provisions with higher levels of educational attainment. Consequently, these three groups rank near the bottom (Mexicans) and the top (Africans and Asians) of the socioeconomic distribution of the immigrant population.

A second feature of immigration policy that has an impact on the socioeconomic distribution of the immigrant population is the use of refugee and asylum provisions to allow certain groups admittance to the United States. These provisions are often employed in accordance with the political goals of the American government, and, as a result, many groups designated as refugees have been those escaping Communist or left-leaning governments, such as those in Cuba, Southeast Asia, and the then-Soviet Union. The effects of these provisions on the socioeconomic characteristics of the immigrant population are more complex. It appears that initially, given the greater ease for the wealthy to escape their countries, refugees are drawn from the upper classes from a sending society. Over time, refugees from lower social strata tend to enter the United States (Portes & Rumbaut, 1996). This decline occurs more quickly for refugees from poorer countries with low levels of education overall, which is why those from Laos and Cambodia have among the lowest socioeconomic profiles in the United States. In 1990, only 5 to 6% of the Laotian and Cambodian foreign born had graduated from college and only one-half were in the labor force (Rumbaut, 1995).

A third influence of immigration policy on the socioeconomic distribution of immigrant families is differential eligibility for federal benefits, depending on immigration status. The immigration provisions of the Personal Responsibility and Work Opportunity Reconciliation Act of 1996 most recently changed these eligibility guidelines. A three-tier system of eligibility is now in place, with refugees and asylees eligible for the full range of federal means-tested benefits, legal immigrants subject to a five-year ban after immigration on all means-tested benefits (including Medicaid, food stamps, WIC, temporary assistance for needy families, and the Children's Health Insurance program), and undocumented immigrants ineligible for nearly all federal benefits. States vary in the extent to which they provide their own benefits to make up for those that the federal government does not provide (Zimmerman & Tumlin, 1999).

TABLE 4.1
Socioeconomic Background of the Foreign Born by Region of Birth

Region	% High School Graduate	% Managerial–Professional Specialty Occupation	Median Household Income
Europe	79.0	37.8	$31,300
Asia	83.9	35.8	$42,900
Africa	88.1	26.1	$31,300
Latin America	47.0	11.4	$24,100
Caribbean	62.4	19.0	$23,900
Central America	35.4	7.0	$23,000
Mexico	31.3	5.8	$22,400
Other	50.7	11.0	$25,400
South America	77.6	23.3	$31,800

Source: Schmidley, A. D., & Gibson, C. (1999). *Profile of the foreign-born population in the United States: 1997*. U.S. Census Bureau Current Population Reports, Series P23–195. Washington, DC: U.S. Government Printing Office.

Although not the only contributing factors, these three features of American-immigration policy help to produce large socioeconomic variations among the immigrant population according to national origin. As shown in Table 4.1, immigrants from Asian countries tend to possess higher levels of education, work in higher status jobs, and have significantly more income than those from Latin America. Those from Africa are approximately equal to their Asian counterparts in terms of education, but they tend to work in lower status occupations and earn lower incomes. The low socioeconomic status (SES) of Latin Americans is largely due to those from Mexico, only a third of whom have graduated from high school.

As suggested by Table 4.1, immigrants as a group actually possess greater economic diversity than the native-born American population. This variation gives rise to the seemingly contradictory findings that the foreign-born, as a whole, are both less likely to have graduated from high school (65% vs. 84%) and equally likely to have received college (24% vs. 24%) and graduate degrees (9% vs. 8%) as the American-born population (Schmidley & Gibson, 1999).

Additional factors also play a role in the socioeconomic features of the immigrant population. Demand for both low-wage and highly skilled workers by American industries, the proximity of certain nations to the United States, and differential rates of illegal immigration according to country of origin all contribute to the socioeconomic characteristics of the foreign born (Portes & Rumbaut, 1996). For example, illegal immigrants tend to have fairly low levels of education (Fix & Passel, 1994). As a result, the amnesty of previously illegal immigrants that took place in the late 1980s and 1990s substantially lowered the average rates of educational and occupational attainment of the foreign-born from Mexico (Rumbaut, 1997).

In summary, immigration is a highly selective process that is subject to many factors beyond the control of the immigrants themselves. The important point for understanding the socioeconomic resources of immigrant families is that the socioeconomic variability among the foreign-born population is due, in large part, to the history and structural features of American-immigration policy.

ASSESSING THE SOCIOECONOMIC RESOURCES OF IMMIGRANT FAMILIES: HUMAN, FINANCIAL, AND SOCIAL CAPITAL

In this section, we discuss issues involved in the measurement of the socioeconomic resources of immigrant families. In order to think about socioeconomic resources in terms of how they may influence parenting and child development, we follow the suggestion of Entwisle and Astone (1994) and break down the socioeconomic background of immigrant families into the three types of capital outlined by Coleman (1988). Human capital refers to the potential nonmaterial resources than can be provided by the parents, such as cognitive stimulation and values regarding achievement, and is usually indexed by parental educational level. Financial capital refers to the financial and physical resources available to the parents and children, and is typically measured by wealth, earnings, and income. Social capital is more complex, as it encompasses the resources that stem from the social relationships and connections both within the family and between the family and the larger community. As we discuss in the following, traditional indicators of human and financial capital can be problematic for immigrant families because these indicators may simultaneously underestimate and overestimate the resources available to parents and children. In addition, social capital may be an especially important socioeconomic resource of immigrant families, providing children in these families with advantages over their peers from American-born families.

Human Capital

Parental educational level is the most common index of human capital because it is thought to capture the extent to which parents can provide the skills and abilities that children need to achieve in school settings and later in their own employment. Yet for immigrant families, the absolute educational level of parents can be both an underestimate and an overestimate of the cognitive stimulation and achievement socialization that takes place within immigrant families.

One reason that parental education may be an underestimate of human capital among immigrant families stems from the differential availability of education around the world. The United States is a world leader in the access to secondary and post-secondary schooling, making it easier for American-born parents to attain high school and college degrees. As a result, some immigrant parents who have lower absolute levels of education are ranked higher then American-born parents

TABLE 4.2

Highest Level of Education Attained Within the Native Countries of the Top Five
Immigrant Groups

Country (Year)	No Schooling	Primary	Secondary	Postsecondary
Mexico (1990)	18.8	19.9	23.4	9.2
Philippines (1995)	3.8	15.1	38.5	22.0
China (1990)	29.3	34.3	34.4	2.0
Vietnam (1989)	23.4	66.2	8.4	1.7
India (1991)	57.5	28.0	7.2	7.3

Notes. Numbers refer to percentages of the total population. Primary refers to the percentage who completed primary school, whereas Secondary and Postsecondary refer to the percentages who attended school at those levels. The year refers to the year in which the data were compiled by the respective countries. Source: *1999 UNESCO statistical yearbook*, Paris, France: UNESCO.

when their educational level is normed within their native societies. For example, only 31% of Mexican immigrants have received a high school education or higher as compared to 84% of American-born individuals (Schmidley & Gibson, 1999). Yet, given that Mexico has only six years of compulsory schooling as compared to 10 years in the United States, a Mexican who has received a high school education or higher is at approximately the 70th percentile in terms of educational level in Mexico, whereas an American with a similar amount of education is at only the 16th percentile in the United States. (UNESCO, 1999). In terms of post-secondary education, a Mexican with at least some college is at approximately the 90th percentile, as compared to an American who would be at the 51st percentile. Virtually all immigrant groups come from societies with lower overall levels of educational attainment than the United States. As shown in Table 4.2, only a minority of the population in all but one of the top five sending countries has received education beyond the primary school level.

What do these dramatic differences in the absolute and relative levels of education of the foreign-born mean in terms of the human capital provided for children within immigrant families? To the extent that each year of education provides parents with additional cognitive and literacy skills, it should not matter where an individual falls within the national distribution. Parents with a high school education or greater should have greater capacity than those with less schooling to provide a cognitively rich environment that will promote children's success in school, thereby making the absolute level of education an accurate estimate of the human capital within immigrant families. Yet this assumes that the same level of education provides parents with the same amount of cognitive and literacy skills in different countries, and the same returns in occupational status, wages, and income. Numerous studies have shown this not to be the case. Cognitive skills of individuals schooled in the United States have often been shown to be lower than those of individuals with the same level of education in several immigrant-sending countries, such as China and Taiwan (Stevenson & Stigler, 1992). It would be wise

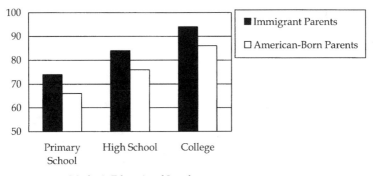

FIGURE 4.1. Perceived parental educational aspirations, according to mother's educational level and immigrant status of parents. *Note.* Aspirations represented by the percent of adolescents in each group who report that their parents want them to receive a 4-year college degree or more. Estimates based upon a regression analysis predicting adolescents' perceptions of their parents' aspirations, controlling for gender. The sample includes approximately 900 adolescents from Asian, Latin American, and European backgrounds. These results do not control for adolescents' ethnic background, but the findings remain similar even with ethnicity is controlled.

for investigators to be aware of such possibilities when equating immigrant and American-born parents in terms of their level of education. If one assumes that the distribution of cognitive skills is similar in different countries and that those with more schooling tend to have more cognitive skills, then the relative position in the formal schooling distribution within each country may reflect the relative position in the distribution of cognitive skills within each country.

In addition to the capacity to provide a cognitively rich environment, parental education is assumed to tap values of education that include high aspirations and expectations for educational attainment (Entwisle & Astone, 1994). In this regard, the absolute educational level of foreign-born parents may be an underestimate of the human capital within an immigrant family. Because high school graduates in Mexico have by definition nearly doubled the number of years of compulsory schooling in their country, such a level of educational attainment may reflect a belief in the value of education that surpasses that of an American high school graduate. Indeed, immigrant parents have stronger values of education and higher educational aspirations than one would predict on the basis of their educational level (Fuligni, 1997; Kao & Tienda, 1995). In one of our own studies, as shown in Figure 4.1, Fuligni (1997) found that adolescents from immigrant families of Asian and Latin American origin reported that their parents wanted them to attain the same level of education as did adolescents from American born-families with higher levels of parental education. For example, the perceived aspirations of immigrant parents with a high school degree were equivalent to those of American parents with a college degree. This difference in the value of education accounted for the tendency for students from immigrant families to receive better grades in school than their counterparts from American-born families, even after controlling for parental education. Fuligni (1997) did not examine whether such an advantage in beliefs could be accounted for by differences in the relative educational level of parents in their native countries, but it would be worthwhile to do so in future research. In addition, delineating changes, pre- vs. post-immigration, in aspirations, expectations, and their relationship to children's educational outcomes, would further elucidate the dynamic shifts in immigrant families' human capital across the immigration divide.

Whereas levels of parent education may underestimate human capital in terms of parents' cognitive skills and value of education, they may overestimate human capital in terms of the direct involvement of parents in their children's schooling and instruction. On average, immigrant parents have less familiarity and comfort with the English language, thereby making it more difficult for them to provide their children with extensive exposure to English on their own (Zhou, 1997). The relatively limited use of English by many immigrant parents may be the reason why many children from immigrant families, despite doing fairly well in school and on standardized tests in mathematics, tend to receive poorer scores on standardized tests in reading than their peers from American-born families (Kao & Tienda, 1995). Along with their English difficulties, many immigrant parents have little knowledge of American schools and instruction (Caplan, Choy, & Whitmore, 1991). As a result, immigrant parents are less likely to talk to their children about topics like programs at school, their children's school activities, and what their children studied in class (Kao & Tienda, 1995). Immigrant parents are also less likely to belong to a parent–teacher group, although they are more likely to attend regular parent–teacher meetings.

In summary, parental educational level may both underestimate and overestimate the human capital that immigrant parents provide for their children's education. Because of the relative lack of access to education beyond primary school in many immigrant-sending nations, immigrant parents with lower levels of education may have similar or even greater educational aspirations as compared to American-born parents with more years of schooling. In contrast, the lack of familiarity with the English language and American schools may result in immigrant parents demonstrating less direct participation in their children's schooling and instruction than an American-born parent with the same level of education. Therefore, in order to obtain the most accurate assessment of the human capital available to the children of immigrant families, investigators should consider both the absolute and relative level of educational attainment of immigrant parents. Analytically, this would mean using both the total number of years of schooling parents have received, as well as the point within the national distribution of educational attainment at which the parents fall to predict parenting behavior and child outcomes. In addition, investigators should directly measure the proposed mediators of parental education, such as the parents' educational aspirations for their children and their involvement in their children's schooling.

Finally, it would be worthwhile to consider the extent to which the educational level of immigrant parents, as well as the proposed mediators of parental education, may change as a result of both the process of immigration and amount of time spent in the United States. Some foreign-born parents came to the United States to pursue post-secondary and graduate education, staying in the country afterwards in order to obtain better economic returns from their training (Portes & Rumbaut, 1996). Immigrant parents may acquire better English skills and more knowledge about American schools after living in the country for several years. Some immigrants come with highly optimistic views of American education and economic opportunities, only to find themselves settling in areas with poor schools and limited occupational options (Portes & Zhou, 1993; Waters, 1994). The extent which these factors may alter the human capital within immigrant families remains to be seen, but it is important to keep in mind that these resources may change over time.

Financial Capital

Compared to parental education, the wealth and income of immigrant families appear at first glance to be relatively unambiguous indicators of the amount of financial capital parents have to provide to their children here in the United States. The same amount of income should give parents the same ability to provide material resources for their children, regardless of whether they are American or foreign born. Nevertheless, there are some unique issues regarding the financial capital of immigrant families of which one should be aware.

First, for all families, it is important to obtain direct measures of family wealth and income rather than infer financial status from other indicators such as education and occupation. This is especially true for immigrant families, as immigrants tend to earn less than American-born workers with the same level of education (Portes & Rumbaut, 1996). Some of this discrepancy is due to the unwillingness on the part of American employers to give equal credit to foreign credentials and certifications, and another part can be attributed to the time it takes immigrants to establish themselves professionally in a new society. The measurement of family income may be particularly difficult to accomplish with immigrant populations, who may come from cultures in which it is frowned on to discuss household finances with strangers, and who may not trust researchers' statements that they are not collecting data for government. It is also important to be aware of whether immigrants received their education in the United States or in their native countries. Some immigrants come to the United States in order to obtain schooling, and those who received their degrees in the United States tend have higher incomes than those with similar degrees obtained elsewhere (Schoeni, McCarthy, & Vernez, 1996).

Second, evidence regarding the patterns of income packaging and expenditures within immigrant households suggests that expected relations among parent income, parenting, and children's development may not hold among this population. Studies using national data sets have found that the relations of family income and income poverty to children's cognitive and socioemotional development are mediated through indicators of the quality of the home environment, such as cognitive stimulation or the physical environment in the home (Duncan, Brooks-Gunn, & Klebanov, 1994). However, parents' income, measured on an individual basis, appears not to reflect the income packaging that immigrants, especially those from low-income backgrounds, employ to make ends meet. Such packaging includes the assembling of income from multiple extended family members, as well as combining formal and informal sources of income. In a recent study of the Little Village neighborhood in Chicago, Tienda and Raijman (2000) found complex patterns of such income packaging in their sample of Mexican-American immigrant families. Measuring income at the household level produced data regarding poverty status and other indicators of economic well-being that were markedly different than methods that measured only the income of individual parents or caregivers. In addition, for those households that reported informal sources of income, such income often made the difference between living below or above the poverty line. Both of these factors may bias traditional measures of income and employment downward as reflections of the true SES of immigrant families.

Data concerning household income packaging such as those of Tienda and Raijman (2000) also suggested dimensions of parenting that may be important to investigate and that diverge from conventional measures. If parents rely on their children to supplement their own income, how are such requests and demands made? How are such interactions perceived by children, and how do the interactions shape their development? Does the quality or quantity of income-generating activities engaged in by children and adolescents affect their school achievement or socioemotional development?

On the expenditure side, evidence suggests that for many immigrant families, large proportions of household income are sent back as remittances to relatives in the country of origin (Schiller, 1999). These data suggest that obtained measures of family income may actually bias SES upward. Income available for spending on the educational opportunities of children living in the household may be lower than one might expect given total family income. On the other hand, some or all of the children of immigrant parents may be in the country of origin, staying with relatives, which is a relatively common pattern among immigrants from Latin America. In either case, expected associations among income, parenting, and child development, based on national data, may not apply so strongly to immigrant families.

Third, although the buying power of immigrants' financial capital may be fairly straightforward, the meaning of their current wealth and income for their children could be better understood when compared to their financial resources prior to entering the United States. For many immigrant families, coming to the United

States can result in a substantial absolute increase in standard of living. At the same time, their relative economic standing in society may drop. It would be important to examine whether the families' economic changes have an impact on parenting and child development within immigrant families, independent of their current financial resources.

Fourth, it is important to take into account the complexities in both the eligibility for and the actual use of governmental social services by immigrant families. For example, immigrant groups differ from one another in terms of their access to social welfare benefits. Those who enter under refugee and asylum provisions are entitled to a package of benefits that are unavailable to other immigrant groups. For example, the Refugee Resettlement Program offers income support, job training, and health and social services to those designated as refugees (Fix & Zimmerman, 1997). As mentioned previously, legal immigrants who entered after the enactment of the legislation in 1996 are ineligible for federal means-tested benefits for at least five years (Fix & Passel, 1999). It appears that post-1996, legal immigrants' applications for benefits for which they are eligible have declined precipitously (Zimmerman & Fix, 1998). The implications of these changes for the financial capital of immigrant families, and thereby the material resources that they can provide for their children's development, are unclear and are still being examined.

Finally, debate exists over the merits of using parental occupational status as an index of financial capital within families. On the one hand, it has been argued occupational status may be a poor indicator of income for certain groups such as women, who tend to be in occupations with relatively high prestige but that offer lower pay (Entwisle & Astone, 1994). One the other hand, parental occupational status may be a better indicator of long-term income than an income measurement at a single point in time, which may be prone to short-term fluctuations (Hauser, 1994). For immigrant families, however, the extent to which the parents' current occupational status taps long-term income can be called into question because of the tendency for some immigrants to work in lower-level occupations than they did in their native countries (Portes & Rumbaut, 1996). In addition, immigration sometimes occurs on the basis job-related networks, which results in foreign-born workers of particular ethnicities being funneled into particular occupations and job sectors. Immigrant parents also may be forced to work in lower-level occupations upon arrival before they are able to obtain jobs that are more in accordance with their skills and qualifications. When using occupational status as an index of financial capital, therefore, investigators should be aware of the potential variability in the jobs of immigrant parents as they become settled in American society.

Social Capital

Although social capital is not a commonly measured indicator of SES in studies of parenting, some observers have argued that it is central to the transmission of human and financial capital from parents to children. According to Coleman

(1988), social capital differs from human and financial capital in that it "inheres in the structure of the relations between actors and among actors" (p. 98). As Portes (1998) recently defined it, social capital is "the ability of actors to secure benefits by virtue of membership in social networks or other social structures" (p. 6). In Coleman's view, effective family relationships are critical for the transmission of human capital from parents to children. Social capital may also be provided for children outside of the family through parents' relationships with other parents and members of the community.

At first blush, immigrant families may be perceived as lacking in social capital on arrival in the United States. Many immigrant parents have left behind extended family and friends (Rogler, 1994), and it is easy to imagine that it would be difficult for immigrant parents to become established in social networks that will support the difficult task of rearing children in a new and different society. Yet social capital appears to be a socioeconomic resource in which immigrant families are at an advantage, at least in terms of the socialization of their children. Just as it helps some children from disadvantaged American-born families to achieve unexpected success (Furstenberg, Cook, Eccles, Elder, & Sameroff, 1999; Furstenberg & Hughes, 1995), social capital may be an important reason why the children from immigrant families often demonstrate better behavioral and educational adjustment than would be predicted by other features of their socioeconomic background (Fuligni, 1998; Zhou & Bankston, 1994).

Numerous studies have suggested that immigrant families and communities, regardless of their country of origin, exhibit high levels of the three elements of social networks deemed especially important by Coleman (1988): obligations, expectations, and trustworthiness. Within their own families, many immigrant parents emphasize a strong sense of obligation between children and adults. The majority of immigrant families hail from cultures (e.g., Latin American, Asian, African) that traditionally place great importance upon the duty of family members to support and assist one another (Fuligni, 1998). Such traditions are evident in the lower rate of divorce among immigrant parents (Hernandez & Charney, 1998) as well as the cultural belief in a type of social exchange between parents and children. Children, in exchange for the care and attention they received from their parents, are often expected to consider their parents' wishes when the children begin to make educational and occupational decisions (Gibson & Bhachu, 1991; Zhou & Bankston, 1998).

Existent within the cultural backgrounds of many immigrant families, the tradition of family obligation becomes especially salient as a result of families' entrance into a new country. The limited knowledge of many immigrant parents about American society, coupled with their difficulty with obtaining well-paying occupations, can create the very real need for children to support and assist their families. Children, usually having more experience with American institutions because of their schooling, often assist their families with the official and unofficial demands of the new society (Zhou, 1997). Yet even more than increasing the need for day-to-day assistance from children, immigration creates in children a sense that their primary duty to the family is to succeed in the new country (Fuligni & Tseng, 1999). Many immigrants leave their native countries for the explicit reason of providing better opportunities for their children. Children are aware of the family's motive for immigrating, as well as the great personal and professional sacrifices their parents have sometimes made in order to come to the United States. As a result, the children from immigrant families often believe that their primary obligations to the family include doing well in school, staying out of trouble, and eventually securing gainful employment (Caplan et al., 1991; Suárez-Orozco & Suárez-Orozco, 1995).

The strong sense of obligation of children from immigrant families, and its connection to academic motivation and avoiding problem behavior, has been a dominant theme in several recent studies of this population. The Suárez-Orozcos, in their ethnographies of Central American and Mexican immigrants, report how both parents and students consistently voice the duty of children to try hard and do well in school (Suárez-Orozco, 1991; Suárez-Orozco & Suárez-Orozco, 1995). Caplan et al. (1991) found that Vietnamese children, when asked to rank the importance of large set of values, listed respect for family members, education and achievement, freedom, family loyalty, and hard work as the top five. Similarly, Zhou and Bankston (1994, 1998) observed that Vietnamese children in New Orleans believed obedience and working hard to be the most important values in their families. These youths, despite coming from families with low levels of parental education and income, tended to do better in school than their counterparts from American-born families.

Fuligni and his colleagues also have observed a stronger sense of family obligation among adolescents from immigrant families as compared to their peers from American-born families (Fuligni, Tseng, & Lam, 1999). As shown in Figure 4.2, first and second generation youths (i.e., those with immigrant parents) place more importance on their role in supporting the family in the future. These youths are more likely to believe that, when they become adults, they should support their parents financially, live or go to college near their parents, and take care of their siblings. What is remarkable about Figure 4.2 is the consistency in the tendency for first and second generations to have a stronger sense of family obligation across the different ethnic groups. That is, despite the fact that Asian and Latin-American adolescents are more likely to endorse their family obligations overall, even adolescents from European immigrant families report a greater sense of familial duty than their peers from American-born families with European backgrounds.

In addition to having greater social capital within the family, immigrant families seem to be able to access greater capital outside of the family within their immigrant communities. Immigrant families often settle in communities with other people from their native societies who share similar values and traditions, in part because of preexisting social ties in their countries of origin (Portes & Rumbaut, 1996). Coleman (1988) highlighted the importance of relationships between the parents

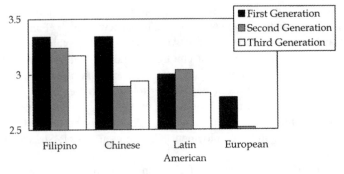

Ethnic Background

FIGURE 4.2. Adolescents' value of future obligations to the family, according to ethnic background and generational status. *Note.* The measure of adolescents' value of future obligations to the family asked youths to rate one a 1 (not at all important) to 5 (very important) scale of how important it is to them that they do things such as help their parents financially in the future, live at home with their parents until they are married, live or go to college near their parents, and have their parents live with them when they get older.

of children from different families, which he called intergenerational closure. Such networks, by setting norms and establishing trust within a community, assist the socialization efforts of parents. Intergenerational closure, often cited as being on the decline among American families, remains quite high within many immigrant communities. These communities often hold rigid standards for members' behavior; gossip spreads quickly (Gibson & Bhachu, 1991; Zhou & Bankston, 1998). As a result, children's transgressions will be noticed by nonfamily members and reported to the parents. In addition, the shared community values of academic success and good behavior mean that doing well in school will bring honor to the family (Gibson, 1995). The shame that poor school performance and problem behavior could bring to the family can act as an effective sanction to keep children on a straight path.

In summary, what many immigrant parents may lack in traditional measures of human and financial capital, they make up with a strong supply of social capital within their families and communities. Children from immigrant families often do better in school and are less likely to get involved in problem behavior when compared to those from American-born families with similar or even higher levels of parental education and income (Fuligni, 1998). As discussed earlier, part of the apparent advantage for children from immigrant families may be due to an underestimate of the human and financial capital of immigrant parents. But another portion of the success of these children seems be due to their orientation toward their cultural traditions and the availability of a community of adults and peers that supports the families' goal of getting their children to succeed in American society (Fuligni, 1997; Harris, 1999).

It is important to note, however, that not all immigrant families settle in neighborhoods that provide for intergenerational closure or other important aspects of community-level social capital, such as social control or collective efficacy (Sampson, 2001). Some foreign-born parents, because of a lack of financial resources, are forced to raise their families in impoverished and high crime areas that afford them little social support and trust between community members. Areas such as these may also compromise the occupational mobility of the parents themselves. These families may be forced to rely on the social capital within their families, which itself may be difficult to cultivate because of the pressures on the children from these families by their peers in these communities (Portes & Zhou, 1993; Waters, 1994).

Finally, as with human and financial capital, it is important to understand how the social capital of immigrant families may change over time. Although he extolled the virtues of social capital, Coleman (1988) also pointed out its fragility and tendency to weaken as individuals perceive less of a return on their investment in such capital. Therefore, greater economic security over time for immigrant families may make it less important for parents to monitor other children in the community and less important for children to provide for the well-being of their parents. Greater involvement and interaction with nonimmigrant communities may also weaken the perceived sense of responsibility to the immigrant community and its members. Extremely high levels of economic distress and sustained blockage of opportunities for mobility can also weaken social capital if immigrant parents and children begin to believe that their efforts toward economic advancement are futile (Portes & Zhou, 1993; Waters, 1994). It is possible that such changes in social capital over time could explain why some of the apparent benefits of being in an immigrant family decline over subsequent generations.

CONCLUSIONS

The many issues of SES that are unique to the immigrant families suggest that prescriptions for research differ from those that may apply to other populations. First, measurement of indicators of SES should acknowledge particular patterns that are more common among immigrant than native-born families. Such patterns include the packaging of income sources from multiple members of family networks (including children) and remittances to relatives in countries of origin.

Second, applying dynamic models to research on the SES of immigrant families is crucial. Without consideration of the trajectory of the immigration experience, from migration within countries of origin to migration within the United States, one cannot accurately account for how particular indicators of SES undergo change at points in the trajectory. Such changes may result in underestimation or overestimation of other indicators of SES, as well as differences in strengths and directions of relations to parenting and child outcomes. Therefore, rather than assessing only one or two indicators of status, it is critical to obtain separate estimates of factors such as parental education, occupation, and income because they do not serve well as proxies for one another among immigrant families.

Third, research should acknowledge differences in cultural norms regarding how and under what conditions various forms of capital—human, financial, and social—are passed on to children in the form of educational opportunities, materials, or variation in socialization patterns. Rather than relying on just these indicators, one must directly measure the socialization processes that various measures of SES are thought to capture. Perhaps more than for any other population, traditional indicators of status may seriously misestimate the parenting and developmental processes that exist within immigrant families.

Finally, research linking changes in SES and child development to changes in immigration policy, such as the ones described in this chapter, is lacking in current research on children in immigrant families. Such research requires attention to dynamic processes at the time scales of policy formation, immigration trajectories, and child development (Yoshikawa & Hsueh, 2001). Although such research presents formidable methodological difficulties, the resulting data might better inform public policies affecting immigrant families, which are all too often based solely on ideology.

The challenges of conceptualizing and measuring the socioeconomic resources of immigrant families are many, but by attempting to meet these challenges, researchers may gain insights into the role of socioeconomic factors in parenting and child development among all families.

ACKNOWLEDGMENTS

Support for the preparation of this chapter was provided by Faculty Scholars Awards from the William T. Grant Foundation to both authors, a FIRST Award from the National Institute of Child Health and Human Development to the first author, and a National Science Foundation award to the second author. We would also like to thank Marc Bornstein, Robert Bradley, and Greg Duncan for their helpful comments on an earlier version of this chapter.

REFERENCES

Bornstein, M. H., & Cote, L. R. (2001). Mother-infant interaction and acculturation: I. Behavioral comparisons in Japanese American and South American families. *International Journal of Behavioral Development, 25,* 549–563.

Caplan, N., Choy, M. H., & Whitmore, J. K. (1991). *Children of the boat people: A study of educational success.* Ann Arbor, MI: The University of Michigan Press.

Coleman, J. S. (1988). Social capital and the creation of human capital. *American Journal of Sociology, 94,* 95–120.

Duncan, G. J., Brooks-Gunn, J., & Klebanov, P. K. (1994). Economic deprivation and early childhood development. *Child Development, 65,* 296–318.

Entwisle, D. R., & Astone, N. M. (1994). Some practical guidelines for measuring youth's race–ethnicity and socioeconomic status. *Child Development, 65,* 1521–1540.

Fix, M., & Passel, J. S. (1994). *Immigration and immigrants: Setting the record straight.* Washington, DC: The Urban Institute.

Fix, M., & Passel, J. S. (1999). *Trends in noncitizens' and citizens' use of public benefits following welfare reform: 1994–1997.* Washington, DC: The Urban Institute.

Fix, M., & Zimmerman, W. (1997). Immigrant families and public policy: A deepening divide. In A. Booth, A. C. Crouter, & N. S. Landale (Eds.), *Immigration and the family: Research and policy on U. S. immigrants* (pp. 237–262). Hillsdale, NJ: Lawrence Erlbaum Associates.

Fuligni, A. J. (1997). The academic achievement of adolescents from immigrant families: The roles of family background, attitudes, and behavior. *Child Development, 68,* 261–273.

Fuligni, A. J. (1998). Adolescents from immigrant families. In V. McLoyd & L. Steinberg (Eds.). *Research on minority adolescents: Conceptual, theoretical, and methodological issues* (pp. 127–143). Hillsdale, NJ: Lawrence Erlbaum Associates.

Fuligni, A. J., & Tseng, V. (1999). Family obligations and the achievement motivation of children from immigrant and American-born families. In T. Urdan (Ed.), *Advances in motivation and achievement* (pp. 159–184). Greenwich, CT: JAI.

Fuligni, A. J., Tseng, V., & Lam, M. (1999). Attitudes toward family obligations among American adolescents from Asian, Latin American, and European backgrounds. *Child Development, 70,* 1030–1044.

Furstenberg, F. F., Cook, T. D., Eccles, J. S., Elder, G. H., & Sameroff, A. (1999). *Managing to make it: Urban families and adolescent success.* Chicago: University of Chicago Press.

Furstenberg, F. F., & Hughes, M. E. (1995). Social capital and successful development among at-risk youth. *Journal of Marriage and the Family, 57,* 580–592.

Gibson, M. A. (1995). Additive acculturation as a strategy for school improvement. In R. G. Rumbaut & W. A. Cornelius (Eds.), *California's immigrant children: Theory, research, and implications for educational policy* (pp. 77–106). San Diego, CA: University of California, San Diego.

Gibson, M. A., & Bhachu, P. K. (1991). The dynamics of educational decision making: A comparative study of Sikhs in Britain and the United States. In M. A. Gibson & J. U. Ogbu (Eds.), *Minority status and schooling: A comparative study of immigrant and involuntary minorities* (pp. 63–96). New York: Garland.

Harris, K. M. (1999). *Family processes and health risk behavior among adolescents in immigrant families.* Paper presented at the urban seminar series on children's health and safety, Harvard University, Cambridge, MA.

Hauser, R. M. (1994). Measuring socioeconomic status in studies of child development. *Child Development, 65,* 1541–1545.

Hernandez, D. J., & Charney, E. (1998). *From generation to generation: The health and well-being of children in immigrant families.* Washington, DC: National Academy Press.

Kao, G., & Tienda, M. (1995). Optimism and achievement: The educational performance of immigrant youth. *Social Science Quarterly, 76,* 1–19.

Portes, A. (1998). Social capital: Its origins and applications in modern sociology. *Annual Review of Sociology, 24,* 1–24.

Portes, A., & Rumbaut, R. G. (1996). *Immigrant America: A portrait.* (2nd ed.). Berkeley, CA: University of California Press.

Portes, A., & Zhou, M. (1993). The new second generation: Segmented assimilation and its variants. *Annals of the American Academy of Political and Social Sciences, 530*, 74–96.

Rogler, L. H. (1994). International migrations: A framework for direction research. *American Psychologist, 49*, 701–708.

Rumbaut, R. G. (in press). Severed or sustained attachments? Language, identity, and imagined communities in the post-immigrant generation. In N. P. Levitt & M. C. Waters (Eds.), *Transnationalism and the second generation*. New York: Russell Sage.

Rumbaut, R. G. (1995). The new Californians: Comparative research findings on the educational progress of immigrant children. In R. G. Rumbaut & W. A. Cornelius (Eds.), *California's immigrant children: Theory, research, and implications for edcuational policy* (pp. 17–70). San Diego, CA: University of California, San Diego.

Rumbaut, R. G. (1997). Ties that bind: Immigration and immigrant families in the United States. In A. Booth, A. C. Crouter, & N. S. Landale (Eds.), *Immigration and the family: Research and policy on U. S. immigrants* (pp. 3–46). Hillsdale, N.J.: Lawrence Erlbaum Associates.

Sampson, R. (2001). How do communities undergird or undermine human development? Relevant contexts and social mechanisms. In A. Booth & A. C. Crouter (Eds.), *Does it take a village? Community effects on children, adolescents, and families* (pp. 3–30). Mahwah, NJ: Lawrence Erlbaum Associates.

Schiller, N. G. (1999). Transmigrants and nation-states: Something old and something new in the U.S. immigrant experience. In C. Hirschman, P. Kasinitz, & J. DeWind (Eds.), *The handbook of international migration* (pp. 94–119). New York: Russell Sage.

Schmidley, A. D., & Gibson, C. (1999). *Profile of the foreign-born population in the United States: 1997.* U.S. Census Bureau Current Population Reports, Series P23–195. Washington, DC: U.S. Government Printing Office.

Schoeni, R. F., McCarthy, K. F., & Vernez, G. (1996). *The mixed economic progress of immigrants.* Santa Monica, CA: Rand Corporation.

Stevenson, H. W., & Stigler, J. W. (1992) *The learning gap.* New York: Summit Books.

Suárez & Orozco, M. M. (1991). Immigrant adaptation to schooling: A Hispanic case. In M. A. Gibson & J. U. Ogbu (Eds.), *Minority status and schooling: A comparative study of immigrant and involuntary minorities* (pp. 37–62). New York: Garland.

Suárez-Orozco, C., & Suárez-Orozco, M. M. (1995). *Transformations: Immigration, family life, and achievement motivation among Latino adolescents.* Stanford, CA: Stanford University Press.

Tienda, M., & Raijman, R. (2000). Immigrants' income packaging and invisible labor force activity. *Social Science Quarterly, 81*, 291–310.

Waters, M. (1994). Ethnic and racial identities of second-generation black immigrants in New York City. *International Migration Review, 28*, 795–820.

UNESCO (1999). *1999 UNESCO statistical yearbook,* Paris, France: Author.

Yoshikawa, H., & Hsueh, J. (2001). Child development and public policy: Towards a dynamic systems perspective. *Child Development, 72*, 1887–1903.

Zhou, M. (1997). Growing up American: The challenge confronting immigrant children and children of immigrants. *Annual Review of Sociology, 23*, 63–95.

Zhou, M., & Bankston, C. L. (1994). Social capital and the adaptation of the second generation: The case of Vietnamese youth in New Orleans. *International Migration Review, 28*, 821–845.

Zhou, M., & Bankston, C. L. (1998). *Growing up American: How Vietnamese children adapt to life in the United States.* New York: Russell Sage.

Zimmerman, W., & Fix, M. (1998). *Declining immigrant applications for Medi-Cal and welfare benefits in Los Angeles county.* Washington, DC: The Urban Institute.

Zimmerman, W., & Tumlin, K. C. (1999). *Patchwork policies: State assistance for immigrants under welfare reform.* Washington, DC: The Urban Institute.

5

Methodological Issues in Studies of SES, Parenting, and Child Development

Lois Wladis Hoffman

Department of Psychology,
The University of Michigan

INTRODUCTION

The importance of socioeconomic status (SES) for children's development has been a subject of research for almost three-quarters of a century (Davis, 1941; Davis & Havighurst, 1946; Hollingshead, 1949; Lynd & Lynd, 1929; Warner & Lunt, 1942). Children's access to health facilities, nutrition, and education; their physical environment, neighborhood, and peers; the kinds of childrearing patterns experienced; the size of their family, its authority structure, and its stability—all are related to social class (L. Hoffman, 1984). So too are a great many child outcomes— health, cognitive performance, social adjustment, educational attainment, and teen pregnancy. Thus, a major challenge for developmental science is to understand the links that connect socioeconomic factors to child outcomes.

There is already a considerable accumulation of data on which to build. As suggested by Ensminger and Fothergill (chap. 1, this volume), a particularly fertile period for research on socioeconomic differences in parenting and children's cognitive development was during the 1960s and early 1970s, when Head Start programs were launched and federal funds were available for research (Deutsch, 1973; Hess, 1970). Although most studies were based on parents' reports of their attitudes or behaviors, some involved direct observation. Hess and his colleagues, for example, demonstrated social class differences in mothers' teaching styles in a structured situation and found these differences related to cognitive measures of children (Hess & Shipman, 1965, 1967; Hess, Shipman, Brophy, & Bear, 1968). As another example, longitudinal data from the Fels Institute using behavioral observations of parent behavior showed a higher use of coerciveness by lower-class mothers (Waters & Crandall, 1964).

Many of the findings from that period have been replicated and amplified in more recent research, and the new research, reviewed by Bornstein and his colleagues (chap. 2, this volume), is conceptually and methodologically more sophisticated. Although attention to social class may have diminished after 1975, as suggested in chapter 1, it may be that the field of child development has grown and expanded with new interest in studying the developmental process itself. The investigations of infant attachment and the development of concepts, categories, and children's thinking may have decreased the proportion of studies concerned with socioeconomic influences, but not necessarily their number. In any case, recent publications suggest a new interest in identifying the specific route by which socioeconomic, ethnic, and cultural differences affect children's socialization and cognitive development (Bradley & Corwyn, 2002; Hart & Risley, 1995; McLoyd, 1998).

This volume has assembled researchers from developmental science, sociology, and the health sciences to reexamine and extend the study of how socioeconomic factors affect parenting and child development and to bring in the sociocultural and ethnic diversity of our society. To do this, we have started out with methodological issues of conceptualization, measurement, and design.

So pervasive is the influence of SES that it is difficult to imagine a child development study where the researcher can avoid controlling on SES or considering its effects in generalizing results. Even if the investigation is not focussed on studying the effects of social class itself, it is related to so many independent and dependent variables in developmental research that it is usually necessary to pull out SES effects in order to examine relations among the variables of interest. Furthermore, because SES is an important context that may affect relations among other variables, it is often necessary to consider it as a moderating variable, or to examine relations of interest separately for each socioeconomic group. For example, certain stresses, such as divorce, lack of parental supervision, chronic illness, or a large sibship, can have more serious consequences for children in poverty than for those in more affluent families (Barber & Eccles, 1992; Clausen & Clausen, 1973; Coley, 1999; Sameroff, Seifer, Baldwin, & Baldwin, 1993). And, as a different example, Hoffman and Youngblade (1999) found that maternal employment had a positive effect on mothers' morale in blue-collar and impoverished families, but not in middle-class families, and furthermore, that mothers' higher morale in the blue-collar and impoverished families mediated a higher reliance on authoritative discipline and a lower reliance on both authoritarian and permissive parenting styles. Thus, because of differences in the socioeconomic context, relations among variables may be quite different in different socioeconomic groups.

In view of the socioeconomically based differences in parents' personal and material resources for coping with stress, in the neighborhood environment, and in parental attitudes, values, goals, and knowledge, attending to socioeconomic factors in studies of parenting and child development is extremely important. Yet it is clear from the chapter by Ensminger and Fothergill that child development journal articles, across disciplines, often fail even to mention the SES of the research population.

These authors also note that many of the *Child Development* articles report data from homogeneous, white, middle-class populations. While this is certainly a limitation of the field, it is very likely a reflection of the kinds of issues currently being addressed and the costs in time and money that much of the research requires. A behavioral observation study of mother–infant interaction, like the one described in the chapter by Bornstein and his colleagues, is rare. Even the job of recruiting such a sample—324 mothers with one 5 1/2 month-old infant—is daunting. Investigations of language development, children's understanding of concepts and categories, and the "theory of mind" research (Wellman, 1990) are dealing with basic developmental processes, but they are labor intensive and numbers are small. When numbers are small, a researcher cannot examine socioeconomic differences, and a homogeneus sample is used to avoid the interference of socioeconomic factors. Because the sample used is most often drawn from the white middle class, it means that much of our knowledge in these areas cannot be generalized beyond that group, and a published article should note this. Even more important, however, replications of this work using lower-class or African American samples should be conducted and rarely are.

This commentary is focussed on methodological issues of conceptualization, measurement, and design. The primary aim is to select topics from the foregoing chapters and to integrate and expand them. In the first section, this discussion will focus on the three major components of SES: income, occupation, and education. The Hollingshead Four-Factor Index of Social Status (HI) will also be discussed because this is the composite measure most commonly used in studies of SES, parenting, and child outcomes (Ensminger & Fothergill, chap. 1, in this volume). In a second section, the challenge of linking SES to parenting and child development is considered. In the final section, special issues that arise in studies of African American and immigrant families are discussed.

CONCEPTUALIZATION
AND MEASUREMENT

An important methodological problem raised in the foregoing chapters is the issue of how SES should be conceptualized and measured. Two major questions emerge: (1) What component of socioeconomic status is most important for a particular study or most responsible for the child outcomes we seek to understand? (2) When a general measure of socioeconomic status is needed, which one is likely to serve developmental science best?

Components

There is consensus throughout this volume, as in other publications, that to understand how SES affects children, we need to look at its specific components (Alwin, 1989; Featherman, Spenner & Tsunematsu,1988; McLoyd, 1998). In chapter 3, Duncan and Magnuson provide an excellent explication of the three major components, income, education, and occupation, as well as a research-based analysis suggesting which are most potent for certain populations, particular developmental periods, and specific outcomes. In this section, we elaborate and extend this discussion.

Income

As these authors note, income is extremely important in studies of poverty where even modest differences can have profound effects, particularly during the early years. For example, Smith and her colleagues (1997) found that the positive impact of family income on young children's IQ and Peabody Picture Vocabulary Test (PPVT) scores was much larger for families at or below the poverty line than for families above the poverty line. Poverty in infancy can affect prenatal care, nutrition, and exposure to environmental hazards and thus have life-long effects. But, as previously noted, low income and job insecurity continue to have negative effects throughout childhood and adolescence because the lack of parental resources augments other life stresses. Economic strains also cause parental stress that can function to diminish the quality of parenting, and income-based differences in the neighborhood environment of the very poor can have a particularly negative effect during adolescence (McLoyd, 1998). In fact, research indicates that changes in income—both increases and decreases—have greater effects on children and adolescents in low-income groups (Dearing, McCartney, & Taylor, 2001; Flanagan & Eccles, 1993).

It is important to keep in mind also, however, that some of the negative effects of poverty, particularly in infancy, may be carried by education. Failure to seek prenatal care, lack of attention to diet during pregnancy, and reliance on bottle feeding, which deprives the child of immunities against many of the infectious diseases of infancy, are often a function of lack of knowledge rather than lack of money.

Duncan and Magnuson (chap. 3, this volume) also point out the frailties of the different components and, for income, its volatility over the years is noted. Thus, income measured at one age may not reflect income at another, and persistent poverty has stronger adverse effects than transitory poverty on the cognitive development of preschool children (McLoyd, 1998). Income volatility presents a problem when income at one stage of development is used to predict child outcomes at another. It can also be valuable, however, when incorporated into the study design. For example, within-family shifts in income level can be important in explaining sibling differences (Featherman et al., 1988; L. Hoffman, 1991). In the case of a family that moves out of poverty during the childbearing years, the early-born children may carry negative effects that the later-born do not. Furthermore, since income loss per se carries some of the negative effects of divorce on children (Barber & Eccles, 1992; Lorenz et al., 1997), the age of each child at the time of divorce can also lead to sibling differences. In Elder's (1974) study of the depression in the early 1930s, different effects of income loss on children were found depending on their age when the loss occurred.

In general, income differences are important predictors of parenting and child outcomes at the low socioeconomic levels, and income loss can have deleterious effects on both parents and children across a wider economic range. However, whether, or to what extent, income per se is related to parenting and child development within the higher income groups is not clear, as suggested both in Duncan and Magnuson's chapter and in the chapter by Bornstein and his colleagues. To use a concrete example, why would one expect parents in the family of a skilled blue-collar worker, whose income is often higher than a school teacher's, to have children with higher academic competence or who obtain more education? Parental values and childrearing goals have been viewed by many researchers as reflecting the parents' beliefs about where success lies (L. Hoffman, 1984, 1986, 1988; Kohn, 1969; Miller & Swanson, 1958) and for the skilled blue-collar worker, it seems unlikely to depend on academic accomplishment. There is no empirical answer to this question, but it would be interesting to compare these two groups, skilled blue-collar workers and public school teachers, with respect to their childrearing patterns and goals, and the academic competence of their children.

A practical problem in using income as an indicator of SES is the difficulty of obtaining income information. Duncan and Magnuson (chap. 3, this volume) discuss this issue at a general level in their chapter, but the problem is amplified in developmental science. To obtain a large sample of children of a specific age, it is often necessary to enlist the cooperation of the public schools. Ensminger and her colleagues (2000) reported problems in obtaining income information from adolescents directly or from parents on permission slips, whereas parental education and occupation can be obtained from permission slips and education from the adolescents directly.

Even when home interviews are conducted with parents, however, it can be unwise to ask about income when the researcher is conducting the study through the schools. To obtain their cooperation throughout the data collection period, and sometimes beyond when a follow-up study is planned, is a delicate task. School administrators have a politically sensitive position. They have little to gain by their cooperation with researchers and risk censure if a parent complains. Sometimes cooperation is obtained with the explicit proviso that income information is not requested, but even if it is not explicit, the seasoned researcher knows it is a question that parents may find intrusive and even one complaining parent can put at risk the entire project.

Occupation

There is considerable consensus that occupation is a major marker of social class. It has been used as the only index in much of the social science research across the years, and it is included in most of the composite indices of SES. Both income and education are implicit in occupation because knowing one's occupation provides a rough estimate of the other two. In the case of the Socioeconomic Index of Occupations, the scores are based on occupation but they are purposely weighted to reflect the other components (see Bornstein et al., chap. 2, this volume).

As a measure of SES, occupation has the advantage of being easily obtained. Parents are freer to report their occupation than even their education, particularly when they are relatively uneducated. If SES information is obtained on parent permission forms, for example, it is more comfortable to write "assembly line at Ford" than to check "less than eighth grade".

However, although there is research examining the effects on children of various aspects of work, such as time schedules and stress levels (L. Hoffman, 1984, 1986; Menaghan & Parcels, 1991), few researchers, with the exception of Kohn (1959a, 1959b, 1969; Parcels & Menaghan, 1994), have examined the link between occupation itself and childrearing patterns, parental values, or child outcomes, and each of the first three chapters in this book referred to the work of Kohn as one of the few researchers who has tried to demonstrate that fathers' occupations directly affect these variables. Kohn pursued the hypothesis that the link between SES and children's development lies in the nature of the occupations that distinguish the middle from the lower class. According to Kohn, middle-class occupations involve manipulating ideas, symbols, and interpersonal relations, and require flexibility, thought, and judgement. Lower-class occupations require manipulating physical objects and are more standardized, less complex, and more supervised. Because of these differences, middle-class fathers would be expected to value self-direction and independence in their children, whereas lower-class fathers would value obedience and conformity. Kohn's data supported this prediction, and he found corresponding differences in the reported childrearing practices: lower-class parents used more physical punishment and judged their children's behavior in terms of the consequences, whereas middle-class parents used more psychological discipline and judged misbehavior in terms of intent.

Many of the social class differences predicted in Kohn's theories have been found in subsequent research. A repeated finding over the years is that lower-class parents in their attempts to influence children are more likely to use power-assertive techniques and less likely to give reasons, to try to induce the child to become intrinsically motivated to comply, or to attend to extenuating circumstances, and these childrearing patterns have been linked to children's cognitive competence, social competence, and moral development (Baumrind, 1971; Dornbusch, Ritter, Leiderman, Roberts, & Fraleigh, 1987; Hess, 1970; M. Hoffman, 1963, 1975; M. Hoffman & Saltzstein, 1967; L. Hoffman & Youngblade, 1999; Krevans, & Gibbs, 1996; Steinberg, Dornbusch, & Brown, 1992). Among the processes seen as connecting the lower-class style of parental control to these outcomes are: (1) they engender in the child a sense of inefficacy; (2) they fail to communicate rationality in life; and (3) they do not provide verbal enrichment.

However, whether or not these differences are a function of the nature of the father's job per se is not clear. Even in Kohn's work, education seemed to have an effect independent of the job itself, and the research of Lueptow, McClendon, and McKeon (1979) suggested education is the more potent variable. In addition, many of the on-the-job experiences that Kohn described are mirrored in experiences in the larger society. Lower-class parents often feel subject to rules and authorities in their relations with other institutions in society where rules are inflexible, rationales are rarely provided, and extenuating circumstances are not considered. Their parenting may reflect these circumstances, as well as their job experiences, but with them in the authority roles (L. Hoffman, 1984).

Thus, occupation is a core aspect of SES and provides a general estimate of income and education, but it is not clear that it has a direct causal relation to parenting or child outcomes. Furthermore, there is a caveat to this discussion. Occupation is a better predictor of men's education than women's, and in the longitudinal research of Gottfried and his colleagues (chap. 8, this volume), the occupations of fathers, but not mothers, were related to child development outcomes.

Education

Some researchers have argued that the key component of SES that affects parenting and child development is education and suggest it may be an adequate alternative to composite indices, such as the Hollingshead Four-Factor Index (Alwin, 1989; Gottfried et al., chap. 8, this volume). Of the three components, education seems to be the most closely related to mother–child interactions, the cognitive stimulation of the environment, and children's cognitive development (Bornstein et al., chap. 2, this volume; Haveman & Wolfe, 1995; Hoff, chap. 6, this volume; Hoff-Ginzberg & Tardif, 1995). It is also the most stable of the three (Gottfried et al., chap. 8, this volume) and the easiest to measure.

However, even though education may be the major SES component in developmental studies, it does not include the full context of SES. If a researcher is interested in SES per se, no single component may be adequate. In the case of education, the fact that it may not reflect occupation or income, particularly for women, is a limitation given the high number of single-mother families in the United States. If it does not reflect income, it can miss the access to resources in times of stress that affects the quality of parenting, and the social milieu of class such as the neighborhood environment and the friends and associates of both parents and children.

In addition, although there are data indicating that parental education does not show a linear relationship to children's academic achievement (Haveman & Wolfe, 1995), how parents' education relates to the quality of *parenting* has not been established. Is there a more significant difference, for example, between high school graduation and 11 years of schooling than between completing eight years of school and seven? Do two years of college make a more marked difference than two years at a lower level? A study investigating this issue would be helpful in unraveling the relation between maternal education and parenting.

Thus, education is useful in child-development studies as an efficient measure of the SES of the sample, and it is essential in most child-development research as a control or moderator variable because so many of the independent and dependent variables studied are related to it. Furthermore, it may be key in carrying the effects of SES on parenting and child development.

Nevertheless, education does not capture the full significance of SES on children's development, and in research with very low-income families, income may be more important in carrying the effects of SES on parenting and children. Furthermore, each of the three major components of SES may affect different aspects of parenting and child outcomes (De Garmo, Forgatch, & Martinez, 1999). Thus, the final decision about which of the components to use depends on the particular study.

The Hollingshead Four-Factor Index of Social Status

Although examining the separate components of SES is important in research on how SES affects parenting and children's development, for many purposes, a general measure of SES is needed. If the researcher is interested in identifying the components of social class that carry effects, a general measure may be useful to first establish that there are effects. If a study is not geared toward examining socioeconomic effects per se, a general measure may be needed as a control, as a possible moderator of effects, or as part of the description of the sample. In the Hoffman and Youngblade (1999) study of the effects of maternal employment, previously mentioned, a general measure, the Hollingshead Four-Factor Index of Social Status (1975), was used to identify three groups, and the analyses were conducted separately for each. Conducting separate analyses for each socioeconomic group seemed important because previous research had indicated different effects of maternal employment in middle-class, working-class, and poverty groups.

These differences, however, were based on different studies, each of which had used a homogeneous, one-class sample. Thus, one goal of this new study was to see if previous class differences would be replicated in a single multi-class sample where the same measures and procedures were used for each group. Furthermore, the dynamics of the relations between the mother's employment status and child outcomes were different for each socioeconomic group and thus could more easily be examined by considering each separately.

The Hollingshead Four-Factor Index has several advantages over other indices. Gottfried (1985) found that, although the HI, the Revised Duncan Socioeconomic Index, and the Siegel Prestige Scale related similarly to a variety of child development measures, the Hollingshead consistently showed the highest correlations. It includes both education and occupation, and scoring takes account of the prevalence of single-mother families. It also considers the fact that many mothers are employed and incorporates the occupation and education of employed mothers. As noted by Gottfried and his colleagues (chap. 8, this volume), it is also stable across childhood. A tribute to the value of this widely-used index is that it has never been published and researchers using it are relying on a Xeroxed copy that is reproduced and passed around among colleagues.

An additional value of the Hollingshead was revealed in an analysis in which Hoffman and Youngblade (1999) compared Hollingshead scores with a measure based on occupation alone. The largest differences occurred among African American families where the mother had a higher occupational level than the father, as well as more education. In several cases, the father was a semi-skilled worker with little education and the mother was a school teacher with a college degree. This pattern of wives' education and occupation exceeding their husbands' is more common among African Americans (Walker, 1988). The inclusion of the wife's education and occupation moved the family from assignment to the working class to the middle class. Thus, the Hollingshead measure corrected an error in social class assignment that affected only African Americans.

Nevertheless, this measure has one serious flaw. Hollingshead was interested in devising a measure of family status. In his unpublished paper that described the measure, he argued well for why family status is derived from the breadwinner role. Thus, the education of a nonemployed mother in a two-parent family is not part of the score. The early studies of social class were conducted by sociologists and social psychologists (Hollingshead, 1949; Warner & Lunt, 1942), and their emphasis was on how families are appraised by others in the community. In developmental science, however, we are interested in the climate in the family— values, attitudes, goals for children, and childrearing patterns. The education of the full-time homemaker contributes to these as much as the education of employed parents. Thus, the value of the HI might be enhanced for developmental science if there were a revision where the same procedures are used, but the education of all mothers is included in the calculations.

LINKING SES TO PARENTING
AND CHILD OUTCOMES

In studying the effects of SES on parenting and child outcomes, whether one starts with a general index or one of the major components, one is still dealing with a distal variable and the task is to identify the process by which the components affect the child. Several of the chapters in this volume have illuminated this process by delineating the mother–child interactions that are related to SES indicators and demonstrating which specific maternal behaviors carry a particular child effect (Bornstein et al., chap. 2, this volume; Bradley & Corwyn, chap. 7, this volume; Hoff, chap. 6, this volume). The analysis by Bradley and Corwyn, in particular, revealed the potential complexities of this task. Using a longitudinal data set obtained from a heterogeneous sample, they examined both contemporaneous parenting and earlier parenting for effects on children's vocabulary attainment, achievement test performance, and problem behaviors. In addition, the moderating effects of ethnicity were considered.

As these analyses show, the task of identifying the process that connects SES to child outcomes is an extremely important one, but it is also a formidable challenge. Furthermore, to unravel the full process, there may be additional links to identify. If, for example, maternal education is the key aspect of SES that affects parenting, what is it about education that carries the effect? Does education promote an orientation toward seeking expert advice about child care (Bronfenbrenner, 1958; Bornstein et al., chap. 2, this volume)? Does it lead to having a reference group that is better informed about the needs and competencies of infants? Does education stimulate the development of a more verbal parenting style? Or, does education induce a greater feeling of efficacy that facilitates effective parenting?

To add to the complexity of the task, there are many mutually reinforcing processes that operate throughout the child's development and thus no single study can yield the full picture. For example, middle-class mothers talk more to their infants and use richer language (Bornstein et al., chap. 2, this volume; Hoff, chap. 6, this volume). When the children are older, middle-class mothers use more inductive control techniques, providing reasons and allowing the child to reason back (Hess, 1970; M. Hoffman & Saltzstein, 1967). Both of these parenting behaviors stimulate verbal ability and the control techniques also encourage reasoning, communicate rationality in the world, and engender a sense of efficacy in the child (L. Hoffman, 1984). These qualities, and the other middle-class styles the children have learned, match the behavior they are expected to exhibit in school. Their peers are more likely to also be middle class so they provide reinforcement. Their parents and their friends' parents expect their children to go to college and know what is needed to get them accepted. School performance is relevant to the goals their parents have passed on to them. Thus, there are so many paths by which middle-class children are environmentally advantaged that no specific investigation can provide the ultimate answer, but each one contributes to our understanding of this important issue.

Policy Implications

Several chapters in this volume have indicated that moving from the broad concept of SES to the specific components facilitates social policy since the specific components—education, income, or even aspects of occupation (Crouter, 1984)—can be enhanced for the benefits accruing to children, whereas changing overall SES is an unrealistic goal. Identifying the *process* that links the SES components to child outcomes, however, can facilitate the effectiveness of the policy and may suggest specific practical intervention programs, parenting classes, and national education efforts (P. Cowan & C. Cowan, 2002). Some of the more successful interventions involved training programs in which lower-class mothers were encouraged to talk to, play with, and stimulate their infants (Belsky, Goode, & Most, 1980; Huebner, 2000; P. Levenstein, 1970; P. Levenstein, S. Levenstein, Shiminski, & Stolzberg, 1998).

The Role of Genes

Although it is sometimes possible to conduct a field experiment when investigating the connections between SES, parenting, and child outcomes (Rozenzsweig & Wolpin, 1994), most studies rely on correlational designs. In correlational research, it is necessary to consider in advance what variables other than the ones under investigation might explain the findings. For example, in a study examining the effects of maternal employment on children, the mother's education needs to be controlled, or examined for moderating effects, because apparent positive effects of mothers' employment might actually reflect the higher educational level of employed mothers.

In recent years, behavioral geneticists have criticized developmental research because it has failed to consider the possibility that SES, parenting, and child outcomes are each reflecting parents' genes, and therefore, a relation between social status or parenting and child outcomes might be a function of the genetic similarity of parents and children (Plomin & Daniels, 1987; Scarr, 1992). A number of developmental scientists have responded to these criticisms, emphasizing the interactive nature of heredity and environment, questioning the assumptions of some of the behavioral genetics research, and clarifying the current approach of developmental theory and research (Collins, Maccoby, Steinberg, Hetherington, & Bronstein, 2000; L. Hoffman, 1991; Lerner, chap. 10, this volume; Wachs, 1983, 1987).

Nevertheless, the challenge from behavioral genetics needs to be considered. A particular strength of the research by Bornstein and his colleagues (chap. 2, this volume) is the inclusion of a measure of the mother's IQ. The analyses indicated that the effects of education held apart from possibly shared genes. Advances in technology and the more sophisticated statistical procedures available make it easier to deal with more links in the causal chain between SES and child outcomes, examine multiple sources of influence, test for mediation effects, introduce potential moderating variables, and test competing hypotheses such as the charge that the results are carried by genetic similarity.

ISSUES IN STUDYING ETHNICITY AND IMMIGRANT POPULATIONS

Studies of ethnic groups or immigrant populations present special methodological issues. Some of these will be considered in this section, first with respect to African Americans and then with respect to recent immigrants.

Research with African Americans

In studies of SES, parenting, and child outcomes, when grouped categories of SES indices are used, African Americans occupy the bottom of each SES group. Within poverty groups, African Americans are not only disproportionately represented, but they are more likely to be in the lowest economic level, to have been in poverty longer, to live in single-mother homes, and to reside in poor neighborhoods that are socioeconomically homogeneous (McLoyd, 1997, 1998). Thus, what appear to be ethnic differences, even when social class seems to be controlled, may actually be socioeconomic differences.

Furthermore, because it is difficult to find an adequate sample of middle-class African American families with a child of a specific age, few studies have examined childrearing patterns in the middle class and generalizations about African American families are based on findings from lower-class samples (Slaughter-Defoe, Nakagawa, Takanishi, & Johnson, 1990). An example of this is the assertion that African American families are more likely to demand obedience and use more authoritarian controls. In fact, however, even within a poor African American sample, education, marital status, and maternal age differentiated childrearing patterns, with less educated, single, and younger mothers placing a stronger emphasis on obedience and relying more on authoritarian controls (Kelley, Power, & Wimbush, 1992). Furthermore, it should be remembered that in the seminal research of Hess and Shipman (1965, 1967), one of the first well-executed studies of social class differences in parenting styles, an all African American sample was used, and the differences they found have subsequently been replicated with European Americans.

Another issue which has been raised in the developmental literature in connection with parenting in low-income groups, and African Americans in particular, is whether authoritarian parenting styles and stress on obedience develop out of the need to protect the child from a dangerous and hostile environment, and whether the effects of such parenting, in that context, are less adverse than those found in more benign living conditions (A. Baldwin, C. Baldwin, & Cole, 1990; Baumrind, 1972; Darling & Steinberg, 1993; Krenichyn, Saegart, & Evans, 2001; Waters, 1996).

Inconsistent with this view is an abundance of research on low-income families, African Americans, European Americans, and Latin Americans, indicating that frequent use of power assertive controls, reliance on physical punishment, and less supportive parenting are tied to maternal stress and depression and have negative consequences for children's socioemotional well-being (Dodge, Pettit, & Bates, 1994; Downey & Coyne, 1990; L. Hoffman & Youngblade, 1999; McLeod & Shanahan, 1993; McLoyd, 1997).

Nevertheless, it is possible that tight parental control has a different meaning in a group that holds a vulnerable position in society. It is also possible that when physical discipline is administered in the context that this is an appropriate parental practice, necessary for protecting children from danger and adverse social influences, the effects are more benign than when it is administered only in exasperation and anger. Few studies have tried to differentiate authoritarian parenting to distinguish punitive and irrational discipline from tight control that may be tempered by explanations, parental support, warmth, and the communication of love. The dichotomous classification of control styles into authoritarian and authoritative may need to be modified. Brody and Flor (1998), for example, in a study of rural, single, African American mothers, identified a pattern of "no nonsense" parenting that included high control but also high warmth and affection. In addition, a recent analysis from one of the few studies that includes a socioeconomically heterogeneous sample of African Americans, as well as a comparable sample of European Americans, indicated both socioeconomic effects and ethnic effects on parenting (Early & Eccles, 2002). With SES controlled, African American mothers reported more controlling parenting, more stress on obedience, and more positive relationships with their adolescent children. The concept of authoritarian control combined with warmth and involvement has been suggested by others as well (Baumrind, 1972; Krenichyn et al., 2001).

This limitation of the standard authoritarian-authoritative distinction has also been indicated for Chinese Americans in research by Chao (2001), which suggests that the warmth or closeness of the parent–child relationship needs to be separated from the control style. Research on socioeconomic effects on parenting and child outcomes relies heavily on the dichotomous distinction in control styles. A reconsideration of these styles with particular attention to the dimensions of warmth and involvement would be especially useful in studies of socioeconomic effects on parenting and children in African American and immigrant families, and it might enhance the research on European American families as well.

Research with Immigrants

The problem of how to conceptualize SES in studies examining parenting and child outcomes in immigrant populations is an important one, particularly in view of the increased rate of immigration and the fact that 20% of the American children under 18 years have immigrant parents (Rumbaut, 2000). The complexities of this problem are discussed by Fuligni and Yoshikawa (chap. 4, this volume). They point out some of the ambiguities of indices, such as education or income, in studies of immigrant families, and suggest that these be supplemented by also considering the concept of social capital, as outlined by Coleman (1988). Social capital includes attitudes and values that the new Americans bring with them that may provide a valuable resource in the socialization of their children. Whether or not they have the positive effect assumed, however, may be affected by the parents' economic resources and by changes that occur as both parents and children deal with the realities of the new environment.

One of the aspects of social capital that many immigrant families, across diverse cultures, seem to share is a strong sense of mutual obligation within the family. The sense of obligation immigrant children feel toward their parents has been cited by several researchers as an important reason why these children have been found to perform better in school than the children of American-born families (Fuligni & Yoshikawa, chap. 4, this volume; Rambaut, 2000). It seems possible, however, that this same sense of obligation to the family could have a very different effect in low-income families. When money is scarce and low-skill jobs are available, filial obligation can operate to push teenagers into the job market as a way of helping the family, rather than into educational pursuits. Because immigrant families from Mexico are more financially pressed than most of the other groups (Rumbaut, 2000; Fuligni & Yoshikawa, chap. 4, this volume), this scenario is a particularly likely one for them, and it is consistent with national data. Thirty-six percent of Latin-American boys leave school without a diploma, compared with 16% and 14% for African American and European American boys (U.S. Bureau of the Census, 2001).

Rumbaut (2000) examined the academic performance of a large sample of children of immigrants from several different Asian countries and from Mexico, using data obtained when the children were in the eighth and 12th grades. Although the children of immigrants as a group received better grades and had fewer drop-outs and suspensions than the school district as a whole, SES, as measured by parental education, occupation, and home ownership, was related to these outcomes within the immigrant group. The Mexican youths had lower grades and a higher rate of drop outs and suspensions than the other children of immigrants. Furthermore, for the three groups whose socioeconomic circumstances were the lowest, those from Mexico, Cambodia, and Laos, educational expectations were the lowest and decreased over the years. Parenting behavior was not examined in this investigation, but the data suggest that cultural attitudes were important and may have moderated socioeconomic effects, but they did not override them.

The study also found within-group differences in the sense of obligation to parents children felt. First, children who had been born in the country of emigration felt this more strongly than those born in the United States; and second, there was a drop in scores between the eighth and the 12th grades, suggesting an acculturation effect. This drop was particularly true for those with a Mexican background. As Fuligni and Yoshikawa (chap. 4, this volume) point out, Mexicans are admitted to the United States on the basis of family reunification. Admission on that basis usually reflects lower SES, but, in addition, it increases the likelihood that the children of immigrants will have contact with peers who have the same national background but are already acculturated to the new country. Thus, the basis on which the immigrants are admitted may affect the extent to which the immigrant family can insulate its values from the larger society.

The questions raised by Fuligni and Yoshikawa (chap. 4, this volume) about the value of the conventional indices of SES, income, occupation, and education, in studies of immigrant populations, are ultimately empirical questions. Research on how the components of SES affect parenting and children may need to be conducted within the particular immigrant group and then contrasted with patterns found in other immigrant or nonimmigrant groups, if possible in parallel studies. Such investigations would need to consider the interacting influences of family attitudes, the community setting, and the impact of the immigration experience. It would be valuable to see how the childrearing patterns brought from the country of emigration functioned in the new environment, whether they changed in the new context, whether they were resisted more by the children, and how socioeconomic factors affected this process.

CONCLUSIONS

Research on the effects of socioeconomic factors on parenting and children's development has been conducted for many years. As a result, a great deal is known about the effects, but there is still a great deal to be learned about the process by which these effects occur. At the present time, there is a need to examine the components of SES and distinguish which component, and what aspect of the component, carries specific effects on parental behavior and child outcomes, at different stages of the child's development. The links in the chain that connect SES to child outcomes need to be identified and explained. To add to this complex task, interactive effects of cultural values, ethnicity, the neighborhood, community resources, schools, and peers need to be considered. The present chapter is an attempt to facilitate this challenge.

REFERENCES

Alwin, D. (1989). Education, occupation, and parental values. In N. Eisenberg, J. Reykowski, & E. Staub (Eds.), *Social and moral values* (pp. 327–346). Hillside, NJ: Erlbaum Associates.

Baldwin, A. L., Baldwin, C., & Cole, R. E. (1990). Stress resistant families and stress resistant children. In J. Rolf, A. S. Masten, D. Cicchetti, K. Neuchterlein, & S. Weintraub (Eds.), *Risk and protective factors in the development of psychopathology.* (pp. 257–280), Cambridge, England: Cambridge University Press.

Barber, B. L. & Eccles, J. S. (1992). Long-term influence of divorce and single-parenting on adolescent family- and work-related values, behavior, and aspirations. *Psychological Bulletin, 111*, 108–126.

Baumrind, D. (1971). Current patterns of parental authority, *Developmental Psychology Monographs, 4* (1, pt. 2), 1–103.

Baumrind, D. (1972). An exploratory study of socialization effects on black children: Some black-white comparisons. *Child Development, 43*, 261–267.

Belsky, J., Goode, M. K., & Most, R. K. (1980). Maternal stimulation and infant exploratory competence: Cross-sectional, correlational, and experimental analyses. *Child Development, 51*, 1168–1178.

Bradley, R. H., & Corwyn, R. F. (2002). SES and child development. *Annual Review of Psychology, 53*, 371–399.

Brody, G. H., & Flor, D. L. (1998). Maternal resources, parenting practices, and child competence in rural, single parent, African American families. *Child Development, 69*, 803–816.

Bronfenbrenner, U. (1958). Socialization and social class through time and space. In E. E. Maccoby, R. M. Newcomb, & E. L. Hartley (Eds.), Readings in social psychology (pp. 400–425). New York: Holt, Rinehart & Winston.

Chao, R. K. (2001). Extending research on the consequences of parenting style for Chinese Americans and European Americans. *Child Development, 72*, 1832–1843.

Clausen, J. A., & Clausen, S. R. (1973). The effects of family size on parents and children. In J. T. Fawcett (Ed.), *Psychological perspectives on population* (pp. 185–208) New York: Basic Books.

Coleman, J. S. (1988). Social capital in the creation of human capital. *American Journal of Sociology, 94*, 95–120.

Coley, R. L. (1999). Nonmaternal care and supervision: Prevalence and effects of child-care arrangements on child well-being. In L. W. Hoffman & L. M. Youngblade (Eds.), *Mothers at work: Effects on children's well-being* (pp. 256–277) Cambridge, England: Cambridge University Press.

Collins, W. A., Maccoby, E. E., Steinberg, L., Hetherington, E. M., & Bornstein, M. H. (2000). Contemporary research on parenting. *American Psychologist, 55*, 218–232.

Cowan, P. A., & Cowan, C. P. (2002). What an intervention design reveals about how parents affect their children's academic achievement and behavior problems. In J. G. Borkowski, S. Ramey, & M. Bristol-Powers (Eds.), Parenting and the child's world: Influences on intellectual, academic, and social-emotional development (pp. 75–97). Mahwah, NJ: Lawrence Erlbaum Associates.

Crouter, A. C. (1984). Participative work as an influence on human development. *Journal of Applied Developmental Psychology, 5*, 71–90.

Darling, N., & Steinberg, L. (1993). Parenting style as context: An integrative model. *Psychological Bulletin, 113*, 487–496.

Davis, A. (1941). American status systems and the socialization of the child. *American Sociological Review, 6*, 345–354.

Davis, A., & Havighurst, R. J. (1946). Social class and color differences in childrearing. *American Sociological Review, 11*, 698–710.

Dearing, E., McCartney, K., & Taylor, B. (2001). Change in family income-to-needs matters more for children with less. *Child Development, 72*, 1779–1793.

Deutsch, C. P. (1973). Social class and child development. In B. M. Caldwell & H. M. Ricciuti (Eds.), *Review of child development research, Vol. 3* (pp. 233–282). Chicago: University of Chicago Press.

De Garmo, D. S., Forgatch, M. S., & Martinez, C. R. (1999). Parenting of divorced mothers as a link between social status and boys' academic outcomes: Unpacking the effects of socioeconomic status. *Child Development, 70*, 1231–1245.

Dodge, K. A., Pettit, G. S., & Bates, J. E. (1994). Socialization mediators of the relation between socioeconomic status and child conduct problems. *Child Development, 65*, 649–665.

Dornbusch, S. M., Ritter, P. L., Leiderman, P. H., Roberts, D. F. & Fraleigh, M. J. (1987). The relation of parenting style to adolescent school performance. *Child Development, 58*, 1244–1257.

Downey, G., & Coyne, J. (1990). Children of depressed parents: An integrative review. *Psychological Bulletin, 108*, 50–76.

Early, D., & Eccles, J. S. (2002). *Understanding the links between socioeconomic status, race, and parenting behaviors.* Unpublished manuscript, University of Michigan, Ann Arbor.

Elder, G. (1974). *Children of the great depression.* Chicago: University of Chicago Press.

Ensminger, M. E., Forrest, C. B., Riley, A. W., Kang, M., Green, B., Starfield, B., & Ryan, S. A. (2000). The validity of measures of socioeconomic status of adolescents. *Journal of Adolescent Research, 15*, 392–419.

Featherman, D. L., Spenner, K. I., & Tsunematsu, N. (1988). Class and the socialization of children: Constancy, change, or Irrelevance? In E. M. Hetherington, R. M. Lerner, & M. Perlmutter (Eds.) *Child development in life-span perspective* (pp. 67–90). Hillside, NJ: Lawrence Erlbaum Associates.

Flanagan, C. A. & Eccles, J. S. (1993). Changes in parental work status and adolescents' adjustment at school. *Child Development, 64*, 246–257.

Gottfried, A. W. (1985). Measures of socioeconomic status in child development research: Data and recommendations. *Merrill-Palmer Quarterly, 31*, 85–92.

Hart, B., & Risley, T. R. (1995). *Meaningful differences in the everyday experience of young American children.* Baltimore, MD: Paul H. Brookes.

Haveman, R., & Wolfe, B. (1995). The determinants of children's attainments: A review of methods and findings. *Journal of Economic Literature, 23*, 1829–1878.

Hess, R. D. (1970). Social class and ethnic influences upon socialization. In P. H. Mussen (Ed.), *Carmichael's manual of child psychology, 3rd ed., Vol.* 2 (pp. 457–557). New York: Wiley.

Hess, R. D., & Shipman, V. (1965). Early experience and the socialization of cognitive modes in children. *Child Development, 34*, 869–886.

Hess, R. D., & Shipman, V. C. (1967). Cognitive elements in maternal behavior. In J. P. Hill (Ed.), *Minnesota symposia on child psychology, Vol. 1*, Minneapolis, MN: University of Minnesota Press.

Hess, R. D., Shipman, V. C., Brophy, J., & Bear, R. (1968). *Cognitive environments of urban preschool Negro children.* Report to the Children's Bureau, Social Security Administration, Health, Education, and Welfare.

Hoff-Ginzberg, E., & Tardiff, T. (1995). Socioeconomic status and parenting. In M. H. Bornstein (Ed.), *Handbook of parenting,* (Vol. 2, pp. 161–188). Mahwah, NJ: Lawrence Erlbaum Associates.

Hoffman, L. W. (1984). Work, family, and the socialization of the child. In R. Parke, R. Ende, H. Mcadoo, & G. Sackett (Eds.) *Review of child development research, Vol. 7* (pp. 223–282). Chicago: University of Chicago Press.

Hoffman, L. W. (1986). Work, family, and the child. In M. S. Pallak & R. O. Perloff (Eds.), *Pschology and work* (pp. 169–220). Washingtin, DC American Psychological Association.

Hoffman, L. W. (1988). Cross-cultural differences in childrearing goals. In R. Levine, P. Miller, & M. M. West, *Parental behavior in diverse societies, new directions for child development* (pp. 99–122). San Francisco: Jossey-Bass.

Hoffman, L. W. (1991). The influence of the family environment on personality: Accounting for sibling differences. *Psychological Bulletin, 110*, 187–203.

Hoffman, L. W., & Youngblade, L. M. (1999). *Mothers at work: Effects on children's well-being.* Cambridge, England: Cambridge University Press.

Hoffman, M. L. (1963). Childrearing practices and moral development: Generalizations from research. *Child Development, 34*, 295–318.

Hoffman, M. L. (1975). Moral internalization, parent power, and the nature of parent-child interaction. *Developmental Psychology, 11*, 228–239.

Hoffman, M. L., & Saltzstein, H. D. (1967). Parent discipline and child's moral development. *Journal of Personality and Psychology, 5*, 45–57.

Hollingshead, A. B. (1949). *Elmtown's youth.* New York: Wiley.

Hollingshead, A. B. (1975). *The four-factor index of social status.* Unpublished manuscript,. Yale University, New Haven, CT.

Huebner, C. E. (2000). Promoting toddlers' language development through community-based intervention. *Journal of Applied Developmental Psychology, 21,* 513–535.

Kelley, M. L., Power, T. G., & Wimbush, D. D. (1992). Determinants of disciplinary practices in low-income black mothers. *Child Development, 63,* 573–582.

Kohn, M. (1959a). Social class and the exercise of parental authority. *American Sociological Review, 24,* 352–366.

Kohn, M. (1959b). Social class and parental values. *American Journal of Sociology, 64,* 337–351.

Kohn, M. (1969). *Class and conformity: A study in values.* Homewood, IL: Dorsey Press.

Krenichyn, K., Saegert, S., & Evans, G. W. (2001). Parents as moderators of psychological and physiological correlates of inner-city children's exposure to violence, *Journal of Applied Developmental Psychology, 22,* 581–602.

Krevans, J., & Gibbs, J. C. (1996). Parents' social use of inductive discipline: Relations to children's empathy and prosocial behavior. *Child Development, 67,* 3263–3277.

Levenstein, P. (1970). Cognitive growth in preschoolers through verbal interaction with mothers. *Americam Journal of Orthopsychiatry, 40,* 426–432.

Levenstein, P., Levenstein, S., Shiminski, J., & Stolzberg, J. E. (1998). Long-term impact of a verbal interaction program for at-risk toddlers: An exploratory study of high school outcomes in a replication of the mother-child home program. *Journal of Applied Developmental Psychology, 19,* 267–285.

Lorenz, F. O., Simons, R. L., Conger, R. D., Elder, G. H., Johnson, C., & Chao, W. (1997). Married and recently divorced mothers' stressful events and distress: Tracing change across time. *Journal of Marriage and the Family, 59,* 219–232.

Lueptow, L., McClendon, M., & McKeon, J. (1979). Father's occupation and son's personality: Findings and questions for the emerging linkage hypothesis. *Sociological Quarterly, 20,* 463–475.

Lynd, R. S., & Lynd, H. M. (1929). *Middletown: A study in contemporary American culture.* New York: Harcourt Brace.

McLeod, J., & Shanahan, M. (1993). Poverty, parenting, and children's mental health. *American Sociological Review, 58,* 351–366.

McLoyd, V. C. (1998). Socioeconomic disadvantage and child development, *American Psychologist, 53,* 185–204.

McLoyd, V. C. (1997). The impact of poverty and low socioeconomic status on the socioemotional functioning of African American children and adolescents: Mediating effects. In R. D. Taylor & M. C. Wang (Eds.), *Social and emotional adjustment and family relations in ethnic minority families* (pp. 7–34). Mahwah, NJ: Lawrence Erlbaum Associates.

Menaghan, E. G., & Parcels, T. L. (1991). Social sources of change in children's home environments: The effects of parental occupational experiences and family conditions. *Journal of Marriage and the Family, 57,* 69–94.

Miller, D., & Swanson, G. E. (1958). *The changing American parent.* New York: Wiley.

Parcels, T. L., & Menaghan, E. G. (1994). *Parents' jobs and children's lives.* New York: deGruyter.

Plomin, R., & Daniels, D. (1987). Why are children in the same family so different from one another? *Behavioral and Brain Sciences, 10,* 1–22.

Rozenzsweig, M. R., & Wolpin, K. I. (1994). Are there increasing returns to intergenerational production of humsn capital? Maternal schooling and child intellectual development. *Journal of Human Resources, 29,* 670–693.

Rumbaut, R. G. (2000). Profiles in resilience: Educational achievement and ambition among children of immigrants in Southern California. In R. D. Taylor & M. C. Wang (Ed.), *Resilience across contexts: Family, work, culture, and community* (pp. 257–294). Mahwah, NJ: Lawrence Erlbaum Associates.

Sameroff, A. J., Seifer, R., Baldwin, A., & Baldwin, B. (1993). Stability of intelligence from preschool to adolescence: The influence of social and family risk factors. *Child Development, 64*, 80–97.

Scarr, S. (1992). Developmental theories of the 1990s: Developmental and individual differences. *Child Development, 63*, 1–19.

Slaughter-Defoe, D. T., Nakagawa, K., Takanishi, R., & Johnson, D. J. (1990). Toward cultural–ecological perspectives on schooling and achievement in African- and Asian-American children. *Child Development, 61*, 363–383.

Smith, J., Brooks-Gunn, J., & Kliebanov, P. (1997). Consequences of living in poverty for young children's cognitive and verbal ability and early school achievement. In G. Duncan & J. Brooks-Gunn (Eds), *Consequences of growing up poor* (pp. 132–189). New York: Russell Sage.

Steinberg, L. D., Dornbusch, S. M., & Brown, B. B. (1992). Ethnic differences in adolescent achievement: An ecological perspective. *American Psychologist, 47*, 723–729.

Wachs, T. D. (1983). The use and abuse of environment in behavior-genetic research. *Child Development, 54*, 396–407.

Wachs, T. D. (1987). The relevance of the concept of nonshared environment to the study of environmental influences: A paradigmatic shift or just some gears slipping? *Behavioral and Brain Sciences, 10*, 41–42.

Walker H. A. (1988). Black-white differences in marriage and family patterns. In S. M. Dornbusch & M. H. Strober (Eds.), *Feminism, children, and the new families* (pp. 87–112). New York: Guilford.

Waters, M. C. (1996). The intersection of gender, race, and ethnicity in identity development of Caribbean American teens. In B. J. Ross-Leadbeater & N. Way (Eds.), *Urban girls: resisting stereotypes, creating identities* (pp. 65–81). New York: New York University Press.

Waters, E., & Crandall, V. J. (1964). Social class and observed maternal behavior from 1940–1960. *Child Development, 35*, 1021–1032.

Warner, W. L., & Lunt, P. S. (1942). *The status system of a modern community.* New Haven, CT: Yale University Press.

Wellman, H. M. (1990). *The child's theory of mind.* Cambridge, MA: MIT Press.

U.S. Bureau of the Census (2001). *Statistical abstract of the United States (121st ed).* Washington, DC: U.S. Government Printing Office.

II

SES: Parenting and Child Development

6

Causes and Consequences of SES-Related Differences in Parent-to-Child Speech

Erika Hoff
Florida Atlantic University

INTRODUCTION

The goal of this chapter is to understand how SES shapes children's language learning environments and their language development, in the larger context of how socioeconomic status (SES) shapes children's lives and developmental trajectories. The literature provides ample evidence that both the environments in which children acquire language and the rate of children's language development vary as a function of family SES. Environmental differences arise, at least in part, from SES-related differences in the ways in which mothers interact with and talk to their children. Compared to lower-SES mothers, higher-SES mothers talk more to their children and are more responsive to their children's verbalizations (Hoff, Laursen, & Tardif, 2002). Higher-SES mothers use speech more for the purpose of initiating and sustaining conversation with their children and less for the purpose of directing their children's behavior; they also use more complex syntax and a more varied vocabulary in talking to their children (Hoff et al., 2002; Huttenlocher, Vasilyeva, Cymerman, & Levine, 2002). SES-related differences in children's language skills are consistently found from at least the age of 2 years (see Arriaga, Fenson, Cronan, & Pethick, 1998; Hoff, in press). The domains of children's language that differ as a function of SES include the functions to which language is put (e.g., Tough, 1982), the grammatical complexity of speech (e.g., Arriaga et al., 1998; Huttenlocher et al., 2002), and vocabulary (e.g., Arriaga et al., 1998).

This chapter seeks to explain how SES has these effects on language environments and language development, first, by describing the SES-related differences in language environments and child language observed in one sample of mid- and high-SES families in the midwestern United States, and, second, by investigating hypothesized processes that link SES to language environments and developmental outcomes. The chapter will be organized around the following four questions:

(1) "What are the SES-related differences in parent-to-child speech?"
(2) "What causes SES-related differences in parent-to-child speech?"
(3) "What are the SES-related differences in children's early language development?"
(4) "Can the SES-related differences in children's vocabularies be attributed to differences in the speech they hear?"

To foreshadow the conclusions, the findings will demonstrate that parent-to-child speech does differ by socioeconomic stratum, even within a relatively advantaged and culturally homogeneous sample. These differences in parent-to-child speech appear to reflect more general SES-related differences in language use. By the time children are 2 years old, they, too, demonstrate SES-related differences in language. This relation of SES to child language is mediated by the nature of the language environment parents create for their children. Parents from higher socioeconomic strata create different language environments than parents from lower socioeconomic strata as a result of both characteristic differences in their language use and differences in the interactive settings they choose.

METHOD USED TO STUDY SES, PARENT-TO-CHILD SPEECH, AND LANGUAGE DEVELOPMENT

Sample

The data come from a sample of 63 mothers and their children who were between $1^1/_2$ and $2^1/_2$ years of age at start of the study. These participants were selected from two different socioeconomic strata, which were defined in terms of parental education and occupation. Thirty of these children came from mid-SES families in which both parents had no education past high school other than technical training and, if employed, they worked in unskilled, semi-skilled, or service positions. Thirty-three of these children came from high-SES families in which both parents had at least two years of college (in fact all but one parent were college graduates), and, if employed, they worked in professional or managerial positions. All the families were European American, monolingual native speakers of English. They lived in the small cities, rural, and suburban areas of southeastern Wisconsin. By design, none of the mothers worked outside the home more than 15 hours per week. According to national census data for the time this research was conducted, approximately 50% of mothers would not meet this criterion, although in the area of the midwestern United States where this study was conducted, this selection criterion probably excluded fewer than 50%. One of the high-SES mothers was a single parent; four of the mid-SES mothers were single parents. All of the fathers who were present in the household were employed, with the exception of one father in the mid-SES sample who was disabled. Income was not a selection criterion but did differ between the groups. According to self-report, the median family income for the mid-SES sample was in the $20,000 to $30,000 category; the median family income for the high-SES sample was in the $30,000 to $40,000. (These numbers reflect the fact that these data were collected in the 1980s from single-income families in Wisconsin. As a benchmark, assistant professors of psychology, at that time and in that area, were being hired at a salary of $24,000.) The two SES groups also differed in maternal age. The mean age of the mid-SES mothers was 26.1 years, $SD = 3.6$; the mean age of the high-SES mothers was 33.3 years, $SD = 4.0$.

This study, then, examines only a portion of the SES continuum—a portion at the high end. There are advantages and disadvantages to such a sample. An advantage is that it affords the opportunity to study differences associated with education and occupation unconfounded by poverty. Although there were income differences between these two groups, neither was living in poverty. None of the children in this study would be described as at-risk. A disadvantage of the nature of this sample, of course, is that the data may not contribute to understanding the factors that affect those children who truly are at risk by virtue of their families' SES.

The children from these two socioeconomic strata were not different in their levels of productive language at the start of the study. They were selected to be at the point where they were all just beginning to combine words but where no more than 50% of their utterances were multiword utterances. There were no significant group differences in either the mean length of the children's utterances (MLU) or in the mean number of different words they produced at the start of the study. Each group contained approximately equal numbers of boys and girls and first born and later born children.

Procedure

Three separate visits were made to the participants in their homes—when the children were an average of 22 months old, 24 months old, and $4\frac{1}{2}$ years old. At the first two visits, the mother and child were videotaped in dyadic interaction in four settings: mealtime, dressing, book reading, and toy play. The books and toys were provided by the researchers. The taping sessions were scheduled to coincide with the child's usual time for eating breakfast or lunch. The durations of the mealtime and dressing interactions were allowed to vary naturally and were taped in their entirety. The reading and toy play interactions were taped for no more than 25 minutes each. The videotapes were transcribed, and those transcripts provide the data base for measures of maternal and child speech at Time 1 and Time 2. Forty-three of these mothers and children were visited again within two weeks of the child's reaching $4^1/_2$ years; 23 of these participants were high SES and 20 were mid SES. At that time, mother–child interaction was recorded during mealtime and toy play. In addition, the child's narrative production was assessed using the frog story procedure (Bamberg, 1987; Berman & Slobin, 1994), and each child was administered two standardized vocabulary tests: the Peabody Picture Vocabulary Test (PPVT; Dunn & Dunn, 1981) and the Expressive One-Word Picture Vocabulary Test (Gardner, 1979). The data at Time 3 consist of the child's spontaneous speech transcribed from recorded mother–child interaction, the child's narrative production, and the child's test scores. These, then, are the sources of data to be drawn on in considering the questions with which we began.

WHAT ARE THE SES-RELATED DIFFERENCES IN PARENT-TO-CHILD SPEECH?

This question was addressed with data from the Time 1 transcripts of the mealtime, dressing, and toy play interactions. The reading session was excluded because it was very overrepresented in the speech samples compared to the proportion of time mothers actually spend reading with their children and because talk during reading has unique characteristics (Hoff-Ginsberg, 1991; Snow, Arlman-Rupp, Hassing, Jobse, Joosten, & Vorster, 1976). The measures, the mean value for each group, and the results of those comparisons are presented in Table 6.1.

The speech high-SES mothers address to their children differs from the speech mid-SES mothers address to their children in the following ways. High-SES mothers produce more speech per unit of time interacting (when the duration of interaction is allowed to vary naturally, it also becomes evident that high-SES mothers sustain conversation longer than mid-SES mothers, thereby further increasing the amount of speech their children hear, Hoff-Ginsberg, 1994), they use a richer vocabulary, they more frequently produce contingent replies to their child's utterances, they issue fewer behavior directives, and they ask more conversation-eliciting questions. There is no SES-related difference in maternal MLU.

These findings suggest that high SES children experience a different language-learning environment from mid-SES children on two dimensions. One dimension is

TABLE 6.1
Properties of Mothers' Child-Directed Speech by SES

	Mid-SES	High-SES
Rate of speech (words/minute)	38.9	48.9 **
	(11.9)	(14.4)
Word tokens	1570	2165 ***
	(538)	(833)
Word types	269	324 **
	(58)	(92)
Mean length of utterance (MLU)	3.48	3.63 ns
	(.35)	(.49)
Topic-continuing replies to the child[1]	34.9	41.8 *
	(11.7)	(12.6)
Directives[2]	24.7	16.3 ***
	(8.0)	(6.3)
Conversation-eliciting questions[2]	28.6	33.7 *
	(9.8)	(8.5)

[1]Calculated as a percent of child-produced utterances.
[2]Calculated as a percent of all utterances in input.
*p < .05, **p < .01, ***p < .001 for difference between mid-SES and high-SES samples by 2-tailed t-test.

social. High-SES mothers are more encouraging of child talk and more responsive to child talk than are mid-SES mothers. In contrast, the speech that mid-SES mothers address to their children is more frequently for the purpose of directing the child's behavior and less frequently for the purpose of eliciting or continuing child talk. Another dimension is what is referred to elsewhere as the data-providing dimension of conversational experience (Hoff & Naigles, 2002; Hoff-Ginsberg, 1986). The children with high-SES mothers hear more speech, and they hear a more varied vocabulary than do the children with mid-SES mothers.

WHAT CAUSES SES-RELATED DIFFERENCES IN PARENT-TO-CHILD SPEECH?

Three hypotheses have been offered in discussions of why parents from different socioeconomic strata differ in the way they talk to their children: (1) they hold different beliefs about their children's communicative abilities and the appropriateness of talking to children (Heath, 1983); (2) they differ in the time available for leisurely conversation—lower SES parents must spend their time in the goal-directed activities of feeding and dressing and do not have time for toy play and book reading (e.g., Snow, Perlmann, & Nathan, 1987); and (3) they have different styles of language use which are manifest in all conversations, regardless of addressee (Hoff-Ginsberg, 1991).

The first hypothesis can be rejected as an explanation for the findings from this sample. All the mothers were interviewed regarding their beliefs about their children's communicative abilities and the age at which they started talking to their children; and there were no SES-related differences on either measure (Hoff-Ginsberg, 1991). The second hypothesis can also be rejected, again for this sample, because it is contradicted by the observed main effects of setting and the setting x SES interactions. The main effects of setting were such that the features that characterized the speech of high-SES mothers more than mid-SES mothers were maximized in book reading, but not at all in toy play. In fact, toy play showed the highest usage of behavior directives of all settings (Hoff-Ginsberg, 1991). (This is not surprising if you think about the nature of the toys designed for 2 year olds. Most involve putting square pegs in square holes, round pegs in round holes, and so on. Mothers guide their children with suggestions. It would be a bizarre mother who tried to have a conversation about something else with a child bent on getting Grover to fit down the chimney.) The Setting x SES interactions were such that the SES-related differences in mothers' speech were greatest in the routine, ostensibly goal-directed settings of dressing and mealtime, and the SES-related differences were attenuated during toy play and book reading.

That leaves the third hypothesis, for which there is support in the data. When the speech that the mothers produced in the interviews about their beliefs and conversational practices is examined, significant SES-related differences in the speech addressed to the researcher emerge. The high-SES mothers produced more utterances, produced longer utterances, and used a richer vocabulary than the mid-SES mothers. Thus, it appears that the SES-related differences in the way these mothers talked to their children are just one manifestation of general SES-related differences in language use and conversational style.

Having established that there are SES-related differences in children's language learning experiences because there are SES-related differences in how adults use language, we now turn to the question of whether there are also SES-related differences in children's language development.

WHAT ARE THE SES-RELATED DIFFERENCES IN CHILDREN'S EARLY LANGUAGE DEVELOPMENT?

The SES-related differences in these children's language at 2 years can be described on the basis of analyses of their spontaneous speech in mother–child conversation (Hoff-Ginsberg, 1998), and the differences at 4½ years can be described on the basis of spontaneous speech in mother–child conversation, elicited narratives (i.e., frog stories), and standardized vocabulary tests.

The samples of the children's speech collected at 2 years were analyzed for their lexical, grammatical, and discourse properties (Hoff-Ginsberg, 1998). In terms of lexical properties, the children from high-SES families used a larger vocabulary in conversation with their mothers—basing the vocabulary estimates on equivalent-sized speech samples for all children. The difference in the range of vocabulary used was particularly pronounced within the domain of object labels. There were no group differences in the grammatical properties of children's speech, as indexed by MLU. In terms of discourse properties, the high-SES children produced more speech that immediately followed a maternal utterance (i.e., adjacent speech), but because the high-SES mothers spoke more, they provided more opportunity for their children to do that. Thus, it is not clear that this difference reflects any greater skill on the part of the high-SES children. In terms of a clear measure of conversational skill, the frequency of contingent replies (Bloom, Rocissano, & Hood, 1976), the groups did not differ. In sum, in this sample of children at age 2 years, there are SES-related differences in the size of the vocabularies they use. This effect of SES holds across birth order and sex. There were also main effects of birth order (Hoff-Ginsberg, 1998), but there were no significant interactions between SES and either birth order or sex.

The speech samples collected at $4^1/_2$ years have thus far been investigated only for their lexical properties. In the context of mother–child conversation, the high-SES children used a larger vocabulary than the mid-SES children, but the difference was observable only when the word count was based on the entire conversation. Like their mothers, the high-SES children talked more than their mid-SES counterparts resulting in more words and more different words produced. There was no difference in the number of different words used in equal-size samples of conversational speech. The high-SES children scored significantly higher on the test of productive vocabulary (EOWPVT), but there was no difference on the test of comprehension vocabulary (PPVT). Last, there was no difference in the vocabulary used in narrative production which was elicited by the researcher. The measures of child speech at 2 and $4^1/_2$ years, the means for each group, and the statistically significant differences are indicated in Table 6.2.

In sum, we can say that of the aspects of language development assessed in this sample (i.e., syntax, vocabulary, and conversational skill), SES-related differences were observed only for vocabulary and only in some contexts. Although this may seem to be a modest effect, several considerations make it worth pursuing. One is the advantaged nature of the lower group in this study. If these differences can be observed between two such similar groups, the differences between high SES-children and truly low-SES children are likely to be much greater. Indeed, several sources of data suggest that they are (e.g., Arriaga et al., 1998; Hart & Risley, 1995). Furthermore, vocabulary is important. Vocabulary is a large component of standard IQ tests, and vocabulary knowledge contributes to success in early reading (Chall, Jacobs, & Baldwin, 1990).

TABLE 6.2

Measures of Child Language Proficiency at Age 2 Years and 4$\frac{1}{2}$ Years by SES

	Mid-SES	High-SES
At 2 years		
Vocabulary		
Number of word types	45.53	51.00 *
	(9.46)	(15.19)
Number of object label types	9.73	12.76 **
	(4.41)	(5.11)
Grammar		
Mean length of utterance (MLU)	1.62	1.63 ns
	(.21)	(.29)
Conversational skill		
Adjacent speech[1]	60.3	66.8 *
	(12.1)	(10.9)
Contingent adjacent speech[2]	51.7	50.5 ns
	(11.9)	(11.5)
At 4$\frac{1}{2}$ years–vocabulary		
Number of word types in mother-child	236.8	271.3 *
conversation	(66.1)	(54.6)
Number of word types in 100 utterances of	116.6	123.0 ns
conversational speech	(14.1)	(23.2)
Number of word types in frog stories	96.1	79.8 ns
	(29.6)	(17.8)
PPVT	56.0	59.8 ns
	(15.1)	(14.3)
EOWPVT	46.8	58.3 **
	(17.6)	(8.7)

[1]Calculated as a percent of child utterances.

[2]Calculated as a percent of adjacent utterances.

*p < .05, **p < .01, ***p < .001 for difference between mid-SES and high-SES samples by 1-tailed t-test.

CAN THE SES-RELATED DIFFERENCES IN CHILDREN'S VOCABULARIES BE ATTRIBUTED TO DIFFERENCES IN THE SPEECH CHILDREN HEAR?

There is first a logically prior question to consider, and that is whether the observed vocabulary differences are real. It has been argued at different times and in different quarters that observed SES-related differences in vocabulary, and in language more generally, are only reflections of bias in the techniques or instruments used to assess vocabulary. Specifically, it has been suggested that children from different social strata do not differ in how many words they know—just in which words they know. Furthermore, it has been argued that interviews with unfamiliar adults depress the language performance of lower-SES children more than they do the performance of higher-SES children (Labov, 1970). There are counter arguments and evidence in the literature (e.g., Arriaga et al., 1998), and the findings of the present study also argue against such views. The differences at age 2 years were observed in spontaneous speech, and thus, those differences could not be a matter of bias in the particular words included on a test. Although at $4^1/_2$ years no differences were observed in equivalent samples of spontaneous speech or in narrative production, it could be that this reflects the fact that ordinary mealtime and toy play conversation and telling a story about a boy, a dog, and a frog are not sufficiently taxing of an average 4 1/2-year-old's vocabulary to reveal differences among children. That is, even at age $4^1/_2$, the vocabulary that discriminates one child from another may be sufficiently rare that these situations do not require it. Furthermore, and contrary to the common view that the most familiar setting elicits the highest performance, we found that the mid-SES children did comparatively better than the high-SES children in the narrative task with the examiner than in conversation with their mothers. The mothers who talk less and use a more restricted vocabulary may not only provide less rich data for vocabulary learning, they may also elicit less advanced vocabulary use concurrently.

With respect to why SES-related differences appear in the standardized test of production vocabulary but not comprehension vocabulary, the data suggest two possibilities. One is that there truly are SES-related differences only in productive vocabularies. The other refers to the fact that the productive vocabulary test is almost exclusively nouns, and this may be where SES-related differences are concentrated. The present data do not provide a way of distinguishing between the two possibilities.

The foregoing arguments suggest that the differences observed in the total vocabulary and object label vocabulary used in spontaneous speech at 2 years and in the vocabulary produced in the EOWPVT at $4^1/_2$ years are real differences, and we turn our attention now to trying to explain them. Because the nature of the differences and the available data are different in each case, the procedures for seeking explanations differ as well.

The search for an explanation of the SES-related differences in children's vocabulary at 2 years begins with the results of other analyses that suggest that variation in vocabulary growth from Time 1 to Time 2 is significantly related to the lexical richness of the speech children hear (i.e., the number of different words used) and to the length of maternal utterances (Hoff & Naigles, 2002). (At this age, where vocabulary development is the outcome, the social-pragmatic features of conversation seem not to have an effect on language development. Growth in object label vocabularies shows a similar pattern of relations to input except that it is specifically related to the number of object label types in input as well (Hoff, 2002). The next analyses asked whether these input effects explain the SES-related differences in children's vocabularies. Separate hierarchical multiple regressions were conducted for both word types and object label types, first entering the properties of input that were significant predictors of individual differences in these out-come measures and then entering SES to ask if there is any variance attributable to SES remaining after variance attributable to properties of input is accounted for.

For number of word types, SES alone (entered as a dummy variable with two values) accounts for 5% of the variance. SES and the input measures together account for 37% of the variance, but the variance uniquely attributable to SES is 1%, which is not significant. It appears that the SES-related differences in charac-teristics of mothers' speech to children fully explain the SES-related differences in the vocabularies children used.

For object labels, however, the multiple regression analyses tell a less complete story. SES alone accounts for 9% of the variance in the number of different object labels children use. SES and the input measures together account for 32% of the variance, and the variance uniquely attributable to SES remains a significant 4%. One possible explanation of this remaining variance associated with SES is that there are other properties of maternal speech that are associated with SES and predictive of language development that were not measured in the present study. One candidate property is the explicit teaching of object labels. It has been sug-gested that high-SES mothers in the United States are more likely to play explicit object-labeling games with their children than lower-SES mothers (Goldfield & Reznick, 1990; Lawrence & Shipley, 1996), and this was not a feature of maternal speech that we coded. To pursue this possibility, we returned to the transcripts of mother–child interaction at Time 1 and counted the frequency of mothers' explicit object naming (e.g., *This is a* _____; *See the* _____) in the toy play and book read-ing sessions. The findings were that there was no difference associated with SES, but there was a significant difference associated with setting. Explicit labeling was more frequent during book reading interaction for both mid-SES and high-SES mothers (Hoff, 2002). Other sources suggest that book reading is a more frequent adult–child activity in higher-SES homes (Heath, 1983, U.S. Department of Edu-cation, 1999). Together, our finding that reading elicits more parental object label teaching and the evidence that reading occurs more frequently in higher-SES homes suggest that family SES affects children's language learning environments—not only via general characteristics of parent-to-child speech but also via the influence on parent-to-child speech of the interactive settings in which mothers chose to spend their time. The SES-related differences in children's language learning en-vironments mediate the relation between SES and early vocabulary development. This conclusion dovetails with findings from older children that language experi-ence also accounts for SES-related differences in school-aged children's syntactic knowledge (Huttenlocher et al., 2002). Together these findings argue that lan-guage experience plays a powerful role in language development, and, thus, social factors that create differences in children's language experience will also create differences in their language development.

Returning to the present data, we consider the source of the difference in the EOWPVT scores at $4^1/_2$. Although analyses of children's language experience and its relation to test performance have not been done for this sample, clues regarding potential sources can be found in analysis of the particular items that differentiated the high-SES children from the mid-SES children. The words that the high-SES children produced correctly at least 10% more frequently than the mid-SES children were the following: *tiger, triangle, square, ear, wheel, typewriter, fireplace, dentist, penguin, rocket, suitcases, fruit, stool, peanut, jewelry, bench, ruler, children, wall, instruments, cloud(s), vegetables, furniture, saddle, well, drinks, binoculars, anchor, Statue of Liberty, propeller, wrench, food, cash register, skeleton, pier,* and *trumpet.*

The question, then, is what explains why one group of children knows these words, and another group at the same age does not. For some words, it seems most likely that the children who got them wrong actually knew the words but got the test item wrong for other reasons. In some cases the stimulus was a picture of several items, and the required response was a superordinate term (e.g., furniture, food). In other cases, the picture itself seemed particularly difficult to interpret. For example, the picture of clouds looks nothing like clouds in the sky—although it does look very much like a line drawing of clouds such as one would see in a book. In other cases, the mid-SES children may really not have known the meanings of the words they missed because of SES-related differences in experience (e.g., tiger, fireplace, trumpet). Of course, the experience that allows a child to know what a tiger is does not have to be an African safari or even a trip to the zoo. Here again, the SES-related differences in children's literacy experiences may result in real differences in vocabulary knowledge at $4^1/_2$ years, just as differences in language input provided by mothers, including, perhaps, language input occasioned by book reading, results in real vocabulary differences at 2 years.

CONCLUSIONS

To conclude, we begin by repeating the questions we set out to answer: (1) "Are there SES-related differences in parent-to-child speech?"; (2) "What causes them?"; (3) "Are there SES-related differences in children's language development?"; and (4) "Are they the result of SES-related differences in parent-to-child speech?" On the basis of data from a sample of 33 college-educated mothers and 30 high school educated mothers and their children, we suggest the following answers:

(1) Yes, there are SES-related differences in parent-to-child speech. In talk-ing to their children, higher-SES mothers sustain conversation longer, elicit more conversation from their children, and are more responsive to

their children's conversational contributions. They also illustrate a larger vocabulary in the speech they produce.

(2) The differences in the nature of child-directed speech parallel SES-related differences in adult-directed speech, suggesting that the differences in child-directed speech are one manifestation of general SES-related differences in language use.

(3) There are SES-related differences in children's rates of vocabulary growth at age 2, in the amount and lexical richness of speech produced in conversation at age $4^1/_2$, and in a standardized measure of productive vocabulary at $4^1/_2$.

(4) These SES-related differences in children's language development can be attributed to differences in their language experience. The SES-related difference in vocabulary at age 2 can be almost fully accounted for by properties of child-directed speech that differ by SES. Ancillary analyses suggest that SES-related differences in the amount of time spent book reading may further contribute to those differences. At age $4^1/_2$, the observed differences are, arguably, attributable to differences in the children's talkativeness and language use that parallel differences observed in adults and to differential experience with book reading.

The results of the research reviewed here provide strong evidence that SES shapes children's language learning environments and, thus, influences their development of language. The influence on language learning environments occurs via influences of SES on the speech parents address to children. Two factors mediate this relation between SES and parents' child-directed speech. One is general SES-related differences in how adults use language. Higher-SES parents talk more and use of a richer vocabulary. The other is SES-related differences in the settings in which parents choose to interact with their children. Higher-SES parents spend more time reading books with their children and book reading is associated with rich vocabulary use and explicit teaching of object labels. These SES-related differences in the language learning environments that parents provide, in turn, produce SES-related differences in children's language development. Higher-SES children develop language, particularly vocabulary, at a faster rate than lower-SES children because, compared to lower SES children, they experience environments that provide them with more information about the lexicon of their language.

ACKNOWLEDGMENTS

The research reported here was supported by grants to the author from the National Institutes of Health and the Spencer Foundation.

REFERENCES

Arriaga, R. J., Fenson, L., Cronan, T., & Pethick, S. J. (1998). Scores on the MacArthur Communicative Development Inventory of children from low- and middle-income families. *Applied Psycholinguistics, 19,* 209–223.

Bamberg, M. (1987). *The acquisition of narratives.* Berlin: deGruyter.

Berman, R. A., & Slobin, D. I. (1994). *Relating events in narrative: A crosslinguistic developmental study.* Hillsdale, NJ: Lawrence Erlbaum Associates.

Bloom, L., Rocissano, L., & Hood, L. (1976). Adult-child discourse: Developmental interaction between information processing and linguistic knowledge. *Cognitive Psychology, 8,* 521–551.

Chall, J. S., Jacobs, V. A., & Baldwin, L. E. (1990). *The reading crisis: Why poor children fall behind.* Cambridge, MA: Harvard University Press.

Dunn, L. M., & Dunn, L. M. (1981). *Peabody picture vocabulary test-revised.* Circle Pines, MN: American Guidance Service.

Gardner, M. F. (1979). *Expressive one-word picture vocabulary test.* Novato, CA: Academic Therapy Publications.

Goldfield, B. A., & Reznick, J. S. (1990). Early lexical acquisition: Rate, content, and the vocabulary spurt. *Journal of Child Language, 17,* 171–184.

Hart, B., & Risley, T. (1995). *Meaningful differences in the everyday experience of young American children.* Baltimore, MD: Brookes.

Heath, S. B. (1983). *Ways with words.* Cambridge, England: Cambridge University Press.

Hoff, E. (in press). Poverty effects. In R. D. Kent (Ed.), *MIT encyclopedia of communication disorders.* Cambridge, MA: MIT Press.

Hoff, E. (2002). *Everyday conversation and book reading: How maternal speech mediates the relation between SES and early vocabulary development.* Unpublished manuscript.

Hoff, E., Laursen, B., & Tardif, T. (2002). Socioeconomic status and parenting. In M. H. Bornstein (Ed.), *Handbook of parenting, 2nd ed.* (pp. 231–252). Mahwah: NJ: Lawrence Erlbaum Associates.

Hoff, E., & Naigles, L. (2002). How children use input in acquiring a lexicon. *Child Development, 73,* 418–433.

Hoff-Ginsberg, E. (1986). Function and structure in maternal speech: Their relation to the child's development of syntax. *Developmental Psychology, 22,* 155–163.

Hoff-Ginsberg, E. (1991). Mother-child conversation in different social classes and communicative settings. *Child Development, 62,* 782–796.

Hoff-Ginsberg, E. (1994). Influences of mother and child on maternal talkativeness. *Discourse Processes, 18,* 105–117.

Hoff-Ginsberg, E. (1998). The relation of birth order and socioeconomic status to children's language experience and language development. *Applied Psycholinguistics, 19,* 603–629.

Huttenlocher, J., Vasilyeva, M., Cymerman, E., & Levine, S. (2002). Language input at home and at school: Relation to child syntax. *Cognitive Psychology, 43.*

Labov, W. (1970). The logic of nonstandard English. In F. Williams (Ed.), *Language and poverty: Perspectives on a theme* (pp. 153–189). Chicago: Markham.

Lawrence, V., & Shipley, E. F. (1996). Parental speech to middle and working class chidren from two racial groups in three settings. *Applied Psycholinguistics, 17,* 233–256.

Snow, C. E., Arlman-Rupp, A., Hassing, Y., Jobse, J., & Vorster, J. (1976). Mothers' speech in three social classes. *Journal of Psycholinguistic Research, 5,* 1–20.

Snow, D., Perlmann, R., & Nathan, D. (1987). Why routines are different: Toward a multiple-factors model of the relation between input and language acquisition. In K. E. Nelson & A. van Kleck (Eds.), *Children's language* (vol. 6, pp. 65–98). Hillsdale, NJ: Lawrence Erlbaum Associates.

Tough, J. (1982). Language, poverty, and disadvantage in school. In L. Feagans, & D. C. Farran (Eds.), *The language of children reared in poverty: Implications for evaluation and intervention* (pp. 3–18). New York: Academic Press.

U.S. Department of Education (1999). National Center for Education Statistics, 1999 National Household Education Survey, published in Federal Interagency Forum on Child and Family Statistics, Table ED1.

7

Age and Ethnic Variations in Family Process Mediators of SES

Robert H. Bradley and Robert F. Corwyn
University of Arkansas at Little Rock

INTRODUCTION

For more than half a century there has been a keen interest in the relation between socioeconomic status (SES) and child development. Researchers throughout the social sciences and health professions have long considered SES to be one of the major influences on child well-being. For the past decade, there has been a concerted effort to identify the processes and factors that mediate the relation, with the hope not only of advancing science but of constructing policies and programs that benefit children. The number of candidate processes proposed for consideration is legion, some occurring prior to birth (e.g., inadequate nutrition and drug exposure during pregnancy), and still others occurring at later points in development (e.g., peer group affiliations, exposure to environmental teratogens, and the quality of school curricula), others occurring throughout postnatal development (e.g., the quality of parental language, the availability of social support, parental responsiveness, and the availability of material resources; see Bradley & Corwyn, 2002, for a review). Researchers in sociology, psychology, economics, and nutrition, as well as other social and health sciences have offered many models (some quite simple, others quite elaborate) depicting links among SES, various mediation processes, and different developmental outcomes (e.g., Baum, Garofalo, & Yali, 1999; Brody et al., 1994; DeGarmo, Forgatch, & Martinez, 1999; Dodge, Petit, & Bates, 1994; Conger, Ge, Elder, Lorenz, & Simons, 1994; Levanthal & Brooks-Gunn, 2000; McLoyd, 1998).

Many of the ecological developmental models that have been proposed to explain the relation between SES and child well-being include aspects of children's home environments (Brooks-Gunn & Duncan, 1997), such as the quality of the physical environment, the amount of cognitive stimulation available, and parental responsiveness. Most researchers have concentrated their efforts on specific developmental periods even though many of the putative mechanisms are assumed to operate throughout most of childhood. Largely unknown is the extent to which particular home environmental processes specified in proposed developmental models actually mediate relations between SES and various aspects of child well-being during each major developmental period. There is both empirical and theoretical support for believing that some mediators will be less potent during adolescence than early childhood. For example, there is Harris' (1995) argument that peers become increasingly important as children enter school and there is the Scarr and McCartney's (1983) argument that as children age they become more active in seeking and constructing environments that suit their needs and interests. Likewise, there is evidence that, as children age, they spend less and less time at home or in the company of their parents (Jessor, 1993). There is also evidence that the association between some home environmental processes and child outcomes slowly subsides with age (Bradley, 1994). Even so, none of these trends translates to a necessary diminution of the mediating role played by most aspects of the home environment. Moreover, Walberg and Marjoribank's (1976) analysis led them to conclude that adolescents may benefit as much as young children from a stimulating home environment.

Except for studies of very young children, findings pertaining to mediation by specific home environment processes during childhood leave unresolved whether the evidence for mediation observed at a particular period of development (e.g., middle childhood) actually reflects an active process of mediation during that period in the life course or whether it reflects mediation by the same process during an earlier period of development. Because aspects of children's home environments (e.g., parental responsiveness, the availability of learning materials) tend to remain somewhat stable through childhood (Bradley, 1994), evidence for significant mediation later in childhood (e.g., middle childhood) may actually reflect the stability of the environment rather than demonstrating that changes in the environment during a later period are associated with changes in development during the same period. Convincing evidence for active mediation during any period of development requires controlling for changes that occurred in earlier periods of development. Relatedly, because the strongest contributor to developmental status in any one period of life tends to be status during the previous period of life (Koutsoulis & Campbell, 2001), it is important to examine mediation during any period of development net (controlling for) status during the previous period.

The main purpose of this study is to examine two aspects of the home environment frequently included in SES–child development mediational models (learning stimulation, maternal responsiveness) from early childhood to adolescence using data from the National Longitudinal Survey of Youth (NLSY). These relations are examined for three developmental outcomes (vocabulary attainment, achievement test performance, and problem behaviors) in three ethnic groups (African American, European American, and Latin American). There are several reasons to examine these relations in different sociocultural groups: (1) the association between SES and particular child outcomes sometimes varies across ethnic and racial groups (Adler, Marmot, McEwen, & Steward, 1999; Fuligni & Yoshikawa, chap. 4, this volume; McLoyd, 1998); (2) there are differences in the likelihood that children from different cultural groups are exposed to certain parenting practices and household conditions independent of SES (Bradley, Corwyn, McAdoo, & Garcia Coll, 2001); (3) the association between particular aspects of the home environment and child outcomes varies as a function of ethnicity (Bradley et al., 1989; Bradley, Corwyn, & Whiteside-Mansell, 1996); (4) the broader context of family life, separate from SES, varies as a function of ethnicity (most notably perhaps, area of residence) which condition the effects of home environmental factors (Bronfenbrenner, 1995; Brooks-Gunn, Duncan, & Aber, 1997); and (5) cultural arguments suggesting that the meaning and significance of particular parenting behaviors vary as a function of culture–ethnicity (Chao, 1994; Garcia-Coll & Magnusson, 1999; Huston, McLoyd, & Garcia-Coll, 1994).

A secondary purpose of this study is to determine whether constituent components of SES (specifically, maternal education and annual household income) bear similar relations to home environmental processes and child development outcomes as the composite index of SES used in the study (i.e., the Duncan Socioeconomic Index of Occupations: SEI). There is reason to believe that constituent components of SES may bear somewhat different relations to outcomes than the composite measure. For example, maternal education may be more strongly implicated in the mother's efforts to teach children and the purchase of learning materials than occupation of head of household (Bradley & Corwyn, 2002; Duncan & Brooks-Gunn, 1997).

SES AND FAMILY MEDIATORS

Sample

Data for this study came from seven biennial NLSY child data files from 1986–1998 (see Center for Human Resource Research (CHHR), 1995; 1997; 1999; U.S. Department of Labor, 2000). The sample consists of those women from the 6,283 originally recruited as part of the NLSY who had at least one child born

TABLE 7.1
Sample Characteristics by 3 Age Groups

Ages (Years)	3 to < 6 (N = 6,954)	6 to < 10 (N = 5,347)	10 to 15 (N = 3,961)
Percent with dad living in household	67%	62%	56%
Age of mother at birth of first child	25.29	23.41	21.67
Highest grade completed by mother (years)	12.42	12.33	12.08
Median family income	$26,800	$29,340	$32,140

prior to the 1998 biennial assessment. However, beginning with the 1990 survey, data were no longer collected from most of the women, $N = 456$, who were neither in the military nor from women who were part of the oversampling of poor European Americans, $N = 901$. Well over 90% of eligible children received Home Observation for Measurement of the Environment—Short Forms (HOME-SF) scores in the biennial surveys. During later surveys, more children were 15 years of age and therefore ineligible to be interviewed. The number of children assessed started at 4,971 in 1986, rose to 6,509 in 1992, and dropped to 4,924 in 1998.

Table 7.1 displays a demographic breakdown of the samples analyzed for each of the three age periods. Because of the structure of the sampling process, the information on older children is somewhat less representative than is the information on younger children. That is, the original NLSY cohort of women was between 33 and 40 years of age on December 31, 1997. Most of their children have been born, but proportionally fewer have reached the maximum age of children being investigated in NLSY. Because age of mother at the birth of her first child is known to be associated with other demographic characteristics of the mother, the sample for older children is likely to be less representative than the sample for younger children. Table 7.1 indicates that children in the older age groups were more likely to have somewhat younger mothers with less education, and were less likely to be living with their fathers. HOME data were available on fewer children older than 10 because the early adolescent version of HOME was not assessed in 1986 and because many children had not reached age 10 by the 1998 interview date. However, the assessment of child outcomes (Peabody Picture Vocabulary Test: PPVT; Peabody Individual Achievement Test: PIAT; and Behavior Problem Index: BPI) further complicated the sample of children who were assessed with both HOME and child outcome scores concurrently. For example, assessment of the PIAT began at age 5, whereas the early childhood version of HOME was assessed from ages 3 through 5. Therefore, only children who were assessed with the HOME at the age of 5 were eligible to participate in the PIAT assessment. For each of the three age-related versions of HOME, a summary of the number of children with both HOME and child outcome measures are shown in Table 7.2.

TABLE 7.2
Number of Children with Both HOME and Child Outcome Scores (1986–1998)

	African American			European American			Latin American		
	PPVT	*PIAT*	*BPI*	*PPVT*	*PIAT*	*BPI*	*PPVT*	*PIAT*	*BPI*
HOME version									
3 to 6 years	1111	598	1102	2465	1223	2399	735	368	765
6 to 10 years	926	1522	1463	1567	2566	2594	558	921	952
10 to 15 years	1102	1210	1258	1488	1625	1720	642	684	726

Note. PPVT = Peabody Picture Vocabulary Test. PIAT = Peabody Individual Achievement Test. BPI = Behavior Problems Index.

Measures

Socioeconomic Status

The Duncan prestige score was used as a measure of SES. The index is a two-digit prestige score ranging from 0 to 97 that is based on education and income distribution ratings of occupations (Duncan, 1961).

Home Observation for Measurement of the Environment—Short Forms

Experienced, specially trained interviewers assessed the quality of the home environments of children born to mothers participating in the NLSY. The home environment was measured with the HOME-SF. Like the original, full-length versions of HOME (Caldwell & Bradley, 1984), the short form is a combination of observer ratings and mother's report on aspects of the environment. Although items on the original HOME inventory are designed to be scored in a dichotomous fashion (yes or no), some of the items from the HOME-SF from NLSY used 3- or 4-choice ordinal scoring. All of the items were converted to the original scoring metric by collapsing the ordinal categories into the original dichotomous ones.

In an effort to organize the findings, items from the four forms of the HOME-SF were clustered with the aid of factor analysis (maximum likelihood with varimax rotation). For this report, two factors from the early childhood form (learning stimulation and parental responsiveness), two factors from the middle childhood form (learning stimulation and parental responsiveness), and two factors from the early adolescent form (learning stimulation and parental responsiveness) were used. Items for the learning stimulation and parental responsiveness subscales are provided in Table 7.3 (early childhood—3 years to less than 6 years, middle childhood—6 years to less than 10 years, and early adolescent—10 years to less than 15 years).

TABLE 7.3
Home Observational Measurement of the Environment

Learning Stimulation Scale
3 years to less than 6 years

About how often do you read stories to your child?	(1 = at least 3 times a week)
About how many children's books does your child have?	(1 = at least 10 books)
About how many magazines does your family get regularly?	(1 = at least 1)
Does child have the use of a CD player, tape deck, tape recorder, or record player here at home and at least 5 children's CDs, tapes, or records? (May be shared with sister or brother)	(1 = yes, 0 = no)
How often does a family member get a chance to take your child on any kind of outing (shopping, park, picnic, drive-in, and so on)?	(1 = at least 2 times a month)
How often has a family member taken or arranged to take your child to any type of museum (children's, scientific, art, historical, etc.) within the past year?	(1 = at least once)

Responsivity Scale

(Mother–Guardian)'s voice conveyed positive feeling about child	(1 = yes)
(Mother–Guardian) conversed with child at least twice	(1 = yes)
(Mother–Guardian) answered child's questions or requests verbally	(1 = yes)
(Mother–Guardian) caressed, kissed, or hugged child at least once	(1 = yes)

Learning Stimulation Scale
6 years to less than 10 years

Is there a musical instrument (for example, piano, drum, guitar, etc.) that your child can use here at home?	(1 = yes)
Does your family get a daily newspaper?	(1 = yes)
Does your family encourage your child to start and keep doing hobbies?	(1 = yes)
Does your child get special lessons or belong to any organization that encourages activities such as sports, music, art, dance, drama, etc.?	(1 = yes)
How often has a family member taken or arranged to take your child to any type of museum (children's, scientific, art, historical, etc.) within the past year?	(1 = at least once)
How often has a family member taken or arranged to take your child to any type of musical or theatrical performance within the past year?	(1 = at least once)

Responsivity scale

(Mother/Guardian) encouraged child to contribute to the conversation.	(1 = yes)
(Mother/Guardian) answered child's questions or requests verbally	(1 = yes)
(Mother/Guardian)'s voice conveyed positive feeling about child	(1 = yes)
(Mother/Guardian) conversed with child at least twice	(1 = yes)

(Continued)

TABLE 7.3

(Continued)

Learning Stimulation Scale *10 years to less than 15 years*	
About how many books does child have?	(1 = at least 3)
Is there a musical instrument (for example, piano, drum, guitar, etc.) that your child can use here at home?	(1 = yes)
Does your family get a daily newspaper?	(1 = yes)
Does your family encourage your child to start and keep doing hobbies?	(1 = yes)
Does your child get special lessons or belong to any organization that encourages activities such as sports, music, art, dance, drama, etc.?	(1 = yes)
How often has a family member taken or arranged to take your child to any type of museum (children's, scientific, art, historical, etc.) within the past year?	(1 = at least once)
How often has a family member taken or arranged to take your child to any type of musical or theatrical performance within the past year?	(1 = at least once)
Responsivity Scale	
How many times in the past week have you shown child physical affection (kiss, hug, stroke hair, etc.)?	(1 = at least 7 times)
How many times in the past week have you praised your child for doing something worthwhile?	(1 = at least 7 times)

Behavior Problems Index

For children aged 4 and older, mothers completed the 28 item BPI. The scale is designed to measure the frequency, range, and type of childhood behavior problems. It was developed by Zill and Peterson of Child Trends, Inc. for use in the National Health Interview Survey. Items were derived from the Achenbach Child Behavior Checklist and other commonly used child behavior scales. Factor analysis of the 28 items indicates that the scale assesses six areas: antisocial, anxious–depressed, headstrong, hyperactive, immature dependency, and peer conflict/social withdrawal. The alpha for young children was estimated at .89, and for adolescents at .91. The test–retest correlation, corrected using the Spearman-Brown formula, was estimated at .92. A same-gender standardized score was used in this study.

Peabody Individual Achievement Test

Children ages 5 and older were administered three subtests from the PIAT battery: mathematics, reading comprehension, and reading recognition. However, because of technical problems with the reading comprehension subtest for younger children and the fact that the two reading subtests were so highly intercorrelated, only the math and reading recognition subtests were analyzed for this report. The PIAT was standardized on 2,887 children in kindergarten through 12th grade in the late 1960s. One-month test–retest was estimated at .74 for the math subtest. Completion rates for this subtest ranged from about 89% for Latin American to 94% for European American and African American children. The test–retest for the reading recognition subtest was .89. Completion rates for this subtest were similar to those for math. The lower rate of completion for Hispanic children was anticipated given that the test was only administered in English.

Peabody Picture Vocabulary Test–Revised

The Peabody Picture Vocabulary Test (PPVT-R) measures receptive (hearing) vocabulary for standard American English, as well as verbal ability (Dunn and Dunn, 1981). The PPVT-R is predictive of achievement test scores and academic success. Children aged 3 and over were given the PPVT-R. Unlike the other child assessments, PPVT-R was not given to all eligible children during each survey. During most assessment years, the PPVT-R was administered to children at the first assessment point possible (ages 3 to 4 for most children, but at later ages for children who were older by the first year that child assessments were done, 1986). In 1992, however, a renewed effort was made to obtain PPVT-R assessments even if the child had received a prior PPVT-R assessment. In addition, only children ages 4 to 5 and 10 to 11 were given the PPVT-R in 1998. Therefore, the number of PPVT-R scores obtained was 2,798 in 1986, 2,216 in 1988, 1,155 in 1990, 4,758 in 1992, 1,866 in 1994, 2,452 in 1996, and 1,272 in 1998.

Total Net Family Income

It is a summary score representing all the income received in the household. Respondent's income from 10 sources including military, wages, business, alimony, and various government subsidies were combined with four sources of partner–spouse income (military, business, wages, and unemployment).

Highest Grade Completed

It was a single question asking mothers what was the highest grade in school they have completed. Responses ranged from 0 = none, to 20 = 8th year in college or more.

Procedures

The mediating role played by learning stimulation and maternal responsiveness in the relation between SES and four outcome measures (PPVT, PIAT Reading, PIAT Math, and BPI) was examined for three ethnic groups (African American, European American, and Latin American) following the procedures for testing mediation outlined by Baron and Kenny (1986). Four conditions are necessary in order to establish mediation: (1) a significant relation when the dependent variable is regressed on the independent variable (first equation); (2) a significant relation when the mediator is regressed upon the independent variable (second equation); (3) the mediator affects the dependent variable while controlling for the independent variable (third equation); and (4) the effect of the independent variable (SES) on the dependent variable in the first equation was reduced when the effect of the mediator was controlled in the third equation. A reduction of at least .03 was considered partial mediation in this study.

Analyses were first performed on the total group, with the inclusion of two dummy variables representing ethnic status (African American versus other, European American versus other) plus their interactions with the mediator and with SES (four interaction terms). The four interaction terms were included in the second block of a hierarchical regression with the first block containing the main effects of the independent variable, the mediator variable, and the two dummy variables representing ethnic group comparisons. If the second block contributed significantly to the explained variance of the dependent variable, while controlling for the effect of the first block, ethnicity had a conditioning effect on the model and, therefore, the mediation model was run separately for each ethnic group. On the other hand, if there were no ethnic group differences found in the model, only the full sample was tested. In order to determine which paths in the model differed across pairs of ethnic groups, tests of significant differences were conducted using Fisher's z' transformations as outlined by Cohen and Cohen (1983, pp. 53–55). Significantly different paths are shown in Figures 7.1 through 7.4.

In each instance that significant mediation was observed, we conducted four additional sets of analyses in an effort to answer the other study questions: (1) "Is there evidence for mediation when controlling for status on the dependent measure during the previous developmental period?"; (2) "Is there evidence for mediation when controlling for level of input from the same environmental process measure during the previous developmental period?"; (3) "Is there evidence for mediation when maternal education is substituted for SES in the equations?"; and (4) "Is there evidence for mediation when total net family income is substituted for SES in the equations?"

To answer question #1, the data were re-analyzed with scores on the dependent variable obtained during the previous developmental period (the pre-score) included in the equations as a control. This allowed us to determine whether the family process mediation observed applied only to current status on the developmental outcome variable or applied to change in the dependent variable during the developmental period being examined. Our approach to analyzing change conformed to the regression procedure outlined by Cohen and Cohen (1983, pp. 413–421). To answer question #2, we used a similar approach, except we used the score on the same family process variable obtained during the previous developmental period as a control variable in the equation rather than the score on the dependent variable

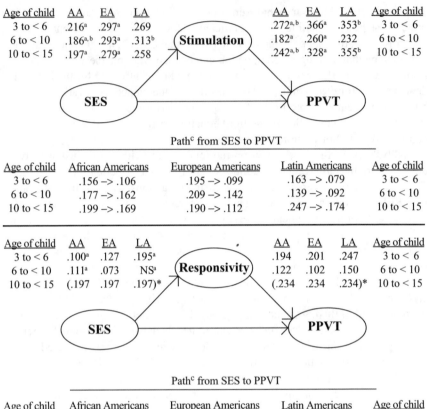

Age of child	AA	EA	LA		AA	EA	LA	Age of child
3 to < 6	.216[a]	.297[a]	.269		.272[a,b]	.366[a]	.353[b]	3 to < 6
6 to < 10	.186[a,b]	.293[a]	.313[b]		.182[a]	.260[a]	.232	6 to < 10
10 to < 15	.197[a]	.279[a]	.258		.242[a,b]	.328[a]	.355[b]	10 to < 15

Path[c] from SES to PPVT

Age of child	African Americans	European Americans	Latin Americans	Age of child
3 to < 6	.156 –> .106	.195 –> .099	.163 –> .079	3 to < 6
6 to < 10	.177 –> .162	.209 –> .142	.139 –> .092	6 to < 10
10 to < 15	.199 –> .169	.190 –> .112	.247 –> .174	10 to < 15

Age of child	AA	EA	LA		AA	EA	LA	Age of child
3 to < 6	.100[a]	.127	.195[a]		.194	.201	.247	3 to < 6
6 to < 10	.111[a]	.073	NS[a]		.122	.102	.150	6 to < 10
10 to < 15	(.197	.197	.197)*		(.234	.234	.234)*	10 to < 15

Path[c] from SES to PPVT

Age of child	African Americans	European Americans	Latin Americans	Age of child
3 to < 6	.146 –> .133	.192 –> .169	.181 –> .139	3 to < 6
6 to < 10	.197 –> .188	.183 –> .178	r =.248	6 to < 10
10 to < 15	(.241 –> .203)*	(.241 –> .203)*	(.241 –> .203)*	10 to < 15

*=No ethnic group differences, so analyses were done on full sample. NS=not significant. AA=African American; EA=European American; LA=Latin American. [a,b]Groups with same superscript are significantly different from each other. [c]First coefficient is bivariate correlation; coefficient following arrow is beta controlling for family process variable.

FIGURE 7.1. Mediation model of the SES/PPVT relationship. Learning stimulation and responsivity as mediators.

measured in the previous developmental period. For example, models in which learning stimulation from the early adolescent HOME were found to mediate a SES/developmental outcome relation, were re-run using learning stimulation from the middle childhood HOME as a control (models in which a mediator from the middle childhood HOME was observed were re-run using the same mediator from the early childhood HOME as a control, and so forth). Evidence that a

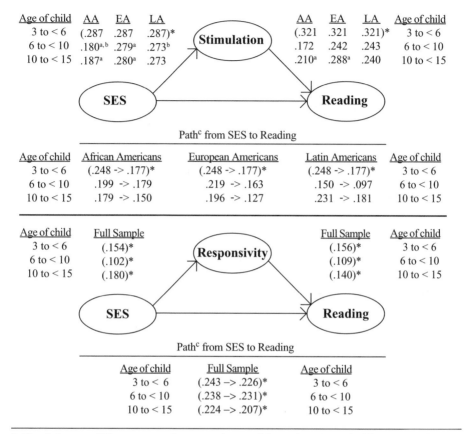

Age of child	AA	EA	LA			AA	EA	LA	Age of child
3 to < 6	(.287	.287	.287)*	**Stimulation**		(.321	.321	.321)*	3 to < 6
6 to < 10	.180[a,b]	.279[a]	.273[b]			.172	.242	.243	6 to < 10
10 to < 15	.187[a]	.280[a]	.273			.210[a]	.288[a]	.240	10 to < 15

Path[c] from SES to Reading

Age of child	African Americans	European Americans	Latin Americans	Age of child
3 to < 6	(.248 -> .177)*	(.248 -> .177)*	(.248 -> .177)*	3 to < 6
6 to < 10	.199 -> .179	.219 -> .163	.150 -> .097	6 to < 10
10 to < 15	.179 -> .150	.196 -> .127	.231 -> .181	10 to < 15

Age of child	Full Sample			Full Sample	Age of child
3 to < 6	(.154)*	**Responsivity**		(.156)*	3 to < 6
6 to < 10	(.102)*			(.109)*	6 to < 10
10 to < 15	(.180)*			(.140)*	10 to < 15

Path[c] from SES to Reading

Age of child	Full Sample	Age of child
3 to < 6	(.243 –> .226)*	3 to < 6
6 to < 10	(.238 –> .231)*	6 to < 10
10 to < 15	(.224 –> .207)*	10 to < 15

*=No ethnic group differences, so analyses were done on full sample. NS=not significant. AA=African American; EA=European American; LA=Latin American. [a,b]Groups with same superscript are significantly different from each other. [c]First coefficient is bivariate correlation; coefficient following arrow is beta controlling for family process variable.

FIGURE 7.2. Mediation model of the SES/PIAT–reading relationship. Learning stimulation and responsivity as mediators.

concurrent, active process of mediation was ongoing during a particular developmental period would be supported if the amount of mediation remained about the same even when controlling for earlier scores on the mediator. If, on the other hand, there was little evidence for mediation once the family process score from the previous developmental period was controlled, then evidence points more to mediation having occurred during some earlier developmental period.

To answer question #3, maternal education was substituted for the Duncan SEI. To answer question #4, total net family income was substituted for the Duncan SEI.

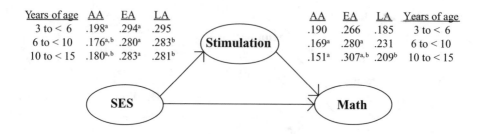

Years of age	AA	EA	LA
3 to < 6	.198[a]	.294[a]	.295
6 to < 10	.176[a,b]	.280[a]	.283[b]
10 to < 15	.180[a,b]	.283[a]	.281[b]

Stimulation

AA	EA	LA	Years of age
.190	.266	.185	3 to < 6
.169[a]	.280[a]	.231	6 to < 10
.151[a]	.307[a,b]	.209[b]	10 to < 15

SES — Math

Path[c] from SES to Math

Age of child	African Americans	European Americans	Latin Americans	Age of child
3 to < 6	.116[a] –> .088	.228[a] –> .171	.218 –> .192	3 to < 6
6 to < 10	.164 –> .143	.198 –> .132	.165 –> .118	6 to < 10
10 to < 15	.184 –> .168	.185 –> .109	.222 –> .170	10 to < 15

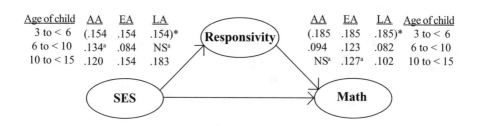

Age of child	AA	EA	LA
3 to < 6	(.154	.154	.154)*
6 to < 10	.134[a]	.084	NS[a]
10 to < 15	.120	.154	.183

Responsivity

AA	EA	LA	Age of child
(.185	.185	.185)*	3 to < 6
.094	.123	.082	6 to < 10
NS[a]	.127[a]	.102	10 to < 15

SES — Math

Path[c] from SES to Math

Age of child	African Americans	European Americans	Latin Americans	Age of child
3 to < 6	(.221 –> .202)*	(.221 –> .202)*	(.221 –> .202)*	3 to < 6
6 to < 10	.201 –> .200	.194 –> .187	r = .195	6 to < 10
10 to < 15	.183 –> .180	.178 –> .163	.181 –> .161	10 to < 15

Note: ( ) = Full sample: Same superscripts=significantly different: NS=not significant. AA=African Americans; EA=European Americans; LA=Latin Americans. [a,b]Groups with same superscript are significantly different from one another. [c]First coefficient is bivariate correlation; coefficient following arrow is beta controlling for family process variable.

FIGURE 7.3. Mediation model of the SES/PIAT–Math relationship. Learning stimulation and responsivity as mediators.

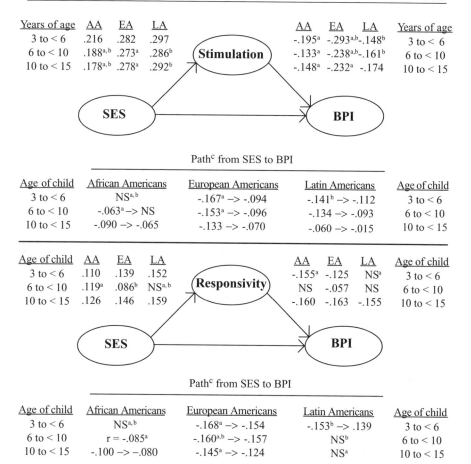

Path[c] from SES to BPI

Age of child	African Americans	European Americans	Latin Americans	Age of child
3 to < 6	NS[a,b]	-.167[a] –> -.094	-.141[b] –> -.112	3 to < 6
6 to < 10	-.063[a] –> NS	-.153[a] –> -.096	-.134 –> -.093	6 to < 10
10 to < 15	-.090 –> -.065	-.133 –> -.070	-.060 –> -.015	10 to < 15

Path[c] from SES to BPI

Age of child	African Americans	European Americans	Latin Americans	Age of child
3 to < 6	NS[a,b]	-.168[a] –> -.154	-.153[b] –> .139	3 to < 6
6 to < 10	r = -.085[a]	-.160[a,b] –> -.157	NS[b]	6 to < 10
10 to < 15	-.100 –> −.080	-.145[a] –> -.124	NS[a]	10 to < 15

*=No ethnic group differences, so analyses were done on full sample. NS=not significant. AA=African American; EA=European American; LA=Latin American. [a,b]Groups with same superscript are significantly different from each other. [c]First coefficient is bivariate correlation; coefficient following arrow is beta controlling for family process variable.

FIGURE 7.4. Mediation model of the SES–BPI relationship. Learning stimulation and responsivity as mediators.

In summary, six sets of analyses were performed: (1) basic tests for mediation on the relation between the Duncan SEI and each outcome variable for learning stimulation and for responsiveness during each developmental period in which outcome data were available, and 2) tests for significant ethnic group differences in each of the three paths in the mediation models. Then for each instance in which significant mediation was observed, four additional sets of analyses were conducted: (3) substituting maternal educational attainment for SES; (4) substituting net family income for SES, and (5) controlling for previous scores on the dependent variable and, (6) controlling for previous scores on the family process variable.

THE MEDIATING ROLE OF HOME
ENVIRONMENTAL PROCESSES

The primary results of analyses done to examine the extent to which learning stimulation and maternal responsiveness function to mediate the relation between SES and the four developmental outcomes examined (PPVT, PIAT Reading, PIAT Math, BPI) are contained in Figures 7.1 through 7.4. Table 7.4 shows the results of the analyses performed to examine questions #1 to #4 for all models where there was evidence of mediation by learning stimulation. There were only two instances of mediation by maternal responsiveness, so those are discussed in text. As an orientation to Table 7.4, there are three columns under the label "Mediation from the Original Model". Column 1 displays the bivariate r between SES and the outcome measure, Column 2 displays the β with the learning stimulation included in the model, and Column 3 displays the change (Δ) as a result of the mediator being included in the model. These coefficients are the same as those found in Figures 7.1 through 7.4. Under the labels, "Maternal Education" and "Family Income" there are also three columns, with coefficients representing the same results as those for the original model (i.e., r, β, and Δ). Under the label "Dependent Variable", there are also three columns. Column 1 contains the β-value for SES when learning stimulation is include in the model, Column 2 contains the β-value for SES when both learning stimulation and the pre-score on the dependent variable are included. Column 3 shows the change (Δ) in β.

Coefficients under the label "Learning Stimulation at Previous Time" are the β-value for SES with learning stimulation during the target developmental period included. This represents the relation between SES and the dependent variable when prescores on learning stimulation are partialled. Column 2 contains the β-value when learning stimulation at both the target developmental period and the previous developmental period are included. Column 3 shows the change (Δ) in β. In effect, prescores on learning stimulation were partialled from the model.

Results pertaining to the basic models relating to mediation, together with results pertaining to questions #1 ("Is there evidence for mediation when controlling for status on the dependent measure during the previous developmental period?") and #2 ("Is there evidence for mediation when controlling for level of input from the same environmental process measure during the previous developmental period?") are described under section headings for each developmental outcome. Because results pertaining to questions #3 ("Is there evidence for mediation when maternal education is substituted for SES in the equations?") and #4 ("Is there

TABLE 7.4

Stimulation as a Mediator of SES, Mother's Education, and Net Family Income

| | | SES | | | Mother's Education | | | Family Income | | | SES Controlling for Previous | | | | | |
| | | | | | | | | | | | Dependent Variable | | | Stimulation | | |
Age	Ethnicity	r	β	Δ	r	β	Δ	r	β	Δ	r	β	Δ	r	β	Δ
							Outcome Variable–PPVT									
3 to < 6	AA	.16	.11	.05	.31	.25	.07	.10	.07	.03		NA		.13	.11	.02
3 to < 6	EA	.20	.10	.10	.23	.14	.09	.10	.04	.06		NA		.16	.11	.05
3 to < 6	LA	.16	.08	.08	.23	.20	.03	.22	.14	.08		NA		.14	.10	.04
6 to < 10	EA	.21	.14	.07	.30	.24	.07	.12	.07	.05		NM		.14	.11	.03
6 to < 10	LA	.14	.09	.05	.35	.30	.04	.10	.07	.03		NM			NM	
10 to > 15	AA	.20	.17	.03	.23	.18	.04	.15	.12	.03		NM		.15	.14	.01
10 to > 15	EA	.19	.11	.08	.26	.19	.08	.11	.06	.06	.15	.09	.06	.11	.09	.02
10 to < 15	LA	.25	.17	.07	.24	.14	.10	.07	.05	.02	.12	.08	.04	.21	.17	.03
							Outcome Variable–Reading Recognition									
3 to < 6	All	.25	.18	.07	.35	.27	.09	.12	.06	.06		NA		.21	.18	.03
6 to < 10	EA	.22	.16	.06	.24	.18	.06	.10	.05	.05	.13	.08	.05	.18	.15	.03
6 to < 10	LA	.15	.10	.05	.22	.16	.06	.08	.06	.02		NM		.10	.08	.02
10 to < 15	EA	.20	.13	.07	.23	.16	.07	.12	.06	.06	.06	$.02^{ns}$	.04	.14	.12	.03
10 to < 15	LA	.23	.18	.05	.18	.11	.07		NM			NM		.19	.17	.03

(Continued)

TABLE 7.4
(Continued)

| Age | Ethnicity | SES | | | Mother's Education | | | Family Income | | | SES Controlling for Previous | | | | | |
| | | | | | | | | | | | Dependent Variable | | | Stimulation | | |
		r	β	Δ	r	β	Δ	r	β	Δ	r	β	Δ	r	β	Δ
Outcome Variable–Piat Math																
3 to < 6	AA	.12	.09	.03	.24	.19	.04		NM			NA		.09	.08	.01
3 to < 6	EA	.23	.17	.06	.27	.20	.07		.04	.04		NA		.20	.18	.02
6 to < 10	EA	.20	.13	.07	.26	.19	.07	.08	.07	.06	.12	.08	.05	.14	.11	.03
6 to < 10	LA	.17	.12	.05	.21	.15	.06	.12	NM		.08	.05^{ns}	.03	.10	.08	.02
10 to < 15	EA	.19	.11	.08	.24	.16	.08	.15	.09	.06	.11	.06	.05	.12	.09	.03
10 to < 15	LA	.22	.17	.05	.16	.10	.06	.15	NM		.15	.09	.05	.19	.17	.02
Outcome Variable–BPI																
3 to < 6	EA	-.17	-.09	.07	-.13	-.06	.07	-.13	-.08	.05		NA		-.10	-.07	.04
6 to < 10	AA	-.06	NM		-.11	-.15	.04		NM		-.07	-.04^{ns}	.03		NM	
6 to < 10	EA	-.153	-.096	.06	-.14	-.08	.06	-.12	.03^{ns}	.10	-.08	-.04	.04	-.10	-.07	.02
6 to < 10	LA	-.13	-.09	.04	-.08	-.04	.05	-.08	-.13	.05	-.08	-.04^{ns}	.05	-.09	-.08	.01
10 to < 15	EA	-.13	-.07	.06	-.14	-.08	.05	-.11	-.07^{ns}	.04		NM		-.10	-.08	.02
10 to < 15	LA	-.06	-.02	.05	-.06	NM		-.11	-.15	.04		NM			NM	

Note. NM = no mediation; NA = not applicable, no previous data available. PPVT = Peabody Picture Vocabulary Test. PIAT = Peabody Individual Achievement Test. BPI = Behavior Problems Index. SES = Socioeconomic Status.

evidence for mediation when total net family income is substituted for SES in the equations?") were so consistent across outcomes, they are described in separate sections.

PPVT

Figure 7.1 displays results for PPVT. During early childhood, learning stimulation was a significant mediator of SES in all three groups, with reductions in β ranging from .05 to .10. There were ethnic differences in the model, with European Americans and Latin Americans showing stronger relations than African Americans. Because PPVT was not assessed during infancy, it was not possible to re-run the analyses using PPVT scores from the previous developmental period to determine the extent to which either learning stimulation or maternal responsiveness during early childhood mediated the relation between SES and change in developmental status from infancy to early childhood. However, when scores on learning stimulation in infancy were controlled, (see results in columns under label "Stimulation at Previous Time" in Table 7.4, the relations between SES and PPVT were reduced somewhat, and the amount of mediation was reduced by about half in all three ethnic groups.

During early childhood, maternal responsiveness was a mediator only for Hispanic Americans, with the β dropping from .18 to .14. There were also small ethnic differences in the models, with Latin Americans showing stronger relations than African Americans. Controlling for maternal responsiveness during infancy slightly reduced the relation between SES and PPVT, however, the amount of mediation increased somewhat (.06 versus .04).

During middle childhood, learning stimulation was a significant mediator for European Americans (β dropping from .21 to .14) and Latin Americans (β dropping from .14 to .09) but not African Americans. There were ethnic group differences in the models, with European Americans and Latin Americans showing stronger relations than African Americans. When PPVT scores from early childhood were included in the model, the conditions for mediation were not met. Similarly, controlling for learning stimulation scores during early childhood significantly reduced the relation between SES and adolescent PPVT, and reduced the amount of mediation among European Americans. The model was not significant for Hispanic Americans.

During early adolescence, learning stimulation was a significant mediator for all three groups, with β dropping from .20 to .17 for African Americans, from .19 to .11 for European Americans, and from .25 to .17 for Latin Americans. Even so, there were ethnic group differences in the model, with European Americans and Latin Americans showing stronger relations than African Americans. Controlling for PPVT during middle childhood had the effect of reducing both the relation between SES and PPVT during adolescence and the amount of variance attributable to mediation by learning stimulation. The model was no longer significant for African Americans, and evidence for mediation was reduced in the other two groups. Controlling for learning stimulation scores during middle childhood reduced the relationship between SES and adolescent PPVT, and reduced the amount of mediation in all three groups to negligible levels. In fact, the drop in β was greater than .03 only among Latin Americans.

During early adolescence, maternal responsiveness was a significant mediator of the SES/PPVT relation for the three groups combined, with β dropping from .24 to .20. In the last two models (controlling for PPVT during middle childhood and controlling for maternal responsiveness during middle childhood), the relationship with PPVT was reduced but the mediational effect remained about the same.

PIAT Reading

Figure 7.2 displays results for PIAT Reading. During early childhood, learning stimulation mediated the relation between SES and PIAT Reading in the three groups combined, with β dropping from .25 to .18. Maternal responsiveness failed to function as a mediator. Because the PIAT was not used in infancy, it was not possible to control for the previous score on PIAT Reading during early childhood. Controlling for learning stimulation during infancy had little effect on the relation with reading scores (.21 versus .25). However, the mediation effect was reduced by about half (.07 versus .03 drop in β).

During middle childhood, learning stimulation mediated the relation for European Americans (β dropped from .22 to .16) and Latin Americans (β dropped from .15 to .10). There was an ethnic group difference in the relations, with relations being stronger for European Americans and Latin Americans than for African Americans. Although there was insufficient evidence that learning stimulation functioned to mediate the relation between SES and reading performance for African Americans, it approached significance. Controlling for PIAT Reading scores during early childhood reduced the relations between SES and reading scores during middle childhood in both ethnic groups, resulting in a nonsignificant relation among Latin Americans. The mediational effect remained the same among European Americans. In both ethnic groups, controlling for learning stimulation during early childhood reduced the relation between SES and reading scores and reduced the mediational effect for middle childhood learning stimulation (from approximately $\beta = .06$ to $\beta = .03$). Maternal responsiveness was not a mediator of the relationship between SES and reading performance.

During early adolescence, learning stimulation mediated the relation between SES and PIAT Reading for European Americans (β dropped from .20 to .13), and for Latin Americans (β dropped from .23 to .18). The mediational effect for African Americans was slightly below the .03 criteria used in this study (β dropped from .18 to .15). There were ethnic group differences, with relations being stronger for European Americans than for African Americans. Controlling for PIAT Reading during middle childhood resulted in a nonsignificant model among Latin Americans. Among European Americans, the relation with reading performance was reduced (.06 versus .20), and the mediation effect was reduced (.04 versus .07 drop in β). Controlling for middle childhood learning stimulation scores reduced the relation with reading and reduced the mediational effect for both ethnic groups. Again, maternal responsiveness was not a mediator of the relation.

PIAT Math

Figure 7.3 displays results for PIAT Math. During early childhood, learning stimulation mediated the relation between SES and PIAT Math for European Americans (β dropped from .23 to .17), but the reduction in β was less than .03 for African Americans and Latin Americans. There was evidence that relations were weaker for African Americans than European Americans. Because the PIAT was not used in infancy, it was impossible to examine the relation between SES and PIAT Math during early childhood controlling for PIAT Math in infancy. Controlling for learning stimulation during infancy reduced the relation with math scores (.20 versus .23) and reduced the amount of mediation (.02 versus .06 drop in β) to a negligible level. Maternal responsiveness was not a significant mediator.

During middle childhood, learning stimulation was a significant mediator for European Americans (β dropped from .20 to .13) and Latin Americans (β dropped from .17 to .12), but the reduction in β was only .02 for African Americans. There were ethnic group differences in the model, with relations being stronger for European Americans and Latin Americans than for African Americans. Controlling for PIAT Math scores in early childhood resulted in reduced relations with math scores and reduced mediation in both ethnic groups. The same reductions were found controlling for learning stimulation during early childhood. Maternal responsiveness failed to mediate the relation. However, there was some evidence that the model that included maternal responsiveness was weaker for Latin Americans than for African Americans.

During adolescence, learning stimulation mediated the relation for European Americans (β dropped from .19 to .11) and Latin Americans (β dropped from .22 to .17). There were ethnic group differences in the model, with the model being weaker for African Americans than for European Americans and Latin Americans. There was also evidence that the relation between learning stimulation and math was stronger for European Americans than for Latin Americans. For both ethnic groups, controlling PIAT Math during middle childhood reduced the relations with adolescent math scores, but the mediational effect remained about the same. Controlling for learning stimulation scores during middle childhood reduced the relations with math scores and resulted in mediational effects below the .03 cut off used in this study. Maternal responsiveness was not a mediator of the relation.

BPI

Figure 7.4 displays results for BPI. During early childhood, learning stimulation mediated the relation between SES and BPI for European Americans (β dropped from $-.17$ to $-.09$). There were ethnic group differences, with relations being stronger for European Americans than for African Americans or Latin Americans. Because the BPI was not used in infancy, it was not possible to examine the relation between SES and BPI during early childhood controlling for earlier BPI. Controlling for learning stimulation scores during infancy reduced the relations with BPI and reduced the mediational effect by about half (from .07 to .04). Maternal responsiveness was not a significant mediator in any group, but there was evidence that the relation between maternal responsiveness and behavior problems was stronger for African Americans than for Latin Americans.

During middle childhood, learning stimulation was a mediator for European Americans (β dropped from $-.15$ to $-.10$), and Latin Americans (β dropped from $-.13$ to $-.09$), and African Americans (β dropped from .06 to non-significance). There were ethnic differences, with relations being strongest for European Americans and weakest for African Americans. Controlling for behavior problems during early childhood resulted in somewhat weaker relations, but the mediational effect remained about the same as when earlier BPI was not controlled in all three ethnic groups. Controlling for the learning stimulation score during early childhood resulted in a nonsignificant model among African Americans, and reduced relations and reduced mediation in the other two groups. Maternal responsiveness was not a significant mediator for any group, but there were indications that the relation between SES and maternal responsiveness was weaker for Latin Americans than the other two groups.

During early adolescence, learning stimulation was a significant mediator for European Americans (β dropped from $-.13$ to $-.07$) and Latin Americans (β dropped from $-.06$ to $-.02$). There were ethnic group differences in the models, with African Americans showing the weakest relations. Controlling for BPI measured in middle childhood resulted in nonsignificant model for European Americans and Latin Americans. Controlling for learning stimulation during middle childhood resulted in a nonsignificant model for Latin Americans and a negligible change in β for European Americans. Maternal responsiveness failed to mediate the relation.

Maternal Education

As Table 7.4 shows, maternal education generally showed as strong or stronger relations with PPVT and PIAT scores than did the Duncan SEI. The differences were most pronounced during early childhood and were negligible during early adolescence. Learning stimulation mediated the relation between maternal education and these three child measures to about the same degree as it mediated the relation between SES and the three child measures. However, during adolescence, maternal responsiveness mediated the relation between maternal education and PPVT to a much greater extent that the relation between SES and PPVT (.16 versus .04).

The situation with respect to BPI was quite different. There was effectively no difference in relations for maternal education and the Duncan SEI.

Total Net Family Income

Total net family income showed somewhat weaker relations with PPVT and PIAT than did the Duncan SEI. Likewise, the amount of mediation by learning stimulation was proportionately smaller. There were exceptions, such as relations involving PPVT during early childhood among Latin Americans, but the relations were generally lower. As was the case for maternal education, maternal responsiveness was a stronger mediator of the relation with PPVT during early adolescence for total net family income than for the Duncan SEI.

The relation between total net family income and the BPI was slightly weaker than the relation between SES and BPI. But, the level of mediation via learning stimulation was very similar.

THE ROLE OF FAMILY MEDIATORS BY AGE AND ETHNICITY

This study focused on the extent to which learning stimulation in the home and maternal responsiveness mediate the relation between SES and child well-being for children ages 4 through 14. Relations were examined for three developmental periods, early childhood, middle childhood, and adolescence, and for three ethnic groups, African Americans, European Americans, and Latin Americans. In addition to answering the basic question of whether either of the two family process variables function as mediators of the relation, the study was designed to address four specific questions: (1) "Is there evidence for mediation when controlling for status on the dependent measure during the previous developmental period?"; (2) "Is there evidence for mediation when controlling for level of input from the same environmental process measure during the previous developmental period?"; (3) "Is there evidence for mediation when maternal education is substituted for SES in the equations?"; and (4) "Is there evidence for mediation when total net family income is substituted for SES in the equations?"

In regard to the basic question of mediation, the correlations between SES and measures of child development (specifically, vocabulary attainment, reading achievement, math achievement, and behavior problems) tended to be low (correlations mostly in the .20 to .30 range). The correlations with intellectual and academic measures were about the same as the average correlation reported by White (1982) in his meta-analysis. The correlations between learning stimulation and measures of child well-being were in the same range as the correlations for SES and child well-being; and are similar to those reported by Bradley (1994) in his review of the literature on the HOME Inventory (perhaps slightly lower on average). The correlations for European Americans tended to be highest, the correlations for African Americans lowest, a finding that is also consistent with previous research (Bradley, 1994). As expected, correlations with vocabulary attainment and achievement (especially PPVT during early childhood) tended to be higher than correlations with behavior problems. The correlations between maternal responsiveness and measures of child well-being, although significant, tended to be lower than those for learning stimulation (more often in the .10 to .15 range); and, curiously, the correlations during middle childhood were little lower than those for early childhood or adolescence. Maternal responsiveness was more strongly associated with vocabulary attainment and achievement than with behavior problems, except during adolescence. Surprisingly, it was uncorrelated with behavior problems during middle childhood and was only correlated with behavior problems among European Americans during early childhood. Overall, the correlations between SES, home conditions, and measures of child well-being were low (only occasionally > .30). These low correlations may reflect the small number of items that compose most of the measures for NLSY, but they are not substantially lower than those reported for longer (perhaps more reliable) measures used in other studies.

Vocabulary Attainment

Learning stimulation partially mediated the relation between SES and PPVT during early childhood. It was a significant mediator for all three ethnic groups. It also mediated the relation during middle childhood and adolescence, but its role as a mediator was more limited in the case of African Americans. In every instance, save one, where learning stimulation was found to mediate the SES/PPVT relation, it also mediated the maternal education/PPVT relation and the total net family income/PPVT relation. The single exception was the relation between family income and PPVT for Latin Americans during early adolescence; and, even in that instance the tendency was the same. Overall, the findings implicating learning stimulation as a mediator of the relation between SES and language proficiency are highly consistent with previous research (Bradley, 1994; Hart & Risley, 1995). Parents with higher levels of education and income tend to engage their children in richer language exchanges and provide them materials and experiences that foster language development (Hoff, chap. 6, this volume). Findings from this study extend previous findings in two important ways. First, results from analyses of the SES/PPVT relation that controlled for PPVT scores in the prior developmental period indicated that SES is related to changes in vocabulary competence from middle childhood to adolescence, as well as to vocabulary attainment during adolescence and that learning stimulation mediates that change (albeit to a lesser degree). By contrast, results provided no evidence that SES was related to changes in vocabulary competence from early childhood to middle childhood, perhaps owing to somewhat homogenizing language exposure in the primary grades of school. Second, results from analyses of the SES/PPVT relation that controlled for level of learning stimulation during the prior developmental period indicated that learning stimulation during each developmental period was associated with vocabulary attainment net prior levels of learning stimulation. The impact of contemporaneous learning stimulation was perhaps greatest during early childhood, but there was evidence for contemporaneous effects even into adolescence. That said, the reduction in mediation effects when the prior level of learning stimulation was controlled also suggests that the effects are cumulative, as well as contemporaneous.

With regard to maternal responsiveness, there were only two instances in which it functioned to mediate relations between SES and child developmental outcomes and both involved PPVT scores. During early childhood, it mediated the relation for Latin Americans, and during adolescence it marginally mediated the relation for the three ethnic groups combined. Even so, the total set of findings in these two instances point to several important conclusions. First, during early childhood maternal responsiveness mediated maternal education/PPVT and family income/PPVT relations to a degree equal to the SES/PPVT relation. However, during adolescence it far more strongly mediated maternal education/PPVT and family income/PPVT relations than overall SES/PPVT relations. Moreover, it mediated changes in vocabulary competence from middle childhood to adolescence (the mediator effect for change in PPVT was actually greater than the mediator effect for PPVT during adolescence), and it mediated the SES/PPVT relation in adolescence net level of maternal responsiveness during middle childhood. The precise reason for this relatively potent effect is not entirely clear, particularly because similar effects did not clearly emerge for the other developmental measures—it did approach significance for PIAT (the reduction in β was .03 for the combined group). It may represent an advantage of generally positive parenting practices during a time when parent–child relationships are often strained (National Research Council, 1993).

Achievement

The findings pertaining to PIAT Reading and PIAT Math scores resemble those pertaining to PPVT. Learning stimulation served as a mediator for both areas of achievement during early childhood, albeit the effect for PIAT Math was marginal for African Americans and Latin Americans. Learning stimulation also functioned as a mediator for achievement test performance during middle childhood, and adolescence, with the effect being marginal in the case of African Americans. Finding that learning stimulation functioned to mediate the relation between SES and achievement was not surprising in view of the long history of research suggesting such a link (Walberg & Marjoribanks, 1976). The findings with respect to achievement were also consistent with the findings of DeGarmo et al. (1999), who reported that both maternal education and predivorce family income were mediated more strongly by skill-building activities at home than by a composite positive-parenting factor that included discipline and negative reinforcement. Like PPVT, there was evidence that learning stimulation mediates the relation between maternal education and achievement and the relation between family income and achievement to about the same degree as it mediates the relation between SES and achievement. Again, like PPVT, there is evidence (somewhat inconsistent) that learning stimulation mediates the relation between SES and change in PIAT scores from one developmental period to another and that learning stimulation during each developmental period mediates the SES/PIAT relation net level of learning stimulation during the prior developmental period. Again, the findings suggest both some contemporaneous mediation and some cumulative effects.

Behavior Problems

Findings pertaining to behavior problems were more complicated. During early childhood, learning stimulation was a mediator for European Americans and Latin Americans (marginal). During middle childhood, learning stimulation was a mediator for all three ethnic groups; and during adolescence, it was a mediator for European Americans and Latin Americans (it approached significance for African Americans). The findings comport with previous research showing that the relation between SES and behavior problems tends not to be as strong as the relation between SES and achievement (Brooks-Gunn & Duncan, 1997). In general, learning stimulation mediated the maternal education/BPI and family income/BPI relations to about the same degree as it mediated SES/BPI relations. However, there were a number of exceptions: (1) in two instances the amount of variance in BPI accounted for by either maternal education or family income actually increased when learning stimulation was added to the model (suggesting a possible suppressor effect), and (2) in one instance the level of mediation by learning stimulation was much higher for family income than for SES (change in $\beta = .15$ versus .06). There was also evidence that learning stimulation mediates the relation between SES and BPI during middle childhood net the child's level of behavior problems in early childhood; but there was no evidence that it mediates the SES–BPI relation in adolescence net the child's level of behavior problems in middle childhood. Moreover, there was limited evidence for active mediation by learning stimulation during any developmental period after early childhood once the level of stimulation in the prior developmental period was controlled. Somewhat surprisingly, there was no evidence that maternal responsiveness mediated the relation between SES and BPI, albeit the findings on that relation are inconsistent in the literature. For example, McLeod and Shanahan (1993) found that mothers' weak emotional responsiveness and use of physical punishment did not explain the relation between persistent poverty and children's mental health even though it did explain part of the relation for current poverty.

The link between SES and behavior problems appears to be a very complex one involving multiple mediators, mediators that may well vary according to sociocultural group (McLoyd, 1998). What the findings pertaining to learning stimulation suggest is that the development of competence may be protective against the development of behavior problems (Masten & Coatsworth, 1998). To test this possible path from SES through learning stimulation to behavior problems, an additional set of analyses was performed. Specifically, a measure of competence (child vocabulary attainment) was introduced into those models where learning stimulation was observed to be a significant mediator of the SES/behavior problems relation. Vocabulary attainment was found to marginally mediate the relation in two of five instances, thus suggesting that other factors principally account for the mediating role of learning stimulation. Perhaps learning stimulation indirectly reflects a connection with institutions (e.g., schools) that afford protection or a separation from peer and neighborhood conditions that increase the likelihood of behavior problems (Levanthal & Brooks-Gunn, 2000). Such an interpretation is consistent with academic mediation theory, which stipulates that for low-SES teens, school bonding increases the likelihood of high academic achievement, staying in school, and low deviant behavior (Battin-Pearson et al., 2000). However, data were not available in the NLSY data set to authoritatively test this alternative explanation. It may also be the case that having a rich opportunity structure reduces the likelihood that children will become bored and frustrated, leading them to engage in social behaviors that arouse negative responses from parents and peers (Saegert & Winkel, 1990). Finally, learning stimulation may reflect deeper commitments to the child, a tendency to be demanding (one of the components of authoritative parenting), and efforts on the part of the parent to connect the child to positive peer groups, all of which may reduce the likelihood that the child will exhibit behavior problems (Sampson, 1992). Again, however, data were not available in the NLSY data set to explore such complex mediational paths.

In overview, there were both age and ethnic group differences in the mediation of the SES/child well-being relation. Learning stimulation was the most consistent mediator, perhaps due to its stronger relation with both SES and intellectual/academic outcomes. Previous studies using NLSY data established that poor families scored lower on all the items that make up the learning stimulation scale than non-poor families (Bradley, et al., 2001). The findings fit a long history of research pertaining to the mediating role played by learning stimulation in the relation between low SES and child cognitive attainment (Hart & Risley, 1995; Walberg & Marjoribanks, 1976). The fact that maternal responsiveness rarely functioned as a mediator was a little surprising in view of the importance attributed to maternal responsiveness in the literature (Bornstein, 1989). Also interesting was the finding the maternal responsiveness was a stronger mediator for adolescents than younger children, given the importance attributed to maternal responsiveness in infancy and early childhood. However, the findings would not appear to refute the general significance of maternal responsiveness in that correlations with most child outcomes during early childhood were significant. Rather, the findings specifically suggest maternal responsiveness does not function as a mediator for SES when children are young. Brody et al., (1994), Conger et al., (1994), and McLoyd (1998), argued that the stresses associated with low SES and persistent poverty gradually diminish the parent's capacity to engage in positive parenting. The findings pertaining to adolescents in this study may be reflective of just such processes. The findings suggest that low-SES parents have a harder time engaging in supportive parenting. The findings also suggest that family processes (most particularly, learning stimulation) actively mediate the SES/child well-being relation during each developmental period and that they are related to changes in well-being during each developmental period. There is some evidence to suggest that contemporaneous effects are strongest during early childhood, with cumulative, early effects, or both, relatively stronger later in childhood—the findings pertaining to maternal responsiveness and vocabulary attainment in adolescence being a notable exception. Finally, results indicate that the family processes examined in this study function to mediate relations between constituent components of SES (maternal education, family income) to a degree as great or greater than they mediate relations for overall SES as measured by Duncan's SEI.

There are a number of limitations to this study. First, the measures used in NLSY were abbreviated versions of the instruments as originally standardized. Thus, the statistical estimates of relations developed in this study may underestimate the actual strength of relations. Second, the data available on older children were not as representative as the data available on younger children given that children born when NLSY mothers were older have not yet reached criterion age.

ACKNOWLEDGEMENTS

Partial support for this study was provided by the Office of Educational Research and Improvement (U. S. Dept. of Education) through a grant to the National Center for Early Development and Learning at the University of North Carolina at Chapel Hill.

REFERENCES

Adler, N. E., Marmot, M. McEwen, B. S., & Steward, J. (Eds.). (1999). *Socioeconomic status and health in industrial nations*. New York: New York Academy of Sciences.
Baron, R. M., & Kenny, D. A. (1986). The moderator-mediator distinction in social psychological research: Conceptual, strategic, and statistical considerations. *Journal of Personality & Social Psychology, 51*, 1173–1182.

Battin-Pearson, S., Newcomb, M. D., Abbott, R. D., Hill, K. B., Catalano, R. F., & Hawkins, J. D. (2000). Predictors of early school dropout: A test of five theories. *Journal of Educational Psychology, 92,* 568–582.

Baum, A., Garofalo, J. P., & Yali, M. (1999). Socioeconomic status and chronic stress. Does stress account for the SES effects on health? In N. E. Adler, M. Marmot, B. S. McEwen, & J. Steward (Eds.), *Socioeconomic status and health in industrial nations* (pp. 131–144). New York: New York Academy of Sciences.

Bornstein, M. (Ed.). (1989). *Maternal responsiveness: Characteristics and consequences.* San Francisco: Jossey-Bass.

Bradley, R. H. (1994). The HOME Inventory: Review and reflections. In. H. W. Reese (Ed.), *Advances in child development and behavior* (Vol. 25, pp. 241–288). San Diego: Academic Press.

Bradley, R. H., Caldwell, B. M., Rock, S. L, Barnard, K., Gray, C., Hammond, M., Mitchell, S., Siegel, L., Ramey, C., Gottfried, A., & Johnson, D. (1989). Home environment and cognitive development in the first 3 years of life: A collaborative study involving six sites and three ethnic groups in North America. *Developmental Psychology, 25,* 217–235.

Bradley, R. H., & Corwyn, R. F. (2002). Socioeconomic status and child development. *Annual Review of Psychology, 53,* 371–399.

Bradley, R. H., Corwyn, R. F., McAdoo, H. P., & Garcia Coll, C. (2001). The home environments of children in the United States: Part 1, Variations in ethnic and income groups. *Child Development, 72,* 1844–1867.

Bradley, R. H., Corwyn, R., & Whiteside-Mansell, L. (1996). Life at home: Same time, different places. An examination of the HOME Inventory in different cultures. *Early Education & Parenting, 5,* 251–269.

Brody, G. H., Stoneman, Z., Flor, D., McCrary, C., Hastings, L., Conyers, O. (1994). Financial resources, parent psychological functioning, parent co-caregiving, and early adolescent competence in rural two-parent African-American families. *Child Development, 65,* 590–605.

Brooks-Gunn, J., & Duncan, G. J. (1997). The effects of poverty on children. *The Future of Children, 7(2),* 55–71.

Brooks-Gunn, J., Duncan, G. J., & Aber, J. L. (Eds.) (1997). *Neighborhood poverty, Vol. 1: Context and consequences for children.* New York: Russell Sage.

Bronfenbrenner, U. (1995). The biological model from a life course perspective: Reflections of a participant observer. In P. Moen, G. H. Elder, & K. Luscher (Eds.), *Examining lives in context* (pp. 599–618). Washington, DC: American Psychological Association.

Caldwell, B. M., & Bradley, R. H. (1984). *Home observation for measurement of the environment.* Little Rock, AR: University of Arkansas at Little Rock.

Center for Human Resource Research. (1995). *NLSY79 user's guide 1995.* Columbus, OH: The Ohio State University.

Center for Human Resource Research. (1997). *1994 child & young adult data users guide.* Columbus, OH: The Ohio State University.

Center for Human Resource Research. (1999). *NLSY79 user's guide 1999.* Columbus, OH: The Ohio State University.

Chao, R. K. (1994). Beyond parental control and authoritarian parenting style: Understanding Chinese parenting through the cultural notion of training. *Child Development, 65,* 1111–1119.

Cohen, J., & Cohen, P. (1983). *Applied multiple regression–correlation analysis for the behavioral sciences* (2nd ed.). Hillsdale, NJ: Lawrence Erlbaum Associates.

Conger, R. D., Ge, X., Elder, G., Lorenz, F., & Simons, R. (1994). Economic stress, coercive family process, and developmental problems of adolescents. *Child Development, 65,* 541–601.

DeGarmo, D. S., Forgatch, M. S., & Martinez, C. R. (1999). Parenting of divorced mothers as a link between social status and boys' academic outcomes: Unpacking the effects of socioeconomic status. *Child Development, 70,* 1231–1245.

Dodge, K. A., Pettit, G. S., & Bates, J. E. (1994). Socialization mediators of the relation between socioeconomic status and child conduct problems. *Child Development, 65,* 649–665.

Duncan G. J., & Brooks-Gunn, J. (1997). *Consequences of growing up poor.* New York: Russell Sage.

Duncan, O. D. (1961). A socioeconomic index for all occupations. In A. J. Reiss (Ed.), *Occupations and social status* (pp. 109–161). New York: The Free Press.

Dunn, L. M., & Dunn, L. M. (1981). *PPVT-revised manual.* Circle Pines, MN: American Guidance Service, Inc.

Garcia Coll, C., & Magnusson, K. (1999). Cultural influences on child development: Are we ready for a paradigm shift? In A. S. Masten (Ed.), *Cultural processes in child development. The Minnesota symposia on child psychology* (Vol. 29, pp. 1–24). Mahweh, NJ: Lawrence Erlbaum Associates.

Harris, J. R. (1995). Where is the child's environment? A group socialization theory of development. *Psychological Review, 102,* 458–489.

Hart, B., & Risley, T. R. (1995). *Meaningful differences in the everyday experience of young American children.* Baltimore, MD: Brookes.

Huston, A. C., McLoyd, V. C., & Garcia Coll, C. (1994). Children and poverty: Issues in contemporary research. *Child Development, 65,* 275–282.

Jessor, R. (1993). Successful adolescent development among youth in high-risk settings. *American Psychologist, 48,* 117–126.

Koutsoulis, M. K., & Campbell, J. R. (2001). Family processes affect students' motivation, and science and math achievement in Cypriot high schools. *Structural Equation Modeling, 8,* 108–127.

Leventhal, T., & Brooks-Gunn, J. (2000). The neighborhoods they live in: The effects of neighborhood residence on child and adolescent outcomes. *Psychological Bulletin, 126,* 309–337.

Masten, A. S., & Coatsworth, J. D. (1998). The development of competence in favorable and unfavorable environments. *American Psychologist, 53,* 205–220.

McLeod, J., & Shanahan, M. (1993). Poverty, parenting, and children's mental health. *American Sociological Review, 58,* 351–366.

McLoyd, V. C. (1998). Socioeconomic disadvantage and child development. *American Psychologist, 53,* 185–204.

National Research Council. (1993). *Losing generations.* Washington, DC: National Academy Press.

Saegert, S., & Winkel, G. H. (1990). Environmental psychology. *Annual Review of Psychology, 41,* 441–477.

Sampson, R. J. (1992). Family management and child development: Insights from social disorganization theory. In J. McCord (Ed.), *Advances in criminological theory* (Vol. 3, pp. 63–93). New Brunswick, NJ: Transactions Books.

Scarr, S., & McCartney, K. (1983). How people make their own environments. *Child Development, 54.* 424–435.

U.S. Department of Labor (2000). *NLS Handbook, 2000.* Washington, DC: Author.

Walberg, H. J., & Marjoribanks, K. (1976). Family environment and cognitive development: Twelve analytic models. *Review of Educational Research, 46,* 527–551.

White, K. R. (1982). The relation between socioeconomic status and academic achievement. *Psychological Bulletin, 91,* 461–481.

8

Socioeconomic Status in Children's Development and Family Environment: Infancy Through Adolescence

Allen W. Gottfried
California State University, Fullerton

Adele E. Gottfried
California State University, Northridge

Kay Bathurst, Diana Wright Guerin, and Makeba M. Parramore
California State University, Fullerton

INTRODUCTION

The concept of socioeconomic status (SES) has had a central and longstanding role in the social sciences. In addition to the study of class differences in social status per se, SES has served as a predictor, outcome, or control variable. Furthermore, it is often utilized to designate characteristics of samples being investigated. In developmental psychology, it has also served as a global index or appraisal of the environmental context in which children are reared. This chapter addresses the following issues: (1) nature of the relations among SES factors in a cohort of families studied longitudinally across an interval of almost two decades; (2) pervasiveness of SES to various domains of children's psychological functioning; and (3) relations between SES and children's family environment.

The findings to be presented are based on a contemporary ongoing prospective investigation known as the Fullerton Longitudinal Study (FLS). In 1979, 130 one year olds and their families were recruited. All infants were normal, and all parents spoke English. The sample comprised 52% males and 48% females. As for racial composition, 90% were European American, and 10% were from other racial/ethnic groups. The families represented a wide range of middle-class socioeconomic families as measured by the Hollingshead Four-Factor Index of Social Status (Hollingshead, 1975; $M = 45.6$, $SD = 11.7$), Revised Duncan Socioeconomic Index (Stevens & Featherman, 1981; $M = 46.5$, $SD = 20.5$), and Siegel Prestige Scores (Siegel, 1971; $M = 47.9$, $SD = 14.2$).

However, for reasons elaborated by A. W. Gottfried (1985), only the Hollingshead Four-Factor Index of Social Status (HI) served as the index of SES throughout the course of investigation. The average index, as well as its constituent educational and occupational factors, increased from 1 to 17 years. The values for the Index of Social Status at 1 and 17 years were $M = 45.6$, $SD = 11.7$ and $M = 48.7$, $SD = 11.3$; Fathers' Occupational Status $M = 6.1$, $SD = 2.1$ and $M = 6.7$, $SD = 2.0$; Mothers' Occupational Status $M = 4.9$, $SD = 1.9$ and $M = 6.3$, $SD = 1.3$; and Fathers' Educational Status (years of parents' educational attainment) $M = 14.7$, $SD = 2.4$ and $M = 15.4$, $SD = 2.5$, Mothers' Educational Status $M = 14.1$, $SD = 2.1$ and $M = 14.9$, $SD = 2.1$, respectively. It is noteworthy that the most dramatic change in the demographic data pertained to mothers' employment status. Specifically, when children were 1 year of age, 36% of the mothers were gainfully employed, whereas at 17 years mothers' employment rate climbed to 83%. Furthermore, in contrast to the employment histories of fathers, those of mothers revealed an inconsistent record (see Gottfried, Bathurst, & Gottfried, 1994; Gottfried & Gottfried, 1988). This in itself has interesting implications when incorporating mothers' work status into a composite or aggregate social status index. Additionally, as the data herein will show, the correspondence between educational attainment and employment status was higher for fathers than for mothers.

Thus far, the FLS comprises 19 laboratory assessments and three home visits, as shown in Table 8.1. From ages 1 through 3.5 years, the children were tested every 6 months; they were tested annually beginning at age 5 through high school completion. During infancy (1.25 years), preschool (3.25 years), and middle-childhood (8 years), direct home assessments were conducted. Data were collected from the children, from parents, as well as from teachers. Hence, a cross-time, multi-context, multi-informant methodology was utilized. Furthermore, numerous ongoing assessments across various developmental domains were conducted. Table 8.2 displays the major standardized psychological and home–family instruments employed. For further details concerning the study sample, research paradigm, and types of assessments, see Gottfried and Gottfried (1984) and Gottfried, Gottfried, Bathurst, and Guerin (1994).

This chapter is delineated into three sections. In the first section, data on the HI, occupation, and education across the longitudinal time frame will be presented to

TABLE 8.1
Assessment Waves of the Fullerton
Longitudinal Study

Developmental Era	Assessment Age (Years)
Laboratory Visit	
Infancy	1, 1.5, 2
Preschool	2.5, 3, 3.5
Elementary school	5, 6, 7, 8, 9, 10, 11
Junior high school	12, 13
High school	14, 15, 16, 17
Home Visit	
Infancy	1.25
Preschool	3.25
Elementary school	8

determine their stability throughout childhood. In the second section, we present the relations of the HI and parents' education and occupation to their children's development in a broad range of domains (intelligence, educational achievement, academic intrinsic motivation, self-concept, social competence, behavioral functioning, and temperament). This analysis was conducted to examine the pervasiveness of SES as a correlate of developmental phenomena. The relations of the HI, parents' education and occupation to children's home and family environments are examined in the third section. This section provides an appraisal of the relation between distal and proximal variables in the context of children's and adolescents' development. Using individuals as the unit of analysis (in contrast to aggregated units; see White, 1982), the extent to which SES and its constituent factors related to developmental and environmental measures in a single cohort across childhood was determined.

Hollingshead Index and Occupational and Educational Status Across Time

In Table 8.3, the cross-time correlations of the HI for every laboratory assessment from 1 through 17 years are presented. A classic simplex intercorrelation matrix emerges. The highest correlations are found at the adjacent ages (i.e., along the diagonal in Table 8.3), with many almost approaching unity. As the time interval increases from the initial assessment (i.e., moving down the columns in Table 8.3), correlation coefficients decrease, but never descend below a moderate level of magnitude. With advancement in age, the correlations increase compared to those observed at earlier ages (i.e., proceeding from left to right across rows of Table 8.3). Succinctly, over short intervals the HI reveals a very high degree of stability, and over long durations throughout childhood, the HI shows a moderate degree of

TABLE 8.2

Major Standardized Psychological and Home–Family Instruments Utilized

Instrument	Assessment Age
Intelligence	
Bayley Scales of Infant Development	1, 1.5, 2
McCarthy Scales of Children's Abilities	2.5, 3, 3.5
Kaufman Assessment Battery for Children	5
Wechsler Intelligence Scale for Children—Revised	6, 7, 8, 12
Wechsler Intelligence Scale for Children—III	15
Wechsler Adult Intelligence Scale—Revised	17
Academic Achievement	
Wide Range Achievement Test—Revised	6
Woodcock-Johnson Psycho-Educational Battery—Revised	7–17
Academic Motivation	
Children's Academic Intrinsic Motivation Inventory	9, 10, 13, 16, 17
Self Concept	
Self-Description Questionnaire I, II	10, 12, 14, 16
Social Competence	
Vineland Adaptive Behavior Scale	6, 8
Behavior Problems	
Child Behavior Checklist	4–17
Teacher Report Form	6–11
Temperament	
Infant Characteristics Questionnaire	1.5
Toddler Temperament Scale	2
Behavioral Style Questionnaire	3, 3.5, 5
Middle Childhood Temperament Questionnaire	8, 10, 12
Dimensions of Temperament Survey—Revised	14, 16
Home–Family Environment	
Home Observation for the Measurement of the Environment	1.25, 3.25, 8
Family Environment Scale	3, 5, 7, 8, 10, 12, 14, 16, 17
Hollingshead Four-Factor Index of Social Status	1–17

stability. It is also noteworthy that there is continuity in the FLS sample with respect to the average SES across the course of investigation. That is, these families with a wide range of middle-SES levels tended to maintain their SES across time. Hence, if developmental researchers seek a stable composite measure of SES per se, the HI meets that criterion. Furthermore, as the following data shows, the HI relates to a comprehensive array of developmental measures throughout childhood.

Henceforth, for ease of presentation and understanding, data are presented for ages 1, 3, 8, 12, and 17 years when available. These ages were selected to represent the various periods in child development (infancy, preschool, middle childhood,

TABLE 8.3

Cross-Time Stability of Socioeconomic Status from 1 to 17 Years

Assessment Age (Years)	Assessment Age (Years)																		
	1	1.5	2	2.5	3	3.5	5	6	7	8	9	10	11	12	13	14	15	16	17
1	—																		
1.5	.96	—																	
2	.93	.95	—																
2.5	.93	.93	.94	—															
3	.89	.90	.89	.96	—														
3.5	.79	.79	.82	.83	.92	—													
5	.78	.78	.81	.77	.81	.85	—												
6	.76	.73	.78	.73	.80	.86	.84	—											
7	.80	.79	.80	.73	.79	.81	.85	.93	—										
8	.76	.74	.77	.78	.73	.72	.76	.78	.87	—									
9	.69	.68	.72	.73	.72	.78	.79	.84	.85	.88	—								
10	.78	.76	.76	.67	.72	.74	.81	.82	.87	.87	.93	—							
11	.74	.73	.74	.72	.71	.68	.75	.73	.83	.86	.83	.93	—						
12	.73	.69	.71	.72	.70	.67	.72	.73	.82	.83	.82	.88	.94	—					
13	.54	.50	.57	.69	.54	.62	.63	.75	.63	.64	.73	.69	.68	.72	—				
14	.48	.44	.50	.48	.49	.55	.55	.64	.54	.55	.66	.62	.61	.64	.87	—			
15	.49	.47	.53	.44	.52	.56	.60	.67	.55	.53	.65	.59	.60	.60	.83	.81	—		
16	.47	.45	.50	.51	.47	.55	.57	.67	.53	.51	.65	.59	.57	.56	.79	.78	.98	—	
17	.48	.48	.47	.47	.44	.41	.47	.56	.52	.50	.54	.55	.58	.57	.75	.73	.97	.98	—
M	45.6	45.3	45.6	45.2	47.0	47.1	47.9	47.8	49.0	49.7	49.8	50.0	49.1	50.0	49.3	48.9	48.5	48.4	48.7
SD	11.9	11.8	12.7	12.6	11.3	11.2	10.8	11.0	9.5	9.3	9.9	8.8	8.6	8.7	10.8	12.5	12.4	12.8	11.3

Note. *N*s range from 80 to 124.

All *p*s < .01.

preadolescence, and adolescence). For certain measures, results for other ages are presented if assessments were conducted at particularly relevant times. For example, data at age 6 are presented for academic achievement because of its relevance to school entry.

The cross-time correlations for occupational status and educational attainment are displayed in Tables 8.4 and 8.5, respectively. Correlations above the diagonal depict values for mothers; those below the diagonal represent the values for fathers. A parent's educational status is entered into the Hollingshead computation only if he or she is gainfully employed. If not employed, only the head of the household is entered into the formula. This procedure tended to eliminate mothers and not fathers, because mothers were less likely to be in the workforce compared to fathers. With traditional families no longer being the norm and various family arrangements emerging (Gottfried & Gottfried, 1994), obvious issues arise as to utility of the concept of a single head of the household. However, for present purposes and for understanding the cross-time relations of occupational status and educational attainment, correlations of the latter were conducted whether mothers were gainfully employed or not.

As for occupational status, the data clearly reveal that fathers maintained a greater degree of cross-time stability in the prestige of their jobs compared to mothers. After all, fathers entered the workforce earlier during the course of having and raising a family, and fathers were more likely to be consistently employed. Mothers, on the other hand, were prone to take parental leaves.

Moreover, as shown in Table 8.6, there tends to be higher correspondence between the educational achievement and occupational status among fathers than there is for mothers. Consequently, mothers' occupational status also bears a differential relation to children's developmental outcome than does fathers— specifically, no relation. Although maternal employment is a worthy and interesting phenomenon to investigate, using a single indicator of occupational status, particularly the mother's, raises concerns. This is especially the case in single mothering family arrangements (see Entwisle & Astone, 1994). It is also important to keep in mind the notion of cohort effects when conducting longitudinal research. This was a population of families studied in the 1980s and 1990s. Mothers were progressively entering the workforce as their children aged. Today, the picture could be quite different, in that most mothers of young children might be employed; economic cycles could obviously affect this trend. Of course, this would make initiating an investigation like the FLS difficult today, because it is more common for mothers to bring children into a developmental research center, as is often the case when bringing children to the pediatrician. However, times are changing in caregiver responsibilities in that fathers have become more involved (Gottfried, Gottfried, & Bathurst, 2002; Parke, 1995).

In contrast to the matrix of occupational status, educational attainment across time depicts a very different picture, as shown in Table 8.5. For both parents, there is a very high degree of stability in education throughout the course of

TABLE 8.4

Cross-Time Stability of Occupations of Mothers[a] (Above Diagonal) and Fathers[b] (Below Diagonal)

Assessment Age (Years)	Assessment Age (Years)				
	1	3	8	12	17
1	—	.72**	.45*	.19	.31
3	.88**	—	.42**	.13	.33*
8	.72**	.72**	—	.72**	.53**
12	.64**	.64**	.83**	—	.51**
17	.72**	.71**	.79**	.94**	—

Note. $^*p < .05.$ $^{**}p < .01.$
[a]ns range from 29 to 67.
[b]ns range from 74 to 113.

TABLE 8.5

Cross-Time Stability of Education of Mothers[a] (Above Diagonal) and Fathers[b] (Below Diagonal)

Assessment Age (Years)	Assessment Age (Years)				
	1	3	8	12	17
1	—	.98	.95	.92	.84
3	.99	—	.97	.94	.85
8	.97	.98	—	.97	.91
12	.96	.97	.99	—	.92
17	.96	.97	.98	.98	—

Note. All *p*s <. 01.
[a]ns range from 91 to 119.
[b]ns range from 85 to 118.

TABLE 8.6

Correlation of Occupation and Education for Fathers[a] and Mothers[b]

Assessment Age (Years)	Fathers	Mothers
1	.70	.60
3	.69	.42
8	.60	.68
12	.54	.48
17	.66	.55

Note. All *p*s < .01.
[a]ns range from 81 to 125.
[b]ns range from 47 to 82.

investigation. This not surprising because educational achievement cannot shift downward, but either remains invariant or increases. Furthermore, for most adults entering parenthood—as in the current study population—most, if not all, of their education has been completed. There was only a very minor increase in the parents' educational attainment across the nearly two decades examined in the FLS. This has significant implications for measuring SES. Additionally, the level of education of both mothers and fathers bears an interesting and close relation to children's psychological functioning across time (see Hoff-Ginsberg & Tardif, 1995).

Relation of SES to Children's Development

The significance and relevance of an SES indicator for developmental scientists rests on the extent to which it relates to aspects of children's development. We examined both the predictive (from 1 year) and concurrent relations of SES and parents' education and occupation to various aspects of development across childhood. For virtually all developmental domains, the network of predictive and concurrent relations was comparable (intrinsic motivation is the exception). Thus, only the predictive relations will be presented. The domains of development investigated include intelligence, educational achievement, academic intrinsic motivation, self-concept, social competence, behavioral functioning, and temperament. Additionally, the relations of SES indictors to proximal components of children's family environment were also studied.

Table 8.7 shows the relation of SES to children's intellectual performance for designated periods from 1 through 17 years. It should first be noted that a significant correlation emerges in the latter part of infancy (1.5–2 years), when symbolic functions begin to develop. This has been repeatedly documented in the literature (e.g., McCall, 1979; Wilson, 1985). In a previous publication examining the relation of various SES indexes and early intellectual functioning, a significant correlation was reported to emerge at 1.5 years in the FLS (A. W. Gottfried, 1985). We hypothesize that the correlation between SES indicators and intellectual performance emerges

TABLE 8.7
Correlations of Socioeconomic Status and Intelligence

	Assessment Age (Years)				
SES at Age 1	1	3	8	12	17
Hollingshead[a]	.10	.42**	.41**	.41**	.44**
Fathers' Education[a]	.04	.40**	.39**	.37**	.40**
Mothers' Education[a]	.11	.42**	.44**	.41**	.45**
Fathers' Occupation[a]	.14	.39**	.36**	.41**	.44**
Mothers' Occupation[b]	−.13	.30	.27	.11	.27

Note. **p < .01.
[a]ns range from 102 to 130.
[b]ns range from 39 to 47.

sooner in infants from families relatively higher in SES because of the quality and consistency of home stimulation received earlier in the course of development.

As can be readily seen in Table 8.7, all SES indicators, except for mothers' occupation, correlate with intellectual performance at a more or less constant magnitude over the years. The lack of relation with mothers' occupation is characteristic in the proceeding matrices as well. The data also reveal that the strength of the relation is comparable across the significant indicators with approximately 20% of the variance being accounted for at best by any one indicator, including the long-term relation of SES appraised at age 1 year and intelligence measured at age 17 years. Cross-cultural longitudinal research by Chen, Lee, and Stevenson (1996) corroborated this finding.

Another aspect of the relation of SES and intelligence in the FLS pertains to our data on intellectually gifted children (A. W. Gottfried et al., 1994). At age 8 years, 20 of the 107 children tested obtained IQ scores at or above 130. We then compared the early developmental aspects of those children who emerged as gifted with those who did not at that point in time. Among the many variables studied were SES, parental occupation, and education. The results revealed that the family SES of gifted children was significantly higher than the family SES of their nongifted cohort peers from infancy onward through age 8. The SES differences were primarily due to parents' educational accomplishments as opposed to occupational status. When we examined the developmental trajectories of SES from 1 through 17 years for the two study groups, the families of the gifted compared to the nongifted children had higher Hollingshead scores throughout the course of investigation (Gottfried, Gottfried, Bathurst, & Guerin, 1997). Hence, even within this predominately middle-class sample, SES is sufficiently potent in differentiating intellectually gifted from nongifted children throughout childhood.

The correlations between the SES indicators and academic achievement for reading and math are displayed in Table 8.8. For both academic subject areas, there is an equivalent pattern of relations to that of intellectual performance. Again,

TABLE 8.8
Correlations of Socioeconomic Status and Academic Achievement

| | Assessment Age and Subject Area | | | | | | | |
| | 6 Years | | 8 Years | | 12 Years | | 17 Years | |
SES at Age 1	Read	Math	Read	Math	Read	Math	Read	Math
Hollingshead[a]	.29**	.27**	.30**	.29**	.26**	.24*	.32**	.39**
Fathers' Education[a]	31**	.26**	.34**	.26**	.32**	.25**	.35**	.40**
Mothers' Education[a]	.35**	.27**	.33**	.40**	.26**	.27**	.28**	.43**
Fathers' Occupation[a]	.25**	.24*	.24*	.29**	.21*	.28**	.27**	.41**
Mothers' Occupation[b]	.13	.14	.16	.20	.07	−.04	.19	.23

Note. *p < .05. **p < .01.
[a]ns range from 102 to 109.
[b]ns range from 39–41.

mothers' occupational status failed to correlate with achievement. Furthermore, the amount of variance accounted for by any single indicator approaches 20%, but is typically less. The latter finding is in accord with White's (1982) meta-analysis of almost 200 studies on the relation between SES and academic achievement in which typically 10% of the variance is accounted for when participants, in contrast to aggregates, are the unit of analysis.

In contrast to performance measures such as intelligence and academic achievement, academic intrinsic motivation refers to the pleasure inherent in school learning. It is characterized by a mastery orientation, curiosity, persistence, task endogeny and the learning of challenging, difficult, and novel tasks (A. E. Gottfried, 1985). This construct is measured by the Children's Academic Intrinsic Motivation Inventory (CAIMI; Gottfried, 1986). The scales are differentiated into the subject areas of reading, math, social studies, and science, and there is also a scale assessing general orientation toward school learning. This standardized instrument was administered to the study sample at 9, 10, 13, 16, and 17 years of age. The relations of the SES indicators with the CAIMI are shown in Table 8.9. SES indicators at age 1 (except mothers' occupation) correlated with subsequent academic intrinsic motivation. Numerous correlations are significant, albeit consistently low in magnitude. The concurrent correlations between SES at 9 through 17 years and academic intrinsic motivation were also highly inconsistent. This is understandable in light of our published structural equation modeling findings (Gottfried, Fleming, & Gottfried, 1998), revealing that SES does not bear a direct relation with academic intrinsic motivation between 9 and 13 years (i.e., the ages studied). Rather SES is only mediated through home environment and motivation during these ages.

Self-concept was appraised by the Self-Description Questionnaire (SDQ; Marsh, 1988, 1990). The view is taken that self-concept is not a unitary construct but differentiated into components. Two higher order rubrics can be formed: an academic self-concept and a general self-concept that does not comprise school-related components. The appropriate versions of the SDQ I and II were administered during preadolescence and adolescence (10, 12, 14, and 16 years of age). The relations between these self-concept measures and the SES indicators are displayed in Table 8.10. Except for mothers' occupation, the SES indicators correlate significantly with self-concept. The correlations reach at best low moderate levels. Overall, the correlations tend to be higher with school self-concept than self-concept in general.

The Vineland Adaptive Behavior Scales (Sparrow, Balla, & Cicchetti, 1984) were administered only upon school entry (ages 6 and 8 years). The Vineland is a well-established measure of social competence, specifically assessing personal and social sufficiency. The scales (communication, daily living, and socialization) result in an overall adaptive behavior composite score, which was employed in the analysis. Table 8.11 presents the relation of SES with this measure of social competence. The SES indicators (with except of mothers' occupation) correlate significantly with the Vineland at both ages.

TABLE 8.9

Correlations of Socioeconomic Status and Intrinsic Motivation

SES at Age 1	Assessment Age (Years)				
	9	10	13	16	17
			Reading		
Hollingshead[a]	.25**	.23*	.27**	.17	.19*
Fathers' Education[a]	.29**	.27**	.18	.13	.15
Mothers' Education[a]	.21*	.17	.03	.07	.10
Fathers' Occupation[a]	.26**	.21*	.29**	.17	.16
Mothers' Occupation[b]	.08	.20	.23	.07	.15
			Mathematics		
Hollingshead[a]	.24*	.27**	.30**	.26**	.23*
Fathers' Education[a]	.23*	.25**	.24*	.24**	.25**
Mothers' Education[a]	.23*	.20*	.20*	.22*	.20*
Fathers' Occupation[a]	.25**	.23*	.30**	.28**	.23*
Mothers' Occupation[b]	.20	.03	−.07	.01	.00
			Social Studies		
Hollingshead[a]	.25**	.18	.23*	.20*	.16
Fathers' Education[a]	.32**	.19	.19	.22*	.14
Mothers' Education[a]	.27**	.20*	.11	.14	.14
Fathers' Occupation[a]	.22*	.19	.21*	.20*	.18
Mothers' Occupation[b]	.17	.25	.17	.03	.02
			Science		
Hollingshead[a]	.17	.28**	.23*	.20*	.30**
Fathers' Education[a]	.14	.17	.20*	.21*	.26**
Mothers' Education[a]	.19	.20*	.15	.14	.19
Fathers' Occupation[a]	.15	.29**	.25**	.20*	.29**
Mothers' Occupation[b]	.16	.09	.04	−.10	.08

Note. $*p < .05.$ $**p < .01.$
[a] ns range from 105 to 111.
[b] ns range from 39 to 41.

Table 8.12 reveals the correlations of SES indicators and behavior problems. The latter were assessed with the Child Behavior Checklist and Teacher Report Form (CBCL and TRF; Achenbach, 1991a, 1991b). These are empirically based contemporary checklists with versions that can be completed by parents and teachers. The individual problem scales form two broad-band nosological categories indicative of distinct types of developmental psychopathology. One rubric represents internalizing types of problems such as being withdrawn, anxious–depressed, somatic problems, etc., and the other characterizes externalizing problems such as attention, and delinquent and aggressive behavior problems. Again, with the exception of mothers' occupation, the SES indicators correlated with both internalizing and externalizing behavior problems. In other words, there is a small but significant tendency for parents relatively higher in SES to have children with fewer

TABLE 8.10

Correlations of Socioeconomic Status and Self-Concept Categories

| | Assessment Age (Years) and Self-Concept Category | | | | | | | |
| | 10 | | 12 | | 14 | | 16 | |
SES at Age 1	Academic	General	Academic	General	Academic	General	Academic	General
Hollingshead[a]	.31**	.18	.32**	.30**	.39**	.21*	.37**	.25**
Fathers' Education[a]	.22*	.15	.37**	.36**	.24*	.19*	.30**	.26**
Mothers' Education[a]	.18	.15	.41**	.28**	.26**	.18	.27**	.22*
Fathers' Occupation[a]	.30**	.17	.26*	.28**	.36**	.21*	.36**	.29**
Mothers' Occupation[b]	.18	-.03	.11	-.04	.17	-.12	.15	-.07

Note. *p < .05. **p < .01.
[a] ns range from 99 to 110.
[b] ns range from 39 to 41.

TABLE 8.11

Correlations of Socioeconomic Status
and Social Competence

	Assessment Age (Years)	
SES at Age 1	6	8
Hollingshead[a]	.33**	.40**
Fathers' Education[a]	.24*	.33**
Mothers' Education[a]	.30**	.33**
Fathers' Occupation[a]	.33**	.37**
Mothers' Occupation[b]	.12*	.16*

Note. *p < .05. **p < .01.
[a] ns range from 100 to 107.
[b] ns range from 39 to 41.

TABLE 8.12

Correlations of Socioeconomic Status and Internalizing and Externalizing
Behavior Problems

	Assessment Age (Years) and Behavior Problem Category					
	8		12		17	
SES at Age 1	Intern	Extern	Intern	Extern	Intern	Extern
Hollingshead[a]	−.28**	−.32**	−.22*	−.27**	−.09	−.25*
Fathers' Education[a]	−.23*	−.24*	−.26**	−.21*	−.11	−.24*
Mothers' Education[a]	−.21*	−.22*	−.10	−.24*	−.13	−.06
Fathers' Occupation[a]	.24*	−.28**	−.18	−.19	−.12	−.21*
Mothers' Occupation[b]	−.06	.03	−.12	−.27	−.03	−.07

Note. *p < .05. **p < .01.
[a] ns ranged from 94 to 105.
[b] ns ranged from 36 to 39.

behavioral difficulties. There is also a tendency for the strength of the correlations to become weaker with advancing age. Perhaps this is not surprising given the role and influence of extrafamilial factors (e.g., peers) increasing with age. There was no relation of SES with teachers' reports on the TRF. Perhaps one reason is because there is low correspondence across informants (i.e., parents and teachers; see Achenbach, McConaughy, & Howell, 1987) on such measures, as well as contextual (i.e., home and school) factors operating. It is important to highlight two points with respect to the measurement of behavior problems. First, the fund of behavioral–observational knowledge of the study children would be greater for the parents than the teachers. Second, the same parents completed the checklists over time, whereas there were hundreds of teachers in providing information about the children's behavioral adjustment in the classroom. This is because children typically have different teachers from 1 year to the next. Furthermore, the study children in the FLS were not selected from one or a few schools, given that the study commenced when the cohort was 1 year of age. In sum, the vast number of teachers in diverse school settings could be contributing a great deal of error variance in such measurements and consequently attenuate the relations (see Guerin, Gottfried, & Thomas, 1997).

The last behavioral dimension studied was temperament. Throughout the course of investigation, temperament was assessed via parents' reports on various questionnaires (Guerin & Gottfried, 1994a, 1994b; Guerin, Gottfried, Oliver, & Thomas, 1994). Succinctly, this was the only dimension researched in which there was no relation with any of the SES indicators. Perhaps this biologically rooted individual difference in behavioral tendency (Bates, 1980) is unrelated to the environmental influences associated with SES.

Relation of SES to Children's Family Environment

The relation of family environment and children's development has been a major theme from the outset of the FLS (see Gottfried, 1984). We have grouped environmental measures into three categories: distal, proximal, and family relationship variables (Gottfried & Gottfried, 1984; A. W. Gottfried et al., 1994). Distal variables refer to the global or descriptive aspects that characterize the environment, but do not measure the specific experiences that impinge on or interact with the child that may influence development. For example, distal variables include SES, parents' occupation, education, etc. Proximal variables, which focus on the process

TABLE 8.13
Socioeconomic Status and Home Environment:
Home Observations for Measurement
of the Environment

	Assessment Age (Years)		
SES at Age 1	1	3	8
Hollingshead[a]	.30**	.49**	.43**
Father's Education[a]	.39**	.49**	.39**
Mother's Education[a]	.38**	.53**	.45**
Father's Occupation[a]	.27**	.40**	.41**
Mothers' Occupation[b]	.11	.47**	.21

Note. **$p < .01$.
[a]ns range from 103 to 129.
[b]ns range from 39 to 47.

or detailed aspects of the environment, include cognitively enriching and stimulating materials and activities, variety of experiences, parental involvement, social and emotional supports, and physical environment. Such variables are measured via direct observation and semi-structured interview with the Home Observation for Measurement of the Environment scales (HOME) developed by Caldwell and Bradley (1984). Family relationships, which may also be considered proximal, comprise the quality of family interactions and the social climate in the home. We have measured this category of environmental characteristics with the Family Environment Scale (FES) developed by Moos and Moos (1986). The FES is a questionnaire that encompasses 10 dimensions: cohesiveness, expressiveness, conflict, independence, achievement orientation, intellectual–cultural orientation, active–recreational orientation, moral–religious emphasis, organization, and control.

Table 8.13 presents the correlations of the SES indicators with the total HOME score. Across time, these indicators (mothers' occupation excluded) consistently correlate with the overall quantity and quality of proximal stimulation furnished by parents to their young children. The relation of SES and proximal processes as measured by the HOME with infants and preschoolers from diverse populations in North America has been documented (Gottfried, 1984; Gottfried & Gottfried, 1986).

Correlations were conducted between the SES indicators and the dimensions of the FES; these are displayed in Table 8.14. One overwhelmingly clear pattern ensued. The SES indicators (again excluding mothers' occupational status) significantly and consistently correlated with a single dimension, intellectual–cultural orientation of the family. Thus, this may explain why the highest correlations in the foregoing matrices of SES and developmental domains were with intelligence and academic achievement.

TABLE 8.14

Relationship of Socioeconomic Status and Intellectual-Cultural Scale of the Family Environment Scale

	Assessment Age (Years)			
SES at Age 1	3	8	12	17
Hollingshead[a]	.44**	.57**	.32**	.42**
Father's Education[a]	.42**	.40**	.24*	.37**
Mother's Education[a]	.45**	.59**	.35**	.54**
Father's Occupation[a]	.37**	.52**	.28**	.37**
Mothers' Occupation[b]	.19	.37*	.24	.20

Note. **$p < .01$.
[a]ns range from 93 to 118.
[b]ns range from 36 to 44.

CONCLUSIONS

SES is quite an encompassing construct. In sociology it has implications for power, prestige, and wealth (Mueller & Parcel, 1981). For developmental scientists, as the present data reveal, it relates to virtually every aspect of human psychological development and across a considerable period of time. It is impressive that a measure of an infant's family SES relates to various aspects of his or her development at the completion of high school. SES permeates almost every component of one's psychological development. One can hardly think of any other variable that is so central in the course of human psychological development.

There are differences of opinion on measuring SES and certainly the research questions posed would dictate the method (Entwisle & Astone, 1994; Hauser, 1994). The present longitudinal investigation employed the HI at the outset. It was selected because it was suitable for estimating SES of unmarried individuals and heads of households of both genders, as well as for families. One never knows the course of events in families who are to be studied longitudinally. Our initial findings also revealed that the Hollingshead correlated higher with early developmental status than did the Revised Duncan Socioeconomic Index or Siegel Prestige Scores (A. W. Gottfried, 1985). As the present data show, the Hollingshead proved to be a reliable index of family SES across almost two decades of investigation, and it displayed a pervasive relation to almost all aspects of development studied.

Issues did arise in the use of the Hollinghead in the course of investigation. Two examples are pertinent. The first pertained to the mother's entry into the workforce. If in a family only the father worked, the index was based exclusively on him and a specific index score ensued. However, if the mother then entered the work force the computation now included her education and occupational status. Typically mothers acquired a job of less prestige than their husbands. The outcome was that the family SES index decreased solely because of her entry into the workforce and lower than if she did not become gainfully employed. Clearly, this makes no sense when in fact the family's power, prestige, and income could be enhanced by her entry into the working world. The lowered index in our opinion is a misrepresentation because it often underestimates dual-earner family arrangements.

A second example involved parents who divorced and parents who remarried. When parents divorced, the issue arose as to whose household should be used to determine family SES (not to mention situations of joint equally shared custody). Using common sense, the home where the child resided mostly or most continuously was deemed the household on which the computation was based. The situation became more complicated when, for example, the child was residing with his or her mother who was not employed and then remarried and the stepfather was employed. "Who enters the index for computations, the natural father who is not living in the home but employed or the gainfully employed stepfather residing in the home?" We chose the latter because, as developmental scientists, we used the child's immediate context or micro-system as the focal point. As families depart from the traditional nuclear arrangement and redefine themselves (see Gottfried & Gottfried 1994), more profound and complex questions will be raised as to the measurement of family SES.

Another issue raised pertains to the amount of variance accounted for by SES. In the present study, no more than 20% of the variance, and typically less, was explained by any one SES indicator. However, keep in mind that individuals were the unit of analysis. As White (1982) pointed out in his meta-analysis of almost 200 studies on the relation between SES and academic achievement, when individuals are used as the unit of analysis as is typically the case, the relation is weak, but when aggregated units are employed the correlations increase substantially. Certainly a researcher can attempt to increase the amount of variance explained by using aggregates, regressions, latent variables, etc. However, we do not view this as a fundamental issue. To us, SES is a central construct that permeates virtually every aspect of a child's development, and what it encompasses and conveys is essential for understanding how environments and development interface. SES is a marker variable that tells us where and what to look for in the more immediate environments of children. As developmental scientists, we view the fundamental issues as how SES enters into children's proximal experiences and what psychological experiences are afforded to children by families varying in SES.

A final point addresses the education variable. It is interesting to note that the nomological network of relations (or correlations) was comparable for education and the HI (as well as fathers'occupational status). Hence, it begs the question as to why would a developmental researcher go though the effort of determining occupational prestige scores or ratings or even computing the HI when the nature of relations with various aspects of development is comparable for such measures and educational attainment per se. The latter is straightforward, easier to obtain, does not eliminate the input of a parent because he or she does not work, and is extraordinarily stable over time. At the very least, we strongly concur with Hauser's (1994) point that, whenever possible paternal, as well as maternal, education should be ascertained. More importantly, the longitudinal data presented herein demonstrate that parents' education not only benefits their lives in terms of occupational status and its implications, but also advantages their children's growth-promoting experiences and development in many ways throughout childhood.

ACKNOWLEDGEMENTS

We thank the children and families of the Fullerton Longitudinal Study for their continuing interest and participation. Gratitude is extended to Pamella Oliver, Jacqueline Coffman, Craig Thomas, Judit Au, Ann Barter, Rachel Mason, Colleen Killian, Michelle Ramos, and Susanne Valdez. This research was supported by grants from the Spencer Foundation, Thrasher Research Fund, and intramural grants from California State University, Fullerton. The data presented, the statements made, and the views expressed are solely the responsibility of the authors.

REFERENCES

Achenbach, T. M. (1991a). *Manual for the Child Behavior Checklist/4-18 and 1991 Profile.* Burlington, VT: University of Vermont.

Achenbach, T. M. (1991b). *Manual for the Teacher's Report Form and 1991 Profile.* Burlington, VT: University of Vermont.

Achenbach, T. M., McConaughy, S. H., & Howell, C. T. (1987). Child–adolescent behavioral and emotional problems: Implications for cross-informant correlations for situational specificity. *Psychological Bulletin, 101,* 213–232.

Bates, J. E. (1980). The concept of difficult temperament. *Merrill-Palmer Quarterly, 26,* 299–319.

Caldwell, B., & Bradley, R. (1984). *Home observation for measurement of the environment.* New York: Dorsey.

Chen, C., Lee, S. Y., & Stevenson, H. H. (1996). Longterm prediction of academic achievement of American, Chinese, and Japanese adolescents. *Journal of Educational Psychology, 88,* 750–759.

Entwisle, D. R., & Astone, N. M. (1994). Some practical guidelines for measuring youth's race–ethnicity and socioeconomic status. *Child Development, 65,* 1521–1540.

Gottfried, A. E. (1985). Academic intrinsic motivation in elementary and junior high school students. *Journal of Educational Psychology, 77,* 631–645.

Gottfried, A. E. (1986). *Children's academic intrinsic motivation inventory.* Odessa, FL: Psychological Assessment Resources.

Gottfried, A. E., Bathurst, K., & Gottfried, A. W. (1994). Role of maternal and dual-earner employment in child development: A longitudinal study. In A. E. Gottfried & A. W. Gottfried (Eds.) *Redefining families: Implications for children's development* (pp. 55–98). New York: Plenum.

Gottfried, A. E., Fleming, J. S., & Gottfried, A. W. (1998). Role of cognitively stimulating environment in children's academic intrinsic motivation: A longitudinal study. *Child Development, 69,* 1448–1460.

Gottfried, A. E., & Gottfried, A. W. (Eds.). (1988). *Maternal employment and children's development: Longitudinal research.* New York: Plenum.

Gottfried, A. E., & Gottfried, A. W. (Eds.). (1994). *Redefining families: Implications for children's development.* New York: Plenum.

Gottfried, A. E., Gottfried, A. W., & Bathurst, K. (2002). Dual earner employment and parenting. In M. H. Bornstein (Ed.), *Handbook of parenting* (2nd ed., pp. 207–229). Mahwah, NJ: Lawrence Erlbaum Associates.

Gottfried, A. W. (Ed.) (1984). *Home environment and early cognitive development.* Orlando, FL: Academic Press.

Gottfried, A. W. (1985). Measures of socioeconomic status in child development research: Data and recommendations. *Merrill-Palmer Quarterly, 31,* 85–92.

Gottfried, A. W., & Gottfried, A. E. (1984). Home environment and cognitive development in young children of middle-socioeconomic-status families. In A.W. Gottfried (Ed.), *Home environment and early cognitive development* (pp. 57–116). Orlando, FL: Academic Press.

Gottfried, A. W., & Gottfried, A. E. (1986). Home environment and children's development from infancy through the school entry years: Results of contemporary longitudinal investigations in North America. *Children's Environment Quarterly, 3,* 3–9.

Gottfried, A. W., Gottfried, A. E., Bathurst, K., & Guerin, D. W. (1994). *Gifted IQ: Early developmental aspects.* New York: Plenum.

Gottfried, A. W., Gottfried, A. E., Bathurst, K., & Guerin, D. W. (1997, April). Intellectual giftedness: A longitudinal study of continuities from infancy through adolescence. In A. W. Gottfried (Chair), *Development of gifted children: Longitudinal studies*. Symposium presented at the biennial meetings of the Society for Research in Child Development, Washington, DC.

Guerin, D. W., & Gottfried, A. W. (1994a). Developmental stability and change in parent reports of temperament: A ten-year longitudinal investigation from infancy through preadolescence. *Merrill-Palmer Quarterly, 40*, 334–355.

Guerin, D. W., & Gottfried, A. W. (1994b). Temperamental consequences of infant difficultness. *Infant Behavior and Development, 17*, 413–421.

Guerin, D. W., Gottfried, A. W., Oliver, P. H., & Thomas, C. W. (1994). Temperament and school functioning during early adolescence. *Journal of Early Adolescence, 14*, 200–225.

Guerin, D. W., Gottfried, A. W., & Thomas, C. W. (1997). Difficult temperament and behavioral problems: A longitudinal study from 1.5 to 12 years. *International Journal of Behavioral Development, 21*, 71–90.

Hauser, R. M. (1994). Measuring socioeconomic status in studies of child development. *Child Development, 65*, 1541–1545.

Hoff-Ginsberg, E., & Tardif, T. (1995). Socioeconomic status and parenting. In M. H. Bornstein (Ed.), *Handbook of parenting* (pp. 161–187). Mahwah, NJ: Lawrence Erlbaum Associates.

Hollingshead, A. B. (1975). *Four factor index of social status*. Unpublished manuscript, Yale University, Department of Sociology, New Haven.

Marsh, H. W. (1988). *Manual for the self-description questionnaire I*. San Antonio, TX: Psychological Corporation/Harcourt Brace Jovanovich.

Marsh, H. W. (1990). *Manual for the self-description questionnaire II*. San Antonio, TX: Psychological Corporation/Harcourt Brace Jovanovich.

McCall, R. B. (1979). The development of intellectual functioning in infancy and the prediction of later IQ. In J. D. Osofsky (Ed.), *Handbook of infant development* (pp. 707–741). New York: Wiley.

Moos, R. H., & Moos, B. S. (1986). *Family environmental scale manual* (2nd ed.). Palo Alto, CA: Consulting Psychologist Press.

Mueller, C. W., & Parcel, T. L. (1981). Measures of socioeconomic status: Alternatives and recommendations. *Child Development, 52*, 13–30.

Parke, R. D. (1995). Fathers and families. In M. H. Bornstein (Ed.), *Handbook of parenting* (pp. 27–64). Mahwah, NJ: Lawrence Erlbaum Associates.

Siegel, P. M. (1971). *Prestige in the American occupational structure*. Unpublished doctoral dissertation, University of Chicago.

Sparrow, S. S., Balla, D. A., & Cicchetti, D. V. (1984). *Vineland Adaptive Behavior Scales survey form manual (Interview edition)*. Circle Pines, MN: American Guidance Service.

Stevens, G., & Featherman, D. L. (1981). A revised socioeconomic index of occupational status. *Social Science Research, 10*, 364–395.

White, K. (1982). The relation between socioeconomic status and academic achievement. *Psychological Bulletin, 91*, 461–481.

Wilson, R. S. (1985). Risk and resilience in early mental development. *Developmental Psychology, 21*, 795–805.

9

Moving on Up: Neighborhood Effects on Children and Families

Tama Leventhal and Jeanne Brooks-Gunn

National Center for Children and Families
Teachers College, Columbia University

INTRODUCTION

Socioeconomic (SES) disparities in well-being have prompted both empirical inquiry and policy attention (Keating & Hertzman, 1999). SES inequities have been documented across most domains of development—cognition/achievement, physical health, and emotional well-being—and across the lifespan for children, youth, and adults (Brooks-Gunn & Duncan, 1997; Duncan & Brooks-Gunn, 1997; Haveman & Wolfe, 1994). Consideration of the role of neighborhood residence as a contributor to SES differentials has been raised. Neighborhood residence may be a source of SES disparities, as a family's resources constrain where they live (Massey & Denton, 1993; Wilson, 1987, 1997). An alternative, yet complementary view, posits that inequities in family SES are transmitted to parents and their children through various mechanisms or processes (i.e., effect indirect), one of which may be neighborhood residence (Brooks-Gunn, Duncan, & Aber 1997a, 1997b; Jencks & Mayer, 1990). In general, studies on child development find that neighborhood conditions, particularly SES, are accounted for, in part, by family SES, yet also have an independent effect on child and adolescent outcomes (Leventhal & Brooks-Gunn, 2000).

A growing body of neighborhood research has used data collected from the United States Decennial Census to examine links among neighborhood SES and a range of child and youth outcomes (controlling for family SES). The census tract is commonly used to define the neighborhood unit, and the census provides information on neighborhood sociodemographic characteristics. Neighborhood SES measures, typically derived from factor or cluster analysis, include a combination of income, percentage of poor residents, percentage of professionals, percentage of residents with high school or college degree, percentage of female-headed households, and percentage of employed (or unemployed) individuals. Separate indicators of affluence/high-SES and poverty/low-SES are used because the presence of poor and affluent neighbors may have differential effects on child and adolescent well-being (Brooks-Gunn, Duncan, Klebanov, & Sealand, 1993; Jencks & Mayer, 1990).

A review of the neighborhood literature found that neighborhood high-SES was positively associated with children's and youths' school readiness, educational, and achievement outcomes, while neighborhood low-SES was adversely associated with their emotional and social outcomes (Leventhal & Brooks-Gunn, 2000). However, after accounting for family characteristics including income/SES, neighborhood SES effects were, generally, small to moderate in magnitude (i.e., accounting for 5 to 10% of variance). It is likely that neighborhood SES effects, particularly on children and youth, may operate through mechanisms such as families, peers, and schools (Elliott et al., 1996; Klebanov, Brooks-Gunn, Chase-Lansdale, & Gordon, 1997; Sampson, 1997; see also Aber, Gephart, Brooks-Gunn, Connell, & Spencer, 1997). In addition, because a majority of evidence linking neighborhood SES to individual-level outcomes (as well as aggregated outcomes) is based on nonexperimental research, these studies are biased by the fact that families have some choice as to where they live (Tienda, 1991). Unmeasured factors, such as literacy, motivation, mental health, and the like may account for any observed neighborhood effects. Consequently, reported effects may be overestimated or underestimated depending on the situation. For example, depressed parents may be less inclined to move out of poor neighborhoods than nondepressed parents, resulting in an overestimation of neighborhood effects. Alternatively, parents who are conserving family economic resources to pay for children's education and extracurricular activities may remain in poor neighborhoods, as opposed to moving to a more affluent neighborhood, leading to an underestimation of neighborhood effects.

This chapter presents three theoretical models for understanding how neighborhood influences may be transmitted to children and youth—institutional resources, relationships, and norms and collective efficacy. This overview highlights how SES disparities at the neighborhood-level may operate. Subsequently, results from the United States Department of Housing and Urban Development's (HUD) Moving to Opportunity for Fair Housing Demonstration (MTO), an experimental study of moving (via randomization) from high- to low-poverty neighborhoods, are reviewed. This study represents a novel policy response to addressing SES disparities, as well as a unique research opportunity; findings are presented for parents, children, and youth.

Models of Neighborhood Influences on Development

In this section, three theoretical frames for understanding how neighborhoods may affect child and adolescent well-being are briefly presented (see Leventhal & Brooks-Gunn, 2000, for detailed presentation). The models include: institutional resources—quality, quantity, and diversity of community resources; relationships—parental attributes, social networks, and behavior and home environment characteristics; and norms and collective efficacy—extent of community formal and informal institutions present to monitor residents' behavior and physical threats to them. These theoretical models draw heavily from a review and analysis by Jencks and Mayer (1990), from work on economic hardship and unemployment (Conger, Ge, Elder, Lorenz, & Simons, 1994; McLoyd, 1990), and from research on social disorganization theory (Sampson, 1992; Sampson, Raudenbush, & Earls, 1997; Shaw & McKay, 1942; see Sampson & Morenoff, 1997, for a review).

Each model focuses on different underlying mechanisms and the utility of the model depends, in part, on the outcome under investigation and, in part, on the age group studied. The present review highlights how SES disparities may operate at the neighborhood level, directly or indirectly, to alter child and adolescent outcomes.

Institutional Resources

Institutional resources in the neighborhood are important to children's and adolescents' health and development. These resources include:

(1) Learning activities: Presence of libraries, family resource centers, literacy programs, and museums;

(2) Social and recreational activities: Presence of parks, sports programs, art and theater programs, and community centers;

(3) Childcare: Availability, quality, and cost of childcare, preschool, and early intervention programs;

(4) Schools: Quality, climate, norms, and demographics of schools;

(5) Health care services: Availability, quality, and affordability of medical and social services; and

(6) Employment opportunities: Supply of jobs, access to jobs (including transportation), and adolescents' expectations about available opportunities.

As described in this section, neighborhood SES, like family SES, is associated with access to institutional resources, as well as the quality of resources obtained. Low-SES neighborhoods generally provide fewer and lower quality resources than more affluent neighborhoods. There are, however, very few studies on links between community-level resources and child development, so we draw on relevant research for each type of resource and address them in turn.

The presence of learning activities in the community is likely to foster children's school readiness and achievement, whereas the availability of social and recreational activities is likely to promote their physical and social development. A comparative ecological study found that low-income communities provide children with fewer literacy resources, such as books, libraries, printed-material, and the like, than middle-income communities (Neuman & Celano, 2001). Qualitative and quantitative studies of families in disadvantaged neighborhoods have found that when learning and social resources are not available in families' own communities, parents will access resources from the larger surrounding community (Elder, Eccles, Ardelt, & Lord, 1995; Jarrett, 1997). This situation is particularly true for African-American parents who are more likely to reside in neighborhoods with fewer of these resources than other groups. One study of young children examined links between learning and social activities and cognitive development and found that activities inside of the home, but not outside of the home, mediated the effect of neighborhood high-SES on children's cognition (Klebanov, Brooks-Gunn, McCarton, & McCormick, 1998).[1] We hypothesize that out-of-home activities may be more relevant for older children who have greater exposure to them than young children, but additional research is needed to test this premise.

Childcare is a salient community resource for young children. As countless studies have documented, childcare quality and early childhood intervention are associated with children's school readiness, behavior, and health in addition to parenting outcomes (see Brooks-Gunn, Berlin, & Fuligni, 2000; Hayes, Palmer, & Zaslow, 1990; McKey et al., 1985; Yoshikawa, 1994, for reviews). A community study found that the availability and quality of childcare were differentially associated with neighborhood SES; low-SES neighborhoods had both a lower supply of and lower quality childcare than higher income neighborhoods (Fuller, Coonerty, Kipnis, & Choong, 1997). In addition, studies of family income report nonlinear effects on childcare availability, suggesting that quantity and quality may be lowest for low- to middle-income families who cannot afford acceptable childcare and do not qualify for government programs (NICHD Child Care Network, 1997).

For older children and youth, schools are a central mechanism through which neighborhood effects may operate. Like childcare, neighborhood low-SES is

---

[1]This example conflicts with our hypothesis regarding the mediating role of community resources. Results may be due to the age of children, as noted, or to the measure of community resources employed. Specifically, the HOME Inventory, largely, taps resources inside the home, as opposed to outside of the home. Further, this inventory assesses resources that are more likely to be provided by affluent parents than low-income parents.

negatively associated with school attributes (e.g., quality, climate, norms, and demographics) and children's and youths' achievement (Jencks & Mayer, 1990).[2] Several studies report that neighborhood conditions are associated with school norms towards risky behaviors, which in turn may be associated with subsequent problem behavior (Ennett, Flewelling, Lindrooth, & Norton, 1997; Teitler & Weiss, 2000).

Research on links between neighborhood characteristics, including SES, and health outcomes, such as low birth weight, injury, mortality, and maltreatment, has not examined the extent of health and social services in communities. There is ample evidence to suggest that access, quality, and variety of health services vary as a function of family SES (Newacheck, Hughes, & Stoddard, 1996; Newacheck, Stoddard, & McManus, 1993). This situation may apply to neighborhood SES as well (Brooks-Gunn, McCormick, Klebanov, & McCarton, 1998).

Another community resource is employment opportunities, which is most important for adolescents. Adolescent employment appears to be differentially associated with youth outcomes, with possibly beneficial effects for low-income youth and more detrimental consequences for middle- to high-income youth (Bachman & Schulenberg, 1993; Gleason & Cain, 1997; Leventhal, Graber, & Brooks-Gunn, 2001; Mortimer, Finch, Ryu, Shanahan, & Call, 1996; Newman, 1999; Steinberg, Fegley, & Dornbusch, 1993; Sullivan, 1989, 1996). Extrapolating from this work, low-SES neighborhoods may provide youth with fewer developmentally enhancing outlets beyond employment, whereas more affluent neighborhoods might have learning and social activities that provide beneficial alternatives to employment. A quasi-experimental study found that poor, minority youth who moved from poor, urban neighborhoods to more affluent suburbs were more likely to be employed, have jobs with benefits, and earn higher wages than youth who stayed in poor, urban neighborhoods (Kaufman & Rosenbaum, 1992). At the individual-level, youths' expectations about opportunities open to them are also shaped by neighborhood contexts, and their expectations may be associated with subsequent behavior, such as substance use, criminal activity, initiation of sexual activity, and child bearing (Billy, Brewster, & Grady, 1994; Ogbu, 1991; Paulter & Lewko, 1987; Willis, 1977).

Relationships

Parental relationships may transmit neighborhood effects to children and youth. Several aspects of relationships are implicated:

(1) Parental characteristics: Mental and physical health, irritability, coping skills, and efficacy;

---

[2]Policies promoting school choice may break the tight link between neighborhood residence and school quality (Shonkoff & Phillips, 2000).

(2) Support networks: Access to friends and family and connections within neighborhood;

(3) Parental behavior: Emotional responsivity, warmth, support, harshness, control, discipline, supervision, and monitoring; and

(4) Home environment: Provision of stimulating experiences (e.g., reading, books, toys), physical environment (e.g., safety, decor, cleanliness), presence of routines and structure (e.g., regular mealtimes and bedtimes), and exposure to violence (e.g., witness, victim).

The overarching framework for this section is based on the family stress model developed from research on economic hardship and unemployment. According to this model, the association between family low-income and child outcomes is mediated by parents' feelings of financial strain, depression, and subsequent parenting behavior (Conger et al., 1994; McLoyd, 1990). Parental relationships, in turn, are thought to intervene or interact with parental physical and emotional health, coping, and efficacy. Here, we extend this model of economic hardship to neighborhood disadvantage; neighborhood low-SES may affect parental well-being and resultant child outcomes by means of parental behavior and home environment. Similar to institutional resource models, there is scant research examining whether the individual and family processes specified transmit neighborhood effects to child well-being. Thus, this section presents relevant research on various components of this model.

Discrepancies in adult physical and mental health outcomes by neighborhood SES have been widely reported at the aggregate or neighborhood level (e.g., Cubbin, LeClere, & Smith, 2000). These studies reveal that neighborhood low-SES is associated with poor adult health outcomes (however, these studies do not usually control for individual- or family-level SES). At the individual level, only a few studies have examined associations among neighborhood conditions and parental health. For instance, a study of parents of young children found that neighborhood poverty and affluence (both compared to middle-income) were not associated with mothers' emotional distress (Klebanov, Brooks-Gunn, & Duncan, 1994). Results from experimental studies presented in the following section suggest to the contrary that such links may exist. In addition, a study of adolescents in disadvantaged communities found that parental efficacy mediated the use of African American parents' family management strategies (Elder et al., 1995).

Parental access to support networks and social connections may act as a vehicle through neighborhood economic resources affect child and adolescent outcomes (Cook, Shangle, & Degirmencioglu, 1997). Such support, particularly within the community, may buffer parents from the stressors of neighborhood violence, disorder, poverty, and material hardship and, consequently, mitigate the negative effects of parental well-being on child outcomes (Conger et al., 1994; Elder et al., 1995; McLoyd, 1990; see also Ross & Jang, 2000). One study found that parental social support had a nonlinear association with neighborhood SES, such that support was higher in middle-income neighborhoods compared with low- and high-income neighborhoods (Klebanov et al., 1994). In addition, social connections within the community might be used to monitor and care for children when parents are unavailable as well as for job referral networks (Coleman, 1988; Logan & Spitze, 1994).

Neighborhood conditions, particularly poverty and violence, are thought to be associated with parental behavior—warmth, harshness, and supervision. Quantitative and qualitative research on family economic hardship indicates that parental stress and anxiety may have the greatest impact on harsh parenting (Conger et al., 1994; McLoyd, 1990). In fact, a quasi-experimental study found that low-income families who moved to more affluent neighborhoods used less harsh behavior than parents who remained in poor neighborhoods (Briggs, 1997). Another study examining mediation models found that quality of parenting (monitoring, warmth/support, inductive reasoning, harsh discipline, hostility, and communication), assessed by means of videotaped parent–child interactions, accounted for the positive association between community disadvantage and adolescents' problem behavior (controlling for family SES; Simons, Johnson, Beaman, Conger, & Whitbeck, 1996); similar results have been reported elsewhere (Paschall & Hubbard, 1998). Parental reports of neighborhood danger also have been linked to use of harsh control and verbal aggression (Earls, McGuire, & Shay, 1994). In addition, one study of young children found that parents in low-income neighborhoods were less warm than their counterparts in middle-income neighborhoods (Klebanov et al., 1994).

Parental supervision and monitoring could intervene between neighborhood effects and child and adolescent outcomes by increasing or decreasing exposure to community influences, with the subsequent impact on well-being dependent on neighborhood context (Gonzales, Cauce, Friedman & Mason, 1996; Lamborn, Dornbusch, & Steinberg, 1996; Pettit, Bates, Dodge, & Meece, 1999). Ethnographic researchers have suggested that parents in dangerous and impoverished neighborhoods might utilize more restrictive monitoring practices with their children to minimize children's exposure to negative community influences (Anderson, 1991; Burton, 1990; Burton & Jarrett, 2000; Furstenberg, 1993; Jarrett, 1997). Along these same lines, a quasi-experimental study of moving from low- to middle-income neighborhoods found that parents who moved to better neighborhoods used less restrictive parenting practices than those who stayed in low-income neighborhoods (Briggs, 1997). Parental monitoring of early dating behavior also has been shown to mediate the positive association between neighborhood low-SES and the odds of teenage childbearing (Hogan & Kitagawa, 1985).

Four aspects of the home environment are hypothesized to transmit neighborhood effects to children and youth—provision of learning activities, physical home environment, presence of routines and structure, and exposure to violence. Several studies of young children, focusing on home learning, have tested this hypothesis. Across two different samples of young children, the beneficial effect of living in a high-SES neighborhood on cognition, verbal ability, and behavior problem scores was accounted for by quality of the home learning environment (controlling for family characteristics; Klebanov et al., 1997). Likewise, another study found that the adverse effects of neighborhood risk, as measured by parent report, on teacher reported social competence and reading achievement were partially mediated by quality of home environment (accounting for child and family characteristics; Greenberg et al., 1999). What parents do with their children in the home (as opposed to outside the home) appears to be the major contributor to child outcomes, particularly cognition (Klebanov et al., 1998; see also Firkowska et al., 1978). This situation may be most applicable for young children because of the primacy of the family context for this age group.

The physical home environment may be most important for children's and youth's health. Neighborhood low-income (compared with middle-income) is associated with low-quality physical home environments after controlling for family SES (Klebanov et al., 1994). In both experimental and nonexperimental work, children and adolescents living in low-SES neighborhoods were at greater risk for injury than their peers in more affluent neighborhoods (Durkin, Davidson, Kuhn, O'Connor, & Barlow, 1994; Katz, Kling, & Liebman, 2001). This situation is likely due, in part, to unsafe play areas in the home.

Routines and structure are thought to be central for children's social development (Boyce, Jensen, James, & Peacock, 1983; Bradley, 1995). At the theoretical level, several scholars have written about their significance, and that such routines may be lacking in low-SES neighborhoods with high poverty and unemployment, marked violence, and low social cohesion (Leventhal & Brooks-Gunn, 2000, Wilson, 1987, 1991). Affluent communities may provide a more optimal context for such practices than poor neighborhoods; although, this premise has not been examined (Leventhal & Brooks-Gunn, in press).

Finally, exposure to violence (witness or victim) may be a process through which neighborhoods influence children's and adolescents' physical and emotional health, in particular (Wright, 1998). Neighborhood low-SES has been found to be associated with children's exposure to violence in the neighborhood as well as the home (Coulton, Korbin, & Su, 1999; Coulton, Korbin, Su, & Chow, 1995; Martinez & Richters, 1993; Richters & Martinez, 1993). How these different levels of exposure interact remains to be tested.

Norms and Collective Efficacy

This frame emanates from social disorganization theory (Shaw & McKay, 1942). Mechanisms of influence operating at the community-level include:

(1) Collective efficacy: Extent of social connections including mutual trust, shared values, and willingness to intervene on behalf of community;

(2) Formal and informal institutions: Regulatory mechanisms that serve to supervise and monitor community activity;
(3) Peers: Group behavior and norms; and
(4) Physical threats: Level of violence, availability of harmful and illegal substances, and other general threats to well-being.

This model posits that collective efficacy modulates the capacity of residents to monitor the behavior of others in accordance with social norms and maintain public order (Sampson et al., 1997). Community formal and informal institutions act as the regulatory mechanisms. The ability of these institutions to monitor residents' behavior, particularly peer groups as well as physical threats, in turn, is thought to be a function of community structural attributes, including low-SES, racial/ethnic composition, residential stability, and single parenthood (Coulton et al., 1995; Sampson, 1992; Sampson & Groves, 1989). Researchers employing this framework have focused on adolescent problem behavior, such as delinquency, crime, violence, and substance use. For instance, in poor, residentially unstable, and racially/ethnically mixed neighborhoods, social organization is often low, leading to the proliferation of problem behaviors, such as public drinking and drug use, crime, and destruction of property. However, when social organization is high, youth are less likely to engage in negative behaviors and may demonstrate more positive behaviors, such as school engagement and civic participation. An emerging body of research from urban sociology has tested this model and is reviewed in this section.

The social connections described by collective efficacy are more diffuse than the social networks discussed under relationship models and operate at the community, as opposed to the individual level (see Sampson, 1999, for further discussion of this distinction). Collective efficacy and social control, measured by means of a community survey, were found to be negatively associated with neighborhood low-SES, rates of crime and violence, and observations of physical and social disorder (Raudenbush & Sampson, 1999; Sampson et al., 1997). In addition, at both the neighborhood and individual levels, mechanisms of social control are negatively associated with rates of adolescent problem behavior (Elliott et al., 1996; Sampson, 1997).

Peers are the central vehicle through which neighborhoods are hypothesized to affect adolescent development, especially social and emotional outcomes. Their influence is thought to be primarily negative because it is exacerbated when community institutions and norms fail to regulate peer group behavior (Sampson & Groves, 1989; Shaw & McKay, 1942). Although peer influences at the neighborhood level are typically discussed in the context of adolescents, these negative peer influences may begin in early childhood (Sinclair, Pettit, Harrist, Dodge, & Bates, 1994). Aggressive and antisocial behavior among peers of all ages may be tolerated in low-SES, low-cohesive neighborhoods because such behavior is more likely to be unstructured and unsupervised (Dishion, Andrews, & Crosby, 1995). In fact, two studies report that, in socially disadvantaged neighborhoods, few formal and informal institutions were present to supervise adolescent peer activities, and this deficit, in turn, was positively associated with delinquent and problem behavior and negative peer group affiliation and negatively associated with prosocial competence (Elliott et al., 1996; Sampson & Groves, 1989; see also Sampson, 1997). Peer support also has been found to moderate neighborhood effects on adolescent antisocial behavior, substance use, and school achievement, such that in high-risk neighborhoods, peer support has adverse effects, and in low-risk neighborhoods, it has more beneficial effects (Dubow, Edwards, & Ippolito, 1997; Gonzales et al., 1996).

Community regulatory mechanisms also are purported to be associated with the presence of risk to residents, especially children and youth, which has the potential to compromise their physical and emotional health. Two housing programs that relocated families from pubic housing to less poor neighborhoods found that parents reported children's safety as the primary reason for wanting to move (Briggs, 1997; Goering et al., 1999). A follow-up of one program found that children who moved to better neighborhoods were less likely to be the victim of a personal crime than children who stayed in public housing (Katz et al., 2001). In addition, adolescents' perceived danger has been shown to mediate the positive association between neighborhood low-SES and emotional problems (Aneshensel & Sucoff, 1996).

In terms of access to illegal and harmful substances, low-income neighborhoods and those with high proportions of African Americans may provide youth with greater access to alcohol and cigarettes than higher income neighborhoods and predominately European American neighborhoods (Briggs, 1997; Landrine, Klonoff, & Alcaraz, 1997). High levels of drug activity in the neighborhood also are associated with elevated school rates of cigarette smoking (Ennett et al., 1997). Finally, a growing body of research on neighborhood-level outcomes has documented that communities characterized by high poverty, residential instability, and high concentrations of racial and ethnic minorities are likely to expose residents to threats to their physical well-being, such as crime, juvenile delinquency, low weight births, infant mortality, morbidity, domestic violence, and child physical abuse (Collins & David, 1990; Coulton et al., 1995; Daly & Wilson, 1997; Drake & Pandey, 1996; Miles-Doan, 1998; see also O'Campo, Xue, Wang, & Caughy, 1997).

MTO: EXPERIMENTAL STUDY
OF NEIGHBORHOOD SES EFFECTS
ON PARENTS AND THEIR CHILDREN

In this section, findings are reviewed from the Moving to Opportunity for Fair Housing Demonstration (MTO). In 1994, HUD initiated the MTO program in five sites across the country (Baltimore, Boston, Chicago, Los Angeles, and New York City). The overarching goal of the program is to examine the impact of residential relocation, particularly the role of neighborhood income/SES, on child and family outcomes. The impetus for MTO was due, in part, to evidence from existing programs suggesting that moving low-income families from poor to more affluent neighborhoods may improve parents' and their children's educational and employment outcomes (Kaufman & Rosenbaum, 1992; Rosenbaum & Popkin, 1991).

Design of MTO

Families who had at least one child younger than 18 years of age and who resided in public housing or received project-based assistance under the Section 8 program were eligible for participation in MTO. Section 8 vouchers are portable rent subsidies that can be used to purchase approved housing in the private market. Participants were recruited from housing projects located in census tracts with poverty rates of 40% percent or higher according to the 1990 U.S. Census. A randomized, experimental design was used in which families who volunteered for the program were assigned to one of three conditions: (1) an experimental or treatment group who received Section 8 housing vouchers and special assistance and counseling to move only to low-poverty neighborhoods (less than 10% poor according to 1990 U.S. Census; experimental group); (2) a control group who received regular, geographically unrestricted Section 8 housing vouchers (Section 8 group); or (3) a second control group who did not receive vouchers or assistance but continued to receive project-based support (in-place control group). Counseling and assistance received by experimental families were provided by local nonprofit organizations and varied across sites. The services generally entailed assisting families with their housing search and finding appropriate units, as well as overcoming obstacles to obtaining housing in low-poverty neighborhoods (see Goering et al., 1999, for further details).

Structured interviews were conducted with heads of households at baseline, prior to random assignment, and subsequent relocation of the two mover groups. These interviews focused on demographic information with limited data on each household member collected. Follow-up evaluations were conducted approximately 2 to 3 years into the program by separate teams of investigators at each site. Consequently, discrepant research methodologies were employed across site evaluations, and a range of outcomes (with some overlap) was examined across site.

Participants

In total, 4,610 families participated in the MTO program (Goering et al., 1999). The profile of families is similar across sites. Families were predominately minority, with about two-thirds African American and the remainder Latino. Over 90% of households were headed by a single parent at baseline. At baseline, approximately 20% of household heads were employed, and 75% of households were receiving welfare at that time. Over three-quarters of applicants cited getting away from drugs and gangs as their primary motivation for joining the program.

Mobility Outcomes

According to 1990 census-based measures, the MTO program was successful at relocating experimental families to low-poverty neighborhoods. Over 90% of experimental families who moved within the program relocated to neighborhoods with poverty rates lower than 10%. In contrast, only 12% of Section 8 families who moved within the program relocated to low-poverty neighborhoods, and a majority, 75%, moved to near poor neighborhoods with poverty rates between 10% and 39%. Approximately 20% of Section 8 families moved to high-poverty neighborhoods with poverty rates of 40% of higher, like those from which they left (Goering et al., 1999).

In the remainder of this section, we summarize results from three of the five site evaluations conducted in Baltimore, Boston, and New York City (see Goering, in press, for a review of all sites). These sites were selected because the evaluations focus on parent, child, and youth outcomes. The Baltimore evaluation relied on administrative data collected from agency records including welfare and revenue records, state standardized educational test scores and reports, and juvenile arrest records (Ludwig, Duncan, & Hirschfield, 2001; Ludwig, Duncan, & Pinkston, 2000; Ludwig, Ladd, & Duncan, 2001). The Boston evaluation also used administrative data on welfare, revenue, and school demographics, as well as information collected during interviews (telephone and in person) with parents in which they reported on themselves and up to two children between the ages of 6 and 15 per household (Katz et al., 2001). The New York City evaluation conducted in-home interviews with families with data collected from parents and up to two children under 18 years of age per household (Leventhal & Brooks-Gunn, in press; Leventhal & Brooks-Gunn, 2001; Leventhal & Brooks-Gunn, 2002). Findings are reviewed separately for parents and for children and youth by outcome including: (1) employment, earnings, welfare, and education, (2) mental health, and (3) physical health (see also Del Conte & Kling, 2001, for an expanded review). Since the MTO is an experimental design, we cannot disentangle the processes that might underlie any observed effects; however, we use our theoretical models to speculate about potential mechanisms of influence.

Employment, Earnings, Welfare, and Education

Parents

One of the primary goals of the MTO program is to improve parents' employment prospects and earnings, and reduce welfare dependence. Results of the initial evaluations, however, suggest that the MTO program had only a modest impact on economic outcomes. Significant reductions in welfare receipt among experimental families relative to in-place control parents were found only at the Baltimore site; this difference was largely attributable to increased employment in the formal labor market. Across the three sites, no program effects were found for parental earnings and employment or household income.

Children and Youth

The MTO program is likely to impact children's and youth's education. At the Baltimore and Boston sites, experimental children and youth, who moved to low-poverty neighborhoods, attended schools with higher achievement test scores than their peers who remained in high-poverty neighborhoods. In Baltimore, Section 8 children and youth, who moved to poor and near poor neighborhoods, also attended schools with significantly higher test scores than in-place control children.

As far as children's educational achievement, the Baltimore evaluation found that, among children aged 5 to 11 at random assignment, reading and math achievement improved significantly for both experimental and Section 8 children compared with in-place control children. In contrast to the findings for children, moving out of high-poverty neighborhoods did not improve the reading achievement of children aged 12 to 18 at random assignment. To the contrary, results from the New York site suggest that only adolescent boys 11 to 18 years of age displayed higher achievement scores as a result of moving to less poor neighborhoods (compared with controls).

Potential Mechanisms

Although findings for parental employment were mixed, results are best interpreted in accordance with institutional resources and relationships models. In terms of resources, moving to less poor neighborhoods may have improved economic self-sufficiency by providing greater access to employment opportunities including jobs with better wages, stability, benefits, or all of the above. With respect to relationship mechanisms, job networks may have been enhanced in high-SES neighborhoods by the presence of middle-income neighbors, who presumably are employed. Alternatively, moving may have restricted access to existing job channels for some parents.

Mover children's enhanced achievement is most likely due to institutional resources. As results indicate, schools in low-poverty neighborhoods are likely to be of superior quality and composed of higher-achieving peers than those in high-poverty neighborhoods. In addition, children's achievement may be enhanced by moving to more advantaged neighborhoods because of additional community resources, such as preschool programs, libraries, and other learning activities. Furthermore, the relationships model would suggest that low-poverty communities are conducive to the provision of high-quality home environments, which promote school readiness and engagement. Finally, the norms/collective efficacy frame would indicate that adolescent boys, in particular, in less poor neighborhoods may affiliate with peers who are more academically engaged than peers in high-poverty neighborhoods.

Mental Health

Parents

The benefits of the MTO program could alter noneconomic outcomes as well. Findings from the Boston and New York sites suggest significant improvements in parental emotional health relative to in-place control parents. At these sites, both experimental and Section 8 parents reported fewer signs of emotional problems indicative of depression and anxiety/distress than in-place control parents, and effects were generally larger for experimental than Section 8 parents.

Children and Youth

Like their parents, children and youth are likely to display improved mental health as a result of moving out of poor neighborhoods. In New York City and Boston, significant improvements in mover children's and youth behavior problems were found relative to in-place controls; however, program effects were generally restricted to boys. Among older male youth, significant program impacts on arrests for violent crime were found in Baltimore, but no significant group differences were found for reported delinquency in New York City.

Potential Mechanisms

Improvements in emotional and social health resulting from moves out of high-poverty neighborhoods are best understood under the norms and collective efficacy model. Lower levels of crime and violence in receiving communities might account for parents' and their children's enhanced mental health, whereas increased collective efficacy and regulatory mechanisms might be responsible for youths' lower crime rates (both compared with in-place controls). In accordance with institutional resource models, more affluent neighborhoods also are likely to have more community resources that promote health than poor neighborhoods, as well as employment opportunities, which may reduce economic hardship and accompanying parental distress and harsh parenting.

Physical Health

Parents

Physical health, like emotional health, may be improved by moving to better neighborhoods. Results of the Boston and New York City evaluations suggest some health benefits of moving out of housing projects in high-poverty neighborhoods into less poor neighborhoods. At the Boston site, experimental parents reported superior health than in-place control parents. In terms of safety, experimental parents in Boston reported that the streets surrounding their homes were significantly safer than those of in-place control families. In New York City, both experimental and Section 8 parents reported less neighborhood physical and social disorder (trash, graffiti, public drinking, public drug use or dealing, and abandoned buildings) than in-place control parents.

Children and Youth

MTO health impacts for children and youth were also anticipated. In Boston, experimental children were less likely than in-place control children to have an injury/accident or an asthma attack requiring medical assistance in the past 6 months. In addition, experimental parents reported that at least one child in the family was less likely to be the victim of a personal crime in the past 6 months than in-place control parents.

Potential Mechanisms

Physical health benefits to parents, children, and youth from moving out of public housing in poor neighborhoods might be interpreted under the norms and collective efficacy model. The chronic stress of living in high-poverty, dangerous neighborhoods may be associated with poor health outcomes (McEwen & Seeman, 1999). As such, moving to more advantaged, socially organized neighborhoods may have led to reductions in health-compromising physiological responses to chronic stress. In line with the relationships model, families' physical home environments are likely to have been improved by moving out of public housing as well. Safer physical environments are likely to have fewer toxins and hazards to health, which may account for movers' superior health (compared with in-place controls).

CONCLUSIONS

This chapter took as its starting point the fact that SES disparities at the neighborhood level are likely to be indirect and operate through several mechanisms. Three models for understanding how neighborhood conditions, particularly SES, might influence child and adolescent outcomes were reviewed—institutional resources, relationships, and norms and collective efficacy. Our goal was to provide a theoretically driven framework for understanding neighborhood effects on development by specifying mechanisms of influence (individual, family, school, peer, and neighborhood) and elucidating how they may operate. In addition, these models were provided to aid empirical explorations of neighborhood effects on development.

A central feature of this framework is that models are complementary rather than conflicting. Some models are most salient for certain developmental age periods, whereas other models are most relevant for a particular class of outcomes. Specifically, for institutional resources, the most influential resource is likely to differ for children across the age span and will, consequently, affect divergent outcomes. For instance, child care and learning activities in the community may be the most salient community resource for young children's school readiness; schools and social activities may be most important for older children's achievement and social outcomes, respectively, and employment opportunities may be most relevant for youth's economic well-being. Quality and availability of health and social services, on the other hand, are likely to be important for physical and mental health outcomes, regardless of child age. Likewise, for relationship models, parental mental health may be important for both children's and youth's emotional health, but specific parenting behaviors and home environment characteristics are likely to vary in importance with developmental period and the respective outcome they alter (e.g., provision of cognitive stimulation for young children's school readiness; discipline for older children's emotional well-being; and supervision for adolescents' problem behavior). Finally, the norms and collective efficacy model, which focuses on community regulation, is most relevant for adolescents' problem behavior, but community-level physical threats to well-being, such as violence, are likely to affect the emotional outcomes of children and youth of all ages.

Findings from a novel social policy experiment also were reviewed. The MTO program afforded the opportunity to examine how a major shift in neighborhood SES (i.e., moving from neighborhoods with poverty rates of 40% or more to 10% or fewer poor) alters child and adolescent development. In addition, the Section 8 group enabled us to explore how more modest changes in neighborhood SES (i.e., moving from neighborhoods with poverty rates of 40% or more to 10%–39% poor) affect well-being. These estimates of neighborhood effects are not biased by omitted variables because the MTO program is based on an experimental design, where families were randomly assigned to certain types of neighborhoods.

Results were highly consistent across sites examining comparable outcomes. The findings presented suggest that the MTO program had a large impact on both noneconomic outcomes—physical and emotional health—and economic outcomes—educational achievement. Parents, children, and youth benefited from moving from high- to low-poverty neighborhoods. Program effects on families in the Section 8 group, who moved to poor and near poor neighborhoods, were generally more modest than those found for the experimental group.

The MTO program provides a unique research and policy opportunity to explore neighborhood SES disparities on child and youth outcomes. To refine our understanding of program effects, we must utilize the theoretical models presented. Because MTO is comprised of low-income families, findings are not necessarily generalizable to the population at large, but provide a window into the experiences of families who are most likely to be affected by policies seeking to address inequities in neighborhood SES.

In neighborhood studies of SES more generally, our ability to point to specific underlying mechanisms at play is necessary to draw policy recommendations. The research presented suggests that the policy lever for addressing neighborhood SES inequalities in health and well-being depends in large part on the outcome of interest and the age of target individuals. Our ability to ask, evaluate, and answer these more nuanced questions is likely to be most fruitful for designing programs and policies targeting neighborhood SES disparities.

ACKNOWLEDGMENTS

The authors would like to thank the United States Department of Housing and Urban Development (HUD), the Russell Sage Foundation, and the National Institute of Child Health and Human Development for their support. We are also grateful to the National Science Foundation, the NICHD Research Network on Child and Family Well-Being, the MacArthur Networks on Family and Work and Economy and Work, and the Spencer Foundation.

REFERENCES

Aber, J. L., Gephart, M., Brooks-Gunn, J., Connell, J., & Spencer, M. B. (1997). Neighborhood, family, and individual processes as they influence child and adolescent outcomes. In J. Brooks-Gunn, G. J. Duncan, & J. L. Aber (Eds.), *Neighborhood poverty: Context and consequences for children (Vol. 1)* (pp. 44–61). New York: Russell Sage.

Anderson, E. (1991). Neighborhood effects on teenage pregnancy. In C. Jencks & P. Peterson (Eds.), *The urban underclass* (pp. 375–398). Washington, DC: The Brookings Institution.

Aneshensel, C. S., & Sucoff, C. A. (1996). The neighborhood context and adolescent mental health. *Journal of Health and Social Behavior, 37*, 293–310.

Bachman, J. G., & Schulenberg, J. (1993). How part-time work intensity relates to drug use, problem behavior, time use, and satisfaction among high school seniors: Are these consequences or merely correlates? *Developmental Psychology, 29*, 220–235.

Billy, O. J., Brewster, K. L., & Grady, W. R. (1994). Contextual effects on the sexual behavior of adolescent women. *Journal of Marriage and the Family, 56*, 387–404.

Boyce, W. T., Jensen, E. W., James, S. A., & Peacock, J. L. (1983). The Family Routines Inventory: Theoretical origins. *Social Sciences and Medicine, 17*, 193–200.

Bradley, R. H. (1995). Environment and parenting. In M. Bornstein (Ed.), *Handbook of parenting* (pp. 235–261). Hillsdale, NJ: Lawrence Erlbaum Associates.

Briggs, X. S. (Ed.). (1997, July). *Yonkers revisited: The early impacts of scattered-site public housing on families and neighborhoods*. Report submitted to the Ford Foundation. New York, Teachers College: Author.

Brooks-Gunn, J., Berlin, L. J., & Fuligni, A. S. (2000). Early childhood intervention programs: What about the family? In J. P. Shonkoff & S. J. Meisels (Eds.), *Handbook on early childhood intervention* (2nd ed., pp. 549–588). New York: Cambridge University Press.

Brooks-Gunn, J., & Duncan, G. J. (1997). The effects of poverty on children. *Futures of Children, 7* (2), 55–71.

Brooks-Gunn, J., Duncan, G. J., & Aber, J. L. (Eds.). (1997a). *Neighborhood poverty: Context and consequences for children (Vol. 1).* New York: Russell Sage.

Brooks-Gunn, J., Duncan, G. J., & Aber, J. L. (Eds.). (1997b). *Neighborhood poverty: Policy implications in studying neighborhoods (Vol. 2).* New York: Russell Sage.

Brooks-Gunn, J., Duncan, G. J., Klebanov, P. K., & Sealand, N. (1993). Do neighborhoods influence child and adolescent development? *American Journal of Sociology, 99*(2), 353–395.

Brooks-Gunn, J., McCormick, M. C., Klebanov, P. K., & McCarton, C. (1998). Young children's health care use: Effects of family and neighborhood poverty. *Journal of Pediatrics, 132,* 971–975.

Burton, L. M. (1990). Teenage childbearing as an alternative life-course strategy in multigenerational black families. *Human Nature, 1*(2), 123–143.

Burton, L. M., & Jarrett, R. L. (2000). In the mix, yet on the margins: The place of families in urban neighborhood and child development research. *Journal of Marriage and the Family, 62*(4), 1114–1135.

Coleman, J. S. (1988). Social capital in the creation of human capital. *American Journal of Sociology, 94,* S95–S120.

Collins, J. W., & David, R. J. (1990). The differential effect of traditional risk factors on infant birthweight among blacks and whites in Chicago. *American Journal of Public Health, 80*(6), 679–681.

Conger, R. D., Ge, X., Elder, G. H., Jr., Lorenz, F. O., & Simons, R. L. (1994). Economic stress, coercive family process, and developmental problems of adolescents. *Child Development, 65*(2), 541–561.

Cook, T. D., Shagle, S. C., & Degirmencioglu, S. M. (1997). Capturing social process for testing mediational models of neighborhood effects. In J. Brooks-Gunn, G. J. Duncan, & J. L. Aber (Eds.), *Neighborhood poverty: Policy implications in studying neighborhoods (Vol. 2)* (pp. 94–119). New York: Russell Sage.

Coulton, C. J., Korbin, J. E., & Su, M. (1999). Neighborhood and child maltreatment: A multi-level study. *Child Abuse and Neglect, 23*(11), 1019–1040.

Coulton, C. J., Korbin, J. E., Su, M., & Chow, J. (1995). Community level factors and child maltreatment rates. *Child Development, 66*(5), 1262–1276.

Cubbin, C., LeClere, F. B., & Smith, G. S. (2000). Socioeconomic status and injury mortality: Individual and neighborhood determinants. *Journal of Epidemiology and Community Health, 54*(7), 517–524.

Daly, M., & Wilson, M. I. (1997). Life expectancy, economic inequality, homicide, and reproductive timing in Chicago neighborhoods. *British Medical Journal, 314,* 1271–1274.

Del Conte, A., & Kling, J. (2001). A synthesis of MTO research on self-sufficiency, safety and health, and behavior and delinquency. *Joint Center for Poverty Research New, 5*(1), 3–7.

Dishion, T. J., Andrews, D. W., & Crosby, L. (1995). Antisocial boys and their friends in early adolescence: Relationship characteristics, quality, and interactional process. *Child Development, 66,* 139–151.

Drake, B., & Pandey, S. (1996). Understanding the relationship between neighborhood poverty and specific types of child maltreatment. *Child Abuse and Neglect, 20,* 1003–1018.

Dubow, E. F., Edwards, S., & Ippolito, M. F. (1997). Life stressors, neighborhood disadvantages, and resources: A focus on inner-city children's adjustment. *Journal of Clinical Child Psychology, 26* (2), 130–144.

Duncan, G. J., & Brooks-Gunn, J. (Eds.). (1997). *Consequences of growing up poor.* New York: Russell Sage.

Durkin, M. S., Davidson, L. L., Kuhn, L., O'Connor, P., & Barlow, B. (1994). Low-income neighborhoods and the risk of severe pediatric injury: A small-area analysis in Northern Manhattan. *American Journal of Public Health, 84*(4), 587–592.

Earls, F., McGuire, J., & Shay, S. (1994). Evaluating a community intervention to reduce the risk of child abuse: Methodological strategies in conducting neighborhood surveys. *Child Abuse and Neglect, 18*(5), 473–485.

Elder, G. H., Eccles, J. S., Ardelt, M., & Lord, S. (1995). Inner-city parents under economic pressure: Perspectives on the strategies of parenting. *Journal of Marriage and the Family, 57*, 771–784.

Elliott, D., Wilson, W. J., Huizinga, D., Sampson, R., Elliott, A., & Rankin, B. (1996). The effects of neighborhood disadvantage on adolescent development. *Journal of Research in Crime and Delinquency, 33*(4), 389–426.

Ennett, S. T., Flewelling, R. L., Lindrooth, R. C., & Norton, E. C. (1997). School and neighborhood characteristics associated with school rates of alcohol, cigarette, and marijuana use. *Journal of Health and Social Behavior, 38*, 55–71.

Firkowska, A., Ostrowska, A., Sokolowska, M., Stein, Z., Susser, M., & Wald, I. (1978). Cognitive development and social policy. *Science, 200*, 1357–1362.

Fuller, B., Coonerty, C., Kipnis, F., & Choong, Y. (1997). *An unfair head start: California families face gaps in preschool and child care availability.* Report published by Berkeley-Stanford PACE Center, Yale University, and the California Child Care Resource and Referral Network: Growing Up in Poverty Project.

Furstenberg, F. F., Jr. (1993). How families manage risk and opportunity in dangerous neighborhoods. In W. J. Wilson (Ed.), *Sociology and the public agenda* (pp. 231–238). Newbury Park, CA: Sage.

Gleason, P. M., & Cain, G. G. (1997). *Earnings of black and white youth and their relation to poverty.* Madison, WI: University of Wisconsin (Discussion Paper #1138-97).

Goering, J. (Ed.). (in press). *Choosing a better life? How public housing tenants selected a HUD experiment to improve their lives and those of their children: The moving to opportunity demonstration program.* Washington, DC: Urban Institute Press.

Goering, J., Kraft, J., Feins, J., McInnis, D., Holin, M. J., & Elhassan, H. (1999, September). *Moving to Opportunity for Fair Housing Demonstration Program: Current status and initial findings.* Washington, DC: U.S. Department of Housing and Urban Development.

Gonzales, N. A., Cauce, A., Friedman, R. J., & Mason, C. A. (1996). Family, peer, and neighborhood influences on academic achievement among African-American adolescents: One-year prospective effects. *American Journal of Community Psychology, 24*(3), 365–387.

Greenberg, M. T., Lengua, L. J., Coie, J. D., Pinderhughes, E. E., Bierman, K., Dodge, K. A., Lochman, J. E., & McMahon, R. J. (1999). Predicting developmental outcomes at school entry using a multiple-risk model: Four American communities. *Developmental Psychology, 33*(35), 403–417.

Haveman, R., & Wolfe, B. (1994). *Succeeding generations: On the effects of investments in children.* New York: Russell Sage.

Hayes, C. D., Palmer, J. L., & Zaslow, M. E. (1990). *Who cares for America's children? Child care policy for the 1990s.* Washington, DC: National Academy Press.

Hogan, D. P., & Kitagawa, E. M. (1985). The impact of social status, family structure, and neighborhood on the fertility of black adolescents. *American Journal of Sociology, 90*(4), 825–855.

Jarrett, R. L. (1997). Bringing families back in: Neighborhoods' effects on child development. In J. Brooks-Gunn, G. J. Duncan, & J. L. Aber (Eds.), *Neighborhood poverty: Policy implications in studying neighborhoods (Vol. 2)* (pp. 48–64). New York: Russell Sage.

Jencks, C., & Mayer, S. (1990). The social consequences of growing up in a poor neighborhood. In L. E. Lynn & M. F. H. McGeary (Eds.), *Inner-city poverty in the United States* (pp. 111–186). Washington, DC: National Academy Press.

Katz, L. F., Kling, J., & Liebman, J. (2001). Moving to Opportunity in Boston: Early results of a randomized mobility experiment. *Quarterly Journal of Economics, May*, 607–654.

Kaufman, J., & Rosenbaum, J. (1992). The education and employment of low-income black youth in white suburbs. *Educational Evaluation and Policy Analysis, 14*(3), 229–240.

Keating, D., & Hertzman, C. (Eds.). (1999). *Developmental health and the wealth of nations: Social, biological and educational dynamics*. New York: Guilford.

Klebanov, P. K., Brooks-Gunn, J., Chase-Lansdale, P. L., & Gordon, R. (1997). Are neighborhood effects on young children mediated by features of the home environment? In J. Brooks-Gunn, G. J. Duncan, & J. L. Aber (Eds.), *Neighborhood poverty: Context and consequences for children (Vol. 1)*; (pp. 119–145). New York: Russell Sage.

Klebanov, P. K., Brooks-Gunn, J., & Duncan, G. J. (1994). Does neighborhood and family poverty affect mothers' parenting, mental health, and social support? *Journal of Marriage and the Family, 56*(2), 441–455.

Klebanov, P. K., Brooks-Gunn, J., McCarton, C. M., & McCormick, M. C. (1998). The contribution of neighborhood and family income upon developmental test scores over the first three years of life. *Child Development, 69*(5), 1420–1436.

Lamborn, S. D., Dornbusch, S. M., & Steinberg, L. (1996). Ethnicity and community context as moderators of the relations between family decision making and adolescent adjustment. *Child Development, 67*, 283–301.

Landrine, H., Klonoff, E. A., & Alcaraz, R. (1997). Racial discrimination in minors' access to tobacco. *Journal of Black Psychology, 23*(2), 135–147.

Leventhal, T., & Brooks-Gunn, J. (2000). The neighborhoods they live in: The effects of neighborhood residence upon child and adolescent outcomes. *Psychological Bulletin, 126*(2), 309–337.

Leventhal, T., & Brooks-Gunn, J. (2001). *Moving to Opportunity: An experimental study of neighborhood effects on mental health*. Manuscript submitted for publication.

Leventhal, T., & Brooks-Gunn, J. (2002). *A randomized study of neighborhood effects on low-income children's educational outcomes*. Manuscript submitted for publication.

Leventhal, T., & Brooks-Gunn, J. (In press). Moving to Opportunity: The early impacts of moving to opportunity on children and youth in New York city. In J. Goering (Ed.), *Choosing a better life? How public housing tenants selected a HUD experiment to improve their lives and those of their children: The moving to opportunity demonstration program*. Washington, DC: Urban Institute Press.

Leventhal, T., Graber, J. A., & Brooks-Gunn, J. (2001). Adolescent transitions into employment: When a job is not just a job. *Journal of Research on Adolescence, 11*(3), 297–323.

Logan, J. R., & Spitze, G. D. (1994). Family neighbors. *American Journal of Sociology, 100*(2), 453–476.

Ludwig, J., Duncan, G. J., & Hirschfield, P. (2001). Urban poverty and juvenile crime: Evidence from a randomized housing-mobility experiment. *Quarterly Journal of Economics, 116*(2), 655–679.

Ludwig, J., Duncan, G. J., & Pinkston, J. C. (2000). Neighborhood effects on economic self-sufficiency: *Evidence from a randomized housing-mobility experiment*. Manuscript in preparation.

Ludwig, J., Ladd, H. F., & Duncan, G. J. (2001). *Urban poverty and educational outcomes*. In W. G. Gale, & J. R. Pack (Eds.), *Brookings-Wharton papers on urban affairs 2001*. Washington, DC: Brookings Institution.

Martinez, J. E., & Richters, P. (1993). The NIMH Community Violence Project: II. Children's distress symptoms associated with violence exposure. *Psychiatry, 56*, 22–35.

Massey, D. S., & Denton, N. A. (1993). *American apartheid: Segregation and the making of the underclass*. Cambridge, MA: Harvard University Press.

McEwen, B. S., & Seeman, T. (1999). Protective and damaging effects of mediators of stress: Elaborating and testing the concepts of allostasis and allostatic load. *Annals of the New York Academy of Sciences, 896*, 30–47.

McKey, R. H., Condelli, L., Granson, H., Barrett, B., McConkey, C., & Plantz, M. (1985). *The impact of Head Start on children, families and communities* (Final report of Head Start Evaluation, Synthesis and Utilization). Washington, DC: U.S. Department of Health and Human Services.

McLoyd, V. C. (1990). The impact of economic hardship on Black families and development. *Child Development, 61*, 311–346.

Miles-Doan, R. (1998). Violence between spouses and intimates: Does neighborhood context matter? *Social Forces, 77*(2), 623–645.

Mortimer, J. T., Finch, M. D., Ryu, S., Shanahan, M. J., & Call, K. T. (1996). The effects of work intensity on adolescent mental health, achievement, and behavioral adjustment: New evidence from a prospective study. *Child Development, 67*, 1243–1261.

Neuman, S. B., & Celano, D. (2001). Access to print in low-income and middle-income communities: An ecological study of four neighborhoods. *Reading Research Quarterly, 36*(1), 8–26.

Newacheck, P. W., Hughes, D. C., & Stoddard, J. J. (1996). Children's access to primary care: Differences by race, income, and insurance status. *Pediatrics, 97*(1), 26–32.

Newacheck, P. W., Stoddard, J. J., & McManus, M. (1993). Enthnocultural variations in the prevalence and impact of childhood chronic conditions. *Pediatrics, 91*(5), 1031–1038.

Newman, K. S. (1999). *No shame in my game: The working poor in the inner city*. New York: Knopf and Russell Sage.

NICHD Child Care Network. (1997). Poverty and patterns of child care. In G. J. Duncan & J. Brooks-Gunn (Eds.), *Consequences of growing up poor* (pp. 100–131). New York: Russell Sage.

O'Campo, P., Xue, X., Wang, M., & Caughy, M. O. (1997). Neighborhood risk factors for low birthweight in Baltimore: A multilevel analysis. *American Journal of Public Health, 87*, 1113–1118.

Ogbu, J. U. (1991). Minority coping responses and school experience. *Journal of Psychohistory, 18*(4), 433–456.

Paschall, M. J., & Hubbard, M. L. (1998). Effects of neighborhood and family stressors on African American male adolescents' self-worth and propensity for violent crime. *Journal of Counseling and Clinical Psychology, 66*(5), 825–831.

Paulter, K. J., & Lewko, J. H. (1987). Children's and adolescents' views of the work world in times of economic uncertainty. In J. H. Lewko (Eds.), *How children and adolescence view the world of work* (pp. 21–31). San Francisco: Jossey-Bass.

Pettit, G. S., Bates, J. E., Dodge, K. A., & Meece, D. W. (1999). The impact of after-school peer contact on early adolescent externalizing problems is moderated by parental monitoring, perceived neighborhood safety, and prior adjustment. *Child Development, 70*(3), 768–778.

Raudenbush, S. W., & Sampson, R. J. (1999). Ecometrics: Toward a science of assessing ecological settings, with application to systematic social observation of neighborhoods. *Sociological Methodology, 29*, 1–41.

Richters, P., & Martinez, J. E. (1993). The NIMH Community Violence Project: I. Children as victims of and witnesses to violence. *Psychiatry, 56*, 7–21.

Rosenbaum, J. E., & Popkin, S. J. (1991). Employment and earnings of low-income blacks who move to middle-class suburbs. In C. Jencks & P. Peterson (Eds.), *The urban underclass* (pp. 342–356). Washington D.C.: Brookings Institution.

Ross, C. E., & Jang, S. J. (2000). Neighborhood disorder, fear, and mistrust: The buffering role of social ties with neighbors. *American Journal of Community Psychology, 28*(4), 401–420.

Sampson, R. J. (1992). Family management and child development: Insights from social disorganization theory. In J. McCord (Ed.), *Advances in criminological theory*, (Vol. 3, pp. 63–93). New Brunswick: Transaction Books.

Sampson, R. J. (1997). Collective regulation of adolescent misbehavior: Validation results from eighty Chicago neighborhoods. *Journal of Adolescent Research, 12*(2), 227–244.

Sampson, R. J. (1999). What "community" supplies. In R. F. Ferguson & W. T. Dickens (Eds.), *Urban problems and community development* (pp. 241–292). Washington, DC: Brookings Institution.

Sampson, R. J., & Groves, W. B. (1989). Community structure and crime: Testing social-disorganization theory. *American Journal of Sociology 94*(4), 774–780.

Sampson, R. J., & Morenoff, J. (1997). Ecological perspectives on the neighborhood context of urban poverty: Past and present. In J. Brooks-Gunn, G. J. Duncan, & J. L. Aber (Eds.), *Neighborhood poverty: Policy implications in studying neighborhoods (Vol. 2)* (pp. 1–22). New York: Russell Sage.

Sampson R. J., Raudenbush S. W., & Earls, F. (1997). Neighborhoods and violent crime: A multilevel study of collective efficacy. *Science, 277*, 918–924.

Shaw, C., & McKay, H. (1942). *Juvenile delinquency and urban areas*. Chicago: University of Chicago Press.

Shonkoff, J. P., & Phillips, D. A. (Eds.). (2000). *From neurons to neighborhoods: The science of early childhood development.* Washington, DC: National Academy Press.

Simons, R. I., Johnson, C., Beaman, J. J., Conger, R. D., & Whitbeck, L. B. (1996). Parents and peer group as mediators of the effect of community structure on adolescent behavior. *American Journal of Community Psychology, 24*(1), 145–171.

Sinclair, J. J., Pettit, G. S., Harrist, A. W., Dodge, K. A., & Bates, J. E. (1994). Encounters with aggressive peers in early childhood: Frequency, age differences, and correlates of risk behaviour problems. *International Journal of Behavioral Development, 17*(4), 675–696.

Steinberg, L., Fegley, S., & Dornbusch, S. M. (1993). Negative impact of part-time work on adolescent adjustment: Evidence from a longitudinal study. *Developmental Psychology, 29*(2), 171–180.

Sullivan, M. L. (1989). *Getting paid: Youth crime and work in the inner city.* Ithaca, NY: Cornell University Press.

Sullivan, M. L. (1996). Developmental transitions in poor youth: Delinquency and crime. In J. A. Graber, J. Brooks-Gunn, & A. C. Petersen (Eds.), *Transitions through adolescence: Interpersonal domains and context* (pp. 141–164). Hillsdale, NJ: Lawrence Erlbaum Associates.

Teitler, J. O., & Weiss, C. C. (2000). Effects of neighborhood and school environments on transitions to first sexual intercourse. *Sociology of Education, 73,* 112–132.

Tienda, M. (1991). Poor people and poor places: Deciphering neighborhood effects on poverty outcomes. In J. Haber (Ed.), *Macro-micro linkages in sociology* (pp. 244–262). Newberry, CA: Sage.

Willis, P. (1977). *Learning to labor: How working-class kids get working-class jobs.* New York: Columbia University Press.

Wilson, W. J. (1987). *The truly disadvantaged: The innercity, the underclass, and public policy.* Chicago: University of Chicago Press.

Wilson, W. J. (1991). Studying inner-city social dislocations: The challenge of public agenda research. *American Sociological Review, 56*(1), 1–14.

Wilson, W. J. (1997). *When work disappears.* New York: Knopf.

Wright, R. J. (1998). *Exposure to violence.* Paper prepared for MacArthur Research Network on Socioeconomic Status and Health.

Yoshikawa, H. (1994). Prevention as cumulative protection: Effects of early family support and education on chronic delinquency and its risks. *Psychological Bulletin, 115*(1), 28–54.

10

What Are SES Effects Effects of?: A Developmental Systems Perspective

Richard M. Lerner
Tufts University

INTRODUCTION

As well documented by the scholarship included in this volume, human developmentalists have a long and rich research tradition of studying associations among socioeconomic status (SES), family structure and function, and child development (for example, see Bornstein, 1995a, 2002; Bronfenbrenner & Crouter, 1983; Fisher, Jackson, & Villarruel, 1998). Despite the voluminous studies of these associations, a—if not the—key theoretical question remains moot. "That is, through what causal mechanism does the set of variables marked by the term socioeconomic status influence parenting and its linkage to child development?" "In other words, by what mechanisms do macro contextual variables represented by SES translate into a developmental process that results in the behaviors of parents or children, or in ontogenetic changes in parent–child relations?"

Several theoretical models of developmental process have been used to provide answers to this question (Lerner, 2002). Across the history of this work, these models have been associated traditionally with ideas that stress the prime influence of variables at one level of organization on the links among SES, family (or parents), and children, and have resulted in the formulation of either sociogenic, psychogenic, or biogenic theories. As explained in the following, these approaches split or separate variables from one level of organization (biological, psychological, or sociological) from variables from other levels; they view the preferred level as real or primary and other levels as, at best, secondary or derivative or, at worst, epiphenomenal (Overton, 1998, in press). In either case, split conceptions reduce variables at nonpreferred levels to ones at the preferred or real level (e.g., Plomin, Corley, DeFries, & Faulkner, 1990; Rowe, 1994; Rushton, 1999, 2000).

In turn, more contemporary models stress that the links among SES, parenting, and child development derive from integrative, or fused, relations among variables associated with the multiple levels of organization existing within the ecology of human development. This relational perspective stresses that syntheses of variables across levels comprise the holistic reality of the human development process (e.g., Gottlieb, 1997, 1998; Magnusson, 1999a, 1999b; Thelen & Smith, 1998; Wapner & Demick, 1998). This focus has been presented within the context of dynamic, developmental systems theories of human development (e.g., Ford & Lerner, 1992; Lerner, 1998, 2002). It is useful to discuss briefly both these split and relational conceptions of the links among SES, parenting, and child development.

THEORIES OF SES–PARENTING–CHILD DEVELOPMENT RELATIONS

Several types of theories of development have provided frames for conceptualizing and studying the linkages among SES, parenting, and child development. One instance (family; Reese & Overton, 1970) of such theories stresses sociogenesis, the idea that societal institutions create categories or sets of behaviors (roles) which individuals are channeled into enacting (e.g., Homans, 1961). Hartup (1978) termed these theories Social Mold models.

Essentially, these sociogenic theories stress social inculcation, and interpret all individual actions as not only societally embedded by as completely societally framed (Dannefer, 1984; Meyer, 1988). Society is, then, the Puppet Master that directs individual behavior and change. There is no agency (primary control) present in individuals and, as such, psychogenesis is epiphenomenal. As Skinner (1971, p. 211) asserted in his book, *Beyond Freedom and Dignity*, "a person does not act upon the world, the world acts upon him."

Psychogenic theories have traditionally stood in contrast to sociogenic models. In psychogenic views, SES marks a context, or represents a social address within which individual—psychological variables develop (Bronfenbrenner & Crouter, 1983). SES may mark interindividual (usually quantitative) variation in individual—psychological variables. As in other split conceptions, psychogenic theories are reductionistic. They see macro level variables as essentially epiphenomenal, conceiving of them as linear combinations of individual—psychological variables (Featherman & Lerner, 1985). For instance, the family is not seen as a level of organization within the ecology of human development that is qualitatively distinct from the individual psychological functioning of the people who comprise the family. Family variables are merely quantitative additions of (and thus reducible to) individual level variables associated with the people comprising the family. Similar reductions—to individual–psychological elements—may be made in regard to social variables more macro than the family. Such combinations of elements constitute the derived societal variables marked by SES.

Biogenic theories are also reductionistic. As noted previously in regard to sociogenic and psychogenic models, biogenic conceptions also split nature from it relation to nurture (Overton, 1998) and (obviously) emphasize the reality of nature and the epiphenominality of nurture. Examples are hereditarian views such as human sociobiology (e.g., Rushton, 1999, 2000) and behavior genetics (Plomin, 2000; Plomin et al., 1990; Rowe, 1994). For instance, as discussed in more detail later in this chapter, Rowe (1994) believed that all socialization can be reduced to the actions of genes on behaviors. Biogenic models such as those proposed by Rowe (and Plomin, et al., 1990, or Rushton, 1999, 2000) reduced the complexity of all levels of organization involved in human development (e.g., individual–psychological and societal levels) to mechanistically acting genetic determinants.

Developmental systems models are integrative conceptions. In contrast to split and reductionistic perspectives, such models take a relational, synthetic approach to understanding the multiple levels of organization involved in human development (Lerner, 2002, Schneirla, 1957; Thelen & Smith, 1998). Theories derived from a developmental systems perspective focus on the integration (relation, fusion) of actions of one variable from one level of organization (e.g., the individual) and actions of variables from the other levels of organization comprising the ecology of human development (e.g., see Brandtstädter, 1998, 1999; Bronfenbrenner, 2001).

From a developmental systems perspective, human beings are active contributors to their own development (Lerner, 1982; Lerner & Busch-Rossnagel, 1981; Lerner & Walls, 1999). Humans are neither passive recipients of genes that compel their actions nor passive recipients of stimuli that impel their behavior. Humans are active, acting, goal oriented, and effective shapers of the complex ecology of human development that influences their development. In addition, humans are relatively plastic organisms (Lerner, 1984) who thus can alter their structure or function to enable adaptation and, in ideal circumstances, well-being (Lerner, Bornstein, & Smith, in press). From this perspective, infants, children, and adolescents as much shape the behavior of their siblings, parents, peers, and teachers as these social groups influence the young person.

In other words, because children both influence and are influenced by their social world, the physical and the social ecology of human life are also active contributors to human development. Accordingly, the basic process of development is relational; it involves the integration, or fusion of the person and the context, or ecology, of human development (Lerner, 1991; Overton, 1998, in press).

Developmental Systems as an Alternative to Behavior Genetics

The developmental process envisioned in this dynamic, relational, developmental systems perspective stands in marked contrast to the conceptualization of the developmental process found in split sociogenic, psychogenic, or biogenic positions. For example, developmental systems models, such as developmental contextualism (Lerner, 2002; Lerner, Rothbaum, Boulos, & Castellino, 2002) and the bioecological perspective (Bronfenbrenner, 2001; Bronfenbrenner & Morris, 1998), have been forwarded to provide alternatives to the biogenic, hereditarian view of parenting in behavior genetics (e.g., Rowe, 1994).

As explained by Gottlieb (1992), in a developmental systems view of process the key "conception is one of a totally interrelated, fully coactional system in which the activity of genes themselves can be affected through the cytoplasm of the cell by events originating at any other level in the system, including the external environment" (Gottlieb, 1992, pp. 144–145). As such, Gottlieb (1992, 1997) and other developmental systems theorists (e.g., Ford & Lerner, 1992; Magnusson, 1999a, 1999b; Sameroff, 1983; Thelen & Smith, 1998; Wapner & Demick, 1998) emphasized that neither genes nor the context by themselves cause development. The fusion among levels within the integrated developmental system means that relations among variables—not splits between nature and nurture—constitute the core of the developmental process.

Accordingly, although hereditarians argue that biological contributions are isomorphic with genetic influences (e.g., Rushton, 1999), this equivalence is not seen as veridical with reality from the perspective of developmental systems theory. For instance, although some hereditarians see constitutional variables (e.g., relating to brain volume, head size, size of reproductive organs, and stature) as all based on heredity (Rushton, 1999), within developmental systems:

> "constitutional" is not equivalent to "genetic," and purposely so. Constitutional includes the expressed functions of genes—which, in themselves require some environmental input—but constitutional includes the operations of the central nervous system and all the biological and environmental experiences that impact organismic functioning and that make constitutional variables part of the dynamic change across the life span as they affect the development of and the decline of behavior. (Horowitz, 2000, p. 8)

In short, developmental science and developmental scientists should stop engaging in the pursuit of theoretically anachronistic and counterfactual conceptions of gene function, or the search for a way to reduce the linkages among SES, parenting, and child development to the independent (split) action of genes (Rowe, 1994; Ruston, 1999, 2000). Indeed, significant advances in the science of human development will rest upon embedding the study of genes within the multiple, integrated levels of organization comprising the dynamic developmental system of person-context relations (Gottlieb, 1997, 1998; Thelen & Smith, 1998).

Questions about the Developmental Systems View of Developmental Process

Several questions are raised by a developmental systems approach to understanding the SES–parenting–child development linkage. First, and most critically, if developmental systems models are to represent a useful alternative to biogenic models such as behavior genetics, we must ask whether SES can be shown to be a plastic component of the developmental system. If so, then we must ask how the variables constituting SES might interact to produce such plasticity. "For instance, how might SES-related variables fuse with individual-psychological ones over the course of life?" "What conditions of the developmental system moderate the level of relations between specific SES-related variables and specific individual-psychological variables?"

The developmental system is embedded in a multitemporal system, for example, as reflected in Bronfenbrenner's (2001) conception of the chronosystems comprising temporality within the bioecology of human development, Elder's (1998) differentiation of ontogenetic time, family time, and historical (or cohort) time across the human life course, or Baltes's (1987; Baltes, Lindenberger, & Staudinger, 1998) notion that age-graded, history-graded, or nonnormative events define experiences across the human life span. Given the embeddedness of human development within time, answers to questions about a developmental systems treatment of SES–parenting–child development relations necessitate an understanding that temporal variation promotes diversity in these relations and provides limits to the generalizabilty of any specific instance of these relations. In other words, in seeking to answer questions about how to delineate the way(s) in which SES relates to parenting and child development, we may be, on the one hand, confident about the ubiquity of dynamic relations being a generic part of the answer. On the other hand, we can also be certain that what specific SES variables relate to what specific parenting behaviors and child development outcomes will vary across time and place (Elder, Modell, & Parke, 1993). Thus, the dynamic systems perspective does not embrace the notion of completeness. In this sense, fusion never happens; rather, only a process of fusing occurs. In turn, hereditarian perspectives such as behavior genetics inherently (and incorrectly) assume that phenomena are in a state rather than passing through a state.

Accordingly, it is paramount to keep in mind the centrality of the Bornstein (1995b) Specificity Principle. Expressed in regard to developmental outcomes in infancy, Bornstein (1995b) noted that "Specific experiences at specific times exert specific effects over specific aspects of infant growth in specific ways" (p. 21). Only through a focus on such diversity of influences, and the plasticity of ontogenetic pathways and developmental outcomes can systems effects—as compared to purported reductionistic effects of one level of organization (e.g., genes) as the prime mover of developmental change—come to the fore of scholarly understanding.

THE PLASTICITY OF SES

Several sources of data suggest that SES is a plastic component of the human developmental system. For instance, Duncan and Magnuson (chap. 3, this volume) provide information about the dynamics of poverty. They note that in the United States more than 25% of people living in poverty in one year report incomes above poverty in the next year. In addition, 60% of poverty spells last less than three years. There are racial differences in probability of experiencing poverty and of length of poverty spells. Similarly, Gottfried, et al. (chap. 8, this volume) report changes in SES scores from ages 1 to 17 years. Correlations among SES scores ranged from a high of .98 (between ages 16 and 17) to a low of .44 (between ages 2.5 and 14).

Other scholarship underscores the plasticity of SES. Featherman, Spenner, and Tsunematsu (1988) discussed class and the socialization of children. They confirm the view of Duncan and Magnuson about the dynamic character of SES—related variables and provide data extending the illustration of the plasticity of SES present in the data of Gottfried et al. (chap. 8, this volume). For instance, Featherman et al. (1988, p. 76) noted that "In their first 17 years of life, 51% of Norwegian children moved between two and five classes, and 11% experienced six or more classes; only a large minority (38%) remained continuously in their class of birth." In regard to class mobility prior to age 7 in Norway and the United States, Featherman et al. (1988) noted that 40% of Norwegian children and more than 50% of American children experienced at least one class change prior to entering school. In regard to the pace of leaving one's class of birth, Featherman et al. (1988) noted that in Norway, 11.3% changed class during the first year of life and that an additional 7.5% changed class in the second year of life. By age 10, 50% were no longer in the class of their birth. In the United States, 34% of the children involved in the analyses conducted by Featherman et al. (1988) had moved from class of birth by age 3, and 50% had moved from class of birth by age 5.

Finally, Featherman et al. (1988) demonstrated the use of person-centered analyses, such as those advanced by Magnusson (1999a, 1999b). Instead of variable-centered analyses, wherein interest is in how variables behave (covary) across people, person-centered analyses are holistic in regard to individuals; such analyses consider how variables combine within a person to constitute his or her individuality. Accordingly, in understanding SES-child development relations, Featherman et al. (1988) did not correlate SES scores across time periods. Instead, using hazard analysis, they assessed the variables related to the probability of a child entering a new SES category at a consequent time after being in another SES category during an antecedent period.

COMPOSITION AND CONTRIBUTION
OF SES—RELATED VARIABLES

If SES is a plastic component of the developmental system, what then are the relations within the system that constitutes SES? How do these variables dynamically interact within the system to influence parenting and child development?

The Composition of SES—
Related Variables

Leventhal and Brooks-Gunn (chap. 9, this volume) provided productive ideas for indexing the relations among variables within the developmental system that constitutes SES. Their work, and the considerable, independent scholarship supporting it, bring to the level of impossibility the contentions of behavior geneticists that SES or its effects can be reduced to the split actions of genes. Leventhal and Brooks-Gunn (chap. 9, this volume) recommended indexing the social organization of both poor and affluent neighborhoods in order to appraise the potentially differential influence of their presence on individual-psychological development. For example, in poor neighborhoods, one might assess percentages of: poor people in the community, female-headed households, high school dropouts, and unemployed. In turn, in affluent neighborhoods, one might assess percentages of: affluent people in the community, intact households, high school or college graduates, and employed. Leventhal and Brooks-Gunn (chap. 9, this volume) also recommended that the constitution of SES can be appraised by indexing institutional deficits and assets (resources).

Kretzmann and McKnight (1993) suggested a methodology to use in pursuing this recommendation. In the content of a discussion of the developmental deficits and assets of communities, Kretzmann and McKnight (1993) offered a community-mapping technique to define and delineate the loci of community strengths and weaknesses. Such community mapping has been used by Sampson, Raudenbush, and Earls (1997) and Sampson, Morenoff, and Earls (1999) to operationalize the community features and their structural distribution within the neighborhoods of Chicago that are marked by the SES construct. Sampson et al. (1997, 1999) found that this mapping enables understanding of the presence of both problems (e.g., violent crime) and strengths (e.g., collective efficacy) in different communities.

The Contribution of SES—
Related Variables

Consistent with the findings of Sampson, et al. (1997, 1999), Leventhal and Brooks-Gunn (chap. 9, this volume) recommended that investigating processes related to family, peer, and school (and other community institutions) facilitates understanding of how variables constituting SES may contribute to parenting and child redevelopment. As an illustration of the utility of the ideas of Leventhal and Brooks-Gunn (chap. 9, this volume) in regard to family processes, Hoff (chap. 6, this volume) noted that children's language learning experience is in large part a function of how mothers structure their children's time. Hoff suggested that SES effects may derive from the settings within which mothers choose to spend time with their children. Such settings may be differentially distributed in neighborhoods varying in the social structures discussed by Leventhal and Brooks-Gunn (chap. 9, this volume) and mapped by Sampson et al. (1997, 1999).

Leventhal and Brooks-Gunn (chap. 9, this volume) noted also that parent's goals and aspirations for their children may produce SES effects. Such parental visions for their children's development are discussed by Harkness and Super (1995) as ethnotheories of parenting, that is, as sets of beliefs held by particular cultural groups about what parents should do or are capable of doing to affect their children's development in specific directions or toward specific goals. An illustration of the possible operation of such enthotheories may be seen in the work of Bradley and Corwyn (chap. 7, this volume). They indicated that stimulation of learning, maternal responsiveness, and punishment practices may mediate relations between SES and individual-psychological variables. In turn, ethnotheories may be enacted at a community level.

For instance, the work of Damon (1997; Damon & Gregory, in press) on community youth charters and of Benson (1997) on individual and ecological developmental assets underscored the presence within communities of collective visions for positive youth development and the way these visions may function to activate and organize means to use community strengths (e.g., present in community-based organizations or programs) to enhance such developmental outcomes. For example, Scales, Benson, Leffert, and Blyth (2000) noted that the individual and ecological assets of communities may combine to promote thriving among adolescents across their high school years.

GOALS OF RESEARCH STUDYING
THE EFFECTS OF SES
ON CHILD DEVELOPMENT

Clearly, SES is constituted by relations among variables at individual, societal, and cultural levels of organization. Through making different social interactions (e.g., among rich and poor, educated and noneducated) more or less probable, and in interrelation with individual parental variables (e.g., ethnotheories, structuring of language developmental opportunities, maternal responsiveness, stimulation of learning, engagement in collective actions with neighbors), SES is associated with variation in child developments (e.g., problem behaviors or positive ones, such as those linked to thriving).

Leventhal and Brooks-Gunn (chap. 9, this volume, pp. 225) noted:

> Our ability to point to specific underlying mechanisms at play is necessary to draw
> policy recommendations . . . Our ability to ask, evaluate, and answer these more nu-
> anced questions is likely to be most fruitful for designing programs and policies
> targeting neighborhood SES disparities.

The mechanisms of developmental change articulated within a dynamic, developmental systems perspective can be expected, then, to have import for policy
development and child- and family-serving program design and implementation.
They do. As may be anticipated by the earlier discussion of the theoretical frames
used to approach the study of SES–parenting–child development relations, these
implications stand in marked contrast to those associated with split, reductionist
positions.

Given the different impact such implications may have for human welfare and
social justice, it is important to discuss these contrasts. Both nature- and nurture-
focused split positions have unfavorable and scientifically undefendable implications. To illustrate the problems with split positions it is useful to focus first on
split conceptions that adopt a biogenetic perspective.

A RETURN TO BIOGENESIS:
THE NONCHALLENGE
OF BEHAVIOR GENETICS

Citing contemporary research using heritability analyses of purportedly contextual influences (e.g., Behrman & Rosenzweig, in press), Duncan and Magnuson
(chap. 3, this volume) suggested that behavior genetics constitutes a challenge to
interpretations of SES effects associated with theories other than biogenic ones.
However, the fatal conceptual and methodological flaws of heritability research
mean that any supposed challenge of behavior genetics to alternative theories,
especially relational, developmental systems ones, is in fact a non-challenge.

According to Plomin (2000):

> Behavioural genetics is the genetic study of behaviour, which includes quantitative
> genetics (twin and adoption studies) as well as molecular genetics (DNA studies) of
> human and animal behaviour broadly defined to include responses of the organism
> from responses measured in the brain such as functional neuroimaging to self-report
> questionnaires. (p. 30)

The goal of behavior genetic analysis is to separate (partition) the variation in
a distribution of scores (e.g., for a personality trait, temperamental characteristic,
or intelligence) into the proportion due to genes and the proportion due to the
environment. Although behavior geneticists admit that genes and environments

may be correlated, may interact, or both, they most typically seek to compute a score (termed a heritability coefficient) that (in its most frequently used form) denotes the independent contribution of genetic variance to the overall differences in the distribution of scores for a given individual characteristic.

For such heritability scores to be meaningful there must be genetic contributions that are independent of (not correlated or interactive with) the context within which genes exist. However, genes do not work in the way that behavior geneticists imagine.

Fatal Flaws in the Behavior Genetics Model of Gene Function

Neither cell biologists (McEwen, 1997, 1998, 1999; Meaney, Aitken, Berkel, Bhatnager, & Sapolsky, 1988) nor molecular geneticists (e.g., Elman, et al. 1998; Ho, 1984; Müller-Hill, 1988; Venter, et al., 2001) place credence in the model of genetic function involved in behavioral genetics. In fact, Venter and his colleagues (2001), the group that successfully mapped the sequence of the human genome, emphasized that there are two conceptual errors that should not be made in the face of the advances they and others are making in understanding the structure and functional consequences of the human genome. They stress that:

> There are two fallacies to be avoided: determinism, the idea that all characteristics of the person are "hard-wired" by the genome; and reductionism, the view that with complete knowledge of the human genome sequence, it is only a matter of time before our understanding of gene functions and interactions will provide a complete causal description of human variability. (Venter, et al. (2001), p. 1348)

These are precisely the fallacies embodied in behavior genetics. Accordingly, contemporary, cutting-edge thought in molecular genetics thus rejects the idea that genes are structures that act on supragenetic levels and, instead, adopts a position consistent with a dynamic, developmental systems view (Gottlieb, 1992, 1997, 1998; Lerner, 2002; Lewis, 1997; Magnusson, 1999a, 1999b; Thelen & Smith, 1998). In essence, then, we have in the field of behavior genetics (e.g., Plomin, 1986, 2000; Rowe, 1994) the use of a model of genetic structure and function that is specifically rejected by those scientists who study the action of genes directly.

Methodological and Interpretational Problems in Heritability Computations

As Hirsch (1997) noted heritability does not mean inheritance. To give an example of how misleading heritability interpretations can be in regard to understanding the role of environmental influences, let us consider first an imaginary example.

Suppose a society had a law pertaining to eligibility for government office. The law was simply that men could be elected to such positions and women could not.

Consider what one would need to know in order to divide completely correctly a group of randomly chosen people from this society into one of two groups. Group 1 would consist of those who had greater than a zero percent chance of being elected to a leadership post and Group 2 would consist of those who had no chance. All that one would need to know to make this division with complete accuracy was whether a person possessed an XX pair of chromosomes or an XY pair. In the first case, the person would be a female (since possession of the XX chromosome pair leads to female development). In the second, the person would be a male. One could thus correctly place all possessors of the XY pair into the greater than zero chance group and all possessors of the XX pair into the no chance group.

In this example, then, all the differences between people with respect to the characteristic in question—eligibility for office—can be summarized by genetic differences between them, that is, possession of either the XX or the XY chromosome pair. In this case the heritability of being eligible would be 1.0. In other words, in this society, eligibility is 100% heritable. But, by any stretch of the imagination, does this mean that the eligibility characteristic is inherited, or that the differences between men and women with respect to this characteristic are genetic in nature? Is there a gene for eligibility, one that men possess and women do not?

Of course, the answers to these questions are no. Although heritability in this case is perfect, it is social (environmental) variables—laws regarding what men and women can and cannot do—that determine whether or not someone has a chance of being elected. Indeed, if the law in question were changed, and women were now allowed to hold office, then the heritability of the eligibility characteristic would—probably rather quickly—fall to much less than 1.0.

Hebb (1970) offered another useful example of the problems associated with the measurement and interpretation of heritability, one drawing on a modest proposal put forth by Mark Twain:

> Mark Twain once proposed that boys should be raised in barrels to the age of 12 and fed through the bung-hole. Suppose we have 100 boys reared this way, with a practically identical environment. Jensen agrees that environment has *some* importance (20% worth?), so we must expect that the boys on emerging from the barrels will have a mean IQ well below 100. However, the variance attributable to the environment is practically zero, so on the "analysis of variance" argument, the environment is not a factor in the low level of IQ, which is nonsense. (p. 578)

In Hebb's example, environment had no differential effect on the boys' IQs; presumably in all boys it has the same (severely limiting) effect. In having this same effect, environment could contribute nothing to differences between the boys. No differences—or variation—existed in the environment, and so the environment could not be said to contribute anything to differences between people.

Yet, it is also obvious that environment had a major influence on the boys' IQ scores. Even with IQ heritability equal to +1.0, the intelligence of each of the boys would have been different had he developed in an environment other than a barrel.

A third example is based on the research of Partanen, Brunn, and Markkanen (1966). These researchers analyzed data from 172 monozygotic and 557 dizygotic male twin pairs. All participants were alcohol users. The aim of the study was to estimate the degree to which alcohol abuse is genetically determined. When measured by frequency of alcohol consumption, alcohol abuse seems to have at least a modest genetic component (heritability of 0.40). However, if one uses the amount of alcohol consumed on each occasion, the heritability estimate drops considerably to 0.27. A third measure of alcohol abuse—the number of citations and other social conflicts resulting from drinking—yields a heritability estimate of 0.02. Thus, judgments concerning heritability can depend largely on the definition and operationalization of the behavior under study. In addition, the confusion between commonality and variability can lead to misinterpretation.

The Inadequacy of Behavior Genetics as a Frame for Studying SES-Parenting-Child Development Relations

Despite this criticism by their colleagues in the field of psychology, and the lack of credence given to behavior genetics by molecular geneticists, eminent population geneticists (e.g., Feldman & Lewontin, 1975), and evolutionary biologists (e.g., Gould, 1981, 1996) many psychologists continue to act as if behavioral genetics provides evidence for the inheritance of behaviors and links between: (1) the role in human development of the environment (Harris, 1998; Plomin, 1986, 2000; Plomin & Daniels, 1987; Rowe, 1994), for example, SES; (2) parenting (e.g., Harris, 1998; Scarr, 1992); and (3) child development outcomes such as intelligence (Jensen, 1969, 1998), morality (Wilson, 1975), temperament (Buss & Plomin, 1984), and even television watching (Plomin et al., 1990).

To understand the problems with the use of behavior genetics as a frame for studying or explaining parent behaviors and of the effects of parenting on child and adolescent development, Collins, Maccoby, Steinberg, Hetherington, & Bornstein, (2000) noted that:

> Large-scale societal factors, such as ethnicity or poverty, can influence group means in parenting behavior—and in the effects of parenting behaviors—in ways that are not revealed by studies of within group variability. In addition, highly heritable traits also can be highly malleable. Like traditional correlational research on parenting, therefore, commonly used behavior-genetic methods have provided an incomplete analysis of differences among individuals. (p. 220)

Accordingly, Collins, et al. (2000) concluded that:

> Whereas researchers using behavior-genetic paradigms imply determinism by hered-
> ity and correspondingly little parental influence (e.g., Rowe, 1994), contemporary
> evidence confirms that the expression of heritable traits depends, often strongly,
> on experience, including specific parental behaviors, as well as predispositions and
> age-related factors in the child. (p. 228)

Moreover, there are reasons to be skeptical about whether the various methodologies associated with behavior genetics can generate useful data pertinent to SES,
parenting, and child development. For example, Collins, et al. (2000) noted that:

> One criticism is that the assumptions, methods, and truncated samples used in
> behavior-genetic studies maximize the effects of heredity and features of the en-
> vironment that are different for different children and minimize the effects of shared
> family environments . . . A second criticism is that estimates of the relative contribu-
> tions of environment and heredity vary greatly depending on the source of data . . .
> heritability estimates vary considerably depending on the measures used to assess
> similarity between children or between parents and children . . . The sizable vari-
> ability in estimates of genetic and environmental contributions depending on the
> paradigms and measures used means that no firm conclusions can be drawn about
> the relative strength of these influences on development. (pp. 220–221)

Similarly, Horowitz (2000) noted that:

> one sees increasing skepticism about what is to be learned from assigning variance
> percentages to genes . . . The skepticism is informed by approaches that see genes, the
> central nervous system and other biological functions and variables as contributors
> to reciprocal, dynamic processes which can only be fully understood in relation to
> sociocultural environmental contexts. It is a perspective that is influenced by the im-
> pressive recent methodological and substantive advances in the neurosciences. (p. 3)

The cutting-edge study of the neurosciences within the developmental systems
perspective noted by Horowitz (2000) is exemplified by the work of Suomi (1997,
2000; Bennett et al., in press), who sought to identify how genes and context fuse
within the developmental system. Because of the close genetic similarity of rhesus
moneys to humans, he studied such organisms as a means to provide a model for
the investigation of this system. In one recent instance of this long-term research
program, Suomi (2000; Bennett et al., in press) found that young rhesus monkeys
show individual differences in their emotional reactivity (or temperament). Some
young monkeys are highly reactive, for example, they become quite excited and
agitated when they experience environmental stress, for instance, separation from
their mothers; other monkeys show low reactivity in such situations, for instance,

they behave calmly in the face of such separation. Suomi (2000; Bennett et al., in press) discovered that these individual differences in behavior are associated with different genetic inheritances related to the functioning of serotonin, a brain chemical involved in neurotransmission and linked to individual differences in such conditions as anxiety, depression, and impulsive violence.

Accordingly, in order to study the interrelation of serotonergic system genes and environmental influences on behavioral development, Suomi (2000; Bennett et al., in press) placed high or low reactivity rhesus young with foster rhesus monkeys who were also either high or low in emotional reactivity. When young monkeys with the genetic inheritance marking high reactivity were reared for the first 6 months of life with a low reactivity mother, they developed normally and, for instance, despite their genes, they did not show high reactivity even when removed from their foster mothers and placed in a group of peers and unknown adults. In fact, these monkeys showed a high level of social skill (e.g., they took leadership positions in their group). However, when young monkeys with this same genetic marker for high reactivity were raised by high reactivity foster mothers, they did not fare well under stressful conditions and proved socially inept when placed in a new social group.

Moreover, Suomi (2000; Bennett et al., in press) found that the interaction between the serotonin transporter genotype and early experience not only influences rhesus monkey behavior but brain chemistry regarding the use of serotonin. Despite having a high reactivity genotype, the monkeys whose early life experiences were with the low reactivity foster mothers had brain chemistry that corresponded to monkeys with a low reactivity genotype. Accordingly, Suomi (2000) concluded that:

> The recent findings that specific polymorphisms in the serotonin transporter gene are associated with different behavioral and biological outcomes for rhesus monkeys as a function of their early social rearing histories suggest that more complex gene-environment interactions actually are responsible for the phenomenon. It is hard to imagine that the situation would be any less complex for humans. (p. 31)

POLICY IMPLICATIONS OF SPLIT VERSUS RELATIONAL CONCEPTIONS OF SES–PARENTING–CHILD DEVELOPMENT RELATIONS

As suggested by Leventhal and Brooks-Gunn (chap. 9, this volume), extensions of flawed ideas to the arena of public policy and social programs can be dangerous to human welfare, social justice, and civil society. Split conceptions of the SES–parenting–child development relations, whether they are biogenic, psychogenic, or sociogenic, can have such negative impacts.

Policy Implications of Split Conceptions

Consider, for example, a society that developed policies derived from a split, sociogenic perspective. Such a society may well deny the value of all genetic inquiry, and would believe in virtually limitless developmental plasticity. For example, in order to capitalize on (beliefs in) the infinite malleability of children's behavioral development, efforts to enhance school achievement might involve policies standardizing the school curriculum for all students, mandating a common performance test for all students, and evaluating all schools by the application of an identical standard. In turn, individual parents taking actions predicated on these strict environmentalist ideas might participate in programs that expose fetuses to classical music, or might place their newborn on the waiting list for entry into an elite preschool, in order to enhance later-life achievements.

By contrast, a society with policies derived from a split, biogenic perspective could well exclusively support policies that invest in genetic counseling programs or in incentives for some people to reproduce more and for others to reproduce less. In addition, miscegenation laws might be enacted to assure that the genes that (purportedly) provided the basis of desirable individual differences would not be diluted by those genes associated with undesirable individual differences (e.g., see Lorenz, 1940). Thus, a split, biogenic belief that fixed genes, given at conception, exclusively or primarily control a child's development has the potential to lead parents, youth-serving professionals, or policy makers to believe that there is little that can be done through childrearing to diminish undesired behaviors or to promote positive ones; such views may lead people to look with favor on reproductive control policies and programs. Pessimism about the role of environmental influences on behavior and development in the face of genes received from parents may be intensified when some scientists claim to have demonstrated that parent socialization strategies are, at best, largely irrelevant or merely epiphenomenal and reducible to genetics actions (e.g., as in Rowe, 1994).

Policy Implications of Relational Conceptions

A society based on relational, dynamic, developmental systems beliefs would more likely support policies that invest in parent education programs that emphasize the importance of assessing a child's individuality and enhancing the goodness-of-fit with the specific characteristics of his or her context (e.g., Chess & Thomas, 1999; Thomas & Chess, 1977). In addition, such a society might provide resources (e.g., grants, scholarships, and tax incentives) to lead all parents to place their children in high quality child care and educational programs that foster such fits while, at the same time, recognizing the significance of and providing support for basic biological research pertinent to both organismic individuality and to the presence of and limits on relative plasticity across the life span (Baltes et al., 1998; Lerner, 2002).

For example, programs derived from this policy perspective would support leave from employment, school, or military service for parents of all socioeconomic levels during times of work, family transition, or crisis. More generally, programs derived from such a policy perspective would enable all parents to provide their children with the key resources needed for child well-being and positive youth development (e.g., Lerner et al., 2002), for example, a healthy start in life, an education linked to marketable skills, the presence of an adult in the child's life committed completely to his or her positive development, a safe living environment, the opportunity to become an active and engaged citizen in a civil society, and freedom from prejudice and discrimination (Lerner, Fisher, & Weinberg, 2000). In short, policies derived from developmental systems theory would suggest social justice, equity among all people, and the creation and maintenance of a level playing field for all racial, ethic, religious, cultural, sexual preference, and socioeconomic groups.

In sum, there is then a significant difference between split and relational perspectives about relations among social context (e.g., the variables marked by SES), parenting, and child development, not only in regard to the character of the scientific activity associated with the study of these relations but, as well, in the degree of confidence parents might have about the efficacy of their agency with their children and in the sorts of policies and programs policy makers and practitioners might support. Building on the concept of ethnotheories of parenting, discussed earlier (and see Lerner, 2002), Table 10.1 presents one view of the implications for policies and programs of split, biogenic conceptions of parenting. The table presents (A) beliefs about whether the hereditarian, split conception is believed to be either (1) true or (2) false, and (B) public policy and social program implications that would be associated with the hereditarian split position were it in fact (1) true or (2) false under either of the two belief conditions involved in A (cf., Jensen, 1973).

In contrast, Table 10.2 presents a view of the different implications for policies and programs of split, sociogenic conceptions of parenting (Lerner, 2002). Moreover, Tables 10.1 and 10.2—in the A.2.B2. quadrant—not only present the policy and program implications of believing that the hereditarian or the strict environmentalist conceptions, respectively, are believed to be false and are in fact false. In addition, they illustrate the policy and program implications of believing relational, developmental systems theory to be true when it is in fact the case (as obviously argued in this chapter) that it is true.

Table 10.1 demonstrates that if the hereditarian conception is believed to be true, then irrespective of whether it is in fact true (and, it must be emphasized that it is incontrovertibly not true; for example, see Collins et al., 2000; Gottlieb, 1997; Hirsch, 1997; Horowitz, 2000; Lerner, 2002; Venter et al., 2001), a range of actions constraining the freedom of association, reproductive rights, and even survival of people would be promoted. However, if the hereditarian conception were correctly regarded as false (and conversely the developmental systems conception were correctly seen as true), then policies and programs aimed at social

TABLE 10.1
Policy and Program Implications that Arise if the Hereditarian (Genetic
Reductionist) "Split" Conception of Genes (A) Were Believed to be True
or False; and (B) Were In Fact True or False

		Public Policy and Social Program Implications if Hereditarian Split Position Were In Fact:	
		True	*False*
Hereditarian split conception is believed to be:	True	• repair inferior genotypes, making them equal to superior genotypes • miscegenation laws • restrictions of personal liberties of carriers of inferior genotypes (separation, discrimination, distinct social tracts) • sterilization • elimination of inferior genotypes from genetic pool	• same as true
	False	• wasteful and futile humanitarian policies • wasteful and futile programs of equal opportunity, affirmative action, equity, and social justice • policies and programs to quell social unrest because of unrequited aspirations of genetically constrained people • deterioration of culture and destruction of civil society	• equity, social justice, equal opportunity, affirmative action • celebration of diversity • universal participation in civic life • democracy • systems assessment and engagement • civil society

Note. Source: Lerner (2002).

TABLE 10.2
Policy and Program Implications that Arise if the Strict Environmentalist (Radical
Contextual) "Split" Conception of Context (A) Were Believed to be True or False;
and (B) Were In Fact True or False

		Public Policy and Social Program Implications if Strict Environmentalist Split Position Were In Fact:	
		True	*False*
Strict environmental split conception is believed to be:	True	• provide all children with same educational or experiential regimen to maximize their common potential–aptitude • eliminate all individualized educational or training programs • standardized assessments for all children • penalties for parents, schools, and communities when children manifest individual differences in achievement • educate all parents, caregivers, and teachers to act in a standard way in the treatment of all children	• same as true
	False	• wasteful and counterproductive diversity-sensitive policies • wasteful and counterproductive programs based on individual differences	• programs that are sensitive to individual differences and that seek to promote a goodness of fit between individually different people and contexts.

(Continued)

TABLE 10.2
(Continued)

| | | Public Policy and Social Program Implications if Strict Environmentalist Split Position Were In Fact: | |
		True	False
		• policies and programs to quell social unrest because of unrequited aspirations of people promised that the individualized program they received would make them equal to all other people • deterioration of culture and destruction of civil society	• affirmative actions to correct ontogenetic or historical inequities in person-context fit • celebration of diversity • universal participation in civic life • democracy • systems assessment and engagement • social justice • civil society

Note. Source: Lerner (2002).

justice and civil society for the diverse families and children of America would be promoted. Similarly, Table 10.2 shows that if the developmental systems perspective is correctly seen as true and if the strict environmentalist conception is correctly regarded as false, corresponding results for social justice and civil society are promoted. This result obtains despite, of course, the fact the strict environmentalist perspective would be associated with a set of problematic policy and program implications that differed from those problems linked to the hereditarian perspective.

CONCLUSIONS

Ideas are powerful organizers of individual behavior and social action. Theories of SES–parenting–child development relations can be linked to a more democratic and socially just nation for families and children or they can be linked to ill-founded inequities, discrimination, or even more horrendous constraints on human freedom and opportunity. The path to pursue in our science and in the applications to policy and practice we support are clear. We should unequivocally pursue and promote developmental systems approaches to parenting research and applications and, just as strongly, speak out against the hereditarian approach (i.e., behavior genetics and sociobiology) and, of course, if it should again gain favor, we should criticize as well strict environmentalist ideas.

This course has been clearly set for some time. In the mid 1960s, T. C. Schneirla wrote about the social policy implications of Konrad Lorenz's hereditarian ideas about the existence of a human instinct for aggression. In a review of Lorenz's (1966) *On Aggression*, Schneirla (1966) wrote:

> It is as heavy a responsibility to inform man about aggressive tendencies assumed to be present on an inborn basis as it is to inform him about "original sin," which Lorenz admits in effect. A corollary risk is advising societies to base their programs of social training on attempts to inhibit hypothetical innate aggressions, instead of continuing positive measures for constructive behavior. (p. 16)

More recently, Horowitz (2000) pointed to the caution about hereditarian ideas made by Elman et al. (1998) in the concluding section of their book, *Rethinking Innateness*; "If our careless, under-specified choice of words inadvertently does damage to future generations of children, we cannot turn with innocent outrage to the judge and say 'But your Honor, I didn't realize the word was loaded'" (p. 8).

To avoid the undesirable policy and program outcomes that may be linked to split conceptions of human development, we will need to alter both our theoretical models and the vocabulary we use to present our beliefs about human development to colleagues and to nonscholarly communities (Hirsch, 1997). We will need to advance models that avoid all splits (Overton, 1998) and that, instead, conceptually embrace the dynamic, fused relations between genes and context that is involved in the developmental system (Gottlieb, 1997). It is this gene-context fusion that gives the developmental system its organismic integrity, its continuity, and its plasticity (Thelen & Smith, 1998).

As illustrated in Tables 10.1 and 10.2, the potential costs, in the form of undemocratic and even life-threatening policies and programs to the health and welfare of diverse families and children, are too great for scholars persuaded by the utility of developmental systems theories to fail to rise to what is in effect a dual challenge–of scientific revision and community outreach. We must pay heed to Lewontin's (1992) caution that the price society must pay for the continued presence of split conceptions is the need to remain vigilant about their appearance. We must be prepared to discuss the poor science they reflect and the inadequate bases they provide for public policy and applications pertinent to improving human life (see too Schneirla, 1966; Tobach, 1994). We must be ready to suggest alternatives, such as developmental systems ones, to split views of research about and applications for human development. Given the enormous, and arguably historically unprecedented, challenges facing the families of America and the world, perhaps especially as they strive to rear healthy and successful children capable of leading civil society productively, responsibly, and morally across the 21st century

(Benson, 1997; Damon, 1997; Lerner, 1995; Lerner et al., 2000), there is no time to lose in the development of such a commitment by the scholarly community.

REFERENCES

Baltes, P. B. (1987). Theoretical propositions of life-span developmental psychology: On the dynamics between growth and decline. *Developmental Psychology, 23*, 611–626.

Baltes, P. B., Lindenberger, U., & Staudinger, U. M. (1998). Life-span theory in developmental psychology. In W. Damon (Series Ed.) & R. M. Lerner (Vol. Ed.), *Handbook of child psychology: Vol. 1 Theoretical models of human development* (5th ed., pp. 1029–1144). New York: Wiley.

Behrman, J. R., & Rosenzweig, M. R. (in press). Does increasing women's schooling raise the schooling of the next generation? *American Economic Review.*

Bennett, A. J., Lesch, K. P., Heils, A., Long, J., Lorenz, J., Shoaf, S. E., Champoux, M., Suomi, S. J., Linnoila, M., & Higley, J. D. (in press). Serotonin transporter genotype and early experience interact to influence nonhuman primate CNS serotonin turnover. *Molecular Psychiatry.*

Benson, P. (1997). *All kids are our kids: What communities must do to raise caring and responsible children and adolescents.* San Francisco: Jossey-Bass.

Bornstein, M. H. (1995). Parenting infants. In M. H. Bornstein (Ed.), *Handbook of Parenting* (Vol. 1, pp. 3–39). Mahwah, NJ: Lawrence Erlbaum Associates.

Bornstein, M. H. (Ed.). (2002). *Handbook of Parenting* (2nd ed.). Mahwah, NJ: Lawrence Erlbaum Associates.

Brandtstädter, J. (1998). Action perspectives on human development. In W. Damon (Series Ed.), & R. M. Lerner (Vol. Ed.), *Handbook of child psychology: Vol. 1 Theoretical models of human development* (5th ed., pp. 807–863). New York: Wiley

Brandtstädter, J. (1999). The self in action and development: Cultural, biosocial, and ontgenetic bases of intentional self-development. In J. Brandtstädter & R.M. Lerner (Eds.), *Action and self-development: Theory and research through the life-span* (pp. 37–65). Thousand Oaks, CA: Sage.

Bronfenbrenner, U. (2001). Human development, bioecological theory of. In N. J. Smelser & P. B. Baltes (Eds.), *International encyclopedia of the social and behavioral sciences* (pp. 6963–6970). New York: Elsevier.

Bronfenbrenner, U., & Crouter, A. C. (1983). The evolution of environmental models in developmental research. In W. Kessen (Series Ed.) & P.H. Mussen (Vol. Ed.), *Handbook of child psychology: Vol. 1 History, theory, and methods* (4th ed., pp. 357–414). New York: Wiley.

Bronfenbrenner, U., & Morris, P. A. (1998). The ecology of developmental process. In W. Damon (Series Ed.) & R. M. Lerner (Vol. Ed.), *Handbook of child psychology: Vol. 1 Theoretical models of human development* (5th ed., pp. 993–1028). New York: Wiley.

Buss, A. H., & Plomin, R. (1984). *Temperament: Early developing personality traits.* Hillsdale, NJ: Lawrence Erlbaum Associates.

Chess, S., & Thomas, A. (1999). *Goodness of fit: Clinical applications from infancy through adult life.* Philadelphia: Brunner/Mazel.

Collins, W. A., Maccoby, E. E., Steinberg, L., Hetherington, E. M., & Bornstein, M. H. (2000). Contemporary research on parenting: The case of nature and nurture. *American Psychologist, 55*, 218–232.

Damon, W. (1997). *The youth charter: How communities can work together to raise standards for all our children.* New York: The Free Press.

Damon, W., & Gregory, A. (in press). In R. M. Lerner & P. L. Benson (Eds.), *Developmental assets and asset-building communities: Implications for research, policy, and practice.* Norwell, MA: Kluwer Academic Publishers.

Dannefer, D. (1984). Adult developmental and socialization theory: A paradigmatic reappraisal. *American Sociological Review, 49*, 100–116.

Elder, G. H., Jr. (1998). The life course and human development. In W. Damon (Series Ed.) & R. M. Lerner (Vol. Ed.), *Handbook of child psychology: Vol. 1 Theoretical models of human development* (5th ed., pp. 939–991). New York: Wiley.

Elder, G. H., Modell, J., & Parke, R. D. (Eds.). (1993). *Children in time and place: Developmental and historical insights.* New York: Cambridge University Press.

Elman, J. L., Bates, E. A., Johnson, M. H., Karmiloff-Smith, A., Parisi, D., & Plunkett, K. (1998). *Rethinking innateness: A connectionist perspective on development (neural network modeling and connectionism).* Cambridge, MA: MIT Press.

Featherman, D. L., & Lerner, R. M. (1985). Ontogenesis and sociogenesis: Problematics for theory about development across the lifespan. *American Sociological Review, 50,* 659–676.

Featherman, D. L., Spenner, K. I., & Tsunematsu, N. (1988). Class and the sociolization of children: Constancy, change, or irrelevance? In E. M. Hetherington, R. M. Lerner, & M. Perlmutter (Eds.), *Child development in life-span perspective* (pp. 67–90). Hillsdale, NJ: Lawrence Erlbaum Associates.

Feldman, M. W., & Lewontin, R. C. (1975). The heritability hang-up. *Science, 190,* 1163–1168.

Fisher, C. B., Jackson, J. F., & Villarruel, F. A. (1998). The study of African American and Latin American children and youth. In R. M. Lerner (Ed.), *Handbook of child psychology: Vol. 1 Theoretical models of human development* (5th ed., pp. 1145–1207). New York: Wiley.

Ford, D. L., & Lerner, R. M. (1992). *Developmental systems theory: An integrative approach.* Newbury Park, CA: Sage.

Gottlieb, G. (1992). *Individual development and evolution: The genesis of novel behavior.* New York: Oxford University Press.

Gottlieb, G. (1997). *Synthesizing nature-nurture: Prenatal roots of instinctive behavior.* Mahwah, NJ: Lawrence Erlbaum Associates.

Gottlieb, G. (1998). Normally occurring environmental and behavioral influences on gene activity: From central dogma to probabilistic epigenesis. *Psychological Review, 105,* 792–802.

Gould, S. J. (1981). *The mismeasure of man.* New York: Norton.

Gould, S. J. (1996). *The mismeasure of man* (Rev. ed.). New York: Norton.

Harkness, S., & Super, C. (1995). Culture and parenting. In M. H. Bornstein (Ed.), *Handbook of Parenting* (Vol. 2, pp. 211–234). Mahwah, NJ: Lawrence Erlbaum Associates.

Harris, J. R. (1998). *The nurture assumption: Why children turn out the way they do.* New York: The Free Press.

Hartup, W. W. (1978). Perspectives on child and family interaction: Past, present, and future. In R. M. Lerner & G. B. Spanier (Eds.), *Child influences on marital and family interaction: A life-span perspective* (pp. 23–46). New York: Academic Press.

Hebb, D. O. (1970). A return to Jensen and his social critics. *American Psychologist, 25,* 568.

Hirsch, J. (1997). Some history of heredity-vs.-environment, genetic inferiority at Harvard, and the (incredible) bell curve. *Genetica, 99,* 207–224.

Ho, M. W. (1984). Environment and heredity in development and evolution. In M.-W. Ho & P. T. Saunders (Eds.), *Beyond neo-Darwinism: An introduction to the new evolutionary paradigm* (pp. 267–289). London: Academic Press.

Homans, G. C. (1961). *Social behavior: Its elementary forms.* New York: Harcourt Brace.

Horowitz, F. D. (2000). Child development and the PITS: Simple questions, complex answers, and developmental theory. *Child Development, 71,* 1–10.

Jensen, A. R. (1969). How much can we boost IQ and scholastic achievement? *Harvard Educational Review, 39,* 1–123.

Jensen, A. R. (1973). *Educability and group differences.* New York: Harper & Row.

Jensen, A. R. (1998). Jensen on "Jensenism." *Intelligence, 26,* 181–208.

Kretzmann, J. P., & McKnight, J. L. (1993). *Building communities from the inside out: A path toward finding and mobilizing a community's assets.* Evanston, IL: Northwestern University.

Lerner, R. M. (1982). Children and adolescents as producers of their own development. *Developmental Review, 2*, 342–370.

Lerner, R. M. (1984). *On the nature of human plasticity*. New York: Cambridge University Press.

Lerner, R. M. (1991). Changing organism-context relations as the basic process of development: A developmental contextual perspective. *Developmental Psychology, 27*, 27–32.

Lerner, R. M. (1995). *America's youth in crisis: Challenges and options for programs and policies*. Thousand Oaks, CA: Sage Publications.

Lerner, R. M. (1998). Theories of human development: Contemporary perspectives. In R. M. Lerner (Ed.), Theoretical models of human development. Volume 1 of the Handbook of child psychology (5th ed., pp. 1–24), Editor-in-chief: W. Damon. New York: Wiley.

Lerner, R. M. (2002). *Concepts and theories of human development* (3rd ed.). Mahwah, NJ: Lawrence Erlbaum Associates.

Lerner, R. M. (2002). Towards a democratic ethnotheory of parenting for families and policy makers: A developmental systems perspective. *Parenting: Science and Practice, 1*, 339–351.

Lerner, R. M., Bornstein, M. H., & Smith C. (in press). Child well-being: From elements to integrations. In M. H. Bornstein, L. Davidson, C. M. Keyes, K. Moore, & The Center for Child Well-Being (Eds.), *Well-being: Positive development across the life course*. Mahwah, NJ: Lawrence Erlbaum Associates.

Lerner, R. M., & Busch-Rossnagel, N. A. (Eds.). (1981). *Individuals as producers of their development: A life-span perspective*. New York: Academic Press.

Lerner, R. M., Fisher, C. B., & Weinberg, R. A. (2000). Toward a science for and of the people: Promoting civil society through the application of developmental science. *Child Development, 71*, 11–20.

Lerner, R. M., Rothbaum, F., Boulos, S., & Castellino, D. R. (2002). A developmental systems perspective on parenting. In M. H. Bornstein (Ed.), *Handbook of parenting* (2nd ed., pp. 315–344). Mahwah, NJ: Erlbaum.

Lerner, R. M., & Walls, T. (1999). Revisiting individuals as producers of their development: From dynamic interactionism to developmental systems. In J. Brandtstädter & R. M. Lerner (Eds.), *Action and self-development: Theory and research through the life-span* (pp. 3–36). Thousand Oaks, CA: Sage.

Lewis, M. (1997). *Altering fate*. New York: Guilford.

Lewontin, R. C. (1992). Foreword. In R. M. Lerner (Ed.), *Final solutions: Biology, prejudice, and genocide* (pp. vii–viii). University Park: Penn State Press.

Lorenz, K. (1940). Durch Domestikation verursachte Störungen arteigenen Verhaltens. *Zeitschrift für angewandte Psychologie and Charakterkunde, 59*, 2–81.

Lorenz, K. (1966). *On aggression*. New York: Harcourt Brace.

Magnusson, D. (1999a). Holistic interactionism: A perspective for research on personality development. In L. A. Pervin & O. P. John (Eds.), *Handbook of personality: Theory and research* (2nd ed., pp. 219–247). New York: Guilford.

Magnusson, D. (1999b). On the individual: A person-oriented approach to developmental research. *European Psychologist, 4*, 205–218.

McEwen, B. S., (1997). Possible mechanisms for atrophy of the human hippocampus. *Molecular Psychiatry, 2*, 255–262.

McEwen, B. S. (1998). Protective and damaging effects of stress mediators, *New England Journal of Medicine, 338*, 171–179.

McEwen, B. S. (1999). Stress and hippocampal plasticity. *Annual Review of Neuroscience, 22*, 105–122.

Meaney, M., Aitken, D., Berkel, H., Bhatnager, S., & Sapolsky, R. (1988). Effect of neonatal handling of age-related impairments associated with the hippocampus. *Science, 239*, 766–768.

Meyer, J. W. (1988). The social constructs of the psychology of childhood: Some contemporary processes. In E. M. Hetherington, R. M. Lerner, & M. Perlmutter (Eds.), *Child development in life-span perspective* (pp. 47–65). Hillsdale, NJ: Lawrence Erlbaum Associates.

Müller-Hill, B. (1988). Murderous science: Elimination by scientific selection of Jews, gypsies, and others. Germany 1933–1945. New York: Oxford University.

Overton, W. F. (1998). Developmental psychology: Philosophy, concepts, and methodology. In W. Damon (Series Ed.) & R. M. Lerner (Ed.), *Handbook of child psychology: Vol. 1 Theoretical models of human development* (5th ed., pp. 107–187). New York: Wiley.

Overton, W. F. (in press). Development across the life span: Philosophy, concepts, theory. In R. M. Lerner, M. A. Easterbrooks, & J. Mistry, (Eds.), *Handbook of psychology: Vol. 6. Developmental psychology*. New York: Wiley.

Partanen, J., Brunn, K., & Markkanen, T. (1966). Inheritance of drinking. *Pediatrics. New Family Science Review, 5*, (1 &2), 97–110.

Plomin, R. (1986). *Development, genetics, and psychology.* Hillsdale, NJ: Lawrence Erlbaum Associates.

Plomin, R. (2000). Behavioural genetics in the 21st century. *International Journal of Behavioral Development, 24*, 30–34.

Plomin, R., Corley, R., DeFries, J. C., & Faulker, D. W. (1990). Individual differences in television viewing in early childhood: Nature as well as nurture. *Psychological Science, 1*, 371–377.

Plomin, R., & Daniels, D. (1987). Why are children in the same family so different from each other? *Behavioral and Brain Sciences, 10*, 1–16.

Reese, H. W., & Overton, W. F. (1970). Models of development and theories of development. In L. R. Goulet & P. B. Baltes (Eds.), *Life-span developmental psychology: Research and theory* (pp. 115–145). New York: Academic Press.

Rowe, D. (1994). *The limits of family influence: Genes, experience, and behavior.* New York: Guilford.

Rushton, J. P. (1999). *Race, evolution, and behavior* (special abridged ed.). New Brunswick, NJ: Transaction Publishers.

Rushton, J. P. (2000). *Race, evolution, and behavior* (2nd special abridged ed.). New Brunswick, NJ: Transaction Publishers.

Sameroff, A. J. (1983). Developmental systems: Contexts and evolution. In W. Kessen (Ed.), *Handbook of child psychology: Vol. 1. History, theory, and methods* (pp. 237–294). New York: Wiley.

Sampson, R., Raudenbush, S. W., & Earls, F. (1997). Neighborhoods and violent crime. A multilevel study of collective efficacy. *Science, 277*, 918–924.

Sampson, R., Morenoff, J., & Earls, F. (1999). Beyond social capital: Spatial dynamics of collective efficacy for children. *American Sociological Review, 64*, 633–660.

Scales, P., Benson, P., Leffert, N., & Blyth, D. A. (2000). The contribution of developmental assets to the prediction of thriving among adolescents. *Applied Developmental Science, 4*, 27–46.

Scarr, S. (1992). Developmental theories for the 1990s: Development and individual differences. *Child Development, 63*, 1–19.

Schneirla, T. C. (1957). The concept of development in comparative psychology. In D. B. Harris (Ed.), *The concept of development: An issue in the study of human behavior* (pp. 78–108). Minneapolis, MN: University of Minnesota Press.

Schneirla, T. C. (1966). Instinct and aggression: Reviews of Konrad Lorenz, *Evolution and modification of behavior* and *On aggression. Natural History, 75*, 16.

Skinner, B. F. (1971). *Beyond freedom and dignity.* New York: Knopf.

Suomi, S. J. (1997). Early determinants of behavior: Evidence from primate studies. *British Medical Bulletin, 53*, 170–184.

Suomi, S. J. (2000). A behavioral perspective on developmental psychopathology: Excessive aggression and serotonergic dysfunction in monkeys. In A. J. Sameroff, M. Lewis, & S. Miller (Eds.), *Handbook of developmental psychopathology* (2nd ed. pp. 237–256). New York: Plenum.

Thelen, E., & Smith, L. B. (1998). Dynamic systems theories. In W. Damon (Series Ed.) & R. M. Lerner (Vol. Ed.), *Handbook of child psychology: Vol. I Theoretical models of human development* (5th ed., pp. 563–633). New York: Wiley.

Thomas, A., & Chess, S. (1977). *Temperament and development.* New York: Brunner/Mazel.

Tobach, E. (1994). Personal is political is personal is political. *Journal of Social Issues*, *50*, 221–224.

Venter, J. C., Adams, M. D., Myers, E. W., Li, P. W., Mural, R. J., [plus 270 others]. (2001). The sequence of the human genome. *Science*, *291*, 1304–1351.

Wapner, S., & Demick, J. (1998). Developmental analysis: A holistic, developmental, systems-oriented perspective. In W. Damon (series Ed.) and R. M. Lerner (Vol. Ed.), *Handbook of child psychology: Vol. 1 Theoretical models of human development* (5th ed., pp. 761–805). New York: Wiely.

Wilson, E. O. (1975). *Sociobiology: The new synthesis*. Cambridge, MA: Harvard University Press.

About the Authors

KAY BATHURST is Professor of Psychology at California State University, Fullerton, and Co-Director of the Fullerton Longitudinal Study. Her PhD is from the University of California at Los Angeles. Bathurst's research interests include psychological assessment, standardized testing, and test-taking behavior, family functioning and divorce, and intellectual giftedness. She is co-author of *Gifted IQ: Early Developmental Aspects*. Bathurst is a member of the American Psychological Association, American Psychological Society, Society for Research in Child Development, and Western Psychological Association. She has served on the editorial board of *Child Development*.

MARC H. BORNSTEIN is Senior Investigator and Head of Child and Family Research at the National Institute of Child Health and Human Development. He holds a B.A. from Columbia College and a PhD from Yale University. Bornstein was a Guggenheim Foundation Fellow, and received a RCDA from the NICHD, the Ford Cross-Cultural Research Award from the HRAF, the McCandless Young Scientist Award from the APA, the US PHS Superior Service Award from the NIH, two Japan Society for the Promotion of Science Fellowships, an Award for Excellence from the American Mensa Education & Research Foundation, and the Arnold Gesell Prize from the Theodor Hellbrügge Foundation. Bornstein has held faculty positions at Princeton University and New York University as well as visiting academic appointments in Munich, London, Paris, New York, and Tokyo. Bornstein is Editor Emeritus of *Child Development* and Editor of *Parenting: Science and Practice*. He has contributed scientific papers in the areas of human experimental, methodological, comparative, developmental, cross-cultural, neuroscientific, pediatric, and aesthetic psychology. Bornstein is coauthor of *Development in Infancy* (4 editions) and general editor of *The Crosscurrents in Contemporary Psychology Series* (10 volumes) and the *Monographs in Parenting* (4 volumes). He also edited the *Handbook of Parenting* (Vols. I-V, 2 editions), and he coedited *Developmental Psychology: An Advanced Textbook* (4 editions) as well as a dozen other volumes. He is author of several children's books and puzzles in *The Child's World* series.

ROBERT H. BRADLEY is Professor in the Center for Applied Studies in Education at the University of Arkansas at Little Rock and Adjunct Professor of Pediatrics and Psychiatry at the University of Arkansas for Medical Sciences. Bradley received his PhD at the University of North Carolina. He was formerly Director of the Center for Research on Teaching and Learning and Director of the University of Arkansas University Affiliated Program in Developmental Disabilities. Bradley serves on the board of editors for *Parenting: Science & Practice* and as president of the Southwestern Society for Research in Human Development. He is a member of the NICHD Child Care and Youth Development Research Network. His primary research interests include the family environment and its relation to children's health and development, particularly children living in poverty and children with disabilities or serious health problems, daycare, fathering, and early intervention. He is the co-author, along with Bettye Caldwell, of the *Home Observation for Measurement of the Environment* (HOME Inventory).

JEANNE BROOKS-GUNN is Virginia and Leonard Marx Professor of Child Development and Education at Teachers College, Columbia University. She is Director of the Center for Children and Families at Teachers College and Co-Director of the Institute for Child and Family Policy at Columbia University. She received her B.A. from Connecticut College, her Ed.M. from Harvard University, and her PhD in human learning and development from the University of Pennsylvania. Her specialty is policy-oriented research focusing on family and community influences upon the development of children and youth. She has served on National Academy of Science Panels and is a member of the Social Science Research Council Committee on the urban underclass focusing on neighborhoods, families and children. She is past president of the Society for Research on Adolescence and is a fellow in the American Psychological Association and the American Psychological Society. She is Associate Editor of the Society for Research in Child Development's *Social Policy Report*. She received the Urie Bronfenbrenner Award from the American Psychological Association, the Vice President's National Performance Review Hammer Award, the Nicholas Hobbs Award from the American Psychological Association's Division of Children, Youth, and Families, and the John B. Hill Award from the Society for Research on Adolescence. She is author of *Adolescent Mothers In Later Life*.

ROBERT FLYNN CORWYN is Research Associate in the Center for Applied Studies in Education at the University of Arkansas at Little Rock. Corwyn received his M.A. at the University of Arkansas at Little Rock and is currently a PhD student at Memphis University. He has taught courses in Gerontology, Family Sociology, Research Methods and Statistics. Corwyn serves on the board of editors of *Marriage and Family: A Christian Journal*. His research interests include adolescent delinquent behavior, the family environment and its effect on child development, and fathering.

GREG J. DUNCAN is Professor of Education and Social Policy and a Faculty Associate in the Institute for Policy Research at Northwestern University. He is Director of the Northwestern University/University of Chicago Joint Center for Poverty Research. Duncan received a PhD from the University of Michigan. Duncan was a Research Scientist at the University of Michigan's Institute for Social for Social Research. He directed the Panel Study of Income Dynamics, a data collection project that has conducted annual interviews with a large and representative set of families all around the country for over 30 years. Duncan's research has focused on issues of economic mobility both within and across generations. He is the author of *Years of Poverty, Years of Plenty* and co-editor of *Consequences of Growing Up Poor* and *Neighborhood Poverty*. His recent research has focused on how economic conditions in families and neighborhoods affect child development and on how welfare reform affects families and children.

MARGARET E. ENSMINGER is Professor in the Health Policy and Management Department, Faculty of Social and Behavioral Sciences, Bloomberg School of Public Health, at The Johns Hopkins University. She received her B.A. at Earlham College, her M.A. at University of Nebraska, and her PhD at the University of Chicago. Ensminger is a member of the American Sociological Association, the Society for Research on Child Development, the Society for Research on Adolescence, the College for Problems of Drug Dependence, the American Public Health Association, and the Society for Life History Research. Her research interests include the study of pathways to educational, family, and antisocial outcomes.

KATE FOTHERGILL is a doctoral student at Bloomberg School of Public Health, The Johns Hopkins University, in the Social Behavioral Sciences Division of the Health Policy and Management Department. She received her B.A. from Tufts University and her M.P.H. from University of North Carolina at Chapel Hill. She has worked for over 10 years on adolescent health issues, and she previously worked as Director of Comprehensive Health Care Programs at Advocates for Youth. Her current research interest is the impact of neighborhood on development of risk behaviors over the life course.

ANDREW J. FULIGNI is Associate Professor in the Departments of Psychiatry and Psychology at the University of California, Los Angeles. He received his PhD from the University of Michigan and was previously at New York University. His research focuses on the family relationships and academic adjustment of adolescents from a variety of cultural groups, with a particular focus on the children of immigrant families. Fuligni was recently selected as a recipient of the APA Division 7 Boyd McCandless Award for Early Career Contribution to Developmental Psychology. He has also served on the editorial boards of the *Journal of Research on Adolescence* and *Child Development*.

ADELE ESKELES GOTTFRIED is Professor in the Department of Educational Psychology and Counseling, California State University, Northridge. She was awarded the PhD from the Graduate School of the City University of New York. Her major research programs are in the areas of maternal- and dual-earner employment and children's development, home environment and children's development, and the development of children's academic intrinsic motivation. Gottfried's books include *Maternal Employment and Children's Development: Longitudinal Research*, *Redefining Families: Implications for Children's Development*, *Gifted IQ: Developmental Aspects*, and she is the author of the *Children's Academic Intrinsic Motivation Inventory*. She is a Fellow of the American Psychological Association, recipient of the MENSA Award for Excellence in Research. She has served as Action Editor for *Child Development*, and currently serves on the Editorial Boards of *Parenting: Science and Practice, the Journal of Educational Psychology*, and *Developmental Psychology*.

ALLEN W. GOTTFRIED is Professor of Psychology, California State University, Fullerton, Clinical Professor of Pediatrics at the University of Southern California School of Medicine, and director of the Fullerton Longitudinal Study. His PhD is from the New School for Social Research. Gottfried is a Fellow of the American Psychological Association, the American Psychological Society, and the Western Psychological Association. His areas of interest include infancy, home/family environment-development relations, intelligence, and longitudinal research. His books include *Home Environment and Early Cognitive Development: Longitudinal Research*; *Maternal Employment and Children's Development: Longitudinal Research*; *Infant Stress under Intensive Care*; *Play Interactions: Role of Play Materials and Parental Involvement to Children's Development*; *Redefining Families: Implications for Children's Development*; *Gifted IQ: Early Developmental Aspects*; and the forthcoming, *Temperament: Infancy through Adolescence—The Fullerton Longitudinal Study*.

DIANA WRIGHT GUERIN is Professor and former Chair of Child and Adolescent Studies at California State University, Fullerton, and Co-Director of the Fullerton Longitudinal Study. She was educated at Long Beach (B.A.), Fullerton (M.A.), and University of California, Los Angeles (PhD). Guerin is a member of the American Psychological Association, Society for Research in Child Development, and National Association for the Education of Young Children. Her research interests include the development of temperament and its implications for development, intellectual giftedness, and public policy. She is co-author of *Gifted IQ: Early Developmental Aspects* and *Temperament from Infancy through Adolescence—The Fullerton Longitudinal Study.* She has served as an editorial consultant to *Child Development.*

CHUN-SHIN HAHN is Research Fellow in Child and Family Research at the National Institute of Child Health and Human Development. She received her M.A. at Stanford University and Sc.D. at the Johns Hopkins University, School of Hygiene and Public Health. Hahn is a member of the American Psychological Association. Her research interests concern the origins of behavioral and emotional adjustments in children, with special interest in the role of parent-child interactions and child temperament.

O. MAURICE HAYNES is Section Statistician in Child and Family Research in the National Institute of Child and Human Development in Bethesda, MD. He received his B.A. at Harding College and M.A. and PhD at Wayne State University. He is a member of the Society for Research in Child Development and the American Statistical Association.

ERIKA HOFF is Professor of Psychology at Florida Atlantic University. She received an A.B. Ed. from the University of Michigan, an M.S. from Rutgers— The State University of New Jersey, and a PhD from the University of Michigan. Her research interests focus on early lexical development and the role of language experience in language development. She is author of *Language Development.*

LOIS WLADIS HOFFMAN is Professor Emerita of Psychology at the University of Michigan, Ann Arbor. She received her education at the State University of New York at Buffalo (B.A.), Purdue University (M.S.), and the University of Michigan (PhD). She has been a Research Associate at the Institute for Social Research, Professor of Psychology, and Chair of the Developmental Area at the University of Michigan. She is a fellow of the American Psychological Association and past president of Divisions 7 and 9. Her research interests include the effects of work on families and children, parenting and the socialization process, the value of children to parents, and gender roles. She co-edited the *Review of Child Development Research* and co-authored *The Employed Mother in America*, *Working Mothers and the Family*, *Mothers at Work: Effects on Children's Wellbeing*, and *Developmental Psychology Today.*

RICHARD M. LERNER is the Bergstrom Chair in Applied Developmental Science at Tufts University. Lerner received a PhD from the City University of New York. He has been a fellow at the Center for Advanced Study in the Behavioral Sciences and is a fellow of the American Association for the Advancement of Science, the American Psychological Association, and the American Psychological Society. He was on the faculty and held administrative posts at Michigan State University, Pennsylvania State University, and Boston College, where he was the

Anita L. Brennan Professor of Education and the Director of the Center for Child, Family, and Community Partnerships. Lerner has held the Tyner Eminent Scholar Chair in the Human Sciences at Florida State University in 1994-1995. Lerner is the author or editor of numerous books and scholarly articles and chapters. He edited Volume 1, on *Theoretical Models of Human Development* for the fifth edition of the *Handbook of Child Psychology*. He is the founding editor of the *Journal of Research on Adolescence* and *Applied Developmental Science*.

TAMA LEVENTHAL is Research Scientist at the Center for Children and Families, Teachers College. She received her B.A. from Colgate University and her PhD from Columbia University, where she was also a graduate fellow at the Center for Children and Families. She was a summer fellow in Putting Children First, a research fellowship in child and family policy, and held a Columbia University Public Policy Fellowship. Her research interests are in linking developmental research with social policy regarding children, youth, and families, particularly low-income families. Her work has focused on understanding how neighborhood contexts affect child and family well-being.

KATHERINE A. MAGNUSON is a doctoral student in Human Development and Social Policy program at Northwestern University. She has an undergraduate degree in History and Political Science from Brown University. Her research focuses on the effects of socioeconomic resources, particularly education and income, on the well-being and children and families.

MAKEBA PARRAMORE is a PhD student at Cornell University. She received her B.A. and M.A. degrees from California State University, Fullerton. She was a research assistant on the Fullerton Longitudinal Study and an editorial assistant for *Structural Equation Modeling*. Her current research focuses on cognition and language development of infants and young children.

JOAN T. D. SUWALSKY is a Research Psychologist in Child and Family Research in the National Institute of Child Health and Human Development. She received her B.A. from Vassar College and her M.A. from Cornell University. She is a member of the Society for Research in Child Development. Her research interests include the study of infancy, social development, family relationships, and adoption.

HIROKAZU YOSHIKAWA is Assistant Professor of Psychology at New York University. He received his PhD at New York University. He has conducted research on effects of early childhood care and education programs, public policies, and prevention programs on the development of children and adolescents in poverty in the United States. He is currently conducting research on effects of experimental welfare reform and anti-poverty policy demonstrations on children and families. He has served on the U.S. Department of Health and Human Services Advisory Committee on Head Start Research and Evaluation, a panel appointed to help design the national impact evaluation of Head Start. He currently serves on the Committee on Family Work Policies of the National Research Council, National Academy of Sciences. In 2001 he was awarded the Louise Kidder Early Career Award of the Society for the Psychological Study of Social Issues (Division 9 of the American Psychological Association), as well as the American Psychological Association Minority Fellowship Early Career Award.

Author Index

Subject Index

f = footnote
t = table